PERSPECTIVES ABOUT THE AUTHOR'S EXPERTISE + PRAISE FOR THIS TOOLBOX

"For more than 15 years, Greg has shared his distilled learning as a social entrepreneur with class after class of social entrepreneurship students at Notre Dame. His unparalleled expertise and matter-of-fact approach to applying these tools to the most challenging social issues of our day left many students not only inspired, but resolute in their own attitudes and beliefs as changemakers. With this toolbox, Greg's vision and learnings from the field are that much more accessible to emergent changemakers across the globe. And I can't wait to put it into practice in my own classroom!

MELISSA PAULSEN
PROGRAM DIRECTOR, ENTREPRENEURSHIP + EDUCATION DIVISION | PULTE INSTITUTE FOR GLOBAL DEVELOPMENT | UNIVERSITY OF NOTRE DAME

"Watching Greg at work is a thing to behold. His skill at design, attention to detail and sense of a group make his work special and uniquely impactful."

DAVID WOFFORD
SENIOR DIRECTOR | UNITED NATIONS FOUNDATION

"It's hard to describe how much I have learned from Greg over the years--from being extremely thoughtful on how to frame challenges to preserving a deep curiosity that inevitably leads to innovation. Every meeting with Greg is an opportunity to think about a challenge through a different lens and broaden/deepen impact. Greg does this with tremendous humility and by empowering everyone around him. His ability to create a collaborative environment means he magnifies impact wherever he goes."

TAMAR BENZAKEN KOOSED
FOUNDER + PRESIDENT | MANAUS CONSULTING

"Greg has the unusual ability to combine high-level strategic thinking with on-the-ground logistical prowess. We partnered in building programs together for nearly twelve years and the quality of the experiences for our students was always top-notch. He is truly an original leader in this field."

ERIC MLYN, PHD
FORMER PETER LANGE EXECUTIVE DIRECTOR | DUKE UNIVERSITY

"Greg is the go-to person when it comes to anything related to social entrepreneurship and innovation. He not only created a program that changed the entire trajectory of my career (Social Entrepreneur Corps), but he also has continued to be a mentor when I have navigated where to go next. His patience and deep expertise enables him to be an outstanding consultant. I would recommend Greg for any project you begin with him; I feel lucky to have him as a mentor and a friend."

COLLEEN SHEEHY
GLOBAL SUSTAINABILITY INNOVATION MANAGER | ACCENTURE

"Greg's unique career designing high-impact social innovations uniquely qualifies him to share the "how" that's so critical to translating mission to execution and creating practices that make organizations resilient, especially in attempting to scale. Greg's guidance has been measurably effective for my teams across several disciplines, from venture-funded startups to childhood literacy initiatives."

KEVIN KUSHMAN
CEO| ELECTRADA

"Greg has been an invaluable thought partner for nearly 20 years. He was instrumental in helping VisionSpring gain traction in the marketplace in Central America. He is innovative, a great communicator and teacher, and someone who has a deep commitment to using business practices and principles to improve the world. I look forward to our continued collaboration."

JORDAN KASSALOW
CO-FOUNDER | EYELIANCE
FOUNDER | VISIONSPRING

"Greg is one of the most insightful people in the social innovation space. Greg has forgotten more about social innovation than I will ever know - and I study it for a living! He has a keen understanding of not only how to develop entrepreneurial solutions with people but also how to implement them on-the-ground in the most challenging of environments. Of all the partners with whom I've ever worked, none has been more focused on creating solutions of mutual value. He combines the intellect and experience of a world-class consultant with the heart and empathy of a life-changing teacher. Simply put, there is none better!"

BRETT SMITH, PHD
CINTAS ENDOWED PROFESSOR OF ENTREPRENEURSHIP | MIAMI UNIVERSITY
FOUNDER | CENTER FOR SOCIAL ENTREPRENEURSHIP - MIAMI UNIVERSITY

"Greg is the rare combination of a thought and action leader. We worked alongside one another as our students participated in the Social Entrepreneur Corps program. He is intelligent, caring, and collegial, and truly believes in the power of social entrepreneurship to change the world."

SARA HERALD
DIRECTOR - SOUTHERN MANAGEMENT LEADERSHIP PROGRAM | UNIVERSITY OF MARYLAND

"I have had the immense pleasure of working for and with Greg for over a decade now, and I have learned so much from his approaches to social innovation and social impact strategy. They are clear, empathy-oriented, iterative, and ultimately very effective. So much of what I learned from Greg shaped me as an innovation leader, and I still find myself reflecting on and applying lessons I gained from him years ago. It is awesome that others can benefit from his wealth of knowledge and resources through this toolkit. And, selfishly, I'm excited to keep learning and problem-solving from it as well!"

ALANNA HUGHES
VICE PRESIDENT - INNOVATION | PER SCHOLAS

"Greg is one of the most skilled facilitators and practitioners I have had the pleasure to work with across my career. When it comes to creating mindset shifts and helping professionals put empathy into action to unlock innovation, Greg is second to none! He is sought after for the impact he helps teams to create and because he is a true asset to any team that he chooses to join."

ANNIE O'CONNOR
EXECUTIVE DIRECTOR | BOLINAS COMMUNITY LAND TRUST

"Greg has shared his wonderful combination of talents as an entrepreneur, innovator and educator with our students for over 8 years through unique and immersive internship and field-based opportunities in the Dominican Republic and Guatemala. He has visited our campus as a guest lecturer and public speaker multiple times to discuss his approach to social entrepreneurship and design thinking. He has a recognized track record and ability to foster collaboration and local leadership through community-driven social impact work that is grounded in empathy, humility and unbridled advocacy for marginalized communities."

PATRICK ECCLES
SR. ASSOCIATE DIRECTOR | BUFFET INSTITUTE FOR GLOBAL AFFAIRS- GLOBAL LEARNING OFFICE - NORTHWESTERN UNIVERSITY

"Greg is that rare combination of purpose-driven entrepreneur who knows how to get results and authentic leader who can share in simple, easily understood terms the principles of innovation and creative problem-solving. His enduring passion is designing solutions that address really hard problems and enabling people from all walks of life to discover their own potential as changemakers."

PAUL ROGERS, PHD
ASSOCIATE PROFESSOR OF WRITING STUDIES | UC SANTA BARBARA
EDITOR - INTERNATIONAL MODELS OF CHANGEMAKER EDUCATION

"In addition to engaging Greg to help build a campus social innovation program (which is now a permanent fixture at the university serving the entire campus community), we served as co-instructors for a social entrepreneurship course at UW-Madison. He is a highly skilled and wise teacher, able to communicate complex and strategic topics with ease, drawing from his remarkable career accomplishments while making key lessons applicable to bright young minds aspiring to change the world."

JEFFREY SNELL, PHD.
INNOVATION & COMMERCIALIZATION SPECIALIST, D2P & TEACHING FACULTY (ENTREPRENEURIALISM), SCHOOL OF HUMAN ECOLOGY | UNIVERSITY OF WISCONSIN-MADISON

"Greg is one of the foremost social impact leaders in the social entrepreneurship space. If you are fortunate to meet him, you'll find his passion is contagious. For those "meeting" him through his writing, you should be excited to embark on this journey. Greg is a masterful designer of structured, pragmatic approaches to breaking down problems, understanding root causes, and working collaboratively with communities. Moreover, his approaches are timeless and broadly applicable to impact-centered problem-solving. I am inspired by his authentic compassion, coupled with the ingenuity he brings when tackling some of the thorniest market problems in low and middle-income economies. Having the opportunity to work with Greg not only shaped my career path, but showed me how to engage in social impact work with both empathy and rigor. I often leverage the concepts and frameworks that I learned from Greg, whether I am working with large tech companies or small nonprofit organizations seeking to create social change. I'm positive readers will find this content similarly empowering."

MICHELLE MULLINS
STRATEGY + OPERATIONS LEAD | IMPACT, NEWS, CIVICS - GOOGLE

"This is a book the world needs now more than ever...and there is simply no one better than Greg to upskill us all in the realm of impact innovation education. Greg has given us a practical, accessible, and empowering playbook to both imagine and shape our own futures in an age of unprecedented complexity and uncertainty. Wherever one may be on the changemaking journey, this is the ultimate resource for any young person, parent, educator, or leader who is interested in the "how" of agency, empowerment, collaborative problem-solving and meaningful engagement for our communities and the planet."

CRAIG VEZINA
CEO | THE SPACESHIP ACADEMY

"Greg's expertise in social innovation and commitment to collaboration makes him a unicorn in education. He has inspired my own work with students-- from guest lectures and sharing tools, to informing my approach and sourcing NGO project partners. He brings wide international practitioner experience but also thinks deeply about how to activate that learning for young people in simple, digestible steps. That is what schools need for us to scale changemaking."

IVAN CESTERO
DIRECTOR OF STRATEGIC PARTNERSHIPS | PORTAL SCHOOLS

"Greg has the most unique combination of being a visionary and a pragmatist. As a visionary, he questions injustices with a never-ending curiosity and the deep belief that change is possible and solutions can be found. But it's the pragmatist in him that leads him to develop sustainable, scalable solutions that solve systemic problems with a continuous focus on collaboration. And now, with the vision to enable anyone to be a changemaker, Greg's created this very practical and easy-to-use how-to toolbox based on his decades of changemaking experience. Why am I not surprised? I have been blessed to have been changed and help create change with many of these tools, and I am so excited that anyone who wishes can now access and accelerate their own changemaking journey. Game on!"

MARY CLAIRE MANDEVILLE
CEO | VENNLI

"One of my favorite mantras is: "The problem is the problem." This deceptively simple concept is actually a radical way to approach the biggest and most complex challenges humanity faces, and Greg's critically important work will help any organization or team identify the problems they are facing and then find the best solutions. This is a must-use for any NGO, corporation, or government agency that is truly invested in changemaking."

JANE EHRENFELD
FORMER EXECUTIVE DIRECTOR | CENTER FOR INSPIRED TEACHING

It's What You Set In Motion: A Comprehensive Toolbox for Collaborative Changemaking Conversations

Published by Gatekeeper Press
7853 Gunn Hwy., Suite 209
Tampa, FL 33626
www.GatekeeperPress.com

Library of Congress Control Number: 2023951634

ISBN (paperback): 9781662937934
eISBN: 9781662937941

To Ali, EvaLuna, and Hudson. Thank you for your love and patience.
I hope this makes you proud.

To Mom and Dad. Boy, I miss you. You empowered me.

To my brothers Bucky and Miguel. And my sisters Luz and Mada.
Son los meros meros.

And to all of the team and community members I've been honored to work with. You're my teachers. Thank you. I'm a conduit.

TOOLBOX CONTENTS

NOTES:

SECTION 03 | CHANGEMAKING TOOLKITS + TOOLS

pp. 73 - 338

SECTION 04 | CHANGEMAKING INNOVATION MINI-CASES

pp. 339 - 376

NOTES:

NOTES:

GVK note -

- Remember we're working in COMPLEX ADAPTIVE SYSTEMS. These are systems comprising a dynamic network of interactions where behavior is constantly changing. This means we need to have both PLANNED strategies and EMERGENT strategies. EMERGENT STRATEGIES adapt to the unpredictable changes that will happen in the system. Don't be rigid and prescriptive.
- This toolbox should help you avoid GLOP (General Labelling of Other People).

SECTION 01 | GETTING STARTED

Madalina B. collaborating with changemaker educators in Romania

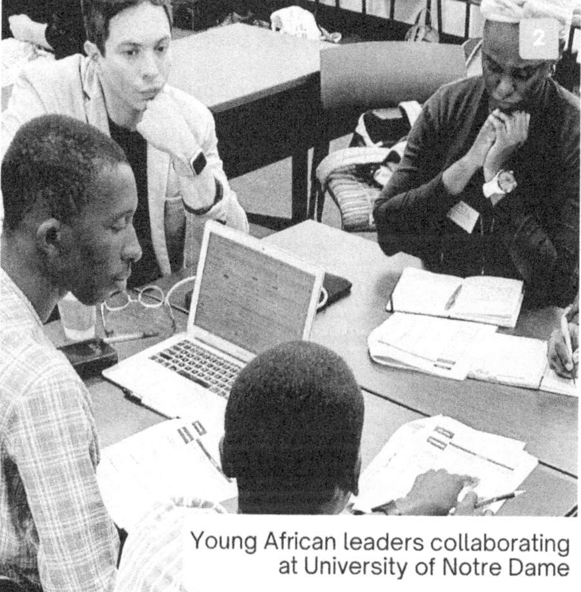

Young African leaders collaborating at University of Notre Dame

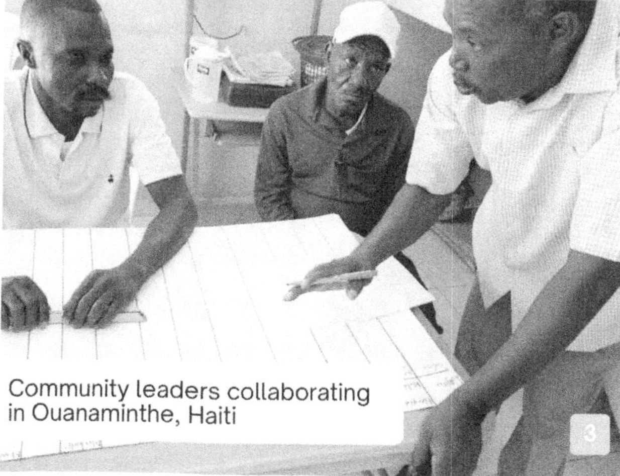

Community leaders collaborating in Ouanaminthe, Haiti

Social Entrepreneur Corps "Community Consultants" en route to collaborative conversations with community members

NOTES:

NOTES:

GVK notes -

- Make sure you're continuously zooming in (human-centered) and zooming out (systems focused)
- Be inductive (specific to general) and deductive (general to specific)
- Empathy is the process and the product
- Ever wonder how sparrows flock in those amazing, dynamic formations that look like swarms? There's no central coordination. There are three simple rules to flocking behavior that make it possible. That's it. They are -
    - Cohesion: Go towards the average position of nearby birds
    - Alignment: Steer towards the average heading of nearby birds
    - Separation: Avoid crowding neighboring birds.

  What are some simple rules your team can follow for "changemaking behavior"? Check out the Changemaking Trimtabs!!!

WHY THIS TOOLBOX?

4 minute read

A mix of personal and professional WHYs inspired me to create and publish this toolbox. I was primarily motivated to get this out in the world for five big reasons. I was also motivated by ongoing frustrations and aspirations. Most of these WHYs are the value proposition.

FIVE BIG REASONS WHY

This is an all-hands-on-deck moment.

Although I'm an optimist by nature, I feel like we're experiencing some of the most challenging times since I've been alive. We're surrounded by accelerating volatility, uncertainty, complexity, and ambiguity (VUCA). So many of our systems are inadequate, inequitable, or just plain broken. We feel disconnected. Overall, it feels like so many problems are outrunning existing solutions. Because of this, we urgently need as many people as possible to feel empowered as changemakers.

> *"It can be scary to go places we've never been. It takes courage to embark on a changemaking journey. However, this is what we need the most. We need a generation who is brave, thinks critically and creatively, and who's not afraid to collaborate and creatively solve the problems we all face."*
>
> **MADALINA BOUROS**
> FOUNDER - ALLGROW

Changemakers need tools to empowered.

Changemakers need tools to develop/ enhance changemaking mindsets and skill sets. And, given that changemaking is a "team sport," these tools should ignite and empower collaboration. They should empower organizations, teams, communities, etc. to work together to diagnose problems and design solutions that are empathetic and equitable.

I believe I can make a helpful contribution.

I've been at this for a while. I've worked in C-suites, communities, and classrooms. I've worn and wear many changemaking hats. During my changemaking journey, I've been blessed to work for, work with, and work on behalf of more amazing changemakers than I can possibly recall. I've learned something from all of them. Along the way, I've designed collaborative changemaking strategies and built collaborative changemaking tools that I use every day. I decided I was finally ready to move everything from my Google Drive to a toolbox that I could offer to aspiring and practicing changemakers. That's what this is.

This is my main thing.

When it comes to changemaking, it's not hard to find the WHAT. There's no shortage of great resources that teach you the WHAT of changemaking (social innovation, social entrepreneurship, etc.) And people show up with all kinds of powerful WHYs. What I've always found lacking, and where I've focused my career, is on the HOW. That's my main thing. The HOW puts the WHAT and the WHY into action. This toolbox is may capstone HOW.

> *"The main thing is to keep the main thing the main thing."*
>
> **STEPHEN COVEY**
> AUTHOR - *SEVEN HABITS OF HIGHLY EFFECTIVE PEOPLE*

I owe it.

As I've shared, over the course of my changemaker journey I've been blessed to learn from inspired and inspiring people from all over the world. I feel a strong sense of obligation to honor these people by sharing what I've learned from them with others. I owe it to them to be a conduit.

Following is a summary list of the frustrations I'm trying to address and aspirations I'm hoping this toolbox will achieve:

FRUSTRATIONS

- ☐ **Inspiration is being wasted.** I can't tell you how many people I've met on my journey who've frustratingly told me, "I want to do something with a purpose, but I don't know how."
- ☐ **Too often we design "for."** Designing "for" leads us to "othering" people. We create undignified solutions. We should be designing "with."
- ☐ **It's chaos or crickets.** I've been in too many meetings where the goal is to diagnose/ solve problems, but where there's no framework/tool to guide the conversation. The result is often either meandering, unproductive conversations or silence.

> *"Everyone is digging deeper into their own trench and rarely standing up to look in the next trench over, even though the solution to their problem happens to reside there."*
>
> **DAVID EPSTEIN**
> AUTHOR - *RANGE: WHY GENERALISTS TRIUMPH IN A SPECIALIZED WORLD*

- ☐ **Tools are often too complicated.** I come across too many tools that are conceptually brilliant but practically overwhelming.
- ☐ **You should be able to step into it where you are.** You shouldn't have to start at zero or follow a specific formula. That's not how innovation works.
- ☐ **You shouldn't have to pick one lane.** Why do you have to choose between human-centered methodologies, systems thinking, business model approaches, etc? Why can't you learn about/ use all of them and then dive deeper into specific approaches as you go?
- ☐ **The business OR social mentality is unproductive.** Business and social strategies are both valuable. And one should inform the other. It should be a two-way street.
- ☐ **People keep reinventing the wheel.** There's so much incredible changemaking going on in the world. There are so many solutions that already exist. People just don't know where to find them.

ASPIRATIONS

- ☐ **Aspiring changemakers will say, "I CAN DO THIS!"** People will feel equipped and empowered with changemaking mindsets and skill sets.
- ☐ **This will contribute to the design of empathetic, equitable, and empowering solutions.**
- ☐ **This will catalyze connections.** In-person, virtually, within communities, and/or across borders, this toolbox is designed to bring people together who share a purpose so that they can create meaningful connections.

> *"Never doubt that a small group of thoughtful, committed citizens can change the world; indeed, it's the only thing that ever has."*
>
> **MARGARET MEAD**
> ANTHROPOLOGIST

- ☐ **New voices will be heard and valued.** Good conversation tools help hidden, marginalized, and/or quiet voices feel empowered to share.
- ☐ **Wonderful, unpredictable things will happen.** Anything is possible when people come together with a common purpose and the right tools.
- ☐ **This will help democratize changemaker education.** This is designed to be approachable and accessible. I'll be sharing this in different formats and through channels to help create the broadest reach possible. Please help with this. Photocopy at will!
- ☐ **People will use this toolbox to strengthen their empathy muscles.** Make a habit of using the resources in this toolbox with teammates, community members, family members, etc. Empathy is like a muscle. You need to use it or it atrophies.
- ☐ **This will help empower resilient changemaking cultures.**
- ☐ **Joy!** Working together with a purpose should be joyful. Look at the Changemaking Video Mini-Cases. The changemakers are joyful. And changemaking is only sustainable when it's joyful.

ABOUT THIS TOOLBOX

4 minute read

Following are a few things to keep in mind:

- This toolbox was **DESIGNED TO FACILITATE** team, group, student, community, etc. **CONVERSATIONS.** You can certainly use it alone, but it's intended to help you work with others.
- Use the components **INDEPENDENTLY** or **INTERDEPENDENTLY**. Think of this toolbox as somewhat of a mutually symbiotic ecosystem. The components benefit from each other.
- Use this **IN PERSON** and/or **VIRTUALLY** by using the links and QR codes.
- This is a **DESTINATION** for changemaking tools and resources. It's also a **DOORWAY** to learn about others that may interest you.

THE CORE COMPONENTS

CHANGEMAKING TRIMTABS

GO TO PAGE 13

These are your strategic principles. They help you set, maintain, and correct your changemaking course.

Buckminster Fuller (see the quote to the right) imaged people as trimtabs. Metaphorically speaking, he believed that, just as a little trim tab can turn a massive ship, a person can change the world. But how? Well, you can't change the world by trying to change the world. That's impossible. You change the world by applying simple, proven strategic principles that, just like a trim tab, require little energy but empower big change. These strategies are what I call Changemaking Trimtabs.

> *"Something hit me very hard once, thinking about what one little man could do. Think of the Queen Elizabeth — the whole ship goes by and then comes the rudder. And there's a tiny thing at the edge of the rudder called a trim tab. It's a miniature rudder. Just moving the little trim tab builds a low pressure that pulls the rudder around. Takes almost no effort at all. So I said that the little individual can be a trim tab."*
>
> **BUCKMINSTER FULLER**
> FUTURIST | DESIGNER

Following are a few things to keep in mind:

- There are 22 Changemaking Trimtabs that I've identified and included. The idea is that, the more you keep in mind, the more successful you're likely to be.
- You might find some of them a bit repetitive. That's a feature, not a bug. Great principles tend to overlap with each other.
- Ideally, over time these will become your heuristics (rules of thumb) for changemaking.
- The Changemaking Innovation Mini-Cases do a fantastic job of showing these in action.
- These are guidance and should be adapted for your particular context.
- Don't get hung up on words or metaphors you don't like. It's a win if you get the idea.

CHANGEMAKING TOOLKITS + TOOLS

GO TO PAGE 73

These empower you and your team/ community to have conversations that put the Changemaking Trimtabs into action.

There are 76 tools curated into 13 toolkits. The tools were inspired by human-centered design methods, systems thinking approaches, Business Model Canvas, and insightful articles and books, amongst other sources. I designed these for my work with communities, as a team leader, as an educator, as a service learning leader, as a facilitator, as a social innovator, and as a strategic consultant.

> <u>THE LAW OF THE INSTRUMENT</u>
>
> *"If the only tool you have is a hammer, it is tempting to treat everything as if it were a nail."*
>
> **ABRAHAM MASLOW**
> PSYCHOLOGIST

Following are a few things to keep in mind

- The toolkits aren't prescriptive. A given tool might fit well in multiple toolkits. And you can make your own toolkits.
- The tools should meet you when you are. Most of them should be valuable if you only have 20 minutes. Depending on the context, you might work with a tool for hours, days, or weeks.
- The tools can be universally applied. You should find a valuable application for at least a handful of these tools regardless of your focus.

CHANGEMAKING INNOVATION MINI-CASES

GO TO PAGE 339

These are 90 short videos that show collaborative changemaking in action.

The changemakers in these videos model what this toolbox is all about. My focus was to curate videos that can be valuable both as stand-alone resources and for scaffolding the Changemaking Trimtabs and Changemaking Tools.

> *"The law of floatation was not discovered by contemplating the sinking of things, but by contemplating the floating of things which floated naturally, and then intelligently asking why they did so."*
>
> **THOMAS TROWARD**
> AUTHOR

Following are a few things to keep in mind:

- They're evergreen. The insights are timeless.
- They're short and snackable. The average length is about three minutes.
- They're joyful and inspiring.
- There are a variety of ways you can search including by SDG.
- There's a balance of for-profit and nonprofit changemaking examples.
- The changemaking strategies are universal and achievable. I've steered away from videos about changemaking that requires massive amounts of resources. The majority of changemaking you'll watch started at a grassroots level. These videos should reinforce your belief that everyone really can be a changemaker!
- They're global. These show changemaking in action in 39 countries. There are many from the United States and English-speaking countries. This is simply a reflection of supply and likely demand.
- I've included as much diversity with regard to gender, age, educational background, strategy, issues, etc. as possible.

CHANGEMAKER COACH

GO TO PAGE 377

This includes the following:

- A dynamic advice/ Ask Me Anything section where you can get your questions answered, learn from others, and ask about how to use the toolbox for your specific changemaking efforts.
- Basic HOW-TO guidance for changemakers
- Recommended resources for changemakers that includes helpful websites and books.

NOTES

- There are CHANGEMAKER COACH TIPS and 50+ extra notes/thoughts throughout the toolbox.
- Don't forget to go to CHOOSE YOUR DONATION DESTINATION.
- Go to INDEX for specific searches.
- This DOES NOT INCLUDE specific tools for in-depth financial analysis.
- Connect and reach out to me (Greg) on LinkedIn for help or with ideas.
- Go to collaborativechangemaking.com for updates, new resources, to report problems, share your ideas, provide feedback, etc.
- Go to youtube.com/@collaborativechangemaking for HOW-TO videos, extra CHANGEMAKING INNOVATION MINI-CASES, etc.

WHO'S THIS TOOLBOX FOR?

1 minute read + 2 minute exercise

This toolbox should be helpful for anyone interested in leading, teaching, facilitating, and/or empowering collaborative changemaking conversations. I designed the tools and resources in this toolbox to support my work in communities, as a team leader, as an educator, as a service learning leader, as a facilitator, as a social innovator, and as a strategic consultant. So, if you wear any of those hats, this toolbox should be of value.

That said, the best way to figure out if this is for you might be by looking at what you're trying to achieve. Which, if any, of the mindsets and skill sets below are priorities for your work? Score yourself from zero to five. The bigger the total at the bottom, the more useful this toolbox should be.

CHANGEMAKING MINDSETS + SKILL SETS	IMPORTANCE TO OUR TEAM, COMMUNITY, OR STUDENTS					
ACTIVE LISTENING	0	1	2	3	4	5
ADAPTIVE LEADERSHIP	0	1	2	3	4	5
BUILDING + EMPOWERING TEAMS/ COMMUNITIES	0	1	2	3	4	5
COMMUNITY ENGAGEMENT + IMPACT	0	1	2	3	4	5
COMPLEX PROBLEM SOLVING	0	1	2	3	4	5
CREATIVITY	0	1	2	3	4	5
CRITICAL THINKING	0	1	2	3	4	5
EQUITABLE DESIGN	0	1	2	3	4	5
GENERATIVE THINKING	0	1	2	3	4	5
GLOBAL COMPETENCE	0	1	2	3	4	5
OPPORTUNITY IDENTIFICATION	0	1	2	3	4	5
PUTTING EMPATHY IN ACTION	0	1	2	3	4	5
RESILIENCE	0	1	2	3	4	5
(SOCIAL) ENTREPRENEUERSHIP	0	1	2	3	4	5
(SOCIAL) INNOVATION	0	1	2	3	4	5
SOCIAL JUSTICE	0	1	2	3	4	5
SYSTEMS CHANGE	0	1	2	3	4	5
YOUR TOTAL SCORE	☐ out of 85					

WHAT'S THIS TOOLBOX FOR?

6 minute read

Big picture, note that "changemaking" is my umbrella term for (social) entrepreneurship, ethical entrepreneurship, (social) innovation, inclusive design, etc. This toolbox is for all of these and more. More specifically, I've included here a dozen recommendations for how you might use this toolbox. Read through these and tick the boxes for the ones you believe might be most helpful for you and your team, community, students, etc. Even more specifically, go to the QR code/ link to the right to download a list of 50+ more detailed ways to use this toolbox.

▢ COLLABORATIVE CHANGEMAKING INNOVATION

This toolbox is for collaborative changemaking innovation. Collaborative changemaking innovation happens when teams/communities work together to diagnose problems and design solutions that create a positive impact. Collaborative changemaking innovation is sector-agnostic. This toolbox should help you if you work in the private sector, social sector, government, education, etc. It's also problem-agnostic. And it's solution-agnostic. You can use this toolbox to design any and all kinds of new products, services, and models. You might also use it to rethink, redesign, reinforce, or repair existing solutions.

▢ COLLABORATIVE CHANGEMAKING CONVERSATIONS

This toolbox is for collaborative changemaking conversations. I think of collaborative changemaking conversations as the process, and changemaking innovations as the product. And the process doesn't have to result in a product to be incredibly valuable. In fact, the relationships created and/or reinforced during the process are often much more valuable over time than any one product. With this in mind, why not pick a few Changemaking Trimtabs and/ or Changemaking Tools to spark collaborative changemaking conversations during your next conference, employee resource group meeting, workshop, class, etc.?

▢ CHANGEMAKER EDUCATION

This toolbox is for changemaker education. Changemaker education focuses on building and/or enhancing the mindsets and skill sets listed on page 7. Changemaker education can be formal or informal. It's "all teach, all learn." Changemaker educators view students/participants as producers of knowledge and insights, not consumers. Following are some examples of how I've used the tools and resources in this toolbox in-person and virtually for changemaker education for children, youth, and adults:

- Social entrepreneurship courses
- New venture design courses
- Social innovation workshops
- Purpose workshops
- Product/ service design conversations
- Professional development workshops
- Community of Practice conversations
- Community engagement conversations
- Community consulting
- Community service programs
- Study abroad programs
- Venture competitions

These examples only scratch the surface. How might you use this toolbox for your changemaker education priorities?

☐ EMPOWERING CHANGEMAKER JOURNEYS

This toolbox is for empowering changemaker journeys. I wish I had this toolbox when I joined the Peace Corps in Guatemala way back in 2001 and really got started on my changemaker journey. Although I had some wonderful teachers during training, HOW-TO resources were in short supply. I kid you not, one day I went to the "library" looking for help, and the only HOW-TO guide I found was a book titled *How to Figure Skate*. Since then, I've had an incredibly diverse changemaker journey. This toolbox includes everything that's helped me along the way. It should help you with your changemaker journey as well.

☐ CREATING + NURTURING CHANGEMAKING CULTURES

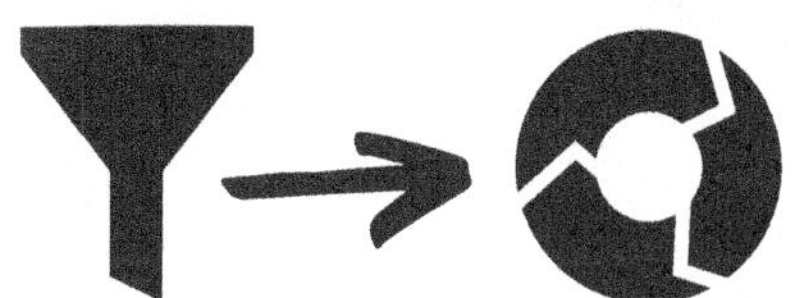

This toolbox will help you and your team go from funnel to flywheel. A funnel approach is a top-down organizational approach. It's a hierarchical, command-and-control approach. In our VUCA (volatile, uncertain, complex, and ambiguous) world, organizational/ team cultures that are dominated by funnel approaches are less than ideal. They're inflexible, unintelligent, slow, and fragile. To succeed n VUCA, the focus should be on building changemaking cultures that prioritize empower-and-trust. To do this, break down funnels and focus on creating changemaking flywheels. What's a flywheel? A flywheel is what you see on a rowing machine. Flywheels store energy and are incredibly efficient. The flywheel concept in business comes from the book ***Good to Great*** by Jim Collins. Collins' big-picture recommendation was that businesses should focus on creating flywheel effects where small wins build on each other over time and gain momentum to the point where success happens on its own, just like the momentum on a flywheel keeps it going. Use this toolbox to create your own changemaking flywheels. Build a habit of engaging in collaborative changemaking conversations to activate a changemaking flywheel effect. Build momentum. Empower a changemaking culture. This won't just help you and your team survive in VUCA, it should help you thrive.

☐ DIRECTING THE RIDER, MOTIVATING THE ELEPHANT + SHAPING THE PATH

This toolbox is for influencing behavior change. Changemaking typically requires behavior change, either within teams and/or communities. Psychologist Jonathan Haidt came up with a helpful analogy for thinking about how to influence behavior change. Chip and Dan Heath built on this analogy in their book ***Switch: How to Change Things When Change Is Hard***. In the analogy, there's an elephant and a person riding it- the rider. The elephant represents the emotional side of the brain. The rider is the rational side. There's also a path. How do you influence the behavior of the rider and elephant so that it goes on the journey using the path? The point of the analogy is that to be successful, you have to work with each of the three - the elephant, the rider, and the path - differently. The elephant requires motivation. If you can't motivate the elephant, you're not going anywhere. This toolbox includes tools for motivating, incentivizing, changing mindsets, etc. The rider needs direction. This toolbox is full of tools focused on defining your WHY and how to get there. And the path needs to be cleared of obstacles. This toolbox is all about problem-solving.

☐ PERSPECTIVE TAKING

This toolbox is for perspective taking. Perspective taking is the ability to look beyond your own point of view to understand how someone else thinks and feels about something. It's essential for empathy. Use this toolbox for perspective taking with both internal and external stakeholders.

▢ CREATING CONNECTION

Use this toolbox to create connections between people. We've encountered massive recent changes in our political culture, the workplace, how we consume media, how we learn, etc., that cause disconnection. The Covid-19 pandemic exacerbated this disconnection. Being intentional about creating meaningful connections seems more important now than ever.

▢ EMPOWERING A SENSE OF OWNERSHIP

This toolbox is for empowering a sense of ownership. When we're empowered to work on problems and solutions, as opposed to being told what to do, we take ownership. A sense of ownership is critical for creative design, smart implementation, and sustainability.

▢ PARTICPATORY + APPLIED LEARNING: PUSHING DOWN THE LEARNING PYRAMID

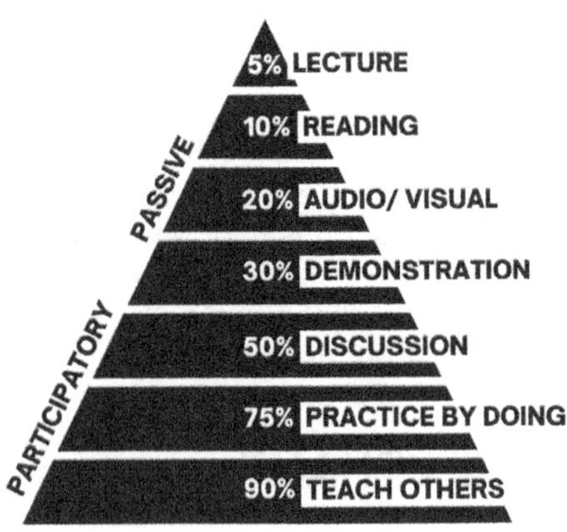

This toolbox is for participatory and applied learning. It's for pushing down the Learning Pyramid. The Learning Pyramid was created by the National Training Laboratories Institute of Applied Behavioral Science. Consider it a guide. It shows how different methods of study lead to different levels of learning and retention. To note, it doesn't mean that you shouldn't lecture, for example. Lecturing might be necessary. Passive learning activities set up participatory learning activities. This toolbox empowers you and your team to teach/ learn at every level of the pyramid by scaffolding. Go to pages 11, 18, 78, and 343 to read about scaffolding and recommended scaffolding strategies. In addition, use this toolbox to scaffold your current curriculum. Reach out to me on LinkedIn or through CHANGEMAKER COACH for ideas.

▢ DEALING WITH WALLS

This toolbox is for dealing with walls. In the words of Michael Jordan, "If you're trying to achieve, there will be roadblocks. I've had them; everybody has had them. But obstacles don't have to stop you. If you run into a wall, don't turn around and give up. Figure out how to climb it, go through it, or work around it." This toolbox will help you "Be like Mike."

▢ SHOOTING TURKEYS INTO ENGINES

Back in my structured finance days, there was a certain business trip that was one of the most coveted by my team members. It was to a Rolls Royce aircraft engine factory in England. Why? Because you got to see them shoot frozen turkeys into engines to test their resilience. I may be a pescatarian but c'mon, that's cool. This toolbox is for shooting turkeys into your engines. It's for testing the resilience of your solutions.

HOW THIS TOOLBOX WORKS

4 minute read

My overarching goal was to make this toolbox simple to use. You should find the design intuitive. Once you dive in, I'm confident you'll feel comfortable using everything and navigating around. Before you start, I'd recommend reading these five HOW-TO's.

1 CHOOSE YOUR OWN JOURNEY

Go through whichever door works best for you. There's a section-specific table of contents at the beginning of the Changemaking Trimtabs, the Changemaking Toolkits and Tools, and the Changemaking Innovation Mini-Cases. Once you've landed somewhere, follow suggestions to jump from section to section and resource to resource. You should be able to use everything in this toolbox independently and interdependantly. You can also go to Changemaker Coach for advice and resources. And the Index should serve as a helpful directory.

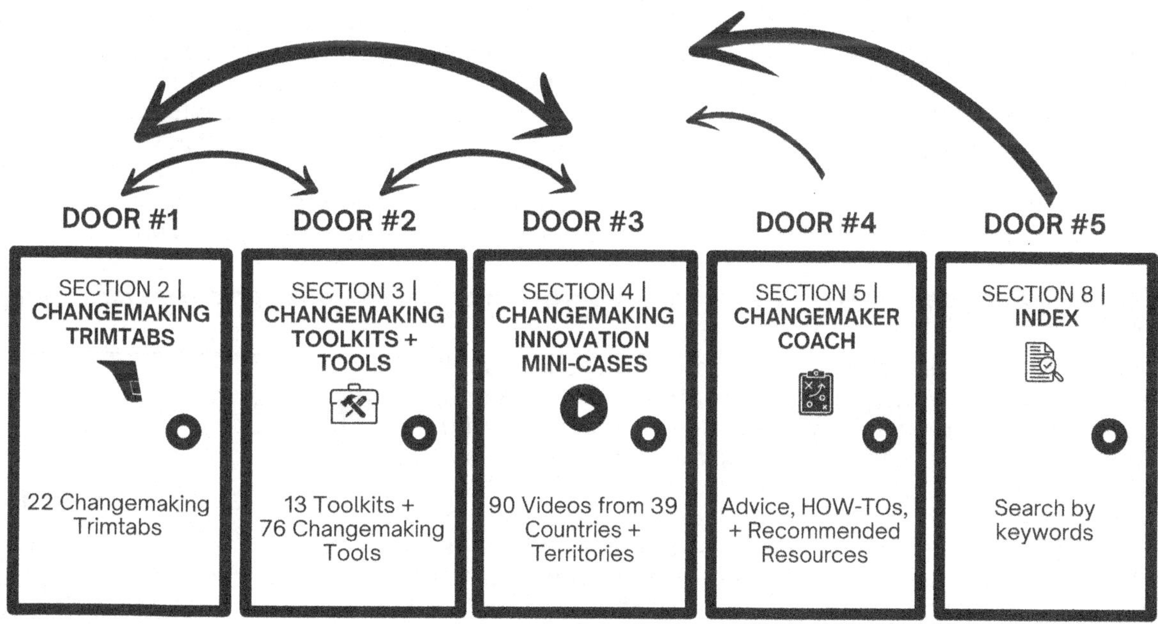

2 SCAFFOLD

For those who aren't familiar, scaffolding is an instructional practice where an educator (Although you could do it alone.) helps students/participants go from "can't do" to "can do with assistance" to "can do independently." The scaffold is the assistance part. I designed this toolbox to help you scaffold each of the primary components, the Changemaking Trimtabs, the Changemaking Tools, and the Changemaking Innovation Mini-Cases, with the others. My goal was to create a 1+1+1=10, so to speak. In addition to being an effective learning strategy, scaffolding is great for working in teams/groups in person and virtually. I've included specific scaffolding guidance in each section. You'll find this on pages 18, 78, and 343.

❸ DIVERGE + CONVERGE

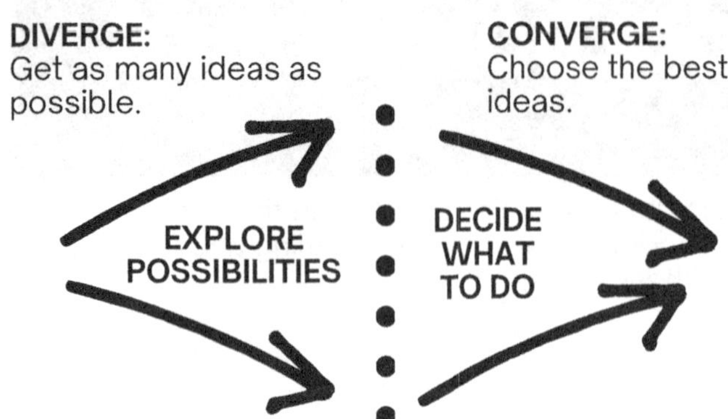
DIVERGE:
Get as many ideas as possible.
CONVERGE:
Choose the best ideas.
EXPLORE POSSIBILITIES
DECIDE WHAT TO DO

The Changemaking Trimtabs and Changemakint Tools are designed for conversations that move from divergence to convergence. This approach is foundational for collaborative changemaking conversations.

Set a time constraint. Make sure people feel a sense of psychological safety. Start by brainstorming. Provide everyone with the opportunity to share their voice. Then narrow down thoughts/ ideas. You'll find a "Now what?" prompt at the bottom of each worksheet to help you with this. I borrowed this from the "What?", "So what?", "Now what?" reflective model.

❹ LEAN INTO THE TOOLBOX METAPHOR

Think of this as a toolbox and use it the same way you'd use any toolbox. For example, a good toolbox is filled with all kinds of different tools. Some of the tools might be ones you already know and use, while others are unfamiliar. It's the same with this toolbox. Also, in a toolbox there are some tools that are your "go-to" tools and others that you rarely, if ever, use. I'm sure you'll also find that to be the case with this toolbox. In a toolbox, there are certain tools that you tend to use together on a project. Same here. And a good toolbox has space to add new tools when needs and opportunities present themselves. This toolbox is the same in two ways. First, I'll be updating this toolbox periodically online at www.collaborativechangemaking.com. And second, throughout this toolbox, you'll find places where you can make and curate your own tools.

❺ DON'T GET HUNG UP ON WORDS. JUST SUBSTITUTE YOUR OWN.

Design is about making choices. By necessity, I've had to choose to use certain words and phrases over others. I've tried to use the most inclusive terminology possible. I'm sure not all of my choices will resonate with you. For example, instead of using the words "customer," "student," or "beneficiary," I use the term "people you aspire to support." I use "team" and "community" interchangeably. "System" can mean a lot of different things. Don't let semantics distract you. Just cross out words or phrases that don't work for you, and pencil in your own.

> *"You say either and I say either. You say neither and I say neither."*
>
> **IRA + GEORGE GERSHWIN**
> SONGRWITERS

NOTES:

GVK notes -

- *There are 22 Changemaking Trimtabs. You could learn/ use/ practice one for each working day in a month.*
- *How about a diet of one Changemaking Innovation Mini-Case per day for three months?*

SECTION 02 | CHANGEMAKING TRIMTABS

What's a Changemaking Trimtab? Go to page 5.

Bucky G. collaborating with community members in South Africa

Mohsin M. collaborating with Mandela Washington Fellows

Corporate leadership teams collaborating to design well-being innovations in Egypt

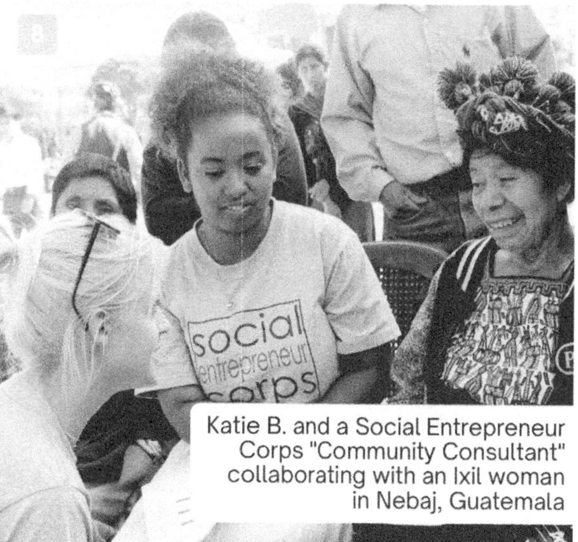

Katie B. and a Social Entrepreneur Corps "Community Consultant" collaborating with an Ixil woman in Nebaj, Guatemala

NOTES:

NOTES:

GVK notes -

- Go to HOW TO FACILITATE GROUP CONVERSATIONS (pg. 379)
- A couple of notes about Changemaking Trimtabs -
    - Realizing that the symbol/icon I've used (a ship's rudder with a trim tab) kind of looks like a thumb. That's interesting, because, put another way, these are "rules of thumb," or heuristics for changemaking.
    - These are for course setting and course correction. Think of the "1 in 60" rule that pilots use. Pilots continually monitor flight positioning and make corrections, because when a plane goes off its course by just 1 degree, it it will miss its destination by 1 mile for every 60 miles it flies. Use Changemaking Trimtabs to pilot your changemaking efforts and stay on course to your desired destination.

50+ SPECIFIC APPLICATIONS

tinyurl.com/cctbpxapps

THE CHANGEMAKING TRIMTABS SECTION OVERVIEW

What's a Changemaking Trimtab? Go to page 5.

HOW THE CHANGEMAKING TRIMTABS WORK pp. 16 - 18

Go here to learn how to use the Changemaking Trimtabs. This includes the following:

- **PART 1: THE DESCRIPTION + RESOURCES PAGE**
- **PART 2: THE COLLABORATIVE CONVERSATION + IDEATION WORKSHEET**
- **GUIDANCE: SCAFFOLDING CHANGEMAKING TRIMTABS**

THE COMPLETE INVENTORY LIST pp. 19 - 21

Go here to find the complete list of 22 Changemaking Trimtabs categorized in pairs by 11 thematic hashtags.

THE CHANGEMAKING TRIMTABS CANVAS pp. 22 - 23

Based on the Business Model Canvas concept, this might help you and your team/ community capture your thoughts/ ideas in one place.

TRIMTABS SCORECARD + PRIORITIZATION HELP p. 24

This includes self-check statements with scoring along with Changemaking Trimtab suggestions to help you and your team decide where to focus your energies.

THE 22 CHANGEMAKING TRIMTABS pp. 25 - 69

This the complete inventory of Changemaking Trimtabs.

REFLECTION + EVALUATION pp. 70 - 71

Go here to reflect on and evaluate each of the Changemaking Trimtabs so that you can prioritize them for future use/ application.

YOUR CHANGEMAKING TRIMTABS p. 72

Go here to note down your modifications to the Changemaking Trimtabs and/or your own Changemaking Trimtabs.

HOW THE CHANGEMAKING TRIMTABS WORK

What's a Changemaking Trimtab? Go to page 5.

THE DESCRIPTION + RESOURCES PAGE

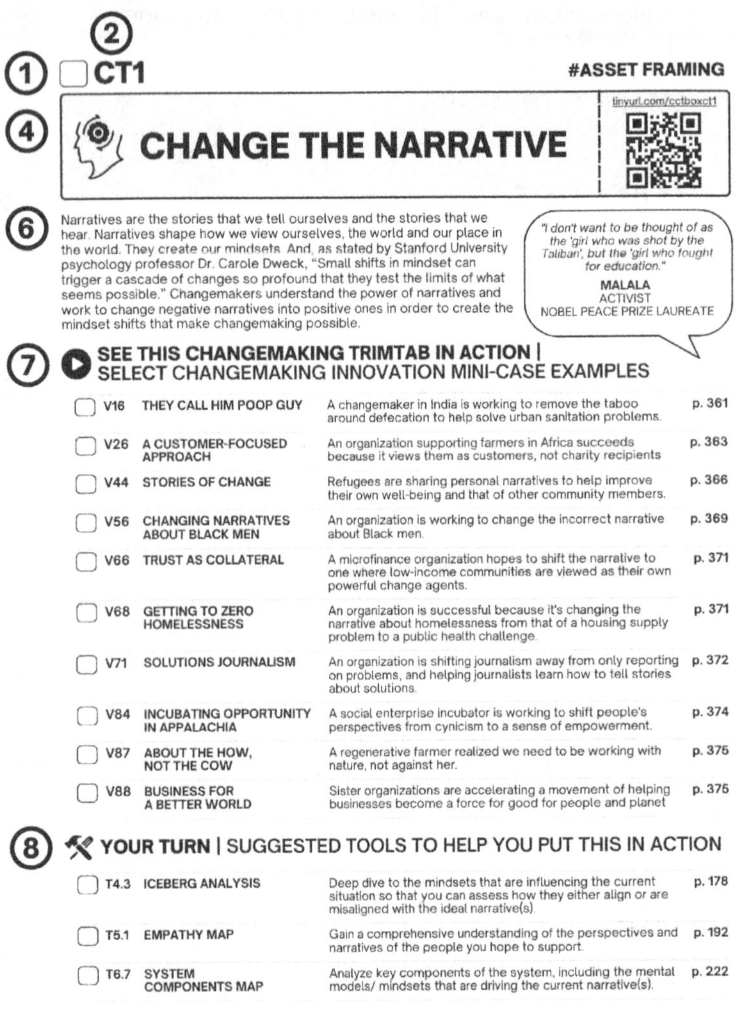

① ☐ CT1 ②   #ASSET FRAMING ③

④ CHANGE THE NARRATIVE   tinyurl.com/cctboxct1 ⑤

⑥ Narratives are the stories that we tell ourselves and the stories that we hear. Narratives shape how we view ourselves, the world and our place in the world. They create our mindsets. And, as stated by Stanford University psychology professor Dr. Carole Dweck, "Small shifts in mindset can trigger a cascade of changes so profound that they test the limits of what seems possible." Changemakers understand the power of narratives and work to change negative narratives into positive ones in order to create the mindset shifts that make changemaking possible.

"I don't want to be thought of as the 'girl who was shot by the Taliban', but the 'girl who fought for education."
MALALA
ACTIVIST
NOBEL PEACE PRIZE LAUREATE

⑦ **SEE THIS CHANGEMAKING TRIMTAB IN ACTION | SELECT CHANGEMAKING INNOVATION MINI-CASE EXAMPLES**

☐	V16	THEY CALL HIM POOP GUY	A changemaker in India is working to remove the taboo around defecation to help solve urban sanitation problems.	p. 361
☐	V26	A CUSTOMER-FOCUSED APPROACH	An organization supporting farmers in Africa succeeds because it views them as customers, not charity recipients	p. 363
☐	V44	STORIES OF CHANGE	Refugees are sharing personal narratives to help improve their own well-being and that of other community members.	p. 366
☐	V56	CHANGING NARRATIVES ABOUT BLACK MEN	An organization is working to change the incorrect narrative about Black men.	p. 369
☐	V66	TRUST AS COLLATERAL	A microfinance organization hopes to shift the narrative to one where low-income communities are viewed as their own powerful change agents.	p. 371
☐	V68	GETTING TO ZERO HOMELESSNESS	An organization is successful because it's changing the narrative about homelessness from that of a housing supply problem to a public health challenge.	p. 371
☐	V71	SOLUTIONS JOURNALISM	An organization is shifting journalism away from only reporting on problems, and helping journalists learn how to tell stories about solutions.	p. 372
☐	V84	INCUBATING OPPORTUNITY IN APPALACHIA	A social enterprise incubator is working to shift people's perspectives from cynicism to a sense of empowerment.	p. 374
☐	V87	ABOUT THE HOW, NOT THE COW	A regenerative farmer realized we need to be working with nature, not against her.	p. 375
☐	V88	BUSINESS FOR A BETTER WORLD	Sister organizations are accelerating a movement of helping businesses become a force for good for people and planet	p. 375

⑧ **YOUR TURN** | SUGGESTED TOOLS TO HELP YOU PUT THIS IN ACTION

☐	T4.3	ICEBERG ANALYSIS	Deep dive to the mindsets that are influencing the current situation so that you can assess how they either align or are misaligned with the ideal narrative(s).	p. 178
☐	T5.1	EMPATHY MAP	Gain a comprehensive understanding of the perspectives and narratives of the people you hope to support.	p. 192
☐	T6.7	SYSTEM COMPONENTS MAP	Analyze key components of the system, including the mental models/ mindsets that are driving the current narrative(s).	p. 222

① **TRACKING BOX:** After using this Changemaking Trimtab, tick this or maybe fill in a number "rating." Use this box however it serves you.

② **CHANGEMAKING TRIMTAB IDENTIFIER:** This is used throughout the toolbox.

③ **THEMATIC CHANGEMAKING HASHTAG:** These are broader themes. The Changemaking Trimtabs are categorized in pairs by 11 of these thematic, changemaking hashtags. Learn about these on pages 19 through 21.

④ **CHANGEMAKING TRIMTAB NAME + ICON**

⑤ **LINK + QR CODE:** These take you to the Google Sheet of the CHANGEMAKING CONVERSATION WORKSHEET described on the next page.
Each Google Sheet has five tabs for community/ team members to work individually and a tab labeled "TEAM" where ideas can be aggregated/ consolidated. Make as many editable copies of the Google Sheet as you'd like. Customize them to meet your needs.

⑥ **BRIEF CHANGEMAKING TRIMTAB DESCRIPTION + COLLABORATIVE CHANGEMAKER QUOTE**

⑦ **"SEE THIS CHANGEMAKING TRIMTAB IN ACTION | SELECT CHANGEMAKING INNOVATION MINI-CASE EXAMPLES":** These short videos show how changemakers working in different fields and contexts are creatively applying the Changemaking Trimtab. These are a handful of examples amongst many that you'll find in the inventory of Changemaking Innovation Mini-Cases. Use these for GUIDANCE: SCAFFOLDING CHANGEMAKING TRIMTABS on page 18.

⑧ **"YOUR TURN | SUGGESTED TOOLS TO HELP YOU PUT THIS IN ACTION":** These are three suggested Changemaking Tools to help you put the Changemaking Trimtab in action in your own work. Use these for GUIDANCE: SCAFFOLDING CHANGEMAKING TRIMTABS on page 18.

THE CHANGEMAKING CONVERSATION WORKSHEET

9

THE CURRENT CONTEXT	
THE CURRENT NARRATIVE(S)	
THE PROBLEM	

10

HOW MIGHT WE CHANGE THE NARRATIVE?

11

PRIORITY FOR OUR CHANGEMAKING EFFORTS	PERCEIVED STRENGTH OF THIS CONCEPT/ IDEA	POTENTIAL POSITIVE IMPACT OF THIS CONCEPT/ IDEA
LOW MEDIUM HIGH	LOW MEDIUM HIGH	LOW MEDIUM HIGH
WHY?	WHY?	WHY?

12

NOW WHAT?	

9 **LEVEL SETTING PROMPTS:** Start with these to create the foundation for your ideation conversation.
To note, **THE CURRENT CONTEXT** prompt is asking "Why are we here having this conversation?", "What's the current situation?", etc. Needless to say, the space allocated will likely be insufficient. Don't let that constrain your conversation.

10 **HOW MIGHT WE - IDEATION SPACE:** How might your community/ team put this Changemaking Trimtab in action in your own work? Jot down notes and/or draw pictures.

11 **CHANGEMAKING TRIMTAB EVALUATION AND REFLECTION PROMPTS:** Use these three prompts after you've had your "How might we..." conversation.

12 **"NOW WHAT?":** Note down agreed-upon action items/ next steps. The relatively small size of the box is due to space constraints and serves as a nudge to encourage you to focus on the most important things.

NOTES:

GVK note -

- Before brainstorming/ ideating as a group, have everyone take a bit of time to note down their personal thoughts. This creates a safe space for everyone and helps you to avoid groupthink.

GUIDANCE: **SCAFFOLDING CHANGEMAKING TRIMTABS**

Go to page 10 to see the Learning Pyramid that informed this design.

This is guidance for scaffolding Changemaking Trimtabs with Changemaking Innovation Mini-Cases and Changemaking Tools. Use this for facilitation/ teaching with teams, in class, in communities, on Zoom calls, etc. Modify this guidance based on your own goals and constraints. Note: You might need to prepare by making photocopies or copies of the Google Sheet links/ QR codes.

GET STARTED

1. **LECTURE/ READING:**
Choose a Changemaking Trimtab. Teach and/or have participants read the BRIEF CHANGEMAKING TRIMTAB DESCRIPTION + QUOTE and review the CHANGEMAKING CONVERSATION WORKSHEET ("WORKSHEET"). This might be an exercise you have participants do before the meeting/ class.

2. **AUDIO/ VISUAL + DEMONSTRATION:**
Go to SEE THIS CHANGEMAKING TRIMTAB IN ACTION | SELECT CHANGEMAKING INNOVATION MINI-CASE EXAMPLES. Select one or a few of these to watch as a full group or in small groups. Share that the goal is to look for and note down how the changemaker(s) in the video(s) is putting the Changemaking Trimtab into action.

3. **DISCUSSION/ TEACH OTHERS:**
Discuss thoughts/ opinions/ takeaways from the videos as a group and/or in small groups.

OPTION 1: **USING CHANGEMAKING INNOVATION MINI-CASES**

4. **PRACTICE BY DOING:**
Tell participants that they're now going to practice using the Changemaking Trimtab's WORKSHEET with a Changemaking Innovation Mini-Case example. Choose and watch another video. Then, in small groups, have participants practice the WORKSHEET. For practice purposes, "How might we..." becomes "How did they...". Rewatch the video as needed.

5. **DISCUSSION/ TEACH OTHERS:**
Have people share their experiences/ what they learned from using the WORKSHEET.

6. **APPLY:**
Break up into existing teams or small groups. Use the WORKSHEET for a real project, venture idea, etc.

OPTION 2: **USING CHANGEMAKING INNOVATION MINI-CASES + CHANGEMAKING TOOLS**

4. **LECTURE/ READING:**
Choose a Changemakaking Tool from YOUR TURN | SUGGESTED TOOLS TO HELP YOU PUT THIS IN ACTION. Teach and/or have participants read/ review the tool's DESCRIPTION, INSTRUCTION + RESOURCES PAGE and CHANGEMAKING CONVERSATION WORKSHEET (the "WORKSHEET"). This might be an exercise you have participants do before the meeting/ class.

5. **PRACTICE BY DOING:**
Tell participants that they're now going to practice using the Changemaking Tool's WORKSHEET with a Changemaking Innovation Mini-Case example. Choose and watch another video. Then, in small groups, have participants practice the Changemaking Tool's WORKSHEET.

6. **DISCUSSION/ TEACH OTHERS:**
Discuss participants' experiences as a group and/ or in small groups. Prompt participants to share how they think this Changemaking Tool might help put the Changemaking Trimtab into action.

7. **STEPS 4, 5 + 6 FROM "OPTION 1: USING CHANGEMAKING INNOVATION MINI-CASES"**

tinyurl.com/cctboxctinv

THE COMPLETE INVENTORY LIST

What's a Changemaking Trimtab? Go to page 5.

Following is the complete list of 22 Changemaking Trimtabs categorized in pairs by 11 thematic hashtags. The changemaking hashtags are as follows:

#ASSET MINDSET
#GENDER EQUALITY
#THINK INSIDE THE COMMUNITY
#TRANSFORMATION
#SOCIAL CAPITAL
#POSITIVE KNOCK-ON OUTCOMES
#DESIGNING FOR CONTEXT
#COUNTER-INTUITIVE DESIGN
#INTRINSIC MOTIVATION
#BUILDING CHANGEMAKING ECOSYSTEMS
#VISION + IMPACT

#ASSET MINDSET

When you apply an asset mindset, you start with a focus on strengths, not weaknesses. You start with assets, not deficits. Changemakers approach their work with an asset mindset. They work to learn aspirations and try to leverage strengths before focusing on weaknesses.

#GENDER EQUALITY

Gender inequality has always been and continues to be pervasive. Changemakers prioritize including gender equality strategies in the DNA of their changemaking innovations.

#THINK INSIDE THE COMMUNITY

Changemakers start by looking for solutions that already exist in communities. Often there's already a solution for a problem. It just hasn't been noticed, optimized, and/or scaled.

#TRANSFORMATION

Oftentimes changemakers innovate by simply adding a dose of imagination and creativity to what's already on hand. Changemakers design innovations that transform the way people view things, produce things, use things, and do things.

#SOCIAL CAPITAL

Social capital is the value derived from relationships in a community. Its existence is essential for sustainable and scalable positive change to happen. It's a cheat code. Changemakers leverage existing social capital and build new opportunities for social capital to take root and flourish.

#POSITIVE KNOCK-ON OUTCOMES

More often than not, the most catalytic positive outcomes happen as a second or third-order consequence of an action. Knock-on outcomes are actually what most changemaking innovation is all about. Changemakers create the conditions for this type of positive domino effect to begin.

#DESIGNING FOR CONTEXT

Just because a solution works in one context doesn't mean it will work in another. Changemakers work to get a deep understanding of the context in order to design innovations that are as empathetic, equitable, and empowering as possible.

#COUNTER-INTUITIVE DESIGN

Our intuitive decisions are affected by a swamp of biases, personal experiences, cultural contexts, and emotions, to name a few. Changemakers recognize that often when something isn't working, success comes from doing things that are contrary to what our intuition tells us.

#INTRINSIC MOTIVATION

Extrinsic motivations such as financial gain, rewards, and acclaim definitely matter. However, changemakers recognize that intrinsic motivations can be the biggest drivers of positive change. Changemakers focus on creating and nurturing opportunities driven by intrinsic motivations such as purpose, joy, community, self-actualization, and personal growth.

#BUILDING CHANGEMAKING ECOSYSTEMS

A changemaking ecosystem is a community of people who continuously work together to create positive change. Changemakers work to build and empower changemaking ecosystems that create systemic and sustainable change.

#VISION + IMPACT

Changemakers aspire to create big, systemic changes. They define what that means and share it broadly. And they understand that, when it comes to changemaking, seeing is believing and inspiring.

NOTES:

GVK notes -

- The size of the problems we're confronted with are asymmetrical with the amount of resources we have to solve them. This means the only way to "win" is by creating "force multipliers" by empowering teams of teams.
- Whenever I'm at a table with a group of people trying to understand and/or solve a problem, I look at an empty chair and ask, "Who isn't here that should be sitting in that chair?" It's usually the person most affected by the problem.

youtube.com/@collaborativechangemaking

Subscribe and find HOW-TO videos, additional Changemaking Innovation Mini-Cases, educational videos, and more.

THE CHANGEMAKING TRIMTABS CANVAS

Capture all of your strategies/ ideas in one place. Take notes, draw pictures, etc.

tinyurl.com/cctboxctcan

#ASSET MINDSET

CT1- CHANGE THE NARRATIVE

CT2- LEAD WITH COMMUNITY VOICE + CHOICE

#GENDER EQUALITY

CT3- FOCUS ON THE WELL-BEING OF GIRLS + WOMEN

CT4- HELP EMPOWER WOMEN AS LAST MILE PROFESSIONALS

#THINK INSIDE THE COMMUNITY

CT5- SPOTLIGHT BRIGHT SPOTS

CT6- OPTIMIZE COMMUNITY ABILITIES + ASSETS

#TRANSFORMATION

CT7- REPURPOSE, REDIRECT, REIMAGINE

CT8- CATALYZE CIRCULARITY

#SOCIAL CAPITAL

CT9- BUILD A PEER-FOR-PEER FRAMEWORK

CT10- BUILD PURPOSE-DRIVEN TEAMS + TEAMS OF TEAMS

#POSITIVE KNOCK ON OUTCOMES

CT11- CREATE OPPORTUNITIES FOR CATALYTIC CONNECTIONS

CT12- SOLVE ONE KIND PROBLEM TO SOLVE ANOTHER

#DESIGNING FOR CONTEXT

CT13- RESTRUCTURE IT

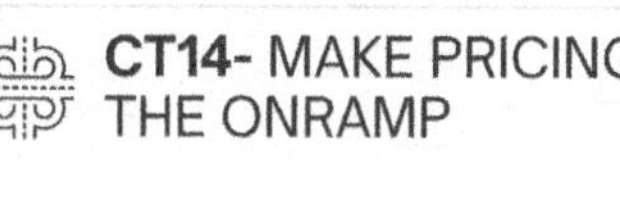

CT14- MAKE PRICING THE ONRAMP

#COUNTER-INTUITIVE DESIGN

CT15- CONFRONT COMPLEXITY WITH SIMPLICITY

CT16- DO THE OPPOSITE

#INTRINSIC MOTIVATION

CT17- FORTIFY EVERYDAY ACTIVITIES

CT18- PRIORITIZE PROXIMITY

#BUILDING CHANGEMAKING ECOSYSTEMS

CT19- BUILD A PRIORITIZATION ECOSYSTEM

CT20- BUILD A MUTUALLY SYMBIOTIC ECOSYSTEM

#VISION + IMPACT

CT21- DEFINE + SHARE THE BHAG

CT22- SHOW IT

TRIMTABS SCORECARD + PRIORITIZATION HELP

Score yourselves to help you decide which trimtabs you might want to prioritize for your changemaking conversations.

SELF-CHECK STATEMENTS	HOW ARE WE DOING?	TRIMTAB SUGGESTIONS
We're talking about how to use/ spread positive and empowering narratives.	0 1 2 3 4 5	CT1
We're having conversations about how community members can take a/ the lead role in diagnosis, discovery, design, and implementation.	0 1 2 3 4 5	CT2
We're focusing on prioritizing the well-being of girls and women within our diagnosis, discovery, design, and implementation process.	0 1 2 3 4 5	CT3
We're looking for ways for women to provide previously inaccessible, vital professional products and/or services to last mile community members.	0 1 2 3 4 5	CT4
We're talking about how to find and spotlight community members who've used their ingenuity to solve the problem(s) within current constraints.	0 1 2 3 4 5	CT5
We're looking for and trying to optimize existing, underappreciated community abilities and/or assets.	0 1 2 3 4 5	CT6
We're creatively thinking about how we can repurpose, redirect and/or reimagine an existing asset or practice to help us solve the problem(s).	0 1 2 3 4 5	CT7
We're talking about how we can create a circular economy in the ecosystem where we're working.	0 1 2 3 4 5	CT8
We're having conversations about how to design ways for people to help each other overcome challenges and become more empowered.	0 1 2 3 4 5	CT9
We've built a team and are having conversations about scaling by building more teams that share the same changemaking purpose.	0 1 2 3 4 5	CT10
We've created mechanisms for people to connect in ways that are frequent and meaningful.	0 1 2 3 4 5	CT11
We're having conversations about how we can solve one problem to also solve another.	0 1 2 3 4 5	CT12
We're talking about how the existing solution does or doesn't achieve the desired outcome of the design, why, and what we can do about it.	0 1 2 3 4 5	CT13
We're having conversations about how to structure pricing that takes context into account and makes it easier for people to adopt our innovation.	0 1 2 3 4 5	CT14
We're always challenging ourselves to keep things as simple as possible.	0 1 2 3 4 5	CT15
We're talking about how we can solve problems by simply doing the opposite of what isn't working now.	0 1 2 3 4 5	CT16
We're leveraging activities that people already participate in and enjoy as a means to address the problem(s).	0 1 2 3 4 5	CT17
We're focusing on building as much proximity as possible into our changemaking innovation efforts and designs.	0 1 2 3 4 5	CT18
We're having conversations about how to build ecosystems that integrate continuous solution discovery and problem diagnosis.	0 1 2 3 4 5	CT19
We're talking about how to build ecosystems that empower people solve each others' problems.	0 1 2 3 4 5	CT20
We're continuously talking about our ambitious, long-term desired outcomes and sharing them far and wide.	0 1 2 3 4 5	CT21
We're having conversations about how to find both small and big ways to make change/ impact as visible as possible.	0 1 2 3 4 5	CT22

THE 22 CHANGEMAKING TRIMTABS

What's a Changemaking Trimtab? Go to page 5.

NOTES:

GVK notes -

- Are you trying to do less bad or more good?
- When a conversation is ending, try to stretch it out for another five minutes or so. Ask another question or two and actively listen. So often I find this is when the most important information/ insights show up.
- Have you heard of "trystorming?" It's like brainstorming, but it's "doing" instead of "talking." Innovation requires continuous trystorming.

Need help, ideas or guidance? Go to CHANGEMAKER COACH "ADVICE/ ASK ME ANYTHING" on page 378.

youtube.com/@collaborativechangemaking

Subscribe and find HOW-TO videos, additional Changemaking Innovation Mini-Cases, educational videos, and more.

☐ CT1

#ASSET MINDSET

CHANGE THE NARRATIVE

What's a Changemaking Trimtab? Go to page 5.

tinyurl.com/cctboxct1

Narratives are the stories that we tell ourselves and the stories that we hear. Narratives shape how we view ourselves, the world, and our place in it. They create our mindsets. And, according to Stanford University psychology professor Dr. Carol Dweck, "Small shifts in mindset can trigger a cascade of changes so profound that they test the limits of what seems possible." Work to change negative narratives into positive ones so that you can create the kind of mindset shifts that make changemaking possible.

"I don't want to be thought of as the 'girl who was shot by the Taliban', but the 'girl who fought for education."

MALALA
ACTIVIST
NOBEL PEACE PRIZE LAUREATE

SEE THIS CHANGEMAKING TRIMTAB IN ACTION | SELECT CHANGEMAKING INNOVATION MINI-CASE EXAMPLES

☐	**V16**	**THEY CALL HIM POOP GUY**	A changemaker in India is working to remove the taboo around defecation while solving urban sanitation problems.	**p. 361**
☐	**V26**	**A CUSTOMER-FOCUSED APPROACH**	An organization supporting farmers in Africa is succeeding because it views them as customers, not charity recipients.	**p. 363**
☐	**V44**	**STORIES OF CHANGE**	Refugees are sharing personal narratives to improve their well-being and that of other community members.	**p. 366**
☐	**V56**	**CHANGING NARRATIVES ABOUT BLACK MEN**	An organization is working to change the incorrect narrative about Black men.	**p. 369**
☐	**V66**	**TRUST AS COLLATERAL**	A microfinance organization hopes to change the narrative so that low-income communities are viewed as powerful change agents.	**p. 371**
☐	**V68**	**GETTING TO ZERO HOMELESSNESS**	An organization is successful because it's changing the narrative about homelessness from that of a housing supply problem to a public health challenge.	**p. 371**
☐	**V71**	**SOLUTIONS JOURNALISM**	An organization is changing the pervasive negative narratives in the the news by helping journalists learn how to tell stories about solutions.	**p. 372**
☐	**V84**	**INCUBATING OPPORTUNITY IN APPALACHIA**	A social enterprise incubator is working to shift people's perspectives from cynicism to a sense of empowerment.	**p. 374**
☐	**V87**	**ABOUT THE HOW, NOT THE COW**	A regenerative farmer realized we need to be working with nature, not against her.	**p. 375**
☐	**V88**	**BUSINESS FOR A BETTER WORLD**	Organizations are changing narratives and showing how business can be a force for good for people and the planet.	**p. 375**

YOUR TURN | SUGGESTED TOOLS TO HELP YOU PUT THIS IN ACTION

☐	**T4.3**	**ICEBERG ANALYSIS**	Dive deep to get to an understanding of the mindsets that are influencing the current situation.	**p. 178**
☐	**T5.1**	**EMPATHY MAP**	Gain a comprehensive understanding of the perspectives and narratives of the people you hope to support.	**p. 192**
☐	**T6.7**	**SYSTEM COMPONENTS MAP**	Analyze key components of the system, including the mental models/ mindsets that are both a result of and that are driving narratives.	**p. 222**

THE CURRENT CONTEXT	
THE CURRENT NARRATIVE(S)	
THE PROBLEM	

HOW MIGHT WE CHANGE THE NARRATIVE?

PRIORITY FOR OUR CHANGEMAKING EFFORTS	PERCEIVED STRENGTH OF THIS CONCEPT/ IDEA	POTENTIAL POSITIVE IMPACT OF THIS CONCEPT/ IDEA
LOW MEDIUM HIGH	LOW MEDIUM HIGH	LOW MEDIUM HIGH
WHY?	WHY?	WHY?

NOW WHAT?	

CT2

#ASSET MINDSET

LEAD WITH COMMUNITY VOICE + CHOICE

tinyurl.com/cctboxct2

We fail as changemakers when we diagnose problems and design solutions FOR people. I've been in more meetings than I can remember where well-intentioned professionals, including me, spent hours discussing THEIR problems, and how we could solve problems for THEM. This is a perniciously easy trap to fall into.

We succeed when we help the people who are the most directly affected by problems take a/the lead role in diagnosing, prioritizing, and solving them. This is the most dignified approach. It's the most effective and efficient approach. And it helps to empower the sense of agency and ownership that's necessary for creativity to thrive and sustainability to become possible.

"Social entrepreneurs...view villagers as the solution, not as the passive beneficiary. They begin with the assumption of competence and unleash resources in the communities they are serving."

DAVID BORNSTEIN
AUTHOR | SOCIAL ENTREPRENEUR

SEE THIS CHANGEMAKING TRIMTAB IN ACTION | SELECT CHANGEMAKING INNOVATION MINI-CASE EXAMPLES

☐	V17	**DESIGNED "WITH," NOT "FOR"**	A social enterprise in India employs a user-centric approach throughout the stove design process.	p. 361
☐	V31	**GIVING CHOICE FOR A CHANGE**	A woman entrepreneur in Kenya is empowered to choose where and how to prioritize money from an organization.	p. 364
☐	V35	**COMMUNITY-OWNED EDUCATION**	A Native American community is now deciding how education is designed for local children and youth.	p. 364
☐	V41	**A STOPLIGHT FOR POVERTY ALLEVIATION**	Community members in Paraguay are using a simple tool to help them analyze and prioritize poverty alleviation strategies.	p. 366
☐	V43	**A COMMUNITY-LED RECOVERY**	Community members in Puerto Rico are leading post-hurricane recovery efforts.	p. 366
☐	V50	**HANDS-ON LEADERSHIP + EMPATHY EDUCATION**	Students are playing critical leadership roles in their school in Thailand.	p. 367
☐	V63	**WELCOMING COMMUNITIES**	Current community members and new immigrants convene to build empathy and understanding.	p. 370
☐	V69	**THE CITIZEN'S JUSTICE LEAGUE**	Family members and friends are playing a central role in the legal defense of their loved ones.	p. 371
☐	V77	**ADVANCING EMPLOYEE OWNERSHIP**	Business ownership is transferred to employees.	p. 373

YOUR TURN | SUGGESTED TOOLS TO HELP YOU PUT THIS IN ACTION

☐	T2.2	**RACI STRUCTURE CHECK-IN**	Establish roles and responsibilities that prioritize leadership by the people who have the most invested in designing successful solutions.	p. 128
☐	T2.4	**STAKEHOLDER ENGAGEMENT LEVEL CHECK-IN**	Analyze engagement levels of key stakeholders and consider what changes should be made so that people most affected can take more leadership/ownership roles.	p. 132
☐	T3.1	**PROXIMITY WHITEBOARD**	Analyze your team's proximity to the people, place and problem. Ideate about how you might get more proximate.	p. 148
☐	T6.8	**STAKEHOLDER POWER MAP**	Analyze the relationships and power dynamics in the system.	p. 226

THE CURRENT CONTEXT	
THE PROBLEM	
WHO'S THE COMMUNITY?	

HOW MIGHT WE LEAD WITH COMMUNITY VOICE + CHOICE?

PRIORITY FOR OUR CHANGEMAKING EFFORTS	PERCEIVED STRENGTH OF THIS CONCEPT/ IDEA	POTENTIAL POSITIVE IMPACT OF THIS CONCEPT/ IDEA
LOW MEDIUM HIGH	LOW MEDIUM HIGH	LOW MEDIUM HIGH
WHY?	WHY?	WHY?

NOW WHAT?	

CT3

#GENDER EQUALITY

FOCUS ON THE WELL-BEING OF GIRLS + WOMEN

tinyurl.com/cctboxct3

It's not exactly "breaking news" to say that girls and women have been, and continue to be, discriminated against, disenfranchised, and disadvantaged. That's both wrong and stupid. Changemakers prioritize the well-being of girls and women as both drivers and desired outcomes of changemaking innovations. That's because it's right and smart. It's right for obvious reasons, and it's smart because it creates better outcomes for everyone.

> *"It's not women's health. It's family health. Women's health really dictates the health of the entire family."*
>
> **DR. GLORIA BACHMANN**
> DIRECTOR | WOMEN'S HEALTH INSTITUTE

SEE THIS CHANGEMAKING TRIMTAB IN ACTION | SELECT CHANGEMAKING INNOVATION MINI-CASE EXAMPLES

☐ V16	**THEY CALL HIM POOP GUY**	An organization in India is focused on ensuring that girls have access to dignified sanitation services.	**p. 361**
☐ V17	**DESIGNED "WITH," NOT "FOR"**	Entrepreneurs in India are designing cookstoves in collaboration with local women to help increase productivity and lower health risks.	**p. 361**
☐ V37	**WE'LL SOLVE IT OURSELVES!**	A group of women in a Nigerian village worked together to solve high rates of infant mortality.	**p. 365**
☐ V40	**EMPOWERING WOMEN-LED TELEMEDICINE**	Women living in last-mile communities and garment workers are getting access to high-quality health care services for the first time.	**p. 365**
☐ V53	**SANITARY PADS FOR EDUCATION**	Young women in Uganda are empowered to continue their education with dignity through access to sanitary pads.	**p. 368**
☐ V66	**TRUST-BASED LENDING**	Women entrepreneurs in Texas are getting first-time access to credit for their small businesses using trust as the collateral.	**p. 371**
☐ V70	**TRUCKERS FIGHTING TRAFFICKING**	Truckers and police are working to create awareness about and prevent human trafficking at truck stops.	**p. 370**
☐ V74	**WALKING FOR TRANSFORMATION**	Black women are walking together and improving their overall well-being.	**p. 372**
☐ V75	**GIRLS FINDING THEIR PACE**	Girls are being empowered to build self-esteem, be healthy, and develop leadership skills through a program based on running.	**p. 372**
☐ V90	**PEDAL POWER**	Women in rural Zambia are getting access to bicycles to help them earn more money for their families.	**p. 375**

YOUR TURN | SUGGESTED TOOLS TO HELP YOU PUT THIS IN ACTION

☐ T5.2	**PERSONA MAP**	Get a better understanding of the whole person to help you find opportunities that might help improve well-being.	**p. 194**
☐ T5.3	**EMPOWERMENT MAP**	Assess where girls and/or women are relatively empowered and relatively disempowered so that you can leverage strengths and address challenges.	**p. 196**
☐ T5.4	**WELL-BEING MAP**	Analyze all of the key components of well-being to help you better understand where you might provide targeted support.	**p. 198**

THE CURRENT CONTEXT	
WHO ARE THE GIRLS AND/ OR WOMEN?	
THE PROBLEM	

HOW MIGHT WE FOCUS ON THE WELL-BEING OF GIRLS + WOMEN?

PRIORITY FOR OUR CHANGEMAKING EFFORTS	PERCEIVED STRENGTH OF THIS CONCEPT/ IDEA	POTENTIAL POSITIVE IMPACT OF THIS CONCEPT/ IDEA
LOW MEDIUM HIGH	LOW MEDIUM HIGH	LOW MEDIUM HIGH
WHY?	WHY?	WHY?

NOW WHAT?	

CT4

#GENDER EQUALITY

HELP EMPOWER WOMEN AS LAST MILE PROFESSIONALS

tinyurl.com/cctboxct4

There are two global problems that, when combined, can create huge opportunities. The first problem is the centralization of vital products and services. Vital products are often geographically centralized in wealthy, urban areas. And vital services tend to be centralized in the offices of licensed professionals. Because of this, billions of people around the world lack equitable access to solutions for their problems.

> *"The seeds of success of every nation on Earth are best planted in women and children."*
>
> **DR. JOYCE BANDA**
> FORMER PRESIDENT OF MALAWI

The second problem is a lack of equitable income generation and employment opportunities for women. For example, according to the International Labor Organization, the global labor force participation rate for women is under 50%. In India, it's roughly 19%. And in many countries, when there are jobs for women, they're low-quality and low paying.

Changemakers turn these two problems into huge opportunities by creating last-mile, professional opportunities for women. People get the products and services they need. And women are afforded dignified opportunities to earn money, support their families, and serve their communities.

SEE THIS CHANGEMAKING TRIMTAB IN ACTION | SELECT CHANGEMAKING INNOVATION MINI-CASE EXAMPLES

☐ V6	**MEDIATING CHANGE**	Women are conflict resolution leaders in Burundi.	p. 359
☐ V12	**MICROCONSIGNMENT FOR THE LAST MILE**	Women are entrepreneurs selling eyeglasses, cookstoves and solar lamps in rural communities.	p. 360
☐ V18	**A VISION FOR IMPACT**	Women are eye care professionals.	p. 361
☐ V40	**EMPOWERING WOMEN-LED TELEMEDICINE**	Underemployed women doctors in Pakistan practice medicine by supporting other women who work as last-mile healthcare professionals.	p. 365
☐ V45	**LIGHTING UP LIVES + LIVELIHOODS**	"Solar Sisters" in Rwanda sell cookstoves and solar lamps in small villages.	p. 366
☐ V47	**BLACK MAMBAS PREVENTING POACHING**	Local young women prevent poaching in South Africa.	p. 367
☐ V52	**FROM PATIENT TO FACILITATOR**	An organization is helping women in rural Uganda become mental healthcare facilitators.	p. 368
☐ V67	**HUMANIZING HEALTHCARE**	Women working within a health care system in the U.S. bridge distances and complexities as community health workers.	p. 371

YOUR TURN | SUGGESTED TOOLS TO HELP YOU PUT THIS IN ACTION

☐ T5.5	**JOURNEY MAP**	Analyze where there might be challenges in someone's journey to gain access to products/ services so that you can ideate about how this might create job opportunities.	p. 200
☐ T6.3	**EQUITABLE ACCESS MAP**	Analyze potential challenges in equitable access to products/ services to help you prioritize where to provide support.	p. 214
☐ T6.9	**FIVE FORCES MAP**	Analyze the forces that influence existing access challenges and the potential for new access opportunities.	p. 226
☐ T8.3	**DISTRIBUTION CHANNEL STRATEGY**	Decide what the most compelling distribution channel strategies might be for women to bridge the last mile.	p. 260

THE CURRENT CONTEXT	
THE ESSENTIAL PRODUCT / SERVICE	
THE PROBLEM	

HOW MIGHT WE HELP EMPOWER WOMEN AS LAST MILE PROFESSIONALS?

PRIORITY FOR OUR CHANGEMAKING EFFORTS	PERCEIVED STRENGTH OF THIS CONCEPT/ IDEA	POTENTIAL POSITIVE IMPACT OF THIS CONCEPT/ IDEA
LOW MEDIUM HIGH	LOW MEDIUM HIGH	LOW MEDIUM HIGH
WHY?	WHY?	WHY?

NOW WHAT?	

☐ CT5 #THINK INSIDE THE COMMUNITY

SPOTLIGHT BRIGHT SPOTS

tinyurl.com/cctboxct5

If you take a good look around your community, you'll discover a person or maybe a few people who've found uncommon solutions for common problems. They've found creative ways to solve problems while working with the same resources and working against the same obstacles, as everyone else in the community. But this isn't just the case in your community. It's the case in most communities. There's a powerful community problem-solving approach based on this reality. It's called "positive deviance."

"The law of floatation was not discovered by contemplating the sinking of things, but by contemplating the floating of things which floated naturally, and then intelligently asking why they did so."

THOMAS TROWARD
AUTHOR

The first step in positive deviance is to help communities discover "bright spots," the outlier problem solvers. The second step is to help empower community members to model the successful behaviors and strategies of the bright spots. So, before designing a new solution, find people who've already designed one. Look for the bright spots. Then shine a spotlight on how they've solved the problem so that everyone else in the community can see and learn.

SEE THIS CHANGEMAKING TRIMTAB IN ACTION | SELECT CHANGEMAKING INNOVATION MINI-CASE EXAMPLES

☐	V9	GROW YOUR OWN RAINFOREST	A man in Ecuador who grew his own rainforest is now working with an organization to help others do the same.	p. 359
☐	V26	A CUSTOMER-FOCUSED APPROACH	An organization working to support farmers in Africa bases its strategies on observing successful farmers who are working next to unsuccessful farmers.	p. 363
☐	V36	NAMING + FAMING	To overcome corruption, the Nepalese government created an "American Idol" inspired game to spotlight exceptional government workers.	p. 365
☐	V37	WE'LL SOLVE IT OURSELVES!	The Nigerian government is trying to scale a strategy designed by a rural women's group to combat infant mortality.	p. 365
☐	V41	A STOPLIGHT FOR POVERTY ALLEVIATION	An organization is using Google maps to spotlight families who've designed successful poverty alleviation strategies.	p. 366
☐	V56	CHANGING THE NARRATIVE ABOUT BLACK MEN	An organization in the U.S. is identifying, convening and spotlighting Black community leaders.	p. 369
☐	V71	SOLUTIONS JOURNALISM	An organization is working to help journalists learn how to write about/ spotlight community solutions.	p. 372
☐	V88	BUSINESS FOR A BETTER WORLD	Organizations are platforming and spotlighting businesses that are creating changemaking cultures and outcomes.	p. 375

YOUR TURN | SUGGESTED TOOLS TO HELP YOU PUT THIS IN ACTION

☐	T3.7	INNOVATION INSIGHTS + APPLICATIONS WHITEBOARD	Research, learn about, and capture insights from existing solutions that might be applicable for your own work.	p. 160
☐	T6.1	BRIGHT SPOTS MAP	Analyze current bright spots to help you decide how you might best spotlight them.	p. 210
☐	T8.4	DIFFUSION STRATEGY DESIGN	Design your strategy to spotlight future bright spots as examples that others can follow.	p. 262

THE CURRENT CONTEXT	
THE PROBLEM	
THE BRIGHT SPOT(S)	

HOW MIGHT WE SPOTLIGHT BRIGHT SPOTS?

PRIORITY FOR OUR CHANGEMAKING EFFORTS	PERCEIVED STRENGTH OF THIS CONCEPT/ IDEA	POTENTIAL POSITIVE IMPACT OF THIS CONCEPT/ IDEA
LOW MEDIUM HIGH	LOW MEDIUM HIGH	LOW MEDIUM HIGH
WHY?	WHY?	WHY?

NOW WHAT?	

☐ CT6 #THINK INSIDE THE COMMUNITY

OPTIMIZE COMMUNITY ABILITIES + ASSETS

tinyurl.com/cctboxct6

What should you do if you run into a problem and something needs fixing in your house? The first thing you should do is to try to figure out if you, someone in the house, or maybe a friendly neighbor has the requisite knowledge, skills, and/or tools to solve the problem. Before you go looking for an outside solution to your problem, it makes the most sense to see if you've got what you need to solve it yourself.

> *"Sometimes, what you're looking for is already there."*
>
> **ARETHA FRANKLIN**
> SINGEER | SONGWRITER

Although I'm oversimplifying, there's actually a community development approach founded on this basic idea. It's called Asset-Based Community Development (ABCD). The point of ABCD is to start the problem solving process by using what's already in the community. It's based on the belief that communities can create positive change for themselves by identifying and optimizing existing, but often unrecognized, abilities and assets. So, when you're working with community members to solve problems, start with ABCD.

SEE THIS CHANGEMAKING TRIMTAB IN ACTION | SELECT CHANGEMAKING INNOVATION MINI-CASE EXAMPLES

☐	V14	**FROM FOREST FIRES TO FUEL**	A community is using pine needles from the local forest floor as fuel for electrification.	**p. 360**
☐	V15	**MOVING KNOWLEDGE INSTEAD OF PATIENTS**	An organization is helping local healthcare providers become more empowered through communities of practice.	**p. 360**
☐	V20	**HARVESTING RAINWATER**	Community members in Indonesia are harvesting rainwater from their roofs.	**p. 361**
☐	V40	**EMPOWERING WOMEN-LED TELEMEDICINE**	Women physicians in Pakistan are at long last becoming more empowered to provide essential care.	**p. 365**
☐	V46	**WRITING A BOOK A DAY**	Educators are coming together to write books for children that are contextually appropriate.	**p. 367**
☐	V47	**BLACK MAMBAS PREVENTING POACHING**	Local women in South Africa are trained and empowered to lead poaching prevention efforts.	**p. 367**
☐	V62	**BUZZING WITH BOOKS**	Barbers in a small U.S. town are helping children learn how to read and improve their confidence.	**p. 370**
☐	V76	**HIP HOP THERAPY**	Youth are using hip hop as a means to address mental health challenges.	**p. 373**
☐	V85	**CODING FOR CHANGE**	An organization mobilzes citizen-led "brigades" to help their communities get better access to government services.	**p. 374**
☐	V89	**INTERGENERATIONAL IMPACT**	An organization is helping older people help younger people create better futures for themselves.	**p. 375**

YOUR TURN | SUGGESTED TOOLS TO HELP YOU PUT THIS IN ACTION

☐	T5.3	**EMPOWERMENT MAP**	Analyze current abilities and resources in order to decide what might be optimized to solve problems.	**p. 196**
☐	T6.4	**COMMUNITY CAPITAL MIX MAP**	Analyze the strengths of all of the forms of capital in the system to help you decide what might be optimized.	**p. 216**
☐	T6.6	**SYSTEM FIVE R'S MAP**	Analyze how current resources, relationships, roles, and rules are influencing the results in the system.	**p. 220**

THE CURRENT CONTEXT	
THE PROBLEM	
THE COMMUNITY ABILITIES + ASSETS	

HOW MIGHT WE OPTIMIZE COMMUNITY ABILITIES + ASSETS?

PRIORITY FOR OUR CHANGEMAKING EFFORTS	PERCEIVED STRENGTH OF THIS CONCEPT/ IDEA	POTENTIAL POSITIVE IMPACT OF THIS CONCEPT/ IDEA
LOW MEDIUM HIGH	LOW MEDIUM HIGH	LOW MEDIUM HIGH
WHY?	WHY?	WHY?

NOW WHAT?	

CT7 #TRANSFORMATION

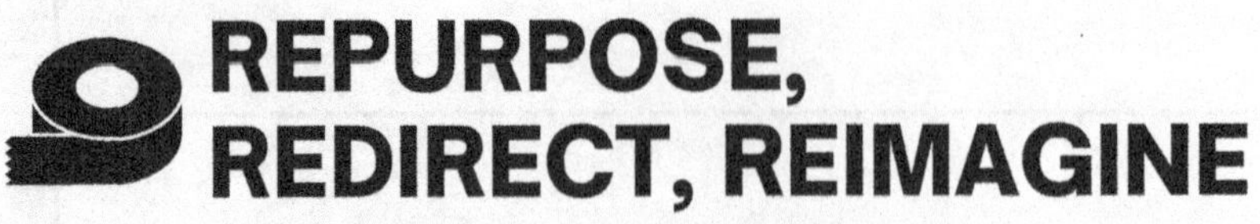

tinyurl.com/cctboxct7

As far as I can tell, duct tape, originally called "duck tape," was first used in the early 1900s for shoes and clothing. Since then, people have found innumerable creative uses for duct tape (I have a duct tape wallet that I love). Duct tape is the ultimate example of something that's been repurposed, redirected, and reimagined. When changemakers look at the world, they metaphorically see duct tape. They ask, "How can we achieve this with that?" They break away from traditional thinking and look at what already exists through a new lens. When you're looking to create positive change, try to repurpose a resource, redirect knowledge or a skill set, and/or reimagine an activity.

> *"Discovery consists of seeing what everybody has seen and thinking what nobody has thought."*
>
> **ALBERT SZENT-GYORGY**
> HUNGARIAN BIOCHEMIST
> NOBEL PRIZE LAUREATE

SEE THIS CHANGEMAKING TRIMTAB IN ACTION | SELECT CHANGEMAKING INNOVATION MINI-CASE EXAMPLES

V7	**WHERE BABIES DO THE TEACHING**	A Canadian organization works with schools to reimagine the natural empathy that children have with babies as a tool to help prevent bullying.	**p. 359**
V10	**MUSHROOM GARAGES**	Unused parking garages in Paris are being repurposed as spaces for small businesses.	**p. 359**
V22	**ULTIMATE PEACEMAKING**	The self-policing component of ultimate frisbee is reimagined as a means for Israeli and Palestinian youth to build relationships and learn conflict resolution strategies.	**p. 362**
V34	**LITERALLY A SCHOOL BUS**	A bus is repurposed as a school for children waiting for asylum on the U.S./Mexico border.	**p. 364**
V39	**HYDROPONIC SHIPPING CONTAINERS**	A Nigerian social enterprise repurposes shipping containers to house hydroponic vegetable farms.	**p. 365**
V59	**PLAY WITH PURPOSE**	An organization in the U.S. reimagines play at recess as a way for children and youth to practice collaboration.	**p. 369**
V61	**FITNESS FUELED SECOND CHANCES**	Formerly incarcerated men redirect their fitness practices into personal training jobs.	**p. 370**
V81	**FOCUSING ON INNOVATION**	A social enterprise is redirecting a portion of revenues to its program that donates eye glasses to organizations working in developing world countries.	**p. 374**
V86	**3D OCEAN FARMING**	A fisherman has reimagined how to get food from the ocean.	**p. 375**

YOUR TURN | SUGGESTED TOOLS TO HELP YOU PUT THIS IN ACTION

T3.4	**SWEET SPOT WHITEBOARD**	Analyze your repurposed, redirected, and/or reimagined innovation to help you ensure that it's sufficiently desirable, viable, feasible, and ethical.	**p. 154**
T7.4	**VALUE PROPOSITION MAP**	Conceptualize how you might repurpose, redirect, and/or reimagine something to relieve pain points and satisfy wants.	**p. 244**
T10.1	**PROBLEM-SOLVING POSITIONING**	Analyze and decide the ideal time/ place to intervene so that you can best consider what you might repurpose, redirect, and/or reimagine to help create positive change.	**p. 284**

THE CURRENT CONTEXT	
THE PROBLEM	
THE CURRENT ASSETS AND/ OR PRACTICES	

HOW MIGHT WE REPURPOSE, REDIRECT AND/OR REIMAGINE?

PRIORITY FOR OUR CHANGEMAKING EFFORTS	PERCEIVED STRENGTH OF THIS CONCEPT/ IDEA	POTENTIAL POSITIVE IMPACT OF THIS CONCEPT/ IDEA
LOW MEDIUM HIGH	LOW MEDIUM HIGH	LOW MEDIUM HIGH
WHY?	WHY?	WHY?

NOW WHAT?	

CT8

#TRANSFORMATION

CATALYZE CIRCULARITY

tinyurl.com/cctboxct8

The Ellen Macarthur Foundation defines a circular economy as "a system where materials never become waste and nature is regenerated. In a circular economy, products and materials are kept in circulation through processes like maintenance, reuse, refurbishment, remanufacture, recycling, and composting." But to be clear, circularity is about so much more than doing "less bad." When we focus on building circular economies, we can create catalytic positive change. Changemakers catalyze circularity to build dignified sanitation solutions, improve healthcare outcomes, protect the environment, improve agricultural yields, generate fuel, create new economic opportunities, and so much more.

"There is no such thing as 'away.' So, when we throw anything away, it must go somewhere."

ANNIE LEONARD
FORMER EXECUTIVE DIRECTOR - GREENPEACE

SEE THIS CHANGEMAKING TRIMTAB IN ACTION | SELECT CHANGEMAKING INNOVATION MINI-CASE EXAMPLES

V11	THE ALCHEMY OF COMPOSTING	A social enterprise in Paris is collecting food waste from restaurants and converting it into jobs and fertilizer.	p. 360
V13	SANITATION TO SOIL	A social enterprise in Haiti is transforming human feces into jobs and fertilizer.	p. 360
V25	FROM WASTE TO WALKWAYS	A young social entrepreneur in Kenya is turning plastic waste into bricks.	p. 362
V30	POO POWER	A social enterprise in Kenya is transforming human waste into cooking fuel.	p. 363
V33	HEROES OF E-WASTE	A couple in Malaysia is turning electronic waste into income generation opportunities.	p. 364
V42	PICKING A DIGNIFIED APPROACH	An organization in Peru is helping informal waste pickers become essential community entrepreneurs.	p. 366
V55	POWERED BY OLD BAGELS	A social enterprise is turning a food waste problem into a money saving and food security solution.	p. 368
V65	A SCRAPPY SOCIAL ENTERPRISE	A social enterprise in Brooklyn is collecting scraps from textile companies and turning them into myriad opportunities.	p. 370
V84	INCUBATING OPPORTUNITY IN APPALACHIA	A social enterprise incubator in Appalachia is working to turn former strip mines into housing sites, solar farm sites etc.	p. 374
V86	3D OCEAN FARMING	An fisherman has created a methodology to grow gardens in the ocean that can be scaled globally.	p. 375
V87	ABOUT THE HOW, NOT THE COW	A generative farmer is creating enterprises while protecting the land and the planet.	p. 375

YOUR TURN | SUGGESTED TOOLS TO HELP YOU PUT THIS IN ACTION

T7.5	NOVEL FEATURES + BENEFITS BLUEPRINT	Prioritize and share the novel features and benefits of your circular economy changemaking innovation.	p. 244
T10.2	TWO ATTRIBUTES POSITIONING DESIGN	Analyze and decide where and how your solution should be positioned relative to existing solutions.	p. 286
T10.4	MARKETING MIX STRATEGY	Discuss and decide the most compelling price, place and promotion strategies for your circular innovation (product).	p. 290

THE CURRENT CONTEXT	
THE "MATERIAL(S)" AND/OR ENVIRONMENT	
THE PROBLEM	

HOW MIGHT WE CATALYZE CIRCULARITY?

PRIORITY FOR OUR CHANGEMAKING EFFORTS	PERCEIVED STRENGTH OF THIS CONCEPT/ IDEA	POTENTIAL POSITIVE IMPACT OF THIS CONCEPT/ IDEA
LOW MEDIUM HIGH	LOW MEDIUM HIGH	LOW MEDIUM HIGH
WHY?	**WHY?**	**WHY?**

NOW WHAT?	

CT9

#SOCIAL CAPITAL

BUILD A PEER-FOR-PEER FRAMEWORK

tinyurl.com/cctboxct9

Who do you go to when you're facing a big challenge? On the one hand, you could turn to family and/or friends. But given the situation, that might not be ideal. On the other hand, there might be a professional who could help. But given factors such as cost, access, and power dynamics, to name a few, this might not be the most practical solution either. Sometimes, the best solution lies somewhere in the middle. This is where peer-for-peer frameworks can be uniquely helpful.

> *"The greatness of a community is most accurately measured by the compassionate actions of its members..."*
> **CORETTA SCOTT KING**
> CIVIL RIGHTS LEADER

There are essentially two peer-for-peer frameworks. The first is peer-to-peer. This framework brings people together who are roughly the same age and in similar situations. The second framework leverages near-peers. This is a relationship where a person who's recently experienced something, a near-peer, mentors/ coaches someone who's about to go through, or who's going through, the same kind of experience. Changemakers build peer-for-peer frameworks to help bring people together to prevent problems, provide mutual support, and build meaningful relationships.

SEE THIS CHANGEMAKING TRIMTAB IN ACTION | SELECT CHANGEMAKING INNOVATION MINI-CASE EXAMPLES

☐	V15	MOVING KNOWLEDGE INSTEAD OF PATIENTS	An organization has built an infrastructure whereby healthcare specialists and front line workers learn from each other.	p. 360
☐	V21	BUDDY BENCHES	Buddy Benches are used in playgrounds to give children a safe space to go to when they want to talk to someone.	p. 362
☐	V24	VIOLENCE INTERRUPTER	A program in Jamaica empowers men who were once part of the problem to become changemaking mentors.	p. 362
☐	V52	FROM PATIENT TO FACILITATOR	In Uganda, an organization created a group therapy program facilitated by other women who've been through the program.	p. 368
☐	V56	CHANGING THE NARRATIVE ABOUT BLACK MEN	A U.S. organization is building communities for Black men and collaborators to support community leadership efforts.	p. 369
☐	V58	DINNER TOGETHER FOR LOSS	Young adults come together over dinner to help each other talk about and deal with loss and grief.	p. 369
☐	V69	THE CITIZENS JUSTICE LEAGUE	An organization empowers families and friends to be defense teams for loved ones and to help other families like them.	p. 372
☐	V74	WALKING FOR TRANSFORMATION	A U.S. nonprofit organization helps Black women practice self-care through walking together.	p. 371

YOUR TURN | SUGGESTED TOOLS TO HELP YOU PUT THIS IN ACTION

☐	T2.8	THREATS + REWARDS CHECK-IN	Analyze how people might feel threatened so that you can prioritize the kind of peer support that might be most helpful.	p. 140
☐	T6.10	VUCA MAP	Identify where and how people are feeling volatility, uncertainty, complexity and/or ambiguity in their lives.	p. 228
☐	T9.1	PEER EMPOWERMENT STRATEGY DESIGN	Design a peer empowerment strategy to help address the most critical challenges/ areas of concern.	p. 270
☐	T9.2	COMMUNITY OF PRACTICE STRATEGY DESIGN	Design a community of practice strategy so that people might share where they need help and build a supportive community.	p. 272

THE CURRENT CONTEXT	
THE PEOPLE	
THE PROBLEM	

HOW MIGHT WE BUILD A PEER-FOR-PEER FRAMEWORK?

PRIORITY FOR OUR CHANGEMAKING EFFORTS	PERCEIVED STRENGTH OF THIS CONCEPT/ IDEA	POTENTIAL POSITIVE IMPACT OF THIS CONCEPT/ IDEA
LOW MEDIUM HIGH	LOW MEDIUM HIGH	LOW MEDIUM HIGH
WHY?	WHY?	WHY?

NOW WHAT?	

CT10

#SOCIAL CAPITAL

BUILD PURPOSE-DRIVEN TEAMS + TEAMS OF TEAMS

tinyurl.com/cctboxct10

The speed of change is accelerating at a faster and faster rate. Given this, successful changemaking requires building purpose-driven teams and teams of teams that are agile, dynamic, fluid, and inclusive.

To start, build a core, purpose-driven team. Make sure the purpose is a commitment. Accelerating change causes volatility, uncertainty, complexity, and ambiguity. Teams that aren't committed to a shared purpose can easily become unmoored and lose their way in this type of environment.

"No matter how brilliant your mind or strategy, if you're playing a solo game, you'll always lose out to a team."

REID HOFFMAN
CO-FOUNDER - LINKEDIN

And second, this core team should be continuously building/ adding additional teams and teams of teams that share the same purpose. This might be smaller, project-focused teams within the core team and/ or teams that include people from different organizations. They might be teams that span geographies and/ or competencies. Some might be temporary, and others might be permanent.

SEE THIS CHANGEMAKING TRIMTAB IN ACTION | SELECT CHANGEMAKING INNOVATION MINI-CASE EXAMPLES

☐	**V15**	**MOVING KNOWLEDGE INSTEAD OF PATIENTS**	An organization is building teams and teams of teams of healthcare professionals to serve patients in remote areas.	**p. 360**
☐	**V32**	**A COOPERATIVE FUTURE**	Community members in Madagascar started cooperatives/ associations to create opportunity and overcome insecurity.	**p. 364**
☐	**V43**	**A COMMUNITY-LED RECOVERY**	Teams and teams of teams in Puerto Rico were created to prioritize and solve problems after a hurricane.	**p. 366**
☐	**V46**	**WRITING A BOOK A DAY**	Teams and teams of teams of educators come together for one day to write contextually appropriate books.	**p. 367**
☐	**V68**	**GETTING TO ZERO HOMELESSNESS**	Teams and teams of teams of stakeholders in cities work together to eradicate homelessness.	**p. 371**
☐	**V69**	**THE CITIZEN'S JUSTICE LEAGUE**	Teams of families and friends work together as part of legal defense teams for their loved ones.	**p. 371**
☐	**V73**	**SURROUNDING STUDENTS WITH SUPPORT**	Teams of dedicated community members work together to support struggling students.	**p. 372**
☐	**V85**	**CODING FOR CHANGE**	Teams and teams of teams of coders improve software to enhance the accessibility of government programs.	**p. 374**

YOUR TURN | SUGGESTED TOOLS TO HELP YOU PUT THIS IN ACTION

☐	**T1.1**	**OUR TEAM**	Identify who you might want to include on your team and team of teams now and in the future.	**p. 110**
☐	**T2.2**	**OUR RACI STRUCTURE CHECK-IN**	Make sure you're distributing roles and responsibilities clearly and thoughtfully.	**p. 128**
☐	**T1.4**	**OUR COLLABORATIVE CULTURE**	Establish the kind of culture that's necessary for your team and teams of teams to collaborate and innovate.	**p. 116**
☐	**T8.2**	**COLLABORATOR COMPATIBILITY ANALYSIS**	Assess the compatibility of potential collaborators that you've identified.	**p. 258**
☐	**T9.4**	**COLLECTIVE IMPACT STRATEGY DESIGN**	Start to build a strategy where multiple organizations work together to solve a big problem.	**p. 258**

THE CURRENT CONTEXT	
THE PURPOSE	
THE PROBLEM	

HOW MIGHT WE BUILD PURPOSE-DRIVEN TEAMS + TEAMS OF TEAMS?

PRIORITY FOR OUR CHANGEMAKING EFFORTS	**PERCEIVED STRENGTH OF THIS CONCEPT/ IDEA**	**POTENTIAL POSITIVE IMPACT OF THIS CONCEPT/ IDEA**
LOW MEDIUM HIGH	LOW MEDIUM HIGH	LOW MEDIUM HIGH
WHY?	**WHY?**	**WHY?**

NOW WHAT?	

CT11

#POSITIVE KNOCK-ON OUTCOMES

CREATE OPPORTUNITIES FOR CATALYTIC CONNECTIONS

tinyurl.com/cctboxct11

Changemakers work to connect people who otherwise wouldn't be connected. This is one of the most catalytic things you can do as a changemaker. At the most basic level, connection creates relationships. And the key to happiness is relationships. This was the big conclusion from the world's longest study of happiness started by Harvard way back in 1938.

However, creating connections can be about so much more than happiness. Connections can be catalytic. They help people become more empathetic and feel more empowered. This is the secret sauce that makes all kinds of amazing changemaking possible.

> *"I define connection as the energy that exists between people when they feel seen, heard, and valued; when they can give and receive without judgment; and when they derive sustenance and strength from the relationship."*
>
> **BRENÉ BROWN**
> PROFESSOR, AUTHOR + SPEAKER

SEE THIS CHANGEMAKING TRIMTAB IN ACTION | SELECT CHANGEMAKING INNOVATION MINI-CASE EXAMPLES

☐	V1	**CLEAN CLOTHES + CONVERSATIONS**	Chairs are set up for community members to converse and build relationships while laundry is being cleaned.	p. 358
☐	V2	**DESIGNING FOR CHANGE**	The CEO of a social enterprise has lunch with her employees every day.	p. 358
☐	V7	**WHERE BABIES DO THE TEACHING**	Schoolchildren in Canada spend time with babies on a continuous basis.	p. 359
☐	V38	**CROWD FARMING**	A crowdfunding platform empowers investors in Nigeria to continually support small scale farmers.	p. 365
☐	V48	**LIVING WITH MANDATORY FRIENDS**	In an apartment building in Sweden, pensioners and younger residents spend two hours per week together to combat loneliness.	p. 367
☐	V54	**COOKING EMPATHY**	Customers return to cooking classes to build relationships with refugees.	p. 368
☐	V63	**WELCOMING COMMUNITIES**	Current community members and new immigrants periodically meet and invite others to join in order to build relationships and create harmony.	p. 370
☐	V73	**SURROUNDING STUDENTS WITH SUPPORT**	A volunteer support and mentor network commits to a ten year relationship with struggling students in Baltimore.	p. 372
☐	V79	**A CIVIC JOURNALISM HUB**	Journalists and local community members meet at a hub to discuss news that should be prioritized.	p. 373

YOUR TURN | SUGGESTED TOOLS TO HELP YOU PUT THIS IN ACTION

☐	T2.1	**LEVEL SETTING CHECK-IN**	Make sure that everyone is starting from the same place at the beginning of every conversation.	p. 126
☐	T2.7	**KANBAN CHECK-IN**	Check-in on the status of shared activities/ projects.	p. 138
☐	T12.3	**COMMUNICATION CHANNEL STRATEGY**	Decide the best communication channel(s) for your continuous communication.	p. 320
☐	T12.5	**TOUCHPOINT STRATEGY**	Decide the ideal frequency and content of your continuous communication.	p. 324

THE CURRENT CONTEXT	
THE PEOPLE WE HOPE TO CONNECT	
THE PROBLEM	

HOW MIGHT WE CREATE OPPORTUNITIES FOR CATALYTIC CONNECTIONS?		
PRIORITY FOR OUR CHANGEMAKING EFFORTS	**PERCEIVED STRENGTH OF THIS CONCEPT/ IDEA**	**POTENTIAL POSITIVE IMPACT OF THIS CONCEPT/ IDEA**
LOW MEDIUM HIGH	LOW MEDIUM HIGH	LOW MEDIUM HIGH
WHY?	**WHY?**	**WHY?**

NOW WHAT?	

CT12 #POSITIVE KNOCK-ON OUTCOMES

SOLVE ONE KIND OF PROBLEM TO SOLVE ANOTHER

tinyurl.com/cctboxct12

Changemakers work to avoid myopic thinking. They look for ways to solve one kind of problem to solve another. Using this approach might be out of necessity or show up as an opportunity. For example, recently schools all across the U.S. have been buying washers and dryers. Why? Because when changemaker educators looked for the root causes of why certain students weren't showing up to school, they discovered that many students from lower-income households couldn't afford to wash their clothes frequently. And they were understandably too embarrassed to come to school wearing dirty clothes. So schools solved the problem by giving students free access to washers and dryers at school. They solved an absenteeism problem by first solving a laundry problem.

> *"The best way to solve a problem is to remove its cause."*
> **DR. MARTIN LUTHER KING JR.**
> CIVIL RIGHTS LEADER | NOBEL PEACE PRIZE LAUREATE

SEE THIS CHANGEMAKING TRIMTAB IN ACTIONN | SELECT CHANGEMAKING INNOVATION MINI-CASE EXAMPLES

☐	**V10**	**MUSHROOM GARAGES**	Paris is solving a vacant parking garage problem to also solve a business infrastructure problem.	**p. 359**
☐	**V13**	**SANITATION TO SOIL**	A social enterprise in Haiti is solving a sanitation problem to also solve an agricultural problem.	**p. 360**
☐	**V47**	**BLACK MAMBAS PREVENTING POACHING**	An organization in South Africa is solving a professional opportunities problem to also solve a poaching problem.	**p. 367**
☐	**V49**	**VEGGIES FOR EDUCATION**	A school in Tanzania is solving a hunger problem to also solve an education problem.	**p. 367**
☐	**V53**	**SANITARY PADS FOR EDUCATION**	A school in Uganda is solving a menstrual health problem to also solve an education problem.	**p. 368**
☐	**V77**	**ADVANCING EMPLOYEE OWNERSHIP**	A U.S. organization is solving the problem of business succession while also helping to empower a new generation of business owners.	**p. 373**
☐	**V80**	**BITE-SIZED CHANGEMAKING**	A social enterprise in the U.S. is solving a portability problem to also solve a plastics problem.	**p. 373**
☐	**V82**	**TURNING BUILDINGS INTO TESLAS**	A social enterprise is solving an energy cost problem to also solve a climate change problem.	**p. 374**
☐	**V89**	**INTERGENERATIONAL IMPACT**	An organization is solving a problem for youth and children by solving a problem confronting older adults.	**p. 375**

YOUR TURN | SUGGESTED TOOLS TO HELP YOU PUT THIS IN ACTION

☐	**T3.9**	**CONSEQUENCES WHITEBOARD**	Analyze the potential second and third-order positive and negative consequences of your solution.	**p. 164**
☐	**T4.1**	**ROOT CAUSE ANALYSIS**	Be methodical about asking "Why?" to get to the root cause of problems and decide where it might be best to intervene.	**p. 174**
☐	**T4.2**	**PROBLEM TREE ANALYSIS**	Analyze all of the the root causes and effects of problems to decide where it might be best to step in.	**p. 176**

THE CURRENT CONTEXT	
ONE PROBLEM	
ANOTHER PROBLEM	

HOW MIGHT WE SOLVE ONE PROBLEM TO ALSO SOLVE ANOTHER?

PRIORITY FOR OUR CHANGEMAKING EFFORTS	**PERCEIVED STRENGTH OF THIS CONCEPT/ IDEA**	**POTENTIAL POSITIVE IMPACT OF THIS CONCEPT/ IDEA**
LOW MEDIUM HIGH	LOW MEDIUM HIGH	LOW MEDIUM HIGH
WHY?	**WHY?**	**WHY?**

NOW WHAT?	

CT13

#DESIGNING FOR CONTEXT

RESTRUCTURE IT

tinyurl.com/cctboxct13

Often the best way to solve a problem is to simply restructure a solution that already exists. It can be a lot easier to make a change to a solution that's already in place than to create an entirely new solution. Restructuring can take many forms. It can mean changing the size, length, shape, taste, capacity, language, location, interface, etc. The solution might be to restructure most of the solution or only one component. So before you create something new, deconstruct what already exists to see if there's a way you can restructure it to achieve your desired outcomes.

> *"The alternative to good design is always bad design. There is no such thing as no design."*
>
> **ADAM JUDGE**
> AUTHOR - *THE LITTLE BLACK BOOK OF DESIGN*

SEE THIS CHANGEMAKING TRIMTAB IN ACTION | SELECT CHANGEMAKING INNOVATION MINI-CASE EXAMPLES

☐	**V8**	**CHILD-CENTERED EDUCATION**	Education is restructured to overcome the challenges that schools face in the developing world.	**p. 359**
☐	**V17**	**DESIGNED "WITH", NOT "FOR"**	In India, a social enterprise is restructuring stoves to fit the needs and wants of local women.	**p. 361**
☐	**V27**	**MICROGRIDS IN ACTION**	Solar energy capacity is restructured to meet the electricity needs of a rural community.	**p. 363**
☐	**V28**	**PIPING THROUGH PROBLEMS**	A system of pipes was restructured to distribute water in a Kenyan city.	**p. 363**
☐	**V46**	**WRITING A BOOK A DAY**	Educators in South Africa restructure books to make them contextually appropriate for local children.	**p. 367**
☐	**V73**	**SURROUNDING STUDENTS WITH SUPPORT**	A program designed to help struggling students provides each one with ten years of continuous community support.	**p. 372**
☐	**V80**	**BITE-SIZED CHANGEMAKING**	An entrepreneur in the U.S. designed individually portion-sized toothpaste to avoid waste.	**p. 373**
☐	**V81**	**FOCUSING ON INNOVATION**	A social enterprise restructures how people try on glasses by sending potential customers five pairs to try on at home.	**p. 374**
☐	**V83**	**CROSS SUBSIDIZING HEALTHY MEALS**	A social enterprise in Los Angeles restructures the ingredients in its meals to meet local tastes and preferences.	**p. 374**
☐	**V85**	**CODING FOR CHANGE**	A U.S. organization is restructuring software programs so that citizens can get equitable access to essential services.	**p. 374**
☐	**V88**	**BUSINESS FOR A BETTER WORLD**	Organizations are restructuring their metrics to help them make positive contributions to the world.	**p. 375**

YOUR TURN | SUGGESTED TOOLS TO HELP YOU PUT THIS IN ACTION

☐	**T5.1**	**EMPATHY MAP**	Get a comprehensive understanding of the unique perspectives of the people you aspire to support.	**p. 192**
☐	**T6.3**	**EQUITABLE ACCESS MAP**	Analyze how current solutions aren't creating equitable access so that you can restructure design features.	**p. 214**
☐	**T11.3**	**USER EXPERIENCE STRATEGY**	Analyze the user experience of your innovation or an existing innovation so that you can identify opportunities for restructuring.	**p. 302**

THE CURRENT CONTEXT	
THE DESIRED OUTCOMES	
THE PROBLEM	

HOW MIGHT WE RESTRUCTURE IT?

PRIORITY FOR OUR CHANGEMAKING EFFORTS	**PERCEIVED STRENGTH OF THIS CONCEPT/ IDEA**	**POTENTIAL POSITIVE IMPACT OF THIS CONCEPT/ IDEA**
LOW MEDIUM HIGH	LOW MEDIUM HIGH	LOW MEDIUM HIGH
WHY?	**WHY?**	**WHY?**

NOW WHAT?	

CT14

#DESIGNING FOR CONTEXT

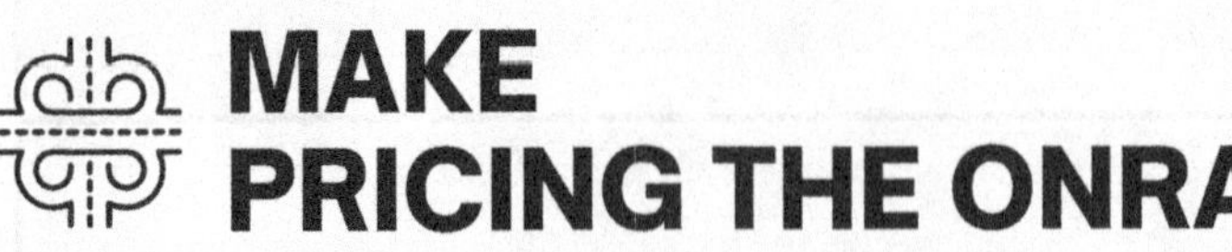

MAKE PRICING THE ONRAMP

tinyurl.com/cctboxct14

Everything has a price. And price is too often seen as an obstacle. It shouldn't be. Changemakers work to understand the context and creatively turn price from obstacle to onramp. Do the same by making sure your pricing strategy creatively passes three tests.

First, make the price affordable to your target market/ community. Second, make it attractive. And third, your price should inspire adoption. This is the ultimate goal. Adoption means people both want to and are able to make a habit of using your changemaking innovation.

> *"Price is what you pay. Value is what you get."*
>
> **WARREN BUFFETT**
> CEO | BERKSHIRE HATHAWAY

SEE THIS CHANGEMAKING TRIMTAB IN ACTION | CHANGEMAKING INNOVATION MINI-CASE EXAMPLES

☐	V9	**GROW YOUR OWN RAINFOREST**	An organization designed a scheme that pays farmers to grow rainforests.	p. 359
☐	V12	**MICROCONSIGNMENT FOR THE LAST MILE**	An organization is empowering opportunities for first-time women entrepreneurs by allowing them to pay for their inventory after they sell it.	p. 360
☐	V31	**GIVING CHOICE FOR A CHANGE**	An organization is giving people in Kenya money with no strings attached.	p. 364
☐	V23	**FREE BEER FOR CYCLING**	Bologna started a program whereby people earn points for riding bicycles that are redeemable at local businesses.	p. 362
☐	V29	**CLEAN COOKING ATM'S**	Lower income families in Kenya can buy cooking fuel from a machine in quantities that they can afford at the moment.	p. 363
☐	V57	**PATIENT CAPITAL**	Social enterprises get access to capital at a price that they're able to pay back over an extended period of time.	p. 369
☐	V81	**FOCUSING ON INNOVATION**	A social enterprise charges a lower price for high-quality glasses than its competitors and then allocates a portion of revenues to donate glasses to people who can't afford them.	p. 374
☐	V82	**TURNING BUILDINGS INTO TESLAS**	Lower income families in apartment buildings pay less for electricity as a part of a model to accelerate solar energy adoption in U.S. cities.	p. 374
☐	V83	**CROSS SUBSIDIZING HEALTHY MEALS**	People pay different prices for meals based on where they live.	p. 374
☐	V86	**3D OCEAN GARDENING**	An organization designed a way for fishermen to start ocean gardens with a reasonable up-front investment.	p. 375
☐	V90	**PEDAL POWER**	Women in Zambia are able to buy bicycles for the first time through a "pay as you go" structure using mobile phones.	p. 375

YOUR TURN | SUGGESTED TOOLS TO HELP YOU PUT THIS IN ACTION

☐	T3.5	**FOUR FITS WHITEBOARD**	Make sure that your pricing strategy fits with your product/service, market, and distribution strategies.	p. 156
☐	T5.2	**PERSONA MAP**	Build a comprehensive profile of the people you aspire to support so that you can consider the best pricing approach.	p. 194
☐	T11.2	**PRICING FOR ADOPTION STRATEGY**	Analyze a variety of pricing strategies to help you decide which might be the best to inspire the adoption of your innovation.	p. 300

THE CURRENT CONTEXT	
THE PEOPLE	
THE PRODUCT/ SERVICE	

HOW MIGHT WE MAKE PRICING THE ONRAMP?

PRIORITY FOR OUR CHANGEMAKING EFFORTS	PERCEIVED STRENGTH OF THIS CONCEPT/ IDEA	POTENTIAL POSITIVE IMPACT OF THIS CONCEPT/ IDEA
LOW MEDIUM HIGH	LOW MEDIUM HIGH	LOW MEDIUM HIGH
WHY?	WHY?	WHY?

NOW WHAT?	

CT15

#COUNTER-INTUITIVE DESIGN

CONFRONT COMPLEXITY WITH SIMPLICITY

tinyurl.com/cctboxct15

The mere thought of trying to solving problems to change systems can make you want to go back to bed and pull the covers over your head. Systems are complex. And confronting complexity can be scary and feel paralyzing. It needn't be. Because you don't solve complex problems with complex solutions. Always start simple. Starting simple helps you get moving. It's the only way to experiment and learn. Simplicity is critical for adoption. And simple scales.

"Everything should be made as simple as possible, but not simpler."

ALBERT EINSTEIN
PHYSICIST

SEE THIS CHANGEMAKING TRIMTAB IN ACTION | CHANGEMAKING INNOVATION MINI-CASE EXAMPLES

☐	V1	CLEAN CLOTHES + CONVERSATIONS	An organization in Australia retrofitted a van with a washer and dryer to provide a mobile laundry solution for the houseless.	p. 358
☐	V21	BUDDY BENCHES	Benches are set up in playgrounds to create a safe space for children who are feeling left out and/or lonely.	p. 362
☐	V34	LITERALLY A SCHOOL BUS	A school bus was retrofitted to serve as the education center for children in limbo on the U.S.-Mexican border.	p. 364
☐	V37	WE'LL SOLVE IT OURSELVES!	Women in a small community in Nigeria bought a car and pay a driver to combat high infant mortality rates.	p. 365
☐	V41	A STOPLIGHT FOR POVERTY ALLEVIATION	An organization in Paraguay created a poverty alleviation diagnostic tool based on the colors of the stoplight.	p. 366
☐	V44	STORIES OF CHANGE	An organization working in refugee camps is using simple storytelling techniques to help people deal with trauma.	p. 366
☐	V63	WELCOMING COMMUNITIES	New immigrants and community members get together to learn each others' perspectives and build empathy.	p. 370
☐	V69	THE CITIZEN'S JUSTICE LEAGUE	An organization is addressing inequities in the justice system by empowering family/ friends as defense team members.	p. 371
☐	V72	BATTLING CASH BAIL	A movement is creating awareness and fighting injustices within the cash bail system by giving people money.	p. 372
☐	V86	3D OCEAN FARMING	A fisherman is combatting the degradation of the oceans by building underwater gardens.	p. 375

YOUR TURN | SUGGESTED TOOLS TO HELP YOU PUT THIS IN ACTION

☐	T3.1	PROXIMITY WHITEBOARD	Start your ideation with the people, place, and/or problem where you have the closest proximity.	p. 148
☐	T3.2	IMPACT + EFFORT WHITEBOARD	Analyze your innovation ideas with the goal of finding one that creates the greatest amount of impact for the least amount of effort.	p. 150
☐	T3.8	TWO LIMITATIONS WHITEBOARD	Make sure that you're accounting for practical limitations to help you design creative, pragmatic solutions.	p. 162
☐	T6.7	SYSTEM COMPONENTS MAP	Analyze five components of the system to help you decide where it might be best to intervene with a simple solution.	p. 222

THE CURRENT CONTEXT	
THE COMPLEX SYSTEM	
THE PROBLEM	

HOW MIGHT WE CONFRONT COMPLEXITY WITH SIMPLICITY?

PRIORITY FOR OUR CHANGEMAKING EFFORTS	**PERCEIVED STRENGTH OF THIS CONCEPT/ IDEA**	**POTENTIAL POSITIVE IMPACT OF THIS CONCEPT/ IDEA**
LOW MEDIUM HIGH	LOW MEDIUM HIGH	LOW MEDIUM HIGH
WHY?	**WHY?**	**WHY?**

NOW WHAT?	

CT16 #COUNTER-INTUITIVE DESIGN

DO THE OPPOSITE

tinyurl.com/cctboxct16

Dating myself, there's a classic episode from the TV show Seinfeld where George, the lovable loser in the show, sits down at a diner with his friend Jerry. He says something to the extent of, "Every instinct I've ever had in my life is wrong, so from now on I'm going to do the opposite." Soon after, he decides to test this new strategy and approaches an attractive woman at the nearby counter and says, "My name's George. I'm unemployed and I live with my parents." She responds with a smile, "I'm Victoria. Hi."

"Humans are allergic to change. They love to say, 'We've always done it this way.' I try to fight that. That's why I have a clock on my wall that runs counter-clockwise."

GRACE HOPPER
COMPUTER SCIENTIST

Doing the opposite doesn't just work in sitcoms. Often, when confronted with a wicked problem, the smartest thing to do is to flip the traditional approach on its head and do the exact opposite. The old way isn't working, so why not try the opposite?! One advantage is that the opposite can be easy to figure out. Trying to make a decision that lies somewhere in the murky middle can be difficult and invites complexity. An added advantage is that doing the opposite is unexpected. It makes people sit up and take notice. So, the next time something isn't working, channel your inner George and try doing the opposite.

SEE THIS CHANGEMAKING TRIMTAB IN ACTION | SELECT CHANGEMAKING INNOVATION MINI-CASE EXAMPLES

V2	**DESIGNING FOR CHANGE**	The CEO of an Australian social enterprise leads with the attitude that she works for her employees.	p. 358
V4	**FOUR-EYED COWS**	Researchers designed a way to protect cattle from lion attacks by focusing on the cattle, not the lions.	p. 358
V8	**CHILD-CENTERED EDUCATION**	An organization in Colombia has flipped classrooms in the developing world from teacher-centered to child-centered learning.	p. 359
V12	**MICROCONSIGNMENT FOR THE LAST MILE**	An organization is empowering first-time women entrepreneurs in Guatemala by having them pay for inventory after they sell it, not before.	p. 360
V31	**GIVING CHOICE FOR A CHANGE**	An organization is giving people in Kenya money with no strings attached.	p. 364
V36	**NAMING + FAMING**	To combat corruption, the Nepalese government designed a program that focuses on rewarding good public servants, as opposed to punishing bad ones.	p. 365
V71	**SOLUTIONS JOURNALISM**	A U.S. non-profit organization is helping journalists write about solutions, not problems.	p. 372
V87	**ABOUT THE HOW, NOT THE COW**	A farmer is working with nature, not against her.	p. 375

YOUR TURN | SUGGESTED TOOLS TO HELP YOU PUT THIS IN ACTION

T3.6	**DESIGN PRINCIPLES WHITEBOARD**	Analyze how well current solutions adhere to design principles so that you can identify where to do the opposite.	p. 158
T6.2	**CURRENT SOLUTIONS LANDSCAPE MAP**	Analyze other solutions to your problem to find out what isn't working. Then do the opposite.	p. 212
T11.4	**MOTIVATION + CAPABILITIES STRATEGY**	Look for what's negatively influencing motivation and capabilities so that you can try the opposite.	p. 304

THE CURRENT CONTEXT	
THE PROBLEM	
THE CONVENTIONAL PRACTICE(S)	

HOW MIGHT WE DO THE OPPOSITE?

PRIORITY FOR OUR CHANGEMAKING EFFORTS	PERCEIVED STRENGTH OF THIS CONCEPT/ IDEA	POTENTIAL POSITIVE IMPACT OF THIS CONCEPT/ IDEA
LOW MEDIUM HIGH	LOW MEDIUM HIGH	LOW MEDIUM HIGH
WHY?	WHY?	WHY?

NOW WHAT?	

CT17 #INTRINSIC MOTIVATIONS

FORTIFY EVERYDAY ACTIVITIES

tinyurl.com/cctboxct17

Rickets is a childhood disease that's caused by a prolonged deficiency of Vitamin D. It softens and weakens bones. In the 1930s, there was a rickets epidemic that primarily affected children from lower-income families in U.S. cities. An innovative solution, which still exists, was to fortify milk with Vitamin D. This was ingenious for three reasons. First, it's compatible. Children drink a lot of milk. Second, it's scalable. A lot of children drink milk. And third, it's inexpensive. The distribution channel for milk already existed.

> *"Life is beautiful not because of the things we see or do. Life is beautiful because of the people we meet."*
>
> **SIMON SINEK**
> AUTHOR- *START WITH WHY: HOW GREAT LEADERS INSPIRE EVERYONE TO TAKE ACTION*

Changemakers often take this same kind of fortification approach when looking for ways to support people. They fortify everyday activities with changemaking activities for the same three reasons that fortifying milk with Vitamin D is so smart. But there are two wonderful differences. First, Vitamin D doesn't make milk taste better, whereas adding a focus on changemaking brings visible new meaning and joy to everyday activities. And second, fortifying milk with Vitamin D does one thing. It prevents a problem. Fortifying everyday activities with changemaking can be about so much more. It can be structured to help people prevent problems and cope with challenges. It can include models to help people build new skill sets and mindsets. And, it helps people build deep, powerful, and purpose-driven relationships.

SEE THIS CHANGEMAKING TRIMTAB IN ACTION | SELECT CHANGEMAKING INNOVATION MINI-CASE EXAMPLES

☐ V1	CLEAN CLOTHES + CONVERSATIONS	Doing laundry is fortified with community conversations.	p. 358
☐ V54	COOKING EMPATHY	Cooking classes are fortified to create job opportunities, build empathy and create friendships.	p. 368
☐ V58	DINNER CONVERSATIONS FOR LOSS	Dinner is fortified as way for people to come together, cope with loss, and build relationships.	p. 369
☐ V59	PLAY WITH PURPOSE	Recess is fortified to help children and youth learn new skill sets and develop new mindsets.	p. 369
☐ V62	BUZZING WITH BOOKS	Haircuts for children are fortified with reading aloud.	p. 370
☐ V74	WALKING FOR TRANSFORMATION	Walking is fortified as a means for Black women to practice self-care.	p. 372
☐ V75	GIRLS FINDING THEIR PACE	Running is fortified as a way for girls to learn life and leadership skills.	p. 372
☐ V76	HIP HOP THERAPY	Hip hop is fortified as a means for youth to improve their mental health.	p. 373
☐ V78	FUTURE READY EDUCATION	School is fortified with global competence skills building.	p. 378

YOUR TURN | SUGGESTED TOOLS TO HELP YOU PUT THIS IN ACTION

☐ T7.5	NOVEL FEATURES + BENEFITS BLUEPRINT	Consider the different features and benefits that might fortify a daily activity.	p. 246
☐ T9.1	PEER SUPPORT STRATEGY DESIGN	Fortify a daily activity with a strategy that brings peers together to support each other.	p. 270
☐ T11.1	KEYS TO INNOVATION ADOPTION	Make sure that your innovation design has the best opportunity of being adopted.	p. 298

THE CURRENT CONTEXT	
THE PEOPLE	
THE PROBLEM	
THE ACTIVITY	

HOW MIGHT WE FORTIFY EVERDAY ACTIVITIES?		
PRIORITY FOR OUR CHANGEMAKING EFFORTS	**PERCEIVED STRENGTH OF THIS CONCEPT/ IDEA**	**POTENTIAL POSITIVE IMPACT OF THIS CONCEPT/ IDEA**
LOW MEDIUM HIGH	LOW MEDIUM HIGH	LOW MEDIUM HIGH
WHY?	**WHY?**	**WHY?**

NOW WHAT?	

☐ CT18

#INTRINSIC MOTIVATIONS

PRIORITIZE PROXIMITY

tinyurl.com/cctboxct18

Changemaking is putting empathy in action. And empathy is driven by proximity, or closeness. The closer we are, emotionally, experientially, and/or physically, the more empathetic we're likely to be. Because of this, changemakers focus on supporting people, working in places, and/or solving problems that they're close to.

Focus your changemaking efforts on the people, places, and/or problems where you have the closest proximity to give yourself the best chance for success.

> *"Leadership is about empathy. It is about having the ability to relate to and connect with people for the purpose of inspiring and empowering their lives."*
>
> **OPRAH WINFREY**
> CHAIRWOMAN + CEO | HARPO PRODUCTIONS

SEE THIS CHANGEMAKING TRIMTAB IN ACTION | SELECT CHANGEMAKING INNOVATION MINI-CASE EXAMPLES

☐	V3	SOLVING THE ARSENIC PROBLEM	A social entrepreneur is helping people in Bangladesh access safe drinking water after seeing the impacts of arsenic poisoning firsthand.	p. 358
☐	V16	THEY CALL HIM POOP GUY	A man in India is motivated to improve sanitation services for girls by thinking about his daughter.	p. 361
☐	V18	A VISION FOR IMPACT	An U.S. optometrist finds his purpose after helping a boy in India get his first pair of glasses.	p. 361
☐	V21	BUDDY BENCHES	Children support fellow classmates who are feeling lonely.	p. 362
☐	V24	VIOLENCE INTERRUPTOR	A Jamaican man is helping others in his hometown to avoid making the same mistakes that he made.	p. 362
☐	V32	A COOPERATIVE FUTURE	A woman in Madagascar is driven by the goal of creating an opportunity for her children to go to college.	p. 364
☐	V51	3D PRINTING SURPRISES + SMILES	Volunteer artists in Turkey are motivated to make their city a more joyful place.	p. 368
☐	V54	COOKING EMPATHY	A woman in the U.K. is motivated to start her organization supporting refugees after visiting Morocco.	p. 368
☐	V58	DINNER TOGETHER FOR LOSS	Friends start an organization to help young adults deal with loss because they've suffered loss themselves.	p. 369
☐	V81	FOCUSING ON INNOVATION	Co-founders launch a social enterprise selling eyeglasses based on their own experiences in the sector and as consumers.	p. 374

YOUR TURN | SUGGESTED TOOLS TO HELP YOU PUT THIS IN ACTION

☐	T1.2	OUR WHY	Align your WHY with your teammates and the community you aspire to support.	p. 112
☐	T1.3	PROXIMITY WHITEBOARD	Analyze the people, places, and problems where you might have the closest proximity.	p. 148
☐	T5.1	EMPATHY MAP	Get the perspectives of the people you aspire to support. Work to see the world through their eyes, words, thoughts, and feelings.	p. 192

THE CURRENT CONTEXT	
THE PEOPLE, PROBLEM AND/OR PLACE	
OUR PROXIMITY	

HOW MIGHT WE PRIORITIZE PROXIMITY?

PRIORITY FOR OUR CHANGEMAKING EFFORTS	PERCEIVED STRENGTH OF THIS CONCEPT/ IDEA	POTENTIAL POSITIVE IMPACT OF THIS CONCEPT/ IDEA
LOW MEDIUM HIGH	LOW MEDIUM HIGH	LOW MEDIUM HIGH
WHY?	WHY?	WHY?

NOW WHAT?	

☐ **CT19** **#BUILDING ECOSYSTEMS**

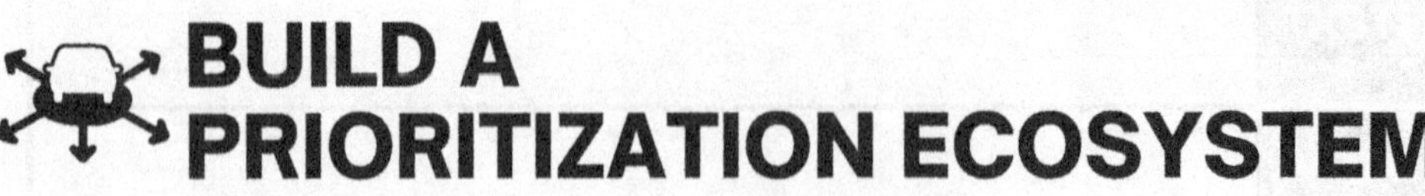

BUILD A PRIORITIZATION ECOSYSTEM

tinyurl.com/cctboxct19

"Measurement is fabulous. Unless you're busy measuring what's easy to measure as opposed to what's important."
SETH GODIN
AUTHOR

Waze is an incredible example of a prioritization ecosystem. You type in your destination. It then gathers information in real-time from users maneuvering through your complex, constantly changing traffic system. It recognizes obstacles and opportunities. It then presents you with a prioritized display of options to help you get to your destination as quickly as possible. And it provides continuous updates and new prioritized suggestions as conditions change.

Changemakers work to build this "Waze-like" functionality in their changemaking innovations. The systems, problems, and opportunities that changemakers encounter are no less complex than traffic patterns. Continuous learning and pivoting are critical. Building ecosystems that provide prioritized information and insights that empowers this is essential for success.

SEE THIS CHANGEMAKING TRIMTAB IN ACTION | SELECT CHANGEMAKING INNOVATION MINI-CASE EXAMPLES

☐	V15	MOVING KNOWLEDGE INSTEAD OF PATIENTS	Healthcare professionals from around the world continuously communicate with each other about how to treat illnesses.	p. 360
☐	V41	A STOPLIGHT FOR POVERTY ALLEVIATION	Community members in Paraguay use a poverty alleviation tool to help them prioritize their efforts.	p. 366
☐	V60	WORKER-LED PRIORITIZATION	Workers use tablets with customized software to crowdsource priorities and participate in campaigns.	p. 369
☐	V63	WELCOMING COMMUNITIES	Established community members and new immigrants continuously meet to build empathy and prioritize challenges.	p. 370
☐	V67	HUMANIZING HEALTHCARE	Community health workers repeatedly go to patients' homes to understand their priority problems and offer support.	p. 371
☐	V68	GETTING TO ZERO HOMELESSNESS	Organizations continuously meet with people experiencing homelessness to prioritize their personal challenges.	p. 371
☐	V70	TRUCKERS FIGHTING TRAFFICKING	Truckers and the police are working together to prioritize where and how they might prevent human trafficking.	p. 371
☐	V73	SURROUNDING STUDENTS WITH FAMILY	Volunteer "families" continuously communicate with students so that they can prioritize how best to provide support.	p. 372
☐	V79	A CIVIC JOURNALISM LAB	Journalists and local citizens meet to discuss the community and prioritize stories.	p. 373

YOUR TURN | SUGGESTED TOOLS TO HELP YOU PUT THIS IN ACTION

☐	T4.5	PROBLEMS VS DESIGN CONSTRAINTS ANALYSIS	Prioritize problems that are currently the most actionable given practical constraints.	p. 182
☐	T4.6	PROBLEM PRIORITIZATION ANALYSIS	Prioritize problems based on an analysis of severity and frequency.	p. 184
☐	T5.6	DECISION MAKING BIASES MAP	Analyze and prioritize some of the most common biases that might be influencing how people are making decisions.	p. 202
☐	T7.6	INNOVATION DISTILLATION BLUEPRINT	Distill the most critical elements of your changemaking innovation so that you can prioritize what scales.	p. 248
☐	T12.4	FEEDBACK PROCESS STRATEGY	Make sure that you're prioritizing all of the key factors for feedback strategy design.	p. 322

THE CURRENT CONTEXT	
THE ECOSYSTEM	
THE PEOPLE	
THE DESIRED INFORMATION/ INSIGHTS	

HOW MIGHT WE BUILD A PRIORITIZATION ECOSYSTEM?		
PRIORITY FOR OUR CHANGEMAKING EFFORTS	PERCEIVED STRENGTH OF THIS CONCEPT/ IDEA	POTENTIAL POSITIVE IMPACT OF THIS CONCEPT/ IDEA
LOW MEDIUM HIGH	LOW MEDIUM HIGH	LOW MEDIUM HIGH
WHY?	WHY?	WHY?

NOW WHAT?	

☐ CT20

#BUILDING ECOSYSTEMS

BUILD A MUTUALLY SYMBIOTIC ECOSYSTEM

tinyurl.com/cctboxct20

> *"Peace requires everyone to be in the circle – wholeness, inclusion."*
>
> **ISABEL ALLENDE**
> CHILEAN NOVELIST

Changemakers are experts in biomimicry. The Biomimicry Institute defines biomimicry as "an approach to innovation that seeks sustainable solutions to human challenges by emulating nature's time-tested patterns and strategies." Possibly the most well-known example of biomimicry is Velcro®. In 1941, while on a walk, Swiss engineer George de Mestral noticed burrs sticking to his socks and dogs. He then studied the burrs and discovered that their clinging property was the result of hundreds of tiny hooks. However, biomimicry doesn't just help with the "what" of design. It also teaches us about the "how." Nature is a master class on the "how.' This is especially true for the "how" of relationships.

In particular, changemakers biomimic the mutually symbiotic relationships found in nature. This is a relationship where two, or multiple organisms, benefit from "working together." Each needs something that the other(s) can offer. Think of the bee and the flower, the clownfish and the anemone, or oxpeckers and rhinos. Oxpeckers eat the parasites that live on the rhino's skin. The oxpecker gets food. The rhino gets pest control.

Work to figure out how one stakeholder's strength might solve another stakeholder's weakness, and vice versa. And build a mutually symbiotic ecosystem where everyone works together and wins.

SEE THIS CHANGEMAKING TRIMTAB IN ACTION | SELECT CHANGEMAKING INNOVATION MINI-CASE EXAMPLES

☐	V23	FREE BEER FOR CYCLING	In Bologna, a "green" points system provides citizens with discounts and local shops with new customer acquisition opportunities.	p. 362
☐	V38	CROWD FARMING	A social enterprise in Nigeria built an ecosystem where young investors and farmers benefit from working together.	p. 365
☐	V48	LIVING WITH MANDATORY FRIENDS	In an apartment building in Sweden, young people and elderly people help each other overcome loneliness.	p. 367
☐	V55	POWERED BY OLD BAGELS	A social enterprise created an app that helps shops solve food waste issues in a way that helps local residents solve food security issues.	p. 368
☐	V64	EXCHANGING PEANUT BUTTER FOR PRODUCE	During the beginning of the Covid-19 pandemic, community members exchanged food to meet each others' needs.	p. 370
☐	V86	3D OCEAN FARMING	A fisherman has created a scalable business model powered by underwater mutually symbiotic ecosystems.	p. 375
☐	V89	INTERGENERATIONAL IMPACT	An organization creates mutually beneficial opportunities for older adults and young people.	p. 375

YOUR TURN | SUGGESTED TOOLS TO HELP YOU PUT THIS IN ACTION

☐	T4.4	SWOT ANALYSIS	Analyze where strengths and weaknesses exist for stakeholders so that you might find matching opportunities.	p. 180
☐	T6.2	CURRENT SOLUTIONS LANDSCAPE MAP	Analyze current solutions so that you might identify potential ecosystem collaborators.	p. 212
☐	T9.2	COMMUNITY OF PRACTICE STRATEGY DESIGN	Design a strategy to help empower people to support and learn from each other on an ongoing basis.	p. 272
☐	T9.3	MUTUAL AID STRATEGY DESIGN	Design a mutual aid strategy whereby community members might solve each others' problems.	p. 274

THE CURRENT CONTEXT	
THE ECOSYSTEM	
THE PEOPLE	
THE PRIORITY PROBLEM	

HOW MIGHT WE BUILD A MUTUALLY SYMBIOTIC ECOSYSTEM?

PRIORITY FOR OUR CHANGEMAKING EFFORTS	PERCEIVED STRENGTH OF THIS CONCEPT/ IDEA	POTENTIAL POSITIVE IMPACT OF THIS CONCEPT/ IDEA
LOW MEDIUM HIGH	LOW MEDIUM HIGH	LOW MEDIUM HIGH
WHY?	WHY?	WHY?

NOW WHAT?	

CT21

#VISION + IMPACT

DEFINE + SHARE THE BHAG

tinyurl.com/cctboxct21

"BHAG" is an acronym for big, hairy, audacious goal. It's a term originally coined by Jim Collins and Jerry Porras in *Built to Last: Successful Habits of Visionary Companies.* Your BHAG is the ambitious, long-term, desired outcome you aspire to achieve. Defining your BHAG helps keep you focused on desired outcomes, as opposed to particular strategies. It helps you avoid being myopic. It keeps you from thinking and acting too small. And when you broadly share your BHAG, you're telling everyone, "This is where we're going, hop on board!" It serves as an inclusive, inspiring, and urgent invitation for people to come together as collaborative changemakers.

> *"We choose to go to the moon in this decade and do the other things, not because they are easy, but because they are hard; because that goal will serve to organize and measure the best of our energies and skills, because that challenge is one that we're willing to accept."*
>
> **JOHN F. KENNEDY**
> 35TH U.S. PRESIDENT

SEE THIS CHANGEMAKING TRIMTAB IN ACTION | SELECT CHANGEMAKING INNOVATION MINI-CASE EXAMPLES

V3	**SOLVING THE ARSENIC PROBLEM**	A changemaker's BHAG is for arsenic poisoning to be eradicated in Bangladesh.	p. 358
V8	**CHILD-CENTERED EDUCATION**	A changemaker's BHAG is for students to have the skill sets and mindsets necessary for democracy to thrive.	p. 359
V26	**A CUSTOMER-FOCUSED APPROACH**	A changemaking organization's BHAG is for Africa to become the "bread basket" for the world.	p. 363
V38	**CROWD FARMING**	A changemaking social enterprise's BHAG is for food to be grown in Nigeria, for Nigerians, and funded by Nigerian investors.	p. 365
V68	**GETTING TO ZERO HOMELESSNESS**	A changemaking organization's BHAG is to get to zero homelessness in the U.S.	p. 371
V72	**BATTLING CASH BAIL**	A movement's BHAG is to eliminate the cash bail system.	p. 372
V77	**ADVANCING EMPLOYEE OWNERSHIP**	Two changemakers' BHAG is to make employee-owned businesses the preferred business model.	p. 373
V82	**TURNING BUILDINGS INTO TESLAS**	A changemaker's BHAG is to make every building in the U.S. electric and reduce greenhouse gas emissions by 30%.	p. 374

YOUR TURN | SUGGESTED TOOLS TO HELP YOU PUT THIS IN ACTION

T1.2	**OUR WHY**	Define and align your team's WHY. Work to ensure that it aligns with a community WHY.	p. 112
T7.1	**LOGIC MODEL BLUEPRINT**	Define your desired outcomes including your long-term desired outcome (BHAG).	p. 238
T7.3	**SUCCESS INDICATORS BLUEPRINT**	Define how you'll know if and when you've achieved your long-term desired outcome (BHAG).	p. 242
T12.1	**INNOVATION STORY STRATEGY**	Design how you'll tell the story of your BHAG.	p. 316

THE CURRENT CONTEXT	
OUR TEAM	
THE PROBLEM	

HOW MIGHT WE DEFINE + SHARE THE BHAG?		
PRIORITY FOR OUR CHANGEMAKING EFFORTS	PERCEIVED STRENGTH OF THIS CONCEPT/ IDEA	POTENTIAL POSITIVE IMPACT OF THIS CONCEPT/ IDEA
LOW MEDIUM HIGH	LOW MEDIUM HIGH	LOW MEDIUM HIGH
WHY?	WHY?	WHY?

NOW WHAT?	

▢ CT22

#VISION + IMPACT

SHOW IT

tinyurl.com/cctboxct22

Telling is important. But whenever you can, show it. Showing creates awareness. Showing overcomes education and language barriers. It can make the complex more simple. Showing makes the abstract concrete. Showing success builds credibility. It can help people overcome skepticism. Showing small wins can make solving big problems feel more possible. Showing can be an invitation to collaboration. And showing can bring joy and inspire.

"Don't tell me the moon is shining; show me the glint of light on broken glass."

ANTON CHEKHOV
RUSSIAN PLAYWRIGHT

SEE THIS CHANGEMAKING TRIMTAB IN ACTION | SELECT CHANGEMAKING INNOVATION MINI-CASE EXAMPLES

▢	**V5**	**PURIFYING WATER WITH THE SUN**	A young changemaker in Brazil designed a water purification device with a dot that changes color to show when the water becomes drinkable.	**p. 358**
▢	**V19**	**REEF STARS TO THE RESCUE**	Organizations restoring coral reefs in Indonesia show what's possible by building the word HOPE.	**p. 361**
▢	**V20**	**HARVESTING RAINWATER**	Changemakers in Indonesia are showing how rainwater harvesting can be a simple and scalable solution.	**p. 361**
▢	**V23**	**FREE BEER FOR CYCLING**	Bologna is implementing a system whereby people earn points for riding bicycles and using public transportation. An app tracks the points that people cash in at local shops.	**p. 362**
▢	**V36**	**NAMING + FAMING**	Nepalese watch at TV program where government employees celebrated for doing their jobs well.	**p. 365**
▢	**V41**	**A STOPLIGHT FOR POVERTY ALLEVIATION**	An organization in Paraguay uses Google Maps to show people where they can find neighbors who've implemented successful poverty alleviation strategies.	**p. 366**
▢	**V74**	**WALKING FOR TRANSFORMATION**	Black women wear blue T-shirts while walking together to show their pride, build community, attract attention, and create awareness.	**p. 372**
▢	**V88**	**BUSINESS FOR A BETTER WORLD**	Organizations show that profitability and positive community impact need not be mutually exclusive.	**p. 375**

YOUR TURN | SUGGESTED TOOLS TO HELP YOU PUT THIS IN ACTION

▢	**T8.1**	**MARKET SIZE ANALYSIS + STRATEGY**	Design a strategy to help innovators and early adopters show how your changemaking innovation creates impact.	**p. 256**
▢	**T11.6**	**NUDGE STRATEGY**	Consider a wide range of nudges that you can incorporate in your design.	**p. 308**
▢	**T12.2**	**STICKY MESSAGING STRATEGY**	Make the messaging about your changemaking innovation capture people's attention and stick.	**p. 318**
▢	**T12.3**	**COMMUNICATION CHANNEL STRATEGY**	Decide which communication channels might be best to showcase your changemaking innovation for your target audience.	**p. 320**

THE CURRENT CONTEXT	
THE PEOPLE WHO WE WANT AS OBSERVERS	
WHAT WE WANT THE PEOPLE TO SEE	

HOW MIGHT WE SHOW IT?

PRIORITY FOR OUR CHANGEMAKING EFFORTS	PERCEIVED STRENGTH OF THIS CONCEPT/ IDEA	POTENTIAL POSITIVE IMPACT OF THIS CONCEPT/ IDEA
LOW MEDIUM HIGH	LOW MEDIUM HIGH	LOW MEDIUM HIGH
WHY?	WHY?	WHY?

NOW WHAT?	

tinyurl.com/cctboxctreflect

REFLECTION + EVALUATION

SCALE:
STRONGLY AGREE = 5, AGREE = 4, NOT SURE = 3, DISAGREE = 2, STRONGLY DISAGREE = 1

	CHANGEMAKING TRIMTABS										
REFLECTION STATEMENTS	**CT1**	**CT2**	**CT3**	**CT4**	**CT5**	**CT6**	**CT7**	**CT8**	**CT9**	**CT10**	**CT11**
This Changemaking Trimtab is easy to understand.											
I/ we understand how this Changemaking Trimtab can be put into practice.											
This Changemaking Trimtab taught me/ us important new knowledge.											
This Changemaking Trimtab provided a helpful framework for new conversations.											
This Changemaking Trimtab helped to spark new ideas/ insights.											
This Changemaking Trimtab should be included in my/ our toolbox for the future.											
I/ we should share this Changemaking Trimtab with other changemakers.											

NOTES:

GVK note -

- *Go to HOW TO DESIGN TEAM REFLECTIONS (pg. 379)*

REFLECTION STATEMENTS	CHANGEMAKING TRIMTAB										
	CT12	CT13	CT14	CT15	CT16	CT17	CT18	CT19	CT20	CT21	CT22
This Changemaking Trimtab is easy to understand.											
I/ we understand how this Changemaking Trimtab can be put into practice.											
This Changemaking Trimtab taught me/ us important new knowledge.											
This Changemaking Trimtab provided a helpful framework for new conversations.											
This Changemaking Trimtab helped to spark new ideas/ insights.											
This Changemaking Trimtab should be included in my/ our toolbox for the future.											
I/ we should share this Changemaking Trimtab with other changemakers.											

NOTES:

GVK note-
"We do not learn from experience...we learn from reflecting on experience." - John Dewey

Would you like to rephrase or modify any of the Changemaking Trimtabs? Do you have your own Changemaking Trimtabs that you've found most helpful? What are they? How would you describe them?

CHANGEMAKING TRIMTAB		DESCRIPTION
CT23		
CT24		
CT25		
CT26		
CT27		
CT28		
CT29		
CT30		

SECTION 03 | CHANGEMAKING TOOLKITS + TOOLS

What are Changemaking Toolkits + Tools?
Go to page 5.

Young African leaders collaborating in South Bend, Indiana

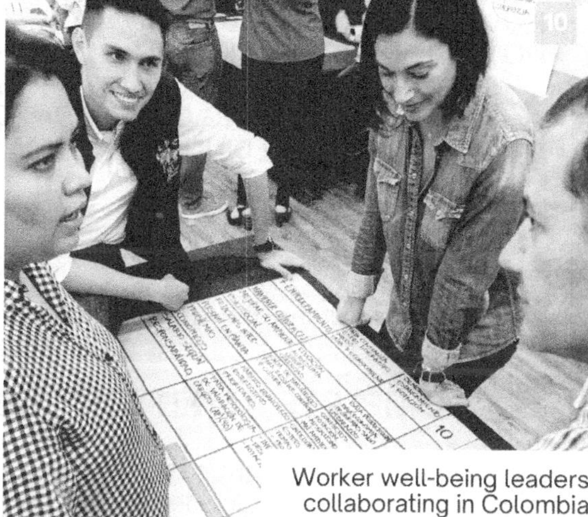

Worker well-being leaders collaborating in Colombia

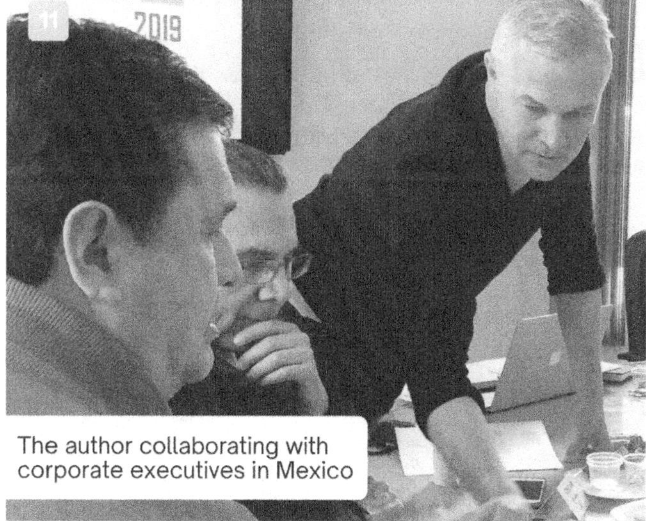

The author collaborating with corporate executives in Mexico

MariaLuz G. collaborating with commmunity leaders

NOTES:

GVK note -

- *Don't fall in love with your solution OR the problem. Fall in love with your search for problems.*

collaborativechangemaking.com

Get updates, new resources, report problems, share your ideas + provide feedback.

CHANGEMAKING TOOLKITS + TOOLS SECTION OVERVIEW

What's are Changemaking Toolkits + Tools? Go to page 5.

HOW THE TOOLKITS + TOOLS WORK pp. 75 - 78

Go here to learn how to use the Changemaking Toolkits + Tools. This includes the following:.

- **HOW THEY'RE STRUCTURED**
- **HOW THE CHANGEMAKING TOOLS WORK**
    - **DESCRIPTION, INSTRUCTIONS + RESOURCES PAGE**
    - **THE CHANGEMAKING CONVERSATION WORKSHEET**
- **GUIDANCE: SCAFFOLDING CHANGEMAKING TOOLS**

MODULES + TOOLKITS INVENTORY DESCRIPTION pp. 79 - 80

Go here to learn about the three modules and 13 Changemaking Toolkits.

COMPLETE INVENTORY WITH HMW QUESTIONS pp. 81 - 90

Go here for the inventory of the 13 Changemaking Toolkits + 76 Changemaking Tools with "How might we..." questions to help you decide which one(s) might be most helpfulf or you and your team.

SNAPSHOT INVENTORY CHECKLIST pp. 91 - 92

Go here for a list of the 13 Changemaking Toolkits + 76 Changemaking Tools with checkboxes. Tick the boxes to track what you've used or maybe fill in a number "rating" to help you prioritize your favorites.

CREATE YOUR OWN TOOLKITS + TOOLS pp. 93 - 97

Go here to find templates for you to create your own Changemaking Toolkits + Tools.

CHANGEMAKING TOOLKITS + TOOLS CANVASES pp. 98 - 99

Based on the Business Model Canvas concept, these might help you and your team capture your thoughts/ ideas. This includes a "Changemaking Team Canvas" and a "Changemaking Innovation Canvas." Both of these include Changmaking Tool prompts for guidance.

TOOLKITS SCORECARD + PRIORITIZATION HELP p. 100

This includes self-check statements with scoring and Changemaking Toolkit suggestions to help you and your team decide where to focus your energies.

THE 13 TOOLKITS + 76 TOOLS p. 101 - 338

This the complete inventory of Changemaking Toolkits + Tools within the three modules.

HOW THE TOOLKITS + TOOLS WORK

What's are Changemaking Toolkits + Tools? Go to page 5.

HOW THEY'RE STRUCTURED

MODULES

The Changemaking Toolkits + Tools are categorized into three modules. This categorization is for guidance purposes and shouldn't be viewed as prescriptive.

CHANGEMAKING TOOLKITS

There are 13 Changemaking Toolkits that include 76 Changemaking Tools. Each of the Changemaking Toolkits is structured in the following manner:

TOOLS INVENTORY

This is a list of the Changemaking Tools in the toolkit with "How might we..." questions to help guide you.

TOOLKIT SCORECARD + PRIORITIZATION HELP

This is a list of self-check statements that you "score." This should help you and your team decide which tools might be most helpful for your changemaking conversations.

COLLABORATIVE CHANGEMAKING VOICES

This includes inspiring and insightful quotes from changemakers from diverse sectors/ backgrounds. Reading these quotes should help you get your changemaking mindset warmed up. There are open speech bubbles for you to note down and share your own unique perspectives and insights.

THE CHANGEMAKING TOOLS

Each Changemaking Toolkit includes four to ten Changemaking Tools. They're all formatted in the same way.

TOOLKIT TOOLS REFLECTIONS

At the end of each Changemaking Toolkit, you'll find a page to evaluate and reflect on the Changemaking Tools you've used.

NOTES:

HOW THE CHANGEMAKING TOOLS WORK

DESCRIPTION, INSTRUCTIONS + RESOURCES PAGE

②

① ☐ T2.2

TOOLS FOR TEAM-FOCUSED CONVERSATIONS | (RE)CALIBRATING OUR TEAM'S EFFORTS  ③

④ **RACI STRUCTURE CHECK-IN**

How might we define clear roles and responsibilities for team members?

tinyurl.com/cctboxt22   ⑤

⑥ **ABOUT THIS TOOL**

Establishing and checking in on individual roles and responsibilities is critically important for team success. This is especially true for diverse changemaking teams that are working to solve complex problems in uncertain and ambiguous environments. This RACI STRUCTURE CHECK-IN tool should help you and your team define clear roles and responsibilities for your projects and activities.

A RACI model is a responsibility matrix that was originally conceived way back in the 1950's. It was designed to help teams ensure that everyone is included while avoiding potentially conflictive situations where team members either don't know their roles and/or are confused about which role they should be playing. RACI is an acronym for the following four roles:

- **(R)ESPONSIBLE:** These are the people who perform the work.
- **(A)CCOUNTABLE:** This is the person who's ultimately accountable for making decisions.
- **(C)ONSULTED:** This is anyone who could be or should be consulted with while the work is in progress and/or before important decisions are made. Their advice may or may not be taken depending on the circumstances.
- **(I)NFORMED:** This is anyone who should be informed of the work periodically and/or when decisions are made. This is a passive role.

HOW TO USE THIS TOOL ⑦

1. First, note down the OVERALL GOAL. What's your team trying to achieve? It's important for everyone to have a clear understanding of the OVERALL GOAL.
2. Next, go to PROJECTS/ ACTIVITIES and note down a DESCRIPTION for each one that's in service of achieving the OVERALL GOAL. Try to describe the PROJECTS/ ACTIVITIES with as much specificity as possible. Next to each DESCRIPTION note down the PROJECTED COMPLETION DATE (IF APPLICABLE).
3. Now go to the RACI TEAM ROLES columns. For each of your PROJECTS/ ACTIVITIES decide and note down WHO'S (R)ESPONSIBLE?, WHO'S (A)CCOUNTABLE?, WHO SHOULD BE (C)ONSULTED?, and WHO SHOULD BE (I)NFORMED?
4. To conclude, go to NOW WHAT? and note down a few priority next steps based on what you've learned and/or new insights you've gained from using this tool.

CHANGEMAKER COACH | TOOL TIPS ⑧

- I'd recommend using this right away once you've created your changemaking team using T1.1 OUR TEAM (p. 110)
- Before you use this, you might want to take a look at T2.4 STAKEHOLDER ENGAGEMENT CHECK-IN (p. 132) and T6.8 STAKEHOLDER POWER MAP (p. 224)

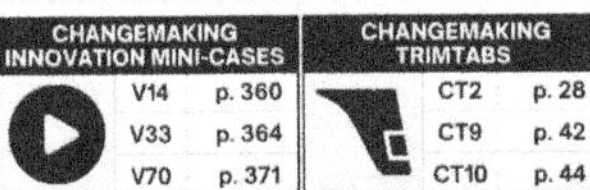

CHANGEMAKING INNOVATION MINI-CASES		CHANGEMAKING TRIMTABS	
V14	p. 360	CT2	p. 28
V33	p. 364	CT9	p. 42
V70	p. 371	CT10	p. 44

⑨

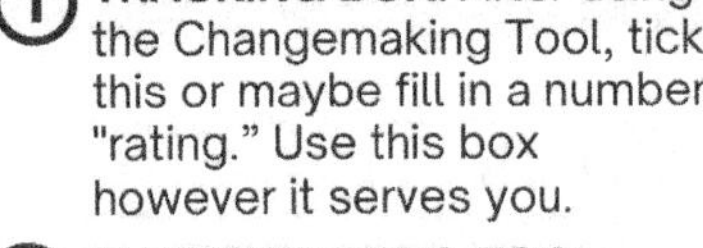

① **TRACKING BOX:** After using the Changemaking Tool, tick this or maybe fill in a number "rating." Use this box however it serves you.

② **CHANGEMAKING TOOL IDENTIFIER:** This is used throughout the toolbox.

③ **MODULE + CHANGEMAKING TOOLKIT:** This is included so that you can easily see the Changemaking Toolkit where this Changemaking Tool has been curated.

④ **CHANGEMAKING TOOL ICON , TITLE + "HOW MIGHT WE" QUESTION**

⑤ **LINK + QR CODE:** These take you to the Google Sheet of the CHANGEMAKING CONVERSATION WORKSHEET described on the next page. Each Google Sheet has five tabs for community/ team members to work individually and a tab labeled "TEAM" where ideas can be aggregated/ consolidated. Make as many editable copies of the Google Sheet as you'd like. Customize them to meet your needs.

⑥ **"ABOUT THIS TOOL":** This describes what the Changemaking Tool is and how it might be helpful.

⑦ **"HOW TO USE THIS TOOL":** These are the step-by-step instructions for how to use THE CHANGEMAKING CONVERSATION WORKSHEET described on the following page.

⑧ **"CHANGEMAKER COACH | TOOL TIPS":** These are the author's tips for using this tool. Go to **SECTION 5: CHANGEMAKER COACH (p. 377)** for more comprehensive guidance/ advice.

⑨ **"CHANGEMAKING INNOVATION MINI-CASES" + "CHANGEMAKING TRIMTABS":** These are three suggestions of each to help you practice and apply the Changemaking Tool. Go to GUIDANCE: SCAFFOLDING CHANGEMAKING TOOLS on page 78 for guidance.

NOTES:

THE CHANGEMAKING CONVERSATIONS WORKSHEET

(10)

OVERALL GOAL					
PROJECTS/ ACTIVITIES		RACI TEAM ROLES			
DESCRIPTION	PROJECTED COMPLETION DATE (IF APPLICABLE)	WHO'S (R)ESPONSIBLE?	WHO'S (A)CCOUNTABLE?	WHO SHOULD BE (C)ONSULTED?	WHO SHOULD BE (I)NFORMED?

(11)

NOW WHAT?	

(10) **CHANGEMAKING TOOL CONVERSATION PROMPTS:** Follow "HOW TO USE THIS TOOL" from DESCRIPTION, INSTRUCTIONS + RESOURCES PAGE. Each Changemaking Tool is structured in a similar manner.

(11) **"NOW WHAT?":** Note down agreed-upon action items/ next steps. The relatively small size of the box is due to space constraints and serves as a nudge to encourage you to focus on the most important things.

NOTES:

GVK notes -

- Make it your priority to help empower the quietest voices to be heard.
- Empathy is the cheat code for changemaking.

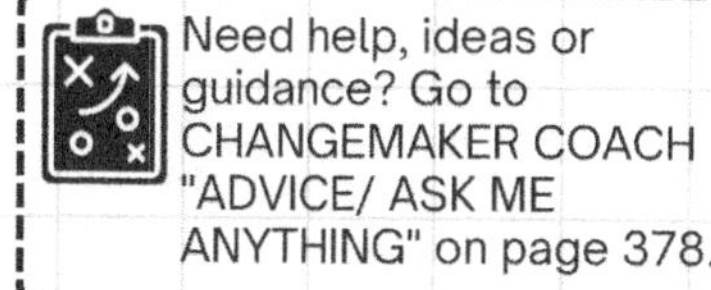

Need help, ideas or guidance? Go to CHANGEMAKER COACH "ADVICE/ ASK ME ANYTHING" on page 378.

GUIDANCE: **SCAFFOLDING CHANGEMAKING TOOLS**

Go to page 10 to see the Learning Pyramid that informed this design.

This is guidance for scaffolding Changemaking Trimtabs with Changemaking Innovation Mini-Cases and Changemaking Tools. Use this for facilitation/ teaching with teams, in class, in communities, on Zoom calls, etc. Modify this guidance based on your own goals and constraints. Note: You might need to prepare by making photocopies or copies of the Google Sheet links/ QR codes.

GET STARTED

1 LECTURE/ READING:
Choose a Changemakaking Tool. Teach and/or have participants read/ review the tool's DESCRIPTION, INSTRUCTION + RESOURCES PAGE and CHANGEMAKING CONVERSATION WORKSHEET (the "WORKSHEET"). This might be an exercise you have participants do before the meeting/ class.

OPTION 1: **USING CHANGEMAKING INNOVATION MINI-CASES**

2 PRACTICE BY DOING:
Tell participants that they're now going to practice using the Changemaking Tool's WORKSHEET with a Changemaking Innovation Mini-Case example. Choose and watch one of three Changemaking Innovation Mini-Cases from the DESCRIPTION, INSTRUCTION + RESOURCES PAGE . Then, in small groups, have participants practice the Changemaking Tool's WORKSHEET. Rewatch the video as needed.

3 DISCUSSION/ TEACH OTHERS:
Have people share their experiences/ what they learned from practicing using the WORKSHEET.

4 APPLY:
Break up into existing teams or small groups. Use the WORKSHEET for a real project, venture idea, etc.

OPTION 2: **USING CHANGEMAKING INNOVATION MINI-CASES + CHANGEMAKING TRIMTABS**

2 LECTURE/ READING:
Choose two to three of the CHANGEMAKING TRIMTAB's from the Changemaking Tool's DESCRIPTION, INSTRUCTION + RESOURCES PAGE. Teach and/or have everyone read the BRIEF CHANGEMAKING TRIMTAB DESCRIPTION + QUOTE from each of the trimtabs. This might be an exercise you have participants do before the meeting/ class.

3 DISCUSSION/ TEACH OTHERS:
Walk through Changemaking Tool's WORKSHEET. As you do this, open up a discussion about how the focus of the Changemaking Trimtabs you reviewed might influence how you go about using the WORKSHEET. How might it affect your approach and perspectives?

4 STEPS 2, 3 + 4 FROM "OPTION 1: USING CHANGEMAKING INNOVATION MINI-CASES"

NOTES:

MODULES + TOOLKITS INVENTORY DESCRIPTION

MODULE 01 | CHANGEMAKING TOOLKITS + TOOLS FOR TEAM-FOCUSED CONVERSATIONS

Go to this module to build and check in with your changemaking team/ community. This module also includes "whiteboards" to help you and your team analyze and ideate about changemaking innovations/ solutions.

toolkit 01 BUILDING OUR CHANGEMAKING TEAM

This toolkit should help you build a team with a shared WHY and a collaborative culture.

toolkit 02 (RE)CALIBRATING OUR TEAM'S EFFORTS

This toolkit includes a variety of tools to help you and your team level set, define roles, prioritize efforts, and self-correct.

toolkit 03 OUR INNOVATION + ANALYSIS WHITEBOARDS

Go to this toolkit to find tools to help you both analyze existing innovations/ solutions and ideate about new changemaking concepts.

MODULE 02 | TOOLKITS + TOOLS FOR DISCOVERY + DIAGNOSIS CONVERSATIONS

Go to this module to equip your team with essential problem/ opportunity discovery and diagnosis tools. This module also includes tools to help you and your team apply both a human-centered and a systems approach.

toolkit 04 FINDING + PRIORITIZING ACTIONABLE PROBLEMS

This toolkit includes essential tools for problem/ opportunity identification and prioritization. Use these in conjunction with all of the other tools in this toolbox.

toolkit 05 HUMAN-CENTERED MAPPING

Go to this toolkit to zoom in. These tools should help you get a granular understanding of the lives and perspectives of the people you aspire to support.

toolkit 06 SYSTEM(S) MAPPING

Go to this toolkit to zoom out. These tools help you get a contextual understanding. Use these to analyze the dynamics of global, community, and organizational systems, etc.

MODULE 03 | TOOLKITS + TOOLS FOR INNOVATION DESIGN CONVERSATIONS

Go to this module to find critical tools for designing and launching your changemaking innovation. This module includes a special toolkit focused on strategies for people to come together to support/ empower each other.

OUR CHANGEMAKING INNOVATION BLUEPRINTS

The tools in this toolkit should help you to comprehensively define and articulate the why, who, what, where, when, and how of your changemaking innovation. They're "blueprints" for sharing with internal and external stakeholders.

LAUNCH + SCALING STRATEGIES

This toolkit includes tools for defining your market and deciding with whom and how you'll launch your changemaking innovation.

SPECIAL: PEOPLE-FOR-PEOPLE STRATEGIES

Go to this toolkit to start designing ways for people/ organizations to come together to support/ empower each other to solve problems.

POSITIONING + MARKETING STRATEGIES

This toolkit includes tools to help you figure out how to differentiate and market your changemaking innovation.

GETTING TO ADOPTION STRATEGIES

Go to these tools to design strategies to get from access to adoption. Focus on ensuring people value using your changemaking innovation.

MESSAGING + COMMUNICATION STRATEGIES

This includes tools to help you articulate the story of your changemaking innovation. They help you make your messaging matter and prioritize communication strategies.

GETTING FUTURE READY

Go to this toolkit to find tools that will help you consider risks and build resilience into your changemaking innovation design.

NOTES:

tinyurl.com/cctboxtools01

What's are Changemaking Toolkits + Tools? Go to page 5.

MODULE 01 | TOOLKITS + TOOLS FOR TEAM-FOCUSED CONVERSATIONS

toolkit 01

BUILDING OUR CHANGEMAKING TEAM

NOTES:

toolkit 02

(RE)CALIBRATING OUR TEAM'S EFFORTS

How might we check-in on our our expectations, responsibilities and priorities? p. 121

toolkit 03

INNOVATION IDEATION + ANALYSIS WHITEBOARDS

How might we ideate about, analyze and evaluate changemaking innovation ideas?

MODULE 02 | TOOLKITS + TOOLS FOR DISCOVERY + DIAGNOSIS CONVERSATIONS

toolkit 04

FINDING + PRIORITIZING ACTIONABLE PROBLEMS

How might we equip ourselves with practical problem identification and prioritization methodologies and tools? p. 169

TOOLS INVENTORY			p. 170
TOOLKIT SCORECARD + PRIORITIZATION HELP			p. 171
COLLABORATIVE CHANGEMAKING VOICES			p. 172
T4.1	ROOT CAUSE ANALYSIS	**How might we** work to understand the root cause(s) of problems?	p. 174
T4.2	PROBLEM TREE ANALYSIS	**How might we** work to understand both the root causes and negative effects of problems?	p. 176
T4.3	ICEBERG ANALYSIS	**How might we** approach problem identification in a way that empowers us to potentially transform a system rather than simply react to an event?	p. 178
T4.4	SWOT ANALYSIS	**How might we** gain insights by analyzing strengths, weaknesses, opportunities and threats?	p. 180
T4.5	PROBLEMS VS DESIGN CONSTRAINTS ANALYSIS	**How might we** make sure we're prioritizing what's currently changeable instead of what isn't?	p. 182
T4.6	PROBLEM PRIORITIZATION ANALYSIS	**How might we** prioritize problems based on frequency and severity?	p. 184
TOOLKIT TOOLS REFLECTIONS			p. 186

NOTES:

GVK notes -

- *Once you start solving problems you stop seeing them as problems and start seeing them as opportunities.*
- *People think inspiration leads to action. I find it's usually the opposite. Once you get started, you engage, you learn, you spark your empathy, and you get inspired.*

toolkit 05

HUMAN-CENTERED MAPPING

How might we zoom in to understand the lives and perspectives of the people we aspire to support?

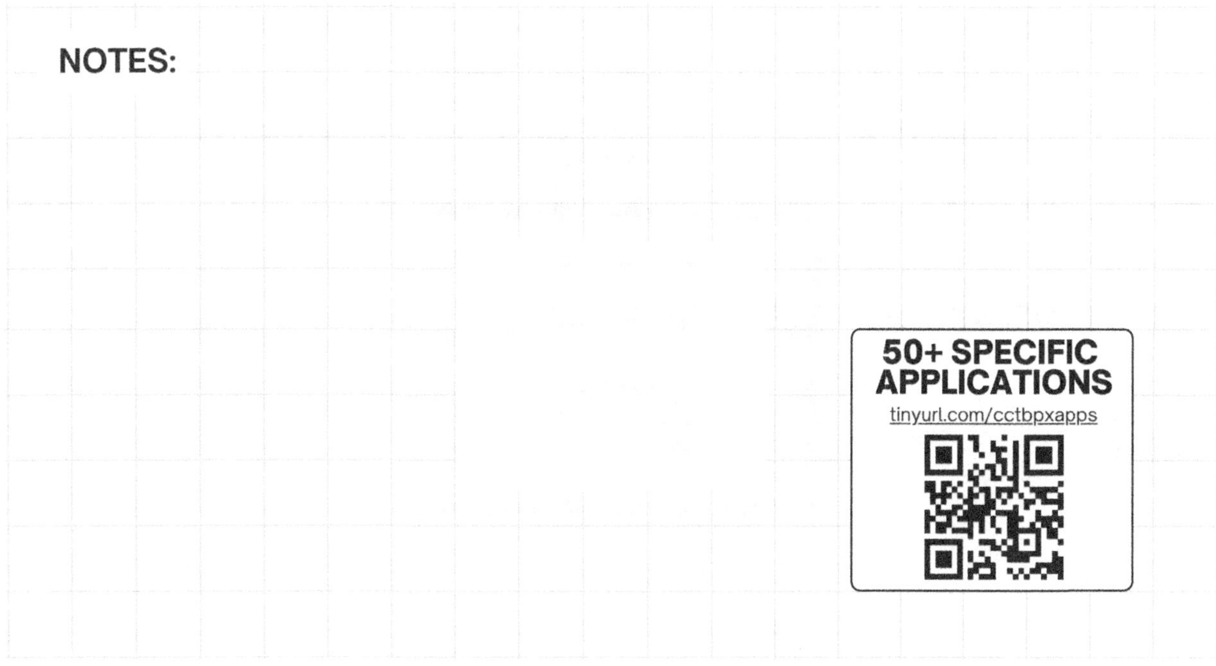

toolkit 06

SYSTEM(S) MAPPING

How might we zoom out to get a 360 degree understanding of the context?

NOTES:

MODULE 03 | TOOLKITS + TOOLS FOR INNOVATION DESIGN CONVERSATIONS

toolkit 07

OUR CHANGEMAKING INNOVATION BLUEPRINTS

How might we clearly define and articulate the why, who, what, where, when, and how of our changemaking innovation? p. 233

TOOLS INVENTORY			p. 234
TOOLKIT SCORECARD + PRIORITIZATION HELP			p. 235
COLLABORATIVE CHANGEMAKING VOICES			p. 236
T7.1	LOGIC MODEL BLUEPRINT	**How might we** describe the desired outcomes of our innovation and the model we've designed to achieve them?	p. 238
T7.2	DRIVER DIAGRAM BLUEPRINT	**How might we** articulate the key drivers of our innovation's success?	p. 240
T7.3	SUCCESS INDICATORS BLUEPRINT	**How might we** design the most optimal ways to measure the success of our innovation over the short, medium and long term?	p. 242
T7.4	VALUE PROPOSITION BLUEPRINT	**How might we** show how our innovation is delivering value?	p. 244
T7.5	NOVEL FEATURES + BENEFITS BLUEPRINT	**How might we** specify the features that make our innovation uniquely beneficial?	p. 246
T7.6	INNOVATION DISTILLATION BLUEPRINT	**How might we** distill the elements that make our innovation tick?	p. 248
TOOLKIT TOOLS REFLECTIONS			p. 250

NOTES:

GVK notes -

- Don't build a metaphorical "Norman Door." This is a door that isn't easy to use. This was named after human-centered design guru Don Norman. To avoid this, make sure your design has -
  - AFFORDANCE: This is a hint/clue about how to use it based on its appearance.
  - FEEDBACK: Makes it clear that action has been taken/ what's been achieved.

toolkit 10

POSITIONING + MARKETING STRATEGIES

toolkit 11

GETTING TO ADOPTION STRATEGIES

SNAPSHOT INVENTORY CHECKLIST

tinyurl.com/cctboxtools02

tinyurl.com/cctboxyours
CREATE YOUR OWN TOOLKITS + TOOLS

Use the following five pages and the link/ QR code above to curate your own Changemaking Toolkits and create your own Changemaking Tools.

CURATE CHANGEMAKING TOOLKITS

On the next three pages you'll find six empty toolkits for you to customize. For example, if you're an educator, you might curate a toolkit called "Three Week Course," "Service Learning Tools," or "January Workshop," for example. If you're leading a team in an organization you might curate toolkits called "ERG Tools," "DEI Workshop Tools," "Offsite Tools," or "Employee Onboarding Tools," for example. You get the idea. Or maybe you just want to create a toolkit that's called "Favorite Tools" or "Tools to Share with Friends?" Curate and update toolkits that fit with your work, life, and goals.

CREATE CHANGEMAKING TOOLS

On pages 96 and 97 you'll find a very basic template to help you create your own tools. Just as I created the tools in this toolbox, there's absolutely no reason why you can't. Or maybe you'd like to assign students or ask employees to create their own tools? Regardless, one way to get started would be to find inspiration and insights from some of the great books and websites I've included in the "Recommended Resources for Changemakers" section starting on page 381.

NOTES:

GVK notes -

- Have your students curate their own toolkits.
- Create a new tool with your team or community.

toolkit 14			
T		How might we	p.
T		How might we	p.
T		How might we	p.
T		How might we	p.
T		How might we	p.

toolkit 15			
T		How might we	p.
T		How might we	p.
T		How might we	p.
T		How might we	p.
T		How might we	p.

toolkit 16			
T		How might we	p.
T		How might we	p.
T		How might we	p.
T		How might we	p.
T		How might we	p.
T		How might we	p.
T		How might we	p.

toolkit 17

T		How might we	p.
T		How might we	p.
T		How might we	p.
T		How might we	p.
T		How might we	p.
T		How might we	p.
T		How might we	p.

toolkit 18

T		How might we	p.
T		How might we	p.
T		How might we	p.
T		How might we	p.
T		How might we	p.
T		How might we	p.

toolkit 19

T		How might we	p.
T		How might we	p.
T		How might we	p.
T		How might we	p.

ABOUT THIS TOOL

HOW TO USE THIS TOOL

NOW WHAT?	

CHANGEMAKING TEAM CANVAS

T1.2 OUR WHY

T1.3 OUR CORE VALUES

T1.1 OUR NETWORK TEAM

T1.1 OUR EXTENDED TEAM

T1.1 OUR CORE TEAM

T1.4 OUR COLLABORATIVE CULTURE

T1.5 OUR SUPERPOWERS

CHANGEMAKING INNOVATION CANVAS

What's the **DESIRED OUTCOME** of our solution? T1.1, T7.1	What are the **SUCCESS INDICATORS**? T7.3	What are the key **DRIVERS** of success for our solution? T7.2, T7.6	What's the **VALUE PROPOSITION** of our solution? T7.4
What's **UNIQUE** about our solution? T3.4, T3.5, T7.5, T10.1, T10.2	Who are the **PEOPLE** we hope to support? T1.1, T3.1, T5.1, T5.2	Where are they? What's the **PLACE**? T1.2, T3.1, T8.1, T8.4, T10.4	How will we **BRAND** and **MARKET** our solution? T10.3, T10.4
What's the **PRICE** of our solution? T10.4, T11.2	What's their **GOAL/ ASPIRATION**? T1.2, MODULE 2	What's the **PROBLEM?** T3.1, MODULE 2	Why will people want to **ADOPT** our solution? TOOLKIT 11
Who will first **ADOPT** our solution? TOOLKIT 8	How will people **HEAR ABOUT** our solution? TOOLKIT 12	How will we gather critical **FEEDBACK?** T12.4	How will we gather critical **SCALE/ GROW** our impact? T8.1, T8.3, T8.4

tinyurl.com/cctboxtkitprior

TOOLKITS SCORECARD + PRIORITIZATION HELP

Score yourselves to help you decide which toolkits you might want to prioritize for your changemaking conversations.

SELF-CHECK STATEMENTS	HOW ARE WE DOING?	TOOLKIT SUGGESTIONS
We're building a joyful, scalable team with an aligned WHY and core values.	0 1 2 3 4 5	TOOLKIT 01
We're being very purposeful about creating and nurturing a collaborative culture.	0 1 2 3 4 5	TOOLKIT 01
We're having continuous, proactive, and productive check-in conversations with our team.	0 1 2 3 4 5	TOOLKIT 02
We're having conversations about our changemaking innovation ideas using a variety of helpful ideation and analysis frameworks.	0 1 2 3 4 5	TOOLKIT 03
We feel well-equipped with problem identification and prioritization methodologies and tools.	0 1 2 3 4 5	TOOLKIT 04
We're zooming in. We're working hard to understand the aspirations, opportunities, and challenges of the people we hope to support from their perspectives.	0 1 2 3 4 5	TOOLKIT 05
We're zooming out. We're analyzing all of the conditions and components of the systems that we're working in.	0 1 2 3 4 5	TOOLKIT 06
We've got blueprints for our changemaking innovation that describe the core components clearly.	0 1 2 3 4 5	TOOLKIT 07
We're having conversations about the overall scale of the problem/opportunity and the best ways for us to get our innovation out there to meet it.	0 1 2 3 4 5	TOOLKIT 08
We're having conversations about how we might design strategies where the key driver is people supporting and empowering other people.	0 1 2 3 4 5	TOOLKIT 09
We feel good about how our changemaking innovation is positioned, how it's branded, and how it's and being marketed.	0 1 2 3 4 5	TOOLKIT 10
We're having ongoing conversations about the best ways to influence adoption.	0 1 2 3 4 5	TOOLKIT 11
We've analyzed our messaging and communication strategies to ensure that we're getting the right messages to the right people in the right ways.	0 1 2 3 4 5	TOOLKIT 12
We're looking over the horizon to consider what might go wrong so that we can make our changemaking innovation as adaptive, flexible, and resilient as possible.	0 1 2 3 4 5	TOOLKIT 13

THE 13 TOOLKITS + 76 TOOLS

NOTES:

GVK notes -

- Go to HOW TO HAVE EFFECTIVE CONVERSATIONS + HOW TO BRAINSTORM EFFECTIVELY (pg. 379)
- Try some "deliberate practice" with select tools. Work on something you're not good at yet. Set a goal. Focus. Be intentional. Get immediate feedback.
- Social capital is the skeleton key for changemaking. It opens every door.
- Sometimes the best way to solve a problem is by simple subtraction, not addition. For example, did you know that NASA reduced the weight of the space shuttle by 600 pounds by simply NOT painting the external fuel tanks? Blind hiring, removing names from resumes, can help traditionally disadvantaged job seekers secure interviews. So, before you start adding things, explore opportunities for some simple subtraction.

NOTES:

collaborativechangemaking.com
for updates, new resources, to report problems, share your ideas, provide feedback, etc.

youtube.com/@collaborativechangemaking
for HOW-TO videos, extra CHANGEMAKING INNOVATION MINI-CASES, etc.

MODULE 01 | TOOLS FOR TEAM-FOCUSED CONVERSATIONS

NOTES:

GVK notes:

- Go to HOW TO CRAFT AN INSPIRING VISION STATEMENT (pg. 379) and HOW TO LEAD CHANGE (pg. 380)
- SERVANT LEADERSHIP: Focus on serving team members, rather than managing for results. Trust and empower. Create the conditions/culture where people can thrive and will model servant leadership themselves. Go to HOW TO PRACTICE SERVANT LEADERSHIP (pg. 380)
- ACCOMPANIMENT: Walk alongside the people you hope to serve and work to solve problems together.
- Break out into 15-minute small team HUDDLES to work on tools. Then come back together, share, and reflect.

NOTES:

50+ SPECIFIC APPLICATIONS
tinyurl.com/cctbpxapps

toolkit 01 TOOLS FOR TEAM-FOCUSED CONVERSATIONS | BUILDING OUR CHANGEMAKING TEAM

A Social Entrepreneur Corps "Community Consultant" collaborating with young changemakers in South Africa

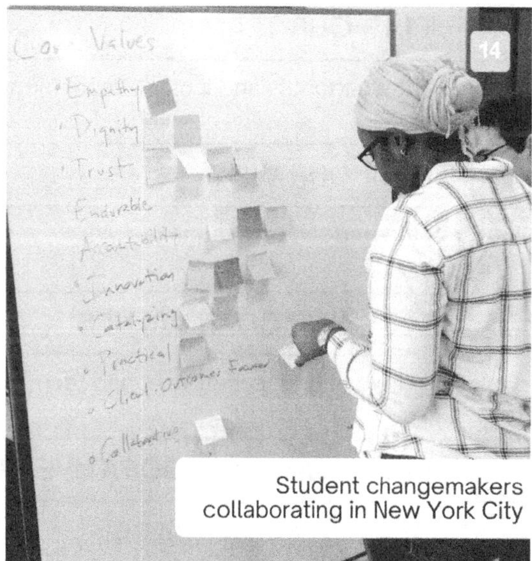

Student changemakers collaborating in New York City

Miguel B. and Conor P. collaborating in Antigua, Guatemala

Social Entrepreneur Corps "Community Consultants" collaborating with changemaker educators in La Pista, Guatemala

NOTES:

toolkit 01

TOOLS FOR TEAM-FOCUSED CONVERSATIONS | BUILDING OUR CHANGEMAKING TEAM

TOOLS INVENTORY

How might we build a team that that feels aligned, empowered and that can grow?

tinyurl.com/cctboxtools01

☐	T1.1 OUR TEAM	p. 110

How might we identify and include team members who'll help us achieve current and futures success?

☐	T1.2 OUR WHY	p. 112

How might we define and align our WHY?

☐	T1.3 OUR CORE VALUES	p. 114

How might we align our individual and team core values?

☐	T1.4 OUR COLLABORATIVE CULTURE	p. 116

How might we ensure that we're creating and nurturing the right culture for successful collaboration?

☐	T1.5 OUR SUPERPOWERS	p. 118

How might we identify and appreciate our individual team members' superpowers?

NOTES:

GVK notes -

- 3 things to prioritize - psychological safety, psychological safety + psychological safety
- Write up and have everyone sign a TEAM MANIFESTO. Include your WHY, Core Values + Collaborative Culture strategies. Keep it to one page.

TOOLS FOR TEAM-FOCUSED CONVERSATIONS | BUILDING OUR CHANGEMAKING TEAM

TOOLKIT SCORECARD + PRIORITIZATION HELP

Score yourselves to help you decide which tool(s) you might want to prioritize for your changemaking conversations.

tinyurl.com/cctboxtoolsprior

SELF-CHECK STATEMENTS	HOW ARE WE DOING?	TOOL SUGGESTIONS
We're having conversations about who should be on our changemaking team now and in the future.	0 1 2 3 4 5	T1.1
We're talking about how we can tap into the experience and expertise of all of the people in our network and our network's network.	0 1 2 3 4 5	T1.1
We've talked about how our team's WHY aligns with our individual WHY'S.	0 1 2 3 4 5	T1.2
We've had conversations about our core values, and have identified the ones that we agree should guide our team.	0 1 2 3 4 5	T1.3
We're having frequent conversations about how to help team members feel psychologically safe.	0 1 2 3 4 5	T1.4
We've established clear rules, roles, responsibilities, and mechanisms to ensure accountability.	0 1 2 3 4 5	T1.4
We've had conversations about and are celebrating our superpowers.	0 1 2 3 4 5	T1.5

TOOLS FOR TEAM-FOCUSED CONVERSATIONS |
BUILDING OUR CHANGEMAKING TEAM

COLLABORATIVE CHANGEMAKING VOICES

Get into the mindset for this toolkit + include your voice in the conversation.

"The fun for me in collaboration is, one, working with other people just makes you smarter; that's proven."

LIN-MANUEL MIRANDA
PLAYWRIGHT | COMPOSER | LYRICIST | ACTOR

"To love one another just may be the fight of our lives."

AMANDA GORMAN
NATIONAL YOUTH POET LAUREATE

"In order to build a great team, you need to understand how each person's job fits into their life goals."

KIM SCOTT
AUTHOR - *RADICAL CANDOR: BE A KICK ASS BOSS WITHOUT LOSING YOUR HUMANITY*

"If you think you are too small to make a difference, try sleeping with a mosquito."

THE DALAI LAMA

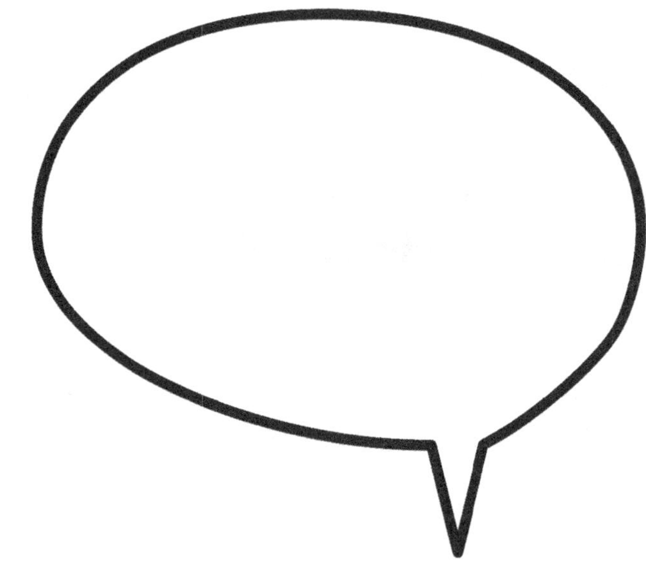

"It's through vulnerability that human beings create connections. The more vulnerable we can be with one another, the more that we'll trust one another and the more we'll be able to collaborate effectively."

NEIL BLUMENTHAL
CO-FOUNDER + CO-CEO - WARBY PARKER

"Now is the accepted time, not tomorrow, not some more convenient season. It is today that our best work can be done and not some future day or future year."

W.E.B DUBOIS
CIVIL RIGHTS ACTIVIST | SOCIOLOGIST

"None of us, including me, ever do great things. But we can all do small things, with great love, and together we can do something wonderful."

MOTHER TERESA
CATHOLIC NUN |
NOBEL PEACE PRIZE LAUREATE

"I have learned you are never too small to make a difference."

GRETA THUNBERG
ENVIRONMENTAL ACTIVIST

T1.1

TOOLS FOR TEAM-FOCUSED CONVERSATIONS | BUILDING OUR CHANGEMAKING TEAM

OUR TEAM

How might we identify and include team members who'll help us achieve current and futures success?

tinyurl.com/cctboxt11

ABOUT THIS TOOL

Changemaking is a team sport. It's best to start out with a small team to keep things simple and manageable. But you should continually be having conversations about who you might want to include in your efforts in the future. Unfortunately, we often don't recognize or appreciate all of the people who might be inspired to contribute to our changemaking work. This OUR TEAM tool should help you to overcome this tendency and to identify current and future potential team members.

Your overall changemaking team should include three "subteams," so to speak. They are as follows:

- **OUR CORE TEAM:** These are team members who are dedicated to your changemaking efforts. As much as possible, this should include people who have very close proximity to and/or a deep understanding of the context in which you're working.
- **OUR EXTENDED TEAM:** These might be other colleagues, other students, good friends, family members, teachers, and the like. It depends on the context. These are people with whom you have a relationship, who are interested in your efforts, and who you can call on for support when needed. They might become involved as community representatives, advisors, mentors, coaches, volunteers, and/or cheerleaders, for example.
- **OUR NETWORK TEAM:** These are people with whom you don't currently have a strong relationship, but who you can access and reach out to as needed. This might include people who provide an essential service, such as lawyers, accountants, and/or investors/funders, for example. They might also be people who do similar work but in other contexts. Be creative and seek out people with a diversity of perspectives, capabilities, and connections.

HOW TO USE THIS TOOL

1. Start by noting down OUR TEAM NAME. If you're an informal team or haven't decided on a name yet, just pick one that resonates with everyone. It can be a temporary name.
2. Next, go to the middle of the tool and note down the names of current and potential future OUR CORE TEAM members. Circle the names of the current ones.
3. After this, do the same for people who are current and potential future OUR EXTENDED TEAM and OUR NETWORK TEAM members. To note, these might be the names of organizations. Circle the names of the current ones.
4. To conclude, go to NOW WHAT? and note down a few priority next steps based on what you've learned and/or new insights you've gained from using this tool.

CHANGEMAKER COACH | TOOL TIPS

- This is a great tool to use when you're forming your team/ community. I'd also use it to refresh periodically as circumstances change.
- This can be very helpful for putting CT9 BUILD PEER-FOR-PEER FRAMEWORKS (p.42) and CT10 BUILD PURPOSE-DRIVEN TEAMS + TEAMS OF TEAMS (p. 44) into practice.
- You might want to use this hand-in-hand with both T2.2 RACI STRUCTURE CHECK-IN (p. 128) and T2.4 STAKEHOLDER ENGAGEMENT LEVEL CHECK-IN (p. 132).

CHANGEMAKING INNOVATION MINI-CASES	
V13	p. 360
V43	p. 366
V79	p. 373

CHANGEMAKING TRIMTABS	
CT2	p. 28
CT9	p. 42
CT10	p. 44

OUR TEAM NAME

OUR NETWORK TEAM

OUR EXTENDED TEAM

OUR CORE TEAM

NOW WHAT?

T1.2

TOOLS FOR TEAM-FOCUSED CONVERSATIONS | BUILDING OUR CHANGEMAKING TEAM

OUR WHY

How might we define and align our WHY?

tinyurl.com/cctboxt12

ABOUT THIS TOOL

What drives you and your changemaking team? What gets you out of bed in the morning? What's your calling? What's your purpose? That's your WHY. In the words of Simon Sinek, author of ***Start with Why: How Great Leaders Inspire Everyone to Take Action***, "All organizations start with WHY, but only the great ones keep their WHY clear year after year." When your team starts with and maintains a clear understanding of its shared WHY, anything is possible. This OUR WHY tool should help you and your team do this.

This tool includes question prompts to help you define your team's WHY in a way that aligns with each team member's personal WHY. It also includes question prompts to help you ensure that your team WHY is aligned with the priority challenges of the community that you hope to support through your changemaking efforts.

Your end goal with this tool is to be able to write your WHY STATEMENT. The template for a WHY STATEMENT is as follows:

TO (your contribution to others)
SO THAT (the impact of your contribution)

Examples:

"TO provide a helpful toolbox for aspiring and practicing changemakers SO THAT they're more empowered to change the world"

"TO offer youth with mental health services SO THAT they feel stronger, more resilient, and more empowered.

CHANGEMAKER COACH | TOOL TIPS

- Two other popular ways to define your WHY are through the Hedgehog Concept and Ikigai. You might want to research these.
- This is great for helping you put CT21 DEFINE + SHARE THE BHAG (p. 66) in action.
- T3.1 PROXIMITY WHITEBOARD (p. 148) can help you figure out your WHY.
- Make sure this aligns with your desired outcome in T7.1 LOGIC MODEL BLUEPRINT (p. 238)

HOW TO USE THIS TOOL

1. First, make photocopies or make sure that everyone can see the tool and has a place to note down their individual responses.
2. Now that you're set up, start by having everyone work individually. Have each person note down the NAME of each of your TEAM MEMBERS at the top. There are spaces for five people. Your team might include fewer or more people.
3. Next, review each of the GETTING TO WHY PROMPTS. Have each person note down their answer for each question prompt. Set a reasonable time limit so that people don't overthink it.
4. Now, go around and have everyone share outloud their answers to each of the questions. People can take notes about what their fellow TEAM MEMBERS' share under their NAME.
5. After this, zoom out and have conversations about where your team aligns for each of the GETTING TO WHY PROMPTS. This might take some iteration. Once you've reached alignment, note down your answers for each of the GETTING TO WHY PROMPTS under the WHAT WE ALIGN ON header.
6. Zoom out again. Can you see a big picture WHY that might resonate with your whole team? Try noting down an OUR WHY STATEMENT at the bottom of the tool. This might require some iteration as well.
7. To conclude, go to NOW WHAT? and note down a few priority next steps based on what you've learned and/or new insights you've gained from using this tool.

CHANGEMAKING INNOVATION MINI-CASES	
V8	p. 359
V47	p. 367
V82	p. 374

CHANGEMAKING TRIMTABS	
CT10	p. 44
CT18	p. 60
CT21	p. 66

	GETTING TO WHY PROMPTS	OUR TEAM MEMBERS					WHAT WE ALIGN ON
PERSONALLY	WHAT DRIVES ME?						
	WHAT'S A CHALLENGE THAT'S REALLY AFFECTED ME OR SOMEONE CLOSE TO ME?						
	WHAT ISSUES/ PROBLEMS DO I REALLY CARE ABOUT?						
	WHAT REALLY FRUSTRATES ME ABOUT THE WORLD RIGHT NOW?						
	WHAT ARE SOME THINGS THAT I BELIEVE NEED TO CHANGED FOR THE BETTER?						
IN MY COMMUNITY	WHAT ARE THE MOST PRESSING PROBLEMS AT THIS MOMENT?						
	WHAT WILL LIKELY BE THE BIGGEST PROBLEMS IN THE FUTURE?						
	WHAT PROBLEMS AREN'T BEING SOLVED EFFECTIVELY, IF AT ALL?						

OUR WHY STATEMENT	TO		SO THAT	

NOW WHAT?	

☐ **T1.3**

TOOLS FOR TEAM-FOCUSED CONVERSATIONS | BUILDING OUR CHANGEMAKING TEAM

OUR CORE VALUES

How might we align our individual and team core values?

tinyurl.com/cctboxt13

ABOUT THIS TOOL

Your core values shouldn't be something you post on your website and forget about. They should be one of your team's most useful assets. They're "guardrails" to help you stay on course to achieve your WHY. They help you make decisions in complex environments where there are no right and wrong decisions, only better and worse ones. With this in mind, this OUR CORE VALUES tool should help you and your team define and align your core values.

To note, the more frequently you use your aligned core values, the more equipped you'll be to empower collaborative changemaking. In particular, use your aligned core values as touchstones during ideation conversations to help you avoid falling into the trap of debating who has the "best" idea or solution. Ask yourselves, "Which idea is most aligned with our core values?" By doing this, your core values keep you metaphorically "sitting on the same side of the table."

CHANGEMAKER COACH | TOOL TIPS

- I always try to use this when I'm starting out with new teams/ groups. It's fast, simple, and establishes a great tone. It also gets people sharing in a positive way.
- T3.6 DESIGN PRINCIPLES WHITEBOARD (p. 158) is a similar tool. It's for changemaking innovations as opposed to changemaking teams.

HOW TO USE THIS TOOL

1. First, make photocopies or make sure that everyone can see the tool and has a place to note down their individual responses.
2. Now that you're set-up, tell everyone they have two minutes to review and check the boxes for (or note down) their top twenty most important CORE VALUES under the ROUND 1 headers. People should feel free to add CORE VALUES that haven't been included in the tool.
3. Next, it's time to start narrowing down. For ROUND 2, give everyone exactly one minute. Ask them to check the boxes for or note down their top ten CORE VALUES from the twenty they just selected.
4. For ROUND 3, give everyone 30 seconds, and ask them to check the boxes or note down their top three CORE VALUES out of the ten.
5. After this, have everyone on the team share how the activity felt for them. Was it easy or difficult? Why? Then have everyone share their top three CORE VALUES aloud and why they chose them.
6. Next, see if you can come up with three to six CORE VALUES that everyone is aligned on. Note these down at the top of the tool next to OUR PRIORITY CORE VALUES.
7. To conclude, go to NOW WHAT? and note down a few priority next steps based on what you've learned and/or new insights you've gained from using this tool.

CHANGEMAKING INNOVATION MINI-CASES	
V56	p. 369
V74	p. 372
V78	p. 373

CHANGEMAKING TRIMTABS	
CT4	p. 32
CT9	p. 42
CT18	p. 60

OUR PRIORITY CORE VALUES		

ROUND 1	ROUND 2	ROUND 3	CORE VALUES	ROUND 1	ROUND 2	ROUND 3	CORE VALUES	ROUND 1	ROUND 2	ROUND 3	CORE VALUES
			ACCEPTANCE				ENVIRONMENT				OPEN-MINDEDNESS
			ACCOMPLISHMENT				EQUITY				OPTIMISM
			ACCOUNTABILITY				ETHICS				ORGANIZATION
			ACHIEVEMENT				EXCELLENCE				ORIGINALITY
			ADAPTABILITY				EXCITEMENT				PATIENCE
			ADVENTURE				EXPLORATION				PASSION
			ALTRUISM				FAIRNESS				PEACE
			AMBITION				FAITH				PERSEVERANCE
			APPRECIATION				FLEXIBILITY				PERSISTENCE
			ARTISTRY				FRIENDSHIP				PLAYFULNESS
			ATTENTIVENESS				FUN				PRACTICALITY
			AWARENESS				GENEROSITY				PRAGMATISM
			BALANCE				GRACE				PREPAREDNESS
			BEAUTY				GRATITUDE				PRESENCE
			BELONGING				GRIT				PROACTIVITY
			BENEVOLENCE				GROWTH				PRODUCTIVITY
			BOLDNESS				HAPPINESS				REFLECTION
			BRAVERY				HEALTH				RELIABILITY
			BRILLIANCE				HELPFULNESS				RESILIENCE
			CALMNESS				HUMILITY				RESOURCEFULNESS
			CAPABILITY				HUMOR				RESPECT
			CHALLENGE				INCLUSION				RESPONSIBILITY
			CHEERFULNESS				IMAGINATION				RISK-TAKING
			COLLABORATION				IMPACT				SACRIFICE
			COMMITMENT				INDEPENDENCE				SELFLESSNESS
			COMMUNITY				INDIVIDUALITY				SELF-RELIANCE
			COMPASSION				INNOVATION				SELF- RESPECT
			CONSCIOUSNESS				INQUISITIVENESS				SENSITIVITY
			CONTRIBUTION				INTEGRITY				SERVICE
			COOPERATION				JOY				SHARING
			COURAGE				JUSTICE				SIMPLICITY
			CREATIVITY				KINDNESS				SINCERITY
			CURIOSITY				KNOWLEDGE				SPIRITUALITY
			DARING				LEADERSHIP				STRUCTURE
			DEPENDABILITY				LEARNING				SUPPORT
			DETERMINATION				LOGIC				SUSTAINABILITY
			DEVOTION				LOVE				TEAMWORK
			DIGNITY				LOYALTY				THANKFULNESS
			DISCIPLINE				MASTERY				THOROUGHNESS
			DIVERSITY				MATURITY				THOUGHTFULNESS
			EDUCATION				MEANING				TRUST
			EMPATHY				MINDFULNESS				TRUTH
			EMPOWERMENT				MODESTY				UNDERSTANDING
			ENCOURAGEMENT				MOTIVATION				UNIQUENESS
			ENERGY				NATURE				WARM-HEARTEDNESS
			ENJOYMENT				NON-CONFORMITY				WISDOM

NOW WHAT?	

T1.4

TOOLS FOR TEAM-FOCUSED CONVERSATIONS | BUILDING OUR CHANGEMAKING TEAM

OUR COLLABORATIVE CULTURE

How might we ensure that we're creating and nurturing the right culture for successful collaboration?

tinyurl.com/cctboxt14

ABOUT THIS TOOL

A team culture that empowers collaborative changemaking is key to success. Roughly 10 years ago, Google launched a research project called "Project Aristotle" to figure out the "secret sauce" for creating and nurturing this kind of culture. This OUR COLLABORATIVE CULTURE tool should help you and your team put what Google learned into practice.

After researching 180 teams and conducting hundreds of double-blind interviews with leaders, the "Project Aristotle" team concluded that there are five critical conditions that must exist for teams to be high-performing. They are as follows:

- **PSYCHOLOGICAL SAFETY:** Teammates have to feel confident that no one on the team will be embarrassed or punished for admitting a mistake, asking a question, or offering a new idea. Everyone's opinions should be solicited, heard, and respected.
- **DEPENDABILITY:** On dependable teams, members reliably complete quality work on time.
- **STRUCTURE + CLARITY:** This is a team member's understanding of expectations, the process for fulfilling expectations, and the consequences of one's performance.
- **PERSONAL MEANING:** The work should personally matter.
- **IMPACT:** Team members must believe that the results of the work will make a meaningful difference.

CHANGEMAKER COACH | TOOL TIPS

- I'd strongly recommend investing time discussing and using this tool. It helps you create a changemaking culture. And just using it sends a really important signal to the team/ community.
- You should also use this as a check-in tool. As they say, "Culture eats strategy for breakfast."
- I find this helpful for putting CT2 LEAD WITH COMMUNITY VOICE + CHOICE (p. 28) into practice.

HOW TO USE THIS TOOL

1. First, go to the top of the tool and note down OUR TEAM NAME. If you're an informal team or haven't decided on a name yet, just pick one that resonates with everyone. It can be temporary.
2. Next, go to the COLLABORATIVE CULTURE QUESTIONS. As a team go through each question and note down OUR STRATEGIES for each. If you don't have a strategy, leave the space blank.
3. After you've completed this, it's time to analyze what you've noted in OUR STRATEGIES for each question. Go to the ANALYSIS header. First, under SATISFACTION WITH STRATEGY circle a number from zero to five. Zero means you're totally unsatisfied. Five means you're completely satisfied. You could either do this after a team conversation, or team members could do this individually and you can then use an average number. After you've circled a number, note down your reason under the WHY THIS LEVEL OF SATISFACTION header.
4. Now pivot the conversation from the current analysis to the future. Consider your ANALYSIS for each of the questions and talk about how you might change your strategy. Note down your thoughts under the IDEAS FOR MODIFICATIONS/IMPROVEMENTS header.
5. To conclude, go to NOW WHAT? and note down a few priority next steps based on what you've learned and/or new insights you've gained from using this tool.

CHANGEMAKING INNOVATION MINI-CASES	
V2	p. 358
V43	p. 366
V58	p. 369

CHANGEMAKING TRIMTABS	
CT2	p. 28
CT17	p. 58
CT20	p. 64

OUR TEAM NAME	

		ANALYSIS		
COLLABORATIVE CULTURE QUESTIONS	**OUR STRATEGIES**	**SATISFACTION WITH STRATEGY**	**WHY THIS LEVEL OF SATISFACTION?**	**IDEAS FOR MODIFICATIONS/ IMPROVEMENTS**
HOW ARE WE CREATING + MAINTAINING A SENSE OF **PSYCHOLOGICAL SAFETY?**		0 1 2 3 4 5		
HOW ARE WE CREATING A CULTURE OF **DEPENDABILITY?**		0 1 2 3 4 5		
HOW HAVE WE ESTABLISHED **STRUCTURE + CLARITY?**		0 1 2 3 4 5		
HOW DOES OUR COLLABORATION TOGETHER HAVE **PERSONAL MEANING?**		0 1 2 3 4 5		
HOW WILL OUR COLLABORATION TOGETHER CREATE TANGIBLE + SIGNIFICANT **IMPACT?**		0 1 2 3 4 5		

NOW WHAT?	

☐ **T1.5**

TOOLS FOR TEAM-FOCUSED CONVERSATIONS | BUILDING OUR CHANGEMAKING TEAM

toolkit 01

OUR SUPERPOWERS

How might we identify and appreciate our individual team members' superpowers?

tinyurl.com/cctboxt15

ABOUT THIS TOOL

Asset-Framing is an approach that defines people by their strengths and aspirations. Changemakers are asset-framers. Use this OUR SUPERPOWERS tool to help you and your team embed this approach in your team's culture by identifying and celebrating team members' strengths.

Needless to say, as with all of the tools, this OUR SUPERPOWERS tool should be helpful with both internal and external stakeholders. You might want to use this with your team, your organization, your partners, and/or in the broader community. Regardless, it should help you start with joy, celebrate how people are showing up, and think creatively about how people might contribute to your changemaking efforts.

CHANGEMAKER COACH | TOOL TIP

- Using this tool can be fun for everyone. It sets a really positive tone and demonstrates that people are valued outside of their "technical" areas of expertise.
- This is definitely a good one for putting CT1 CHANGE THE NARRATIVE (p. 26) into action.

HOW TO USE THIS TOOL

1. First, make photocopies or make sure that everyone can see the tool and has a place to note down their own responses.
2. Now that you're set-up, start by having everyone work individually. Have everyone go to the top of the tool and note down OUR TEAM NAME. If you're an informal team or haven't decided on a name yet, just pick one that resonates with everyone. It can be temporary.
3. After this, have everyone note down the NAME of each of your TEAM MEMBERS. There are spaces for five people. Your team might include fewer or more people.
4. Review the SUPERPOWERS. If you're a new team where people don't know each other, have each person put an "X" in the boxes next to their own SUPERPOWERS. If you're an established team, have each person put an "X" in the boxes next to their TEAM MEMBERS' SUPERPOWERS.
5. Now it's time to share and celebrate. Have each person share what they noted down either for themselves or for their TEAM MEMBERS. Celebrate each person as you do this.
6. To conclude, go to NOW WHAT? and note down a few priority next steps based on what you've learned and/or new insights you've gained from using this tool.

CHANGEMAKING INNOVATION MINI-CASES	
V6	p. 359
V62	p. 370
V69	p. 371

CHANGEMAKING TRIMTABS	
CT1	p. 26
CT4	p. 32
CT9	p. 42

OUR TEAM NAME	

	OUR TEAM MEMBERS				
SUPERPOWERS					
ADAPTIVE					
ATTENTIVE					
CALM					
CARING					
COLLABORATIVE					
COMPASSIONATE					
CURIOUS					
EMPATHETIC					
ENTHUSIASTIC					
GIVING					
JOYFUL					
PASSIONATE					
PATIENT					
PRESENT					
TRUSTING					

NOW WHAT?	

TOOLS FOR TEAM-FOCUSED CONVERSATIONS | BUILDING OUR CHANGEMAKING TEAM

TOOLKIT TOOLS REFLECTIONS

SCALE:
STRONGLY AGREE = 5, AGREE = 4, NOT SURE = 3, DISAGREE = 2, STRONGLY DISAGREE = 1

tinyurl.com/cctboxtoolsrflect

	CHANGEMAKING TOOLS				
REFLECTION STATEMENTS	**T1.1**	**T1.2**	**T1.3**	**T1.4**	**T1.5**
This tool is easy to understand.					
This tool is easy to use.					
This tool taught me/ us important new knowledge.					
This tool empowered new changemaking conversations.					
This tool helped to spark new ideas/ insights.					
This tool should be included in my/ our toolbox for the future.					
I/ we should share this tool with other changemakers.					

NOTES:

GVK note -

- *Go to HOW TO DESIGN TEAM REFLECTIONS (pg. 379)*

toolkit 02

TOOLS FOR TEAM-FOCUSED CONVERSATIONS | (RE)CALIBRATING OUR TEAM'S EFFORTS

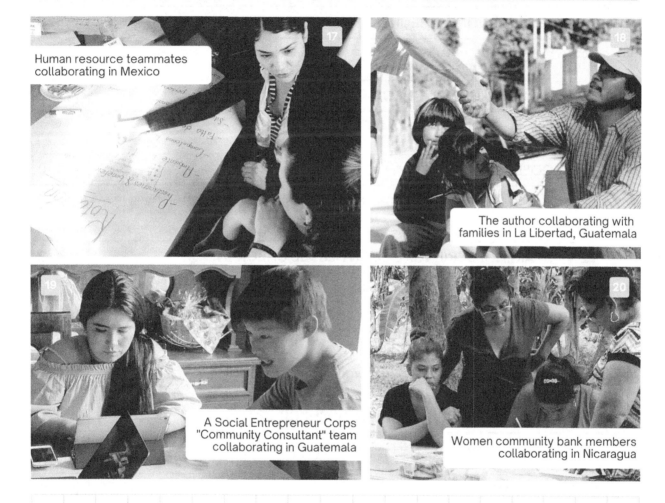

17 Human resource teammates collaborating in Mexico

18 The author collaborating with families in La Libertad, Guatemala

19 A Social Entrepreneur Corps "Community Consultant" team collaborating in Guatemala

20 Women community bank members collaborating in Nicaragua

GVK note -

"THE CLOSET RULE": Most closets are full or overstuffed. Why? When we have space, we fill it. It's just human nature. Same goes with work. Assume team members' closets are full. So, if want someone to put something new in the closet (new job, task, etc.), make sure you empower them to take something out first. And be proactive. Don't put someone in the position where they have to tell you their closet's overstuffed.

TOOLS FOR TEAM-FOCUSED CONVERSATIONS | (RE)CALIBRATING OUR TEAM'S EFFORTS

TOOLS INVENTORY

How might we check-in on our our expectations, responsibilities and priorities?

tinyurl.com/cctboxtools01

☐	**T2.1 LEVEL SETTING CHECK-IN**	**p. 126**

How might we make sure we're starting our conversations with everyone "on the same page?"

☐	**T2.2 RACI STRUCTURE CHECK-IN**	**p. 128**

How might we define clear roles and responsibilities for team members?

☐	**T2.3 GOLDILOCKS CHECK-IN**	**p. 130**

How might we work to achieve a good balance between our short-term focused and long-term focused efforts?

☐	**T2.4 STAKEHOLDER ENGAGEMENT LEVEL CHECK-IN**	**p. 132**

How might we work together to empower the most appropriate level of engagement for each stakeholder?

☐	**T2.5 EISENHOWER CHECK-IN**	**p. 134**

How might we prioritize our efforts by analyzing urgency and importance?

☐	**T2.6 EFFECTIVENESS + EFFICIENCY CHECK-IN**	**p. 136**

How might we analyze our work through the lens of effectiveness and efficiency?

☐	**T2.7 KANBAN CHECK-IN**	**p. 138**

How might we organize and prioritize our workflow?

☐	**T2.8 THREATS + REWARDS CHECK-IN**	**p. 140**

How might we work to minimize perceived threats and maximize rewards?

TOOLKIT SCORECARD + PRIORITIZATION HELP

Score yourselves to help you decide which tool(s) you might want to prioritize for your changemaking conversations.

tinyurl.com/cctboxtoolsprior

SELF-CHECK STATEMENTS	HOW ARE WE DOING?	TOOL SUGGESTIONS
We're starting our meetings/ conversations with shared expectations.	0 1 2 3 4 5	T2.1
We're having periodic conversations to check in on the roles everyone should, and shouldn't, be playing for each project/activity.	0 1 2 3 4 5	T2.2
We're having check-in conversations to find the right balance between being short-term and long-term focused.	0 1 2 3 4 5	T2.3
We're having conversations to check in on everyone's engagement levels.	0 1 2 3 4 5	T2.4
We're having check-in conversations to discuss what's urgent versus what's important.	0 1 2 3 4 5	T2.5
We're analyzing both efficiency and effectiveness.	0 1 2 3 4 5	T2.6
We're having conversations to check in on the status of our activities/ projects.	0 1 2 3 4 5	T2.7
We're having conversations to check in on what might be making team members feel either threatened or rewarded.	0 1 2 3 4 5	T2.8

NOTES:

GVK note -

- Help your team avoid "amygdala hijack" - anger, fear, anxiety, uncertainty, etc. impair the prefrontal cortex, the part of the brain in the frontal lobe that regulates rational thought. This causes the "fight or flight" reaction.

TOOLS FOR TEAM-FOCUSED CONVERSATIONS |
(RE)CALIBRATING OUR TEAM'S EFFORTS

COLLABORATIVE CHANGEMAKING VOICES

Get into the mindset for this toolkit + include your voice in the conversation.

"Although the invention of the Post-It note might have been somewhat accidental, the creation of the 3M environment that allowed it was anything but an accident."

JERRY I. PORRAS + JIM COLLINS
AUTHORS - *BUILT TO LAST: SUCCESSFUL HABITS OF VISIONARY COMPANIES*

"I have to constantly re-identify myself to myself, reactivate my own standards, my own convictions about what I'm doing and why."

NINA SIMONE
SINGER + SONGWRITER |
CIVIL RIGHTS ACTIVIST

"It's okay to admit what you don't know. It's okay to ask for help. And it's more than okay to listen to the people you lead – in fact, it's essential."

MARY BARRA
CEO - GENERAL MOTORS

"Go easy on yourself. Whatever you do today, let it be enough."

SIMONE BILES
GYMNAST | OLYMPIAN

"I realized something the other day. I'd been getting so annoyed because people keep bringing me problems. Then I stepped back for a moment and realized that solving problems is what I do. And how lucky I am that I get to help people solve problems."

GEORGE "BUCKY" GLICKLEY
CO-FOUNDER - COMMUNITY ENTERPRISE SOLUTIONS + SOCIAL ENTREPRENEUR CORPS

"Self-awareness is probably the most important thing towards being a champion."

BILLIE JEAN KING
TENNIS CHAMPION | ACTIVIST

"Trust is earned in the smallest of moments. It is earned not through heroic deeds, or even highly visible actions, but through paying attention, listening, and gestures of genuine care and connection."

BRENÉ BROWN
AUTHOR | PROFESSOR

"Action expresses priorities."

MAHATMA GHANDI
NONVIOLENT ADVOCATE + LEADER

"I can't change the direction of the wind, but I can adjust my sails to always reach my destination."

JAMES (JIMMY) DEAN
COUNTRY MUSIC SINGER | ENTREPRENEUR

☐ **T2.1**

TOOLS FOR TEAM-FOCUSED CONVERSATIONS | (RE)CALIBRATING OUR TEAM'S EFFORTS

LEVEL SETTING CHECK-IN

How might we make sure that we're starting our conversations with everyone "on the same page?"

tinyurl.com/cctboxt21

ABOUT THIS TOOL

Before diving into any collaborative changemaking conversation, it's important to make sure that everyone's "on the same page." This means there's an agreed-upon starting point, and there are shared expectations. This LEVEL SETTING CHECK-IN tool should help your team do this.

This tool helps your team reach agreement about the following:

- **WHAT WE'RE CONFIDENT WE KNOW**
- **WHAT WE THINK WE KNOW, BUT WE'RE NOT SURE**
- **WHAT WE THINK WE DON'T KNOW**
- **WHAT WE'RE CONFIDENT WE DON'T KNOW**

CHANGEMAKER COACH | TOOL TIPS

- This is an approach as much as it's a tool. Ideally you and your team will get into the habit of level setting without the need for a tool.
- You might want to use this with T2.7 KANBAN CHECK-IN (p. 138).

HOW TO USE THIS TOOL

1. First, briefly describe THE CONTEXT. This is the current circumstance/ situation. What's this conversation about? What's the issue? Why are you having this conversation?

2. Next, work your way down the tool. Start with a conversation about WHAT WE'RE CONFIDENT WE KNOW. Note down what everyone says and agrees upon. As always, be specific.

3. Following this, do the same for WHAT WE THINK WE KNOW, BUT WE'RE NOT SURE, WHAT WE THINK WE DON'T KNOW, and WHAT WE'RE CONFIDENT WE DON'T KNOW.

4. To conclude, go to NOW WHAT? and note down a few priority next steps based on what you've learned and/or new insights you've gained from using this tool.

CHANGEMAKING INNOVATION MINI-CASES	
V26	p. 363
V34	p. 364
V73	p. 372

CHANGEMAKING TRIMTABS	
CT5	p. 34
CT11	p. 46
CT19	p. 62

THE CONTEXT	

WHAT WE'RE CONFIDENT WE KNOW
WHAT WE THINK WE KNOW, BUT WE'RE NOT SURE
WHAT WE THINK WE DON'T KNOW
WHAT WE'RE CONFIDENT WE DON'T KNOW

NOW WHAT?	

T2.2

TOOLS FOR TEAM-FOCUSED CONVERSATIONS | (RE)CALIBRATING OUR TEAM'S EFFORTS

RACI STRUCTURE CHECK-IN

How might we define clear roles and responsibilities for team members?

tinyurl.com/ccltoolbox22

ABOUT THIS TOOL

Establishing and checking in on individual roles and responsibilities is critically important for team success. This is especially true for diverse changemaking teams that are working to solve complex problems in uncertain and ambiguous environments. This RACI STRUCTURE CHECK-IN tool should help you and your team do this.

A RACI model is a responsibility matrix that was originally conceived way back in the 1950's. It was designed to help teams ensure that everyone is included while avoiding potentially conflictive situations where team members either don't know their roles and/or are confused about which role they should be playing. RACI is an acronym for the following four roles:

- **(R)ESPONSIBLE:** These are the people who perform the work.
- **(A)CCOUNTABLE:** This is the person who's ultimately accountable for making decisions.
- **(C)ONSULTED:** This is anyone who could be or should be consulted with while the work is in progress and/or before important decisions are made. Their advice may or may not be taken depending on the circumstances.
- **(I)NFORMED:** This is anyone who should be informed of the work periodically and/or when decisions are made. This is a passive role.

HOW TO USE THIS TOOL

1. First, note down the OVERALL GOAL. What's your team trying to achieve? It's important for everyone to have a clear understanding of the OVERALL GOAL.
2. Next, go to PROJECTS/ ACTIVITIES and note down a DESCRIPTION for each one that's in service of achieving the OVERALL GOAL. Try to describe the PROJECTS/ ACTIVITIES with as much specificity as possible. Next to each DESCRIPTION note down the PROJECTED COMPLETION DATE (IF APPLICABLE).
3. Now go to the RACI TEAM ROLES columns. For each of your PROJECTS/ ACTIVITIES decide and note down WHO'S (R)ESPONSIBLE?, WHO'S (A)CCOUNTABLE?, WHO SHOULD BE (C)ONSULTED?, and WHO SHOULD BE (I)NFORMED?
4. To conclude, go to NOW WHAT? and note down a few priority next steps based on what you've learned and/or new insights you've gained from using this tool.

CHANGEMAKER COACH | TOOL TIPS

- I'd recommend using this once you've created your changemaking team using T1. 1 OUR TEAM (p. 110)
- Before you use this, you might want to take a look at T2.4 STAKEHOLDER ENGAGEMENT LEVEL CHECK-IN (p. 132) and T6.8 STAKEHOLDER POWER MAP (p. 224)

CHANGEMAKING INNOVATION MINI-CASES	
V14	p. 360
V33	p. 364
V70	p. 371

CHANGEMAKING TRIMTABS	
CT2	p. 28
CT9	p. 42
CT10	p. 44

OVERALL GOAL	

PROJECTS/ ACTIVITIES		**RACI TEAM ROLES**			
DESCRIPTION	**PROJECTED COMPLETION DATE (IF APPLICABLE)**	**WHO'S (R)ESPONSIBLE?**	**WHO'S (A)CCOUNTABLE?**	**WHO SHOULD BE (C)ONSULTED?**	**WHO SHOULD BE (I)NFORMED?**

NOW WHAT?	

☐ T2.3

TOOLS FOR TEAM-FOCUSED CONVERSATIONS | (RE)CALIBRATING OUR TEAM'S EFFORTS

GOLDILOCKS CHECK-IN

How might we work to achieve a good balance between our short-term focused and long-term focused efforts?

tinyurl.com/cctboxt23

ABOUT THIS TOOL

In the 19th-century fairy tale ***Goldilocks and the Three Bears***, Goldilocks ventures into the house of the three bears, who aren't home at the time. She's hungry. She sees three bowls of porridge. She tries one bowl. It's too hot. She tries another. It's too cold. The third is "just right." She then gets sleepy and goes through this process with beds. One's too hard, another's too soft, and the third one's "just right." This is where the Goldilocks Principle comes from, also known as the "just right" concept. The general idea is that success usually lies in a "just right" place between two extremes. In particular, as changemakers, it's easy to slide into being either too short-term focused or too long-term focused. This GOLDILOCKS CHECK-IN tool should help you and your team self-correct when this happens.

This tool prompts the following questions:

How do we find the "just right" balance between...

- being REACTIVE and PROACTIVE?
- focusing on EXECUTION and INNOVATION?
- focusing on IMMEDIATE RESULTS and CONTINUOUS LEARNING?
- ZOOMING-IN and ZOOMING-OUT?
- DOING or PLANNING?
- focusing on URGENT THINGS and IMPORTANT THINGS?
- spending time on INDIVIDUAL WORK and TEAMWORK?
- MANAGING TEAMS and BUILDING TEAMS AND NETWORKS?
- spending time on DELEGATION and EMPOWERMENT?
- DOING IT OURSELVES and CAPACITY BUILDING?
- EFFECTIVENESS or EFFICIENCY?
- focusing on TRANSACTIONS and RELATIONSHIPS?
- spending time RECEIVING and GIVING?

HOW TO USE THIS TOOL

1. First, briefly describe OUR CURRENT CONTEXT. This is the current circumstance/situation. What's brought the team together at this moment? What's the conversation about? What's the issue?
2. Next, go to the OUR SELF-ASSESSMENT header. Work your way down the tool, and circle the number your team believes represents where you are at this point in time. For example, ask yourselves, "Are we being more REACTIVE or PROACTIVE?" If the consensus answer is, "We believe we're being a bit more REACTIVE at the moment.", you might want to circle the number "1" that's closer to REACTIVE.
3. After you've worked your way to the bottom of the tool, zoom out and have a big-picture conversation about why you assessed yourselves the way that you did for each row. Are you being pulled too far in one direction or another? What should "just right" be for each row?
4. Now go back to the top to the IDEAS FOR CHANGES header. Work your way down the tool again noting down ideas to help you get to "just right" for each row.
5. To conclude, go to NOW WHAT? and note down a few priority next steps based on what you've learned and/or new insights you've gained from using this tool.

CHANGEMAKER COACH | TOOL TIPS

This is good for self-correcting. I originally designed this for a changemaking organization that was growing very quickly. They wanted to make sure that they didn't lose the special culture they had created.

CHANGEMAKING INNOVATION MINI-CASES	
V15	p. 360
V45	p. 366
V84	p. 374

CHANGEMAKING TRIMTABS	
CT15	p. 54
CT19	p. 62
CT20	p. 64

OUR CURRENT CONTEXT	

OUR SELF-ASSESSMENT (MORE SHORT-TERM FOCUSED ← → MORE LONG-TERM FOCUSED)

									IDEAS FOR CHANGES
REACTIVE	3	2	1	0	1	2	3	PROACTIVE	
EXECUTION	3	2	1	0	1	2	3	INNOVATION	
IMMEDIATE RESULTS	3	2	1	0	1	2	3	CONTINUOUS LEARNING	
ZOOMING IN	3	2	1	0	1	2	3	ZOOMING OUT	
DOING	3	2	1	0	1	2	3	PLANNING	
URGENT THINGS	3	2	1	0	1	2	3	IMPORTANT THINGS	
INDIVIDUAL WORK	3	2	1	0	1	2	3	TEAMWORK	
MANAGING TEAMS	3	2	1	0	1	2	3	BUILDING TEAMS + NETWORKS	
DELEGATION	3	2	1	0	1	2	3	EMPOWERMENT	
DOING IT OURSELVES	3	2	1	0	1	2	3	CAPACITY BUILDING	
EFFECTIVENESS	3	2	1	0	1	2	3	EFFICIENCY	
TRANSACTIONS	3	2	1	0	1	2	3	RELATIONSHIPS	
RECEIVING	3	2	1	0	1	2	3	GIVING	
	3	2	1	0	1	2	3		

NOW WHAT?	

T2.4

TOOLS FOR TEAM-FOCUSED CONVERSATIONS | (RE)CALIBRATING OUR TEAM'S EFFORTS

toolkit 02

STAKEHOLDER ENGAGEMENT LEVEL CHECK-IN

How might we work together to empower the most appropriate level of engagement for each key stakeholder?

tinyurl.com/cctboxt24

ABOUT THIS TOOL

How engaged are all of the key stakeholders in your changemaking efforts? Are the right stakeholders currently engaging in the right ways? Do you know? You need to. This STAKEHOLDER ENGAGEMENT LEVEL CHECK-IN tool should help you consider and (re)calibrate engagement levels for key internal and/or external stakeholders.

From highest to lowest, the eight engagement levels included in this tool are as follows:

- **OWNING:** Feels a deep sense of responsibility for achieving success and demonstrates being fully committed
- **LEADING:** Leads people/ decisions and makes sure work is completed
- **PARTICIPATING:** Takes part in and supports the work
- **ADVISING:** Provides advice, coaching, and/or mentoring
- **INTERESTED:** Demonstrates curiosity and/or concern
- **OBSERVING:** Periodically watches what's going on from a distance
- **AWARE:** Knows about the work, but only on a superficial level
- **NOT ENGAGED:** Isn't engaged at all

To note, as a general rule, the people who have the closest proximity to problems should be the most engaged. They should be OWNING and LEADING as soon and as much as possible. They have the highest level of empathy. They have the best contextual understanding, hold the most important relationships, and likely care the most about solving the problem. Conversely, people further away should play a less engaged role. They should act as PARTICIPANTS or ADVISORS. In addition, over time you'll want to get more and more stakeholders AWARE, OBSERVING, and INTERESTED. This is important for scaling.

HOW TO USE THIS TOOL

1. First, briefly describe the PROJECT/ ACTIVITY NAME. This could be anything from your overall team project, to a small, short-term activity.
2. Next, go to the KEY STAKEHOLDERS header. Underneath this, work your way down the tool noting down one name per row. There are eight rows. You may have fewer or more KEY STAKEHOLDERS.
3. Now go to the first KEY STAKEHOLDER you noted down. Go to the ENGAGEMENT LEVEL header to the right of this person and/or organization's name. Circle both the CURRENT and OPTIMAL ENGAGEMENT LEVEL for this KEY STAKEHOLDER. For example, let's assume Maria is this first KEY STAKEHOLDER. For this project, your team believes her CURRENT ENGAGEMENT LEVEL is PARTICIPATING. So you circle CURRENT under PARTICIPATING. However, the team believes she should be playing a more central role. You decide her OPTIMAL ENGAGEMENT LEVEL should be OWNING. So you circle OPTIMAL under OWNING.
4. Go to ANALYSIS and note down why you circled the CURRENT and OPTIMAL. What are your reasons?
5. Go to the IDEAS FOR HOW TO CHANGE ENGAGEMENT LEVEL header. If CURRENT and OPTIMAL are the same, leave this blank. If there's a difference between the two, use this space to note down what you think you need to do to get from one to the other.
6. Repeat steps 3, 4, and 5 for each KEY STAKEHOLDER.
7. To conclude, go to NOW WHAT? and note down a few priority next steps based on what you've learned and/or new insights you've gained from using this tool.

CHANGEMAKING INNOVATION MINI-CASES	
V15	p. 360
V24	p. 362
V60	p. 369

CHANGEMAKING TRIMTABS	
CT2	p. 28
CT11	p. 46
CT20	p. 64

PROJECT/ ACTIVITY NAME	

	ENGAGEMENT LEVEL									
KEY STAKEHOLDERS	**OWNING**	**LEADING**	**PARTICIPATING**	**ADVISING**	**INTERESTED**	**OBSERVING**	**AWARE**	**NOT ENGAGED**	**ANALYSIS**	**IDEAS FOR HOW TO CHANGE ENGAGEMENT LEVEL**
	CURRENT OPTIMAL	CURRENT OPTIMAL	CURRENT OPTIMAL	CURRENT OPTIMAL	CURRENT OPTIMAL	CURRENT OPTIMAL	CURRENT OPTIMAL	CURRENT OPTIMAL		
	CURRENT OPTIMAL	CURRENT OPTIMAL	CURRENT OPTIMAL	CURRENT OPTIMAL	CURRENT OPTIMAL	CURRENT OPTIMAL	CURRENT OPTIMAL	CURRENT OPTIMAL		
	CURRENT OPTIMAL	CURRENT OPTIMAL	CURRENT OPTIMAL	CURRENT OPTIMAL	CURRENT OPTIMAL	CURRENT OPTIMAL	CURRENT OPTIMAL	CURRENT OPTIMAL		
	CURRENT OPTIMAL	CURRENT OPTIMAL	CURRENT OPTIMAL	CURRENT OPTIMAL	CURRENT OPTIMAL	CURRENT OPTIMAL	CURRENT OPTIMAL	CURRENT OPTIMAL		
	CURRENT OPTIMAL	CURRENT OPTIMAL	CURRENT OPTIMAL	CURRENT OPTIMAL	CURRENT OPTIMAL	CURRENT OPTIMAL	CURRENT OPTIMAL	CURRENT OPTIMAL		
	CURRENT OPTIMAL	CURRENT OPTIMAL	CURRENT OPTIMAL	CURRENT OPTIMAL	CURRENT OPTIMAL	CURRENT OPTIMAL	CURRENT OPTIMAL	CURRENT OPTIMAL		
	CURRENT OPTIMAL	CURRENT OPTIMAL	CURRENT OPTIMAL	CURRENT OPTIMAL	CURRENT OPTIMAL	CURRENT OPTIMAL	CURRENT OPTIMAL	CURRENT OPTIMAL		

NOW WHAT?	

T2.5

TOOLS FOR TEAM-FOCUSED CONVERSATIONS | (RE)CALIBRATING OUR TEAM'S EFFORTS

EISENHOWER CHECK-IN

How might we prioritize our efforts by analyzing urgency and importance?

tinyurl.com/cctboxt25

ABOUT THIS TOOL

This tool is named after U.S. President Dwight D. Eisenhower. He was known for being incredibly adept at time management and prioritization. One of his most famous quotes is, "What is important is seldom urgent, and what is urgent is seldom important." This EISENHOWER CHECK-IN tool should help you and your team make decisions like Eisenhower by prioritizing projects, programs, processes, etc. by analyzing urgency and importance.

This tool is set up as a matrix with four quadrants. The four quadrants are as follows :

- **QUADRANT 1 - DO (URGENT + IMPORTANT):** These should dealt with immediately.
- **QUADRANT 2 - DELEGATE (URGENT + NOT IMPORTANT):** These tend to be more trivial. Their importance is low, but they still should be dealt with as soon as possible.
- **QUADRANT 3 - DECIDE (NOT URGENT + IMPORTANT):** Plan for when these will be done, and don't lose sight of them simply because they aren't urgent. Make sure someone(s) has responsibility for these, and that they're on the calendar.
- **QUADRANT 4 - DELETE (NOT URGENT + NOT IMPORTANT):** Get rid of these. They're a waste of time.

HOW TO USE THIS TOOL

1. First, go to OUR GOAL(S) and note down the relevant organizational/ team goal(s).
2. Next, go to QUADRANT 1- DO and note down all of the IMPORTANT and URGENT projects/ processes/ activities, etc. required to achieve OUR GOAL(S). Be as specific as possible.
3. Do the same for the remaining three quadrants. Needless to say, the flow of your conversation might not be this linear. You'll likely end up jumping back and forth to different quadrants.
4. To conclude, go to NOW WHAT? and note down a few priority next steps based on what you've learned and/or new insights you've gained from using this tool.

CHANGEMAKING INNOVATION MINI-CASES		CHANGEMAKING TRIMTABS	
V31	p. 364	CT15	p. 54
V41	p. 366	CT16	p. 56
V43	p. 366	CT19	p. 62

OUR GOAL(S)	

IMPORTANCE		**URGENCY**	
		URGENT	**NOT URGENT**
	IMPORTANT		
	NOT IMPORTANT		

NOW WHAT?	

T2.6

TOOLS FOR TEAM-FOCUSED CONVERSATIONS | (RE)CALIBRATING OUR TEAM'S EFFORTS

toolkit 02

EFFECTIVENESS + EFFICIENCY CHECK-IN

How might we analyze our work through the lens of effectiveness and efficiency?

tinyurl.com/cctboxt26

ABOUT THIS TOOL

Effectiveness means "doing the right things." Efficiency means "doing things right." This EFFECTIVENESS + EFFICIENCY CHECK-IN tool helps you and your team prioritize programs, processes, etc. based on your analysis of their relative effectiveness and efficiency.

This tool is set up as a matrix with four quadrants. The quadrants are as follows:

- **QUADRANT 1 - THRIVES (EFFECTIVE + EFFICIENT):** This is the goal. Prioritize what falls in this quadrant.
- **QUADRANT 2 - SURVIVES (EFFECTIVE + INEFFICIENT):** These are things that show potential, but that aren't meeting goals in the most productive way.
- **QUADRANT 3 - QUICKLY DIES (INEFFECTIVE + EFFICIENT):** These things will fail fast unless emergency action is taken.
- **QUADRANT 4 - SLOWLY DIES (INEFFECTIVE + INEFFICIENT):** This is typically the result of poor strategy, management, processes, and/or execution. Think really hard about whether things that land in this quadrant are worth continuing.

HOW TO USE THIS TOOL

1. First, go to OUR GOAL(S) and note down the relevant organizational/ team goal(s).
2. Next, go to QUADRANT 1- THRIVES and note down all of the EFFICIENT and EFFECTIVE projects/ processes/ activities, etc. required to achieve OUR GOAL(S). Be as specific as possible.
3. Do the same for the remaining three quadrants. Needless to say, the flow of your conversation might not be this linear. You'll likely end up jumping back and forth to different quadrants.
4. To conclude, go to NOW WHAT? and note down a few priority next steps based on what you've learned and/or new insights you've gained from using this tool.

CHANGEMAKING INNOVATION MINI-CASES	
V1	p. 358
V29	p. 363
V46	p. 367

CHANGEMAKING TRIMTABS	
CT5	p. 34
CT6	p. 36
CT19	p. 62

OUR GOAL(S)	

		EFFECTIVENESS	
		EFFECTIVE	**INEFFECTIVE**
EFFICIENCY	**EFFICIENT**	QUADRANT 1 - THRIVES	QUADRANT 3 - QUICKLY DIES
	INEFFICIENT	QUADRANT 2 - SURVIVES	QUADRANT 4 - SLOWLY DIES

NOW WHAT?	

T2.7

TOOLS FOR TEAM-FOCUSED CONVERSATIONS | (RE)CALIBRATING OUR TEAM'S EFFORTS

KANBAN CHECK-IN

How might we organize and prioritize our workflow?

tinyurl.com/cctboxt27

ABOUT THIS TOOL

Kanban originated as a workflow scheduling system for the lean manufacturing (just-in-time manufacturing) strategy designed by industrial engineer and businessman Taiichi Ohno at Toyota. All kinds of teams and organizations, especially those using an Agile approach, work with Kanban boards to optimize work delivery and make the management of complex projects faster and simpler. This KANBAN CHECK-IN tool should help you and your team organize and prioritize your changemaking activities and projects.

This tool uses the following categories to help you track the status of projects and activities:

- **WAITING:** Hasn't been started yet
- **IN-LEARNING:** In discovery and diagnosis
- **IN-DESIGN:** Actively designing
- **IN-REVIEW:** Sharing with team members and/or key stakeholders to get their opinions and recommendations
- **IN-TEST:** In the hands of a select number of people to get their feedback
- **READY:** Seems ready for launch
- **STUCK:** Something that you're having trouble figuring out, or that's bottlenecked for some reason

Frequently revisiting this KANBAN CHECK-IN tool should help your team focus, reduce uncertainty, increase efficiency, and reduce wasted work/ time.

HOW TO USE THIS TOOL

1. Start by noting down the PROJECT and GOAL(S) at the top of the tool.
2. Next, go to the WAITING header. Below this note down all of the key activities/ processes that belong in this category.
3. Do the same under each header. Needless to say, the flow of your conversation might not be this linear. You'll likely end up jumping back and forth between categories.
4. To conclude, go to NOW WHAT? and note down a few priority next steps based on what you've learned and/or new insights you've gained from using this tool.

CHANGEMAKER COACH | TOOL TIPS

- This is a simple project/activity management tool that works well with T2.1 LEVEL SETTING CHECK-IN (p. 126).
- I'd encourage taking a look at T6.5 SYSTEM STATUS MAP (p. 218). Are you working in chaos, complexity, complication, or stability? The "status" of the situation should have a big impact on how you plan, prioritize, and design your work.

CHANGEMAKING INNOVATION MINI-CASES	
V24	p. 362
V65	p. 370
V83	p. 374

CHANGEMAKING TRIMTABS	
CT3	p. 30
CT6	p. 36
CT13	p. 50

PROJECT	
GOAL(S)	

WAITING	**IN LEARNING**	**IN DESIGN**	**IN REVIEW**	**IN TEST**	**READY**	**STUCK**

NOW WHAT?	

T2.8

TOOLS FOR TEAM-FOCUSED CONVERSATIONS | (RE)CALIBRATING OUR TEAM'S EFFORTS

THREATS + REWARDS CHECK-IN

How might we work to minimize perceived threats and maximize rewards?

tinyurl.com/cctboxt28

ABOUT THIS TOOL

Evolution has wired our brains to respond to perceived threats and rewards in particular ways. These responses are instinctive and emotional. They can either hinder or help our collaborative changemaking efforts. Inspired by Dr. David Rock's SCARF® Model, this THREATS + REWARDS CHECK-IN tool should help you and your team design strategies to help minimize threats and maximize rewards.

The SCARF® Model explains how human motivation is driven by our desire to minimize threats and maximize rewards. Threats hinder our creativity, problem-solving abilities, and communication skills. Rewards help us feel more self-confident, empowered, and collaborative. SCARF itself is an acronym for five "domains" that influence our behavior in social situations. The five SCARF domains with examples of common threat and reward activators are as follows:

(S)TATUS: This is our relative importance to others. It's how we view ourselves and how we believe others view us.

- Reward activators: Inclusion, positive feedback, public acknowledgment
- Threat activators: Exclusion, criticism, unsolicited advice

(C)ERTAINTY: This is how we feel about our ability to, and confidence in, predicting the future.

- Reward activators: Clear goals and expectations, feasible workloads
- Threat activators: Lack of transparency, unreliability, erratic behavior

(A)UTONOMY: This is our sense of control over our lives/ events.

- Reward activators: Offering choices, trust, self-responsibility, self-organization
- Threat activators: Micromanagement, command and control

(R)ELATEDNESS: This is how connected to and safe we feel with others.

- Reward activators: Mentoring, coaching, supportive relationships
- Threat activators: Excess competition, judgment, isolation

(F)AIRNESS: This is how fair we feel decisions are that affect us.

- Reward activators: Transparent decisions, equitable access and incentives
- Threat activators: Unequal conditions, favoritism, gender inequality

HOW TO USE THIS TOOL

1. First, go to the INFLUENCING SOCIAL DOMAINS header and go to (S)TATUS.
2. Next, go to the THREATS header to the right of (S)TATUS. As a team, ask yourselves HOW ARE WE DOING AVOIDING THREATS? and score yourselves from "5" (excellent) to "1" (very poorly). Under the ANALYSIS header note down why you gave yourselves this score. And under IDEAS FOR CHANGES note down how you think you might be able to improve your score.
3. Go to the REWARDS header on the right and work through the same process.
4. After you've completed THREATS and REWARDS for (S)TATUS, do the same for the rest of the INFLUENCING SOCIAL DOMAINS.
5. To conclude, go to NOW WHAT? and note down a few priority next steps based on what you've learned and/or new insights you've gained from using this tool.

CHANGEMAKING INNOVATION MINI-CASES	
V26	p. 363
V54	p. 368
V84	p. 374

CHANGEMAKING TRIMTABS	
CT3	p. 30
CT9	p. 42
CT14	p. 52

	THREATS			REWARDS		
INFLUENCING SOCIAL DOMAINS	**HOW ARE WE DOING AVOIDING THREATS?**	**ANALYSIS**	**IDEAS FOR CHANGES**	**HOW ARE WE DOING MAXIMIZING REWARDS?**	**ANALYSIS**	**IDEAS FOR CHANGES**
(S)TATUS	5 4 3 2 1			5 4 3 2 1		
(C)ERTAINTY	5 4 3 2 1			5 4 3 2 1		
(A)UTONOMY	5 4 3 2 1			5 4 3 2 1		
(R)ELATEDNESS	5 4 3 2 1			5 4 3 2 1		
(F)AIRNESS	5 4 3 2 1			5 4 3 2 1		

NOW WHAT?	

TOOLS FOR TEAM-FOCUSED CONVERSATIONS | (RE)CALIBRATING OUR TEAM'S EFFORTS

TOOLKIT TOOLS REFLECTIONS

SCALE:
STRONGLY AGREE = 5, AGREE = 4, NOT SURE = 3, DISAGREE = 2, STRONGLY DISAGREE = 1

tinyurl.com/cctboxtoolsrflect

	CHANGEMAKING TOOLS							
REFLECTION STATEMENTS	**T2.1**	**T2.2**	**T2.3**	**T2.4**	**T2.5**	**T2.6**	**T2.7**	**T2.8**
This tool is easy to understand.								
This tool is easy to use.								
This tool taught me/ us important new knowledge.								
This tool empowered new changemaking conversations.								
This tool helped to spark new ideas/ insights.								
This tool should be included in my/ our toolbox for the future.								
I/ we should share this tool with other changemakers.								

NOTES:

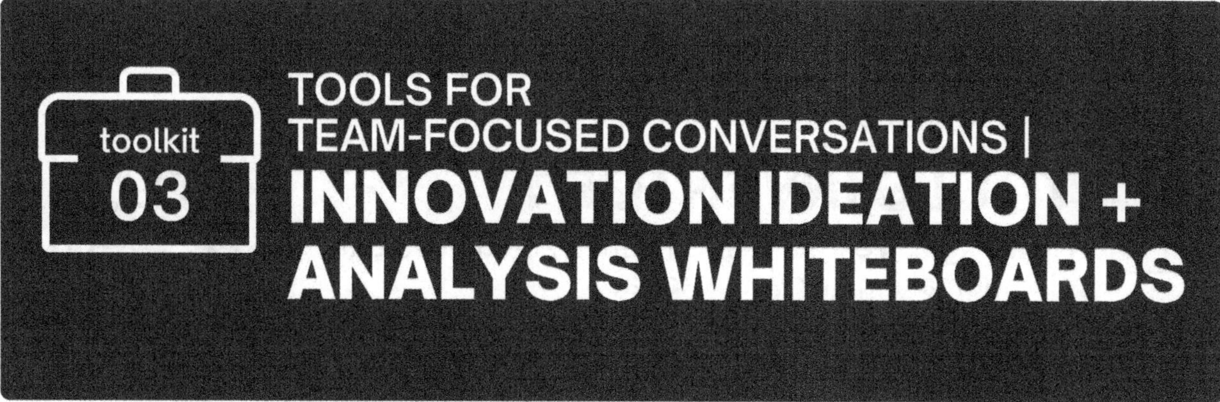

TOOLS FOR TEAM-FOCUSED CONVERSATIONS | INNOVATION IDEATION + ANALYSIS WHITEBOARDS

21

Luke B. collaborating with entrepreneurs in rural Guatemala

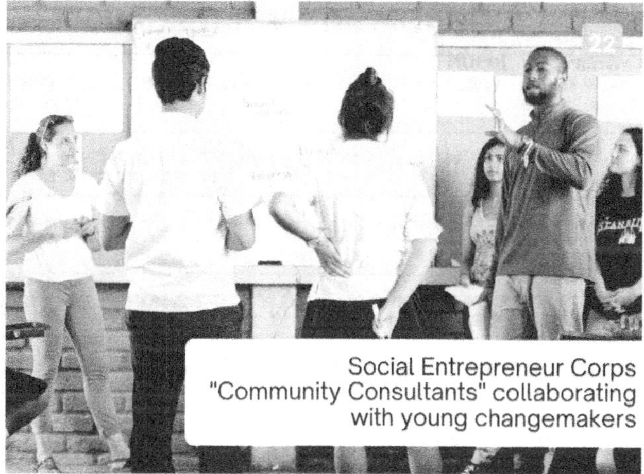
22

Social Entrepreneur Corps "Community Consultants" collaborating with young changemakers

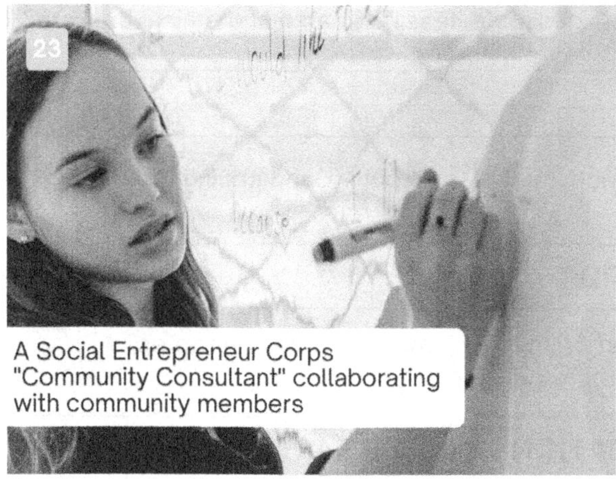
23

A Social Entrepreneur Corps "Community Consultant" collaborating with community members

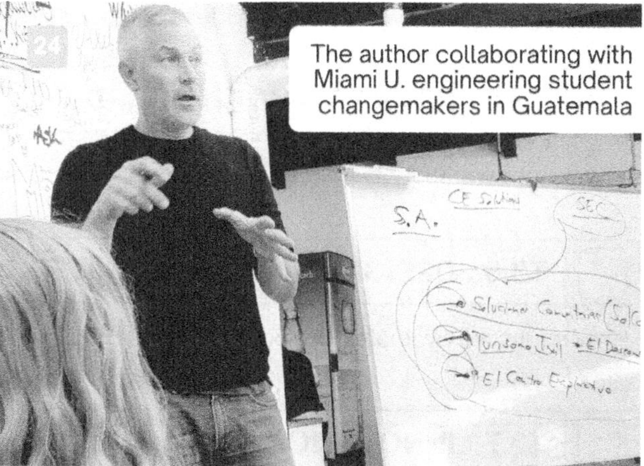
24

The author collaborating with Miami U. engineering student changemakers in Guatemala

NOTES:

GVK note -

- Just try to do the "adjacent possible." This is an opportunity that's next to you. It's practical, feasible, and it also helps you to expand to have new adjacent possible opportunities.

toolkit 03 TOOLS FOR TEAM-FOCUSED CONVERSATIONS | INNOVATION IDEATION + ANALYSIS WHITEBOARDS

TOOLS INVENTORY

How might we ideate about, analyze and evaluate changemaking innovation ideas?

tinyurl.com/cctboxtools01

	Tool	Page
☐	**T3.1 PROXIMITY WHITEBOARD**	p. 148

How might we prioritize based on where we have the closest proximity?

	Tool	Page
☐	**T3.2 IMPACT + EFFORT WHITEBOARD**	p. 150

How might we prioritize innovation ideas by analyzing projected positive impact and required effort?

	Tool	Page
☐	**T3.3 IMPACT + UNCERTAINTY WHITEBOARD**	p. 152

How might we prioritize innovation ideas by analyzing projected positive impact and uncertainty?

	Tool	Page
☐	**T3.4 SWEET SPOT WHITEBOARD**	p. 154

How might we analyze innovation ideas by assessing how desirable, feasible, viable and ethical they are?

	Tool	Page
☐	**T3.5 FOUR FITS WHITEBOARD**	p. 156

How might we analyze the fit between our product/ service, market, distribution, and pricing strategy?

	Tool	Page
☐	**T3.6 DESIGN PRINCIPLES WHITEBOARD**	p. 158

How might we evaluate how our innovation concept aligns with changemaking design principles?

	Tool	Page
☐	**T3.7 INNOVATION INSIGHTS + APPLICATIONS WHITEBOARD**	p. 160

How might we gain strategic insights from other innovations that can be applied to our own innovation?

	Tool	Page
☐	**T3.8 TWO LIMITATIONS WHITEBOARD**	p. 162

How might we assess what's achievable keeping practical limitations in mind?

	Tool	Page
☐	**T3.9 CONSEQUENCES WHITEBOARD**	p. 164

How might we analyze the intended and unintended consequences of innovations?

TOOLS FOR TEAM-FOCUSED CONVERSATIONS | INNOVATION IDEATION + ANALYSIS WHITEBOARDS

toolkit 03

TOOLKIT SCORECARD + PRIORITIZATION HELP

Score yourselves to help you decide which tool(s) you might want to prioritize for your changemaking conversations.

tinyurl.com/cctboxtoolsprior

SELF-CHECK STATEMENTS	HOW ARE WE DOING?	TOOL SUGGESTIONS
We're having conversations about our proximity to the people, place, and problem.	0 1 2 3 4 5	3.1
We're having conversations about prioritizing innovation ideas that strike the right balance between projected positive impact and effort.	0 1 2 3 4 5	3.2
We're having conversations about prioritizing innovation ideas that strike the right balance between projected positive impact and uncertainty.	0 1 2 3 4 5	3.3
We're discussing how feasible, desirable, viable, and ethical our innovation ideas are.	0 1 2 3 4 5	3.4
We're having conversations about how well the product/ service, market/ community, distribution strategy, and pricing strategy fit together.	0 1 2 3 4 5	3.5
We're talking about how well innovations incorporate the most important principles for designing changemaking innovations.	0 1 2 3 4 5	3.6
We're not trying to reinvent the wheel. We're continuously working to get helpful ideas and insights from innovations that are already working well.	0 1 2 3 4 5	3.7
We're having conversations about how our innovation ideas work within practical limitations.	0 1 2 3 4 5	3.8
We're discussing the potential positive and negative consequences of our innovations.	0 1 2 3 4 5	3.9

NOTES: GVK note -

- Go to HOW TO TEST YOUR INNOVATION CONCEPTS (pg. 380)

TOOLS FOR TEAM-FOCUSED CONVERSATIONS | INNOVATION IDEATION + ANALYSIS WHITEBOARDS

COLLABORATIVE CHANGEMAKING VOICES

Get into the mindset for this toolkit + include your voice in the conversation.

"Rarely are opportunities presented to you in a perfect way, in a nice little box with a yellow bow on top. 'Here, open it, it's perfect. You'll love it.' Opportunities – the good ones – are messy, confusing, and hard to recognize. They're risky. They challenge you."

SUSAN WOJCICKI
FORMER CEO - YOUTUBE

"The more constraints one imposes, the more one frees one's self of the chains that shackle the spirit."

IGOR STRAVINSKY
COMPOSER

"I have not failed. I've just found 10,000 ways that won't work."

THOMAS EDISON
INVENTOR

"Setting oneself on a predetermined course in unknown waters is the perfect way to sail straight into an iceberg."

STANLEY MCCHRYSTAL
AUTHOR - *TEAM OF TEAMS - NEW RULES OF ENGAGEMENT FOR A COMPLEX WORLD*

"All great changes are preceded by chaos."

DEEPAK CHOPRA
AUTHOR

"The responsibility is to keep pushing it forward, and not relying on the same old gimmicks. You have to push it forward."

JAY-Z
RAPPER | PRODUCER | ENTREPRENEUR

"It is better to light a candle than curse the darkness."

ELEANOR ROOSEVELT
FORMER FIRST LADY | ACTIVIST

"I never lose. I either win or I learn."

NELSON MANDELA
NOBEL PEACE PRIZE LAUREATE

"When they say you're ridiculous, you know you're onto something."

ABBY WAMBACH
RETIRED USWNT SOCCER PLAYER | COACH

☐ **T3.1**

TOOLS FOR TEAM-FOCUSED CONVERSATIONS | INNOVATION IDEATION + ANALYSIS WHITEBOARDS

PROXIMITY WHITEBOARD

How might we prioritize our efforts based on where we have the closest proximity?

tinyurl.com/cctboxt31

ABOUT THIS TOOL

You should prioritize working with people, in places, and on problems where you have close proximity. Proximity drives empathy, and empathy drives changemaking. This PROXIMITY WHITEBOARD tool should help you and your team analyze and increase your proximity.

This tool is designed to help you get started, iterate, and/ or get unstuck.
When you think about where to dedicate your changemaking efforts, you usually have proximity to the PEOPLE, the PLACE, and/or the PROBLEM. The good news is that you only need to have close proximity to one of these to get close proximity to the others.

For example, you might have a connection with certain PEOPLE whom you feel a desire to support. You can start there and then have conversations with these PEOPLE about a priority PLACE and PROBLEM. Or maybe there's a particular PLACE that really matters to you. Once you decide this, you can do research and talk to PEOPLE in this PLACE to decide what PROBLEM to prioritize. Finally, you might not know the exact PEOPLE or PLACE, but there might be a pressing PROBLEM that really frustrates you. If you know this, you can then research the PLACE and PEOPLE who are most negatively affected by this PROBLEM.

HOW TO USE THIS TOOL

1. Start by noting down OUR TEAM DESCRIPTION at the top of the tool.
2. Next, go to the SUMMARY DESCRIPTIONS header. In no particular order, note down as much information as you can next to the specific prompts about THE PEOPLE, THE PLACE, and THE PROBLEM.
3. After you've noted down all of the SUMMARY DESCRIPTIONS you're able to, go to the OUR PROXIMITY header. In each row, circle HIGH, MED, or LOW under CURRENT STATUS. Then note down WHY THIS STATUS? For each row where you circled MED or LOW, try to answer HOW WE MIGHT GET MORE PROXIMATE?
4. To conclude, go to NOW WHAT? and note down a few priority next steps based on what you've learned and/or new insights you've gained from using this tool.

CHANGEMAKER COACH | TOOL TIPS

- I designed this for student teams trying to figure out where they should focus their changemaking efforts. The goal was to answer the question, "Where should we start?" You should always start with something you know and then work to understand the things you don't. Start with something where you have close proximity.
- This tool goes hand in glove with CT18 PRIORITIZE PROXIMITY (p. 60).
- You can use this as an additional way to figure out your WHY.

CHANGEMAKING INNOVATION MINI-CASES	
V41	p. 366
V51	p. 368
V52	p. 368

CHANGEMAKING TRIMTABS	
CT6	p. 36
CT18	p. 60
CT19	p. 62

OUR TEAM DESCRIPTION	

		SUMMARY DESCRIPTIONS	**OUR PROXIMITY**		
			CURRENT STATUS	**WHY THIS STATUS?**	**HOW MIGHT WE GET MORE PROXIMATE?**
THE PEOPLE	**GOALS/ ASPIRATIONS**		HIGH MED LOW		
	AGE RANGE		HIGH MED LOW		
	GENDER		HIGH MED LOW		
	WORK/ SCHOOL SITUATION		HIGH MED LOW		
	FAMILY SITUATION		HIGH MED LOW		
	HOUSING SITUATION		HIGH MED LOW		
	ECONOMIC SITUATION		HIGH MED LOW		
THE PLACE	**THE PHYSICAL SPACE**		HIGH MED LOW		
	THE COMMUNITY		HIGH MED LOW		
	THE TOWN/ CITY		HIGH MED LOW		
	THE REGION		HIGH MED LOW		
THE PROBLEM	**THE SPECIFIC PROBLEM**		HIGH MED LOW		
	THE CAUSES		HIGH MED LOW		
	THE NEGATIVE EFFECTS		HIGH MED LOW		

NOW WHAT?	

T3.2

TOOLS FOR TEAM-FOCUSED CONVERSATIONS | INNOVATION IDEATION + ANALYSIS WHITEBOARDS

IMPACT + EFFORT WHITEBOARD

How might we prioritize our innovation ideas by analyzing projected positive impact and required effort?

tinyurl.com/cctboxt32

ABOUT THIS TOOL

You've got limited time, knowledge, and resources. Because of this, your goal should be to prioritize changemaking efforts where you're most likely to achieve the biggest positive impact with the least amount of required effort. This IMPACT + EFFORT WHITEBOARD tool should help you and your team prioritize innovations with this goal in mind.

This tool is set up as a matrix with four quadrants. The four quadrants are as follows:

- **QUADRANT 1 - QUICK WINS (HIGH PROJECTED POSITIVE IMPACT + LOW PROJECTED REQUIRED EFFORT):** These should be pursued as soon as possible to create quick and substantial impact.
- **QUADRANT 2 - INCREMENTAL (LOW PROJECTED POSITIVE IMPACT + LOW PROJECTED REQUIRED EFFORT):** Although these require minimum effort, they shouldn't be prioritized. They should be given attention after QUADRANT 1 and 3 opportunities.
- **QUADRANT 3 - BIG PROJECTS (HIGH PROJECTED POSITIVE IMPACT + HIGH PROJECTED REQUIRED EFFORT):** These are difficult, but likely offer the biggest rewards. These require long-term, deep commitment
- **QUADRANT 4 - NOT WORTH IT (LOW PROJECTED POSITIVE IMPACT + HIGH PROJECTED REQUIRED EFFORT):** These should likely be discarded. This is thankless and useless work.

HOW TO USE THIS TOOL

1. Start at QUADRANT 1- QUICK WINS. Note down all of your innovation ideas/ concepts that have a PROJECTED POSITIVE IMPACT that's HIGH and a PROJECTED REQUIRED EFFORT that's LOW. Be as specific as possible.
2. Do the same for the remaining three quadrants. Needless to say, the flow of your conversation might not be this linear. You'll likely end up jumping back and forth to different quadrants.
3. To conclude, go to NOW WHAT? and note down a few priority next steps based on what you've learned and/or new insights you've gained from using this tool.

CHANGEMAKER COACH | TOOL TIPS

- This is a great tool to help you stay grounded and be realistic. I'd run every idea you have through this tool.
- I find this very helpful for putting CT15 CONFRONT COMPLEXITY WITH SIMPLICITY (p. 54) in action.

CHANGEMAKING INNOVATION MINI-CASES	
V34	p. 364
V41	p. 366
V42	p. 366

CHANGEMAKING TRIMTABS	
CT5	p. 34
CT8	p. 40
CT15	p. 54

PROJECTED POSITIVE IMPACT		LOW (EFFORT)	HIGH (EFFORT)
	HIGH		
	LOW		

PROJECTED REQUIRED EFFORT

NOW WHAT?	

T3.3

TOOLS FOR TEAM-FOCUSED CONVERSATIONS | INNOVATION IDEATION + ANALYSIS WHITEBOARDS

IMPACT + UNCERTAINTY WHITEBOARD

How might we prioritize our innovation ideas by analyzing projected positive impact and uncertainty?

tinyurl.com/cctboxt33

ABOUT THIS TOOL

When designing changemaking innovations, you can't know in advance what's going to work and what isn't. That's the nature of innovation. There's uncertainty. Given this, your goal should be to prioritize opportunities that strike the right balance between the level of uncertainty and the projected positive impact. This IMPACT + UNCERTAINTY WHITEBOARD tool should help you and your team prioritize innovations with this goal in mind.

This tool is set up as a matrix with four quadrants. The four quadrants are as follows:

- **QUADRANT 1 - SAFER + BIGGER OPPORTUNITIES (HIGH PROJECTED POSITIVE IMPACT + LOW UNCERTAINTY):** These should go on the top of your priority list.
- **QUADRANT 2 - SAFE + SMALLER OPPORTUNITIES (LOW PROJECTED POSITIVE IMPACT + LOW UNCERTAINTY):** These should be pursued, but aren't a priority.
- **QUADRANT 3 - RISKY OPPORTUNITIES (HIGH PROJECTED POSITIVE IMPACT + HIGH UNCERTAINTY):** These are risks. David Hillson, aka "The Risk Doctor," says "Risk is uncertainty that matters." These matter and should be strongly considered. They have the potential to be long-term game changers.
- **QUADRANT 4 - OPPORTUNITIES TO AVOID (LOW PROJECTED POSITIVE IMPACT + HIGH UNCERTAINTY):** These should be crossed off.

HOW TO USE THIS TOOL

1. Start at QUADRANT 1 - SAFER + BIGGER OPPORTUNITIES. Note down all of your innovation ideas/ concepts that have a PROJECTED POSITIVE IMPACT that's HIGH and UNCERTAINTY that's LOW. Be as specific as possible.
2. Do the same for the remaining three quadrants. Needless to say, the flow of your conversation might not be this linear. You'll likely end up jumping back and forth to different quadrants.
3. To conclude, go to NOW WHAT? and note down a few priority next steps based on what you've learned and/or new insights you've gained from using this tool.

CHANGEMAKER COACH | TOOL TIPS

- It's really important to keep in mind that everyone has different comfort levels with uncertainty. And something that might feel like a reasonable risk to one person might feel incredibly uncertain to another. That's why using this tool as a team/ community is important. It can have the extra benefit of helping your team "level set" on uncertainty.
- Another helpful tool that addresses uncertainty is T6.10 VUCA MAP (p. 228)

CHANGEMAKING INNOVATION MINI-CASES		CHANGEMAKING TRIMTABS	
V12	p. 360	CT3	p. 30
V13	p. 360	CT14	p. 52
V38	p. 365	CT18	p. 60

PROJECTED POSITIVE IMPACT			
	HIGH		
	LOW		
		LOW	HIGH
		UNCERTAINTY	

NOW WHAT?	

T3.4

TOOLS FOR TEAM-FOCUSED CONVERSATIONS | INNOVATION IDEATION + ANALYSIS WHITEBOARDS

SWEET SPOT WHITEBOARD

How might we analyze innovation ideas by assessing how desirable, feasible, viable, and ethical they are?

tinyurl.com/cctboxt34

ABOUT THIS TOOL

This tool is inspired by IDEO, the global design thinking organization. Years ago, the IDEO team recognized that innovations succeed when they satisfy three criteria. They have to be DESIRABLE (Is there a need and want?), FEASIBLE (Is it technically possible?) and VIABLE (Does it make organizational sense?). The goal is to find the "sweet spot" where all three of these criteria are simultaneously optimized. In addition, for changemaking innovations, I find it helpful to add one more important criterion. Innovations must be ETHICAL (Is this morally right?). This SWEET SPOT WHITEBOARD tool should help you analyze, ideate, and prioritize innovations using these four criteria.

As you work with this tool, consider the following questions (not all-inclusive).

DESIRABLE:
- How's this innovation getting people what they really need and want?
- How's this innovation solving a clear and urgent problem in a compelling way?
- How are people drawn to and excited by this innovation?

FEASIBLE:
- Is this an innovation that you can actually build given resource, time, and financial constraints?
- Can you distribute this innovation effectively?
- Is there a supportive ecosystem in place?

VIABLE:
- Will this work economically?
- Can you access the required investment(s)/ funding?
- Are the costs manageable?
- Can you set a price and/or solicit donations that will generate sufficient revenues?

ETHICAL:
- Are you positively impacting stakeholders?
- Are you being contextually and culturally respectful?
- Are you taking power dynamics into account?
- Are you watching out for unintended negative consequences?

HOW TO USE THIS TOOL

1. Start at the top of the tool. Jot down descriptions of THE PEOPLE you hope to support, THE GOAL they're trying to achieve, THE PROBLEM that's getting in the way of them achieving THE GOAL, and THE INNOVATION IDEA to solve THE PROBLEM.
2. Next, go to the DESIRABLE header. Use the spaces under HOW? to describe how you believe THE INNOVATION IDEA might be DESIRABLE. Be specific. Then rate the STRENGTH of desirability to the right of each HOW? on a scale of "1" (very weak) to "5" (very strong).
3. Do the same for FEASIBLE, VIABLE, and ETHICAL.
4. To conclude, go to NOW WHAT? and note down a few priority next steps based on what you've learned and/or new insights you've gained from using this tool.

CHANGEMAKER COACH | TOOL TIPS

Although I have them in design toolkits, three other super helpful tools to help you evaluate innovations are T7.4 VALUE PROPOSITION BLUEPRINT (p. 244), T11.1 KEYS TO INNOVATION ADOPTION (p. 298), and T11.3 USER EXPERIENCE STRATEGY (p. 302). Note that all of the tools in the design module can also be used for diagnosis/ evaluation of existing innovations.

CHANGEMAKING INNOVATION MINI-CASES	
V25	p. 362
V27	p. 363
V82	p. 374

CHANGEMAKING TRIMTABS	
CT7	p. 38
CT12	p. 48
CT13	p. 50

THE PEOPLE	
THE GOAL	
THE PROBLEM	
THE INNOVATION IDEA	

DESIRABLE		FEASIBLE		VIABLE		ETHICAL	
HOW?	STRENGTH	HOW?	STRENGTH	HOW?	STRENGTH	HOW?	STRENGTH
	1 2 3 4 5		1 2 3 4 5		1 2 3 4 5		1 2 3 4 5
	1 2 3 4 5		1 2 3 4 5		1 2 3 4 5		1 2 3 4 5
	1 2 3 4 5		1 2 3 4 5		1 2 3 4 5		1 2 3 4 5
	1 2 3 4 5		1 2 3 4 5		1 2 3 4 5		1 2 3 4 5
	1 2 3 4 5		1 2 3 4 5		1 2 3 4 5		1 2 3 4 5

NOW WHAT?	

T3.5

TOOLS FOR TEAM-FOCUSED CONVERSATIONS | INNOVATION IDEATION + ANALYSIS WHITEBOARDS

FOUR FITS WHITEBOARD

How might we analyze the fit between our product/ service, market, distribution, and pricing strategy?

tinyurl.com/cctboxt35

ABOUT THIS TOOL

Pioneering internet entrepreneur and venture capitalist Marc Andreessen popularized the term "product-market fit" in the mid-2000s. He defined this as "being in a good market with a product that can satisfy that market." The product is the value proposition, and the market is the unmet needs of the target constituents. Building on this, there are additional characteristics of innovations that need to "fit" holistically in order to achieve success. And each one affects the others. This FOUR FITS WHITEBOARD tool should help you and your team analyze and ideate how the product/service, market, distribution strategy, and pricing strategy all "fit" together.

The four "fits" included in this tool can be briefly defined as follows:

- **PRODUCT/ SERVICE-MARKET FIT:** This is the degree to which a product/ service satisfies a market demand. Does the product/ service relieve pains? Does it satisfy wants? Is this "a unique product offering that people desperately want?"
- **MARKET-DISTRIBUTION STRATEGY FIT:** This is the degree to which the distribution strategy creates the best and most compelling opportunity to reach the market.
- **PRICING STRATEGY-DISTRIBUTION STRATEGY FIT:** Do the distribution strategy and pricing strategy align? Changing one of these will most likely affect the other.
- **PRICING STRATEGY-PRODUCT/ SERVICE FIT:** The kind of product/ service that's being offered should be a primary driver of the pricing strategy. Different things are priced differently for different reasons.

CHANGEMAKER COACH | TOOL TIPS

I recognize that this is a bit of a complicated tool. It requires a lot of knowledge, and there's no way the space provided is sufficient. The most important thing is to simply make sure that you're considering how everything needs to fit together. Use this to zoom out with your team and discuss how, when you change one component, others will be affected and might become misaligned.

HOW TO USE THIS TOOL

1. Start at the top under the PRODUCT/ SERVICE-MARKET FIT header.
2. First, note down the PRODUCT/ SERVICE DESCRIPTION.
3. Second, note down the MARKET DESCRIPTION.
4. Now zoom out and analyze how well they fit together. Go to FIT ANALYSIS between them and note down your thoughts. Then circle a FIT RATING. After this, note down your team's IDEAS FOR IMPROVEMENT. These are changes you might make to create a better fit.
5. Next, go to the MARKET-DISTRIBUTION STRATEGY FIT and go through the same process. The MARKET DESCRIPTION is obviously already filled in.
6. Continue with PRICING STRATEGY-DISTRIBUTION STRATEGY FIT, and then conclude with PRICING STRATEGY-PRODUCT/ SERVICE FIT.
7. To conclude, go to NOW WHAT? and note down a few priority next steps based on what you've learned and/or new insights you've gained from using this tool.

CHANGEMAKING INNOVATION MINI-CASES	
V53	p. 368
V80	p. 373
V81	p. 374

CHANGEMAKING TRIMTABS	
CT8	p. 40
CT13	p. 50
CT15	p. 54

PRODUCT/ SERVICE - MARKET FIT

PRICING STRATEGY - PRODUCT/ SERVICE FIT

MARKET - DISTRIBUTION STRATEGY FIT

PRODUCT/ SERVICE DESCRIPTION	FIT ANALYSIS FIT RATING 0 1 2 3 4 5 IDEAS FOR IMPROVEMENT	MARKET DESCRIPTION
FIT ANALYSIS FIT RATING 0 1 2 3 4 5 IDEAS FOR IMPROVEMENT		FIT ANALYSIS FIT RATING 0 1 2 3 4 5 IDEAS FOR IMPROVEMENT
PRICING STRATEGY DESCRIPTION	FIT ANALYSIS FIT RATING 0 1 2 3 4 5 IDEAS FOR IMPROVEMENT	DISTRIBUTION STRATEGY DESCRIPTION

PRICING STRATEGY - DISTRIBUTION STRATEGY FIT

NOW WHAT?	

T3.6

TOOLS FOR TEAM-FOCUSED CONVERSATIONS | INNOVATION IDEATION + ANALYSIS WHITEBOARDS

toolkit 03

DESIGN PRINCIPLES WHITEBOARD

How might we evaluate how our innovation concept aligns with changemaking design principles?

tinyurl.com/cctboxt36

ABOUT THIS TOOL

All high-impact changemaking innovations are designed in adherence to certain principles. These are changemaking design principles. This DESIGN PRINCIPLES WHITEBOARD tool will help you and your team evaluate how well innovations are adhering to these design principles.

The following changemaking design principles are included in this tool:

- **ADAPTIVE:** The innovation has the ability to change to suit changing conditions whilst maintaining its integrity.
- **CATALYTIC:** It creates a spark that accelerates positive change in often unpredictable ways.
- **COMPATIBLE:** It fits with the people and the context.
- **DIGNIFIED:** It's respectful and high quality.
- **EMPATHETIC:** The design is guided by the perspectives of the user. It's responsive to their needs, wants, limitations, opportunities, and aspirations.
- **EMPOWERING:** It helps people take more control of their lives and become better equipped to achieve their goals now and in the future.
- **ENDURABLE:** The solution and impact stand the test of time.
- **EQUITABLE:** It accounts for the differences in people's starting points and situations.
- **INCLUSIVE:** It involves all of the key stakeholders throughout the changemaking process.
- **INNOVATIVE:** It employs creative and practical new ways to solve the problem.
- **MEASURABLE:** The changemaking process and impact can be quantified.
- **OUTCOMES-FOCUSED:** It focuses on creating positive change over the short, medium, and long- term.
- **REGENERATIVE:** It renews, restores, revives, and/or revitalizes.
- **RESILIENT:** It's able to withstand and/or recover quickly from difficult conditions.
- **SCALABLE:** It's able to serve a growing number of people in different contexts over time.
- **SIMPLE:** It's easy to understand and use.
- **SYSTEMS-CHANGING:** It changes the way a system works, improves a suboptimal system, and/or creates a whole new system.
- **TRUSTING:** It assumes goodwill, honesty, integrity, and treats others the way we would want others to treat us.

HOW TO USE THIS TOOL

1. First, go to the top of the tool and note down THE INNOVATION CONCEPT/ IDEA.
2. Next, go to ADAPTIVE. Go to the HOW? prompt and jot down how you believe THE INNOVATION CONCEPT/ IDEA is ADAPTIVE. Then circle a RATING. In this example, "1" would mean that it's not ADAPTIVE at all, and "5" would mean that it seems to be very ADAPTIVE.
3. Continue this process for each of the DESIGN PRINCIPLES in this tool.
4. To conclude, go to NOW WHAT? and note down a few priority next steps based on what you've learned and/or new insights you've gained from using this tool.

CHANGEMAKING INNOVATION MINI-CASES	
V31	p. 364
V35	p. 364
V81	p. 374

CHANGEMAKING TRIMTABS	
CT2	p. 28
CT13	p. 50
CT16	p. 56

THE INNOVATION CONCEPT/ IDEA	

ADAPTIVE	**CATALYTIC**	**COMPATIBLE**
HOW?	HOW?	HOW?
RATING: 1 2 3 4 5	RATING: 1 2 3 4 5	RATING: 1 2 3 4 5
DIGNIFIED	**EMPATHETIC**	**EMPOWERING**
HOW?	HOW?	HOW?
RATING: 1 2 3 4 5	RATING: 1 2 3 4 5	RATING: 1 2 3 4 5
ENDURABLE	**EQUITABLE**	**INCLUSIVE**
HOW?	HOW?	HOW?
RATING: 1 2 3 4 5	RATING: 1 2 3 4 5	RATING: 1 2 3 4 5
INNOVATIVE	**MEASURABLE**	**OUTCOMES-FOCUSED**
HOW?	HOW?	HOW?
RATING: 1 2 3 4 5	RATING: 1 2 3 4 5	RATING: 1 2 3 4 5
REGENERATIVE	**RESILIENT**	**SCALABLE**
HOW?	HOW?	HOW?
RATING: 1 2 3 4 5	RATING: 1 2 3 4 5	RATING: 1 2 3 4 5
SIMPLE	**SYSTEMS-CHANGING**	**TRUSTING**
HOW?	HOW?	HOW?
RATING: 1 2 3 4 5	RATING: 1 2 3 4 5	RATING: 1 2 3 4 5

NOW WHAT?	

☐ T3.7

TOOLS FOR TEAM-FOCUSED CONVERSATIONS | INNOVATION IDEATION + ANALYSIS WHITEBOARDS

INNOVATION INSIGHTS + APPLICATIONS WHITEBOARD

How might we gain strategic insights from other innovations that can be applied to our own innovation?

tinyurl.com/cctboxt37

ABOUT THIS TOOL

This INNOVATION INSIGHTS + APPLICATIONS WHITEBOARD tool is designed to help you and your team learn from existing innovations, and consider how you might apply insights from what you've learned to your own changemaking efforts.

One of my favorite quotes is "Knowledge is knowing that a tomato is a fruit, wisdom is knowing not to put it in fruit salad." The bridge between knowledge and wisdom is experience. And if you don't have your own experiences to build this bridge, the best thing to do is to learn from the experiences of others. This brings me to another quote by Douglas Noël Adams, an author and humorist, best known for writing ***The Hitchhiker's Guide to the Galaxy***. "Human beings, who are almost unique in having the ability to learn from the experience of others, are also remarkable for their apparent disinclination to do so." We have the ability to learn from the experiences of others, and yet so often we don't. Because of this, we end up needlessly putting tomatoes in fruit salad. This tool should ideally help you avoid making this mistake.

CHANGEMAKER COACH | TOOL TIPS

- This should be one of the first tools you use when designing changemaking innovations. There are so many incredible innovations out there waiting to be discovered. Just check out the Changemaking Innovation Mini-Cases for proof of this!
- I highly recommend going to the Solutions Journalism Network's Story Tracker® - https://www.solutionsjournalism.org/storytracker to find innovations. You should also go to Ashoka (Ashoka Fellows), Echoing Green, and Skoll, to name a few.
- This tool goes hand-in-hand with T6.1 BRIGHT SPOTS MAP (p. 210) and T6.2 CURRENT SOLUTIONS LANDSCAPE MAP (p. 212)

HOW TO USE THIS TOOL

1. Go to the INNOVATIONS header at the top of the tool. Start with the box on the left, and write the name of an innovation you've been learning about over the words INNOVATION NAME. Use whatever name works for you. This tool provides you with columns for four INNOVATIONS. You might be learning from fewer or more innovations.
2. Next, go to the INFORMATION, LEARNING, INSIGHTS + APPLICATIONS header. Work your way down the prompts/questions, and note down your team's responses/ thoughts.
3. Repeat this process for each innovation you're analyzing with this tool.
4. To conclude, go to NOW WHAT? and note down a few priority next steps based on what you've learned and/or new insights you've gained from using this tool.

CHANGEMAKING INNOVATION MINI-CASES	
V41	p. 366
V55	p. 368
V81	p. 374

CHANGEMAKING TRIMTABS	
CT5	p. 34
CT12	p. 48
CT22	p. 68

	INNOVATIONS			
INFORMATION, LEARNING, INSIGHTS + APPLICATION	INNOVATION NAME	INNOVATION NAME	INNOVATION NAME	INNOVATION NAME
SOURCE				
WHO DOES THE INNOVATION HELP?				
WHAT'S THE PROBLEM IT'S SOLVING?				
HOW'S IT SOLVING THE PROBLEM?				
WHO'S INVOLVED IN SOLVING THE PROBLEM?				
LEARNING/ INSIGHT #1				
HOW MIGHT WE APPLY THIS LEARNING/ INSIGHT TO OUR WORK?				
LEARNING/ INSIGHT #2				
HOW MIGHT WE APPLY THIS LEARNING/ INSIGHT TO OUR WORK?				
LEARNING/ INSIGHT #3				
HOW MIGHT WE APPLY THIS LEARNING/ INSIGHT TO OUR WORK?				
WHAT REALLY MAKES THIS INNOVATION TICK?				

NOW WHAT?	

T3.8

TOOLS FOR TEAM-FOCUSED CONVERSATIONS | INNOVATION IDEATION + ANALYSIS WHITEBOARDS

TWO LIMITATIONS WHITEBOARD

How might we assess what's achievable keeping practical limitations in mind?

tinyurl.com/cctboxt38

ABOUT THIS TOOL

When we get inspired by innovative new ideas, we have a tendency to set unrealistic goals. Our eyes get bigger than our stomachs. We fail to account for real-world limitations. This TWO LIMITATIONS WHITEBOARD tool should help you and your team avoid this.

As you and your team use this tool, it's important to keep in mind that limitations aren't bad. They aren't constraints. Limitation is what drives innovation. It forces creativity. In the words of legendary filmmaker Orson Wells, "The enemy of art is the absence of limitation."

Following is a list of limitations that you and your team might consider for this tool.

- **TIME:** This could be anywhere from hours to years.
- **RESOURCES:** This might include resources such as:
  - Money
  - Human resources
  - Equipment/ technology
  - Facilities
  - Land
  - Water
  - Energy
  - Partners/collaborators
- **KNOWLEDGE:** Depending on the context, this might refer to expertise in a technical subject, industry knowledge, customer discovery, etc.
- **SCALING**: These might be geographical, systemic, market size limitations, etc.

CHANGEMAKER COACH | TOOL TIPS

- This should help you put CT7 REDUCE, REDIRECT, REIMAGINE (p. 38) into action. Although not listed below, this is also great for putting CT8 CATALYZE CIRCULARITY (p. 40) into action.
- This tool should help you analyze the "effort" part of T3.2 IMPACT + EFFORT WHITEBOARD (p. 150).
- You might want to also look at T4.5 PROBLEMS VS DESIGN CONSTRAINTS ANALYSIS (p. 182).
- This could help you think about how you launch your changemaking innovation when you're using T8.1 MARKET SIZE ANALYSIS + STRATEGY (p. 256)

HOW TO USE THIS TOOL

1. First, go to the top of the tool and note down THE INNOVATION CONCEPT/ IDEA.
2. Next, note down THE QUESTION you're analyzing. For example, a question might be, "How many reading glasses can we distribute in rural Guatemala?"
3. Then note down the LIMITATION CATEGORY #1 and LIMITATION CATEGORY #2. For example, let's assume these are "time" and "funding," respectively.
4. Go to the LIMITATION CATEGORY #1 header. In the three boxes under this, note down three limitations. Start with the most limiting at the top. For example, you might note "Within 3 months" in the top box, "Within 6 months" in the middle, and "Within one year" at the bottom.
5. Once you've done this, go to the LIMITATION CATEGORY #2 header and do the same thing, only horizontally this time. For example, you might note "$1,000" in the left box, "$5,000" in the middle one, and "$10,000" in the box on the right.
6. Now it's time for you to project your achievable goals. Start with the most limiting for each limitation category. Using THE QUESTION and limitation examples, for "Within 3 months" and with "$1,000," your ACHIEVABLE GOAL might be "500 pairs of glasses." This is what you'd note down in the box. Try to note down an ACHIEVABLE GOAL in all nine boxes in the tool.
7. To conclude, go to NOW WHAT? and note down a few priority next steps based on what you've learned and/or new insights you've gained from using this tool

CHANGEMAKING INNOVATION MINI-CASES	
V1	p. 358
V15	p. 360
V19	p. 361

CHANGEMAKING TRIMTABS	
CT6	p. 36
CT7	p. 38
CT15	p. 54

THE INNNOVATION CONCEPT/ IDEA	
THE QUESTION	
LIMITATION CATEGORY #1	
LIMITATION CATEGORY #2	

	LIMITATION CATEGORY #2		
LIMITATION CATEGORY #1	*(most limiting)*		*(least limiting)*
(most limiting)	ACHIEVABLE GOAL	ACHIEVABLE GOAL	ACHIEVABLE GOAL
	ACHIEVABLE GOAL	ACHIEVABLE GOAL	ACHIEVABLE GOAL
(least limitiing)	ACHIEVABLE GOAL	ACHIEVABLE GOAL	ACHIEVABLE GOAL

NOW WHAT?	

T3.9

TOOLS FOR TEAM-FOCUSED CONVERSATIONS | INNOVATION IDEATION + ANALYSIS WHITEBOARDS

toolkit 03

CONSEQUENCES WHITEBOARD

How might we analyze the intended and unintended consequences of innovations?

tinyurl.com/cctboxt39

ABOUT THIS TOOL

Every action has consequences. Sometimes they're intentional, other times they're not. Sometimes they're positive. A virtuous circle gets started where one good thing causes another good thing to happen, and so on and so on. Other times they're negative and, as the proverb goes, "The road to hell is paved with good intentions."

As a changemaker, it's your job to both avoid negative consequences and ideally, ignite opportunities for positive ones. At the very least, your baseline should always be "first, do no harm" ("primum non nocere"). This CONSEQUENCES WHITEBOARD tool should help you and your team consider the potential negative and positive consequences of your changemaking innovation(s).

This tool includes space to note down the OVERALL GOAL of the innovation and the INNOVATION DESCRIPTION. The heart of the tool is where you note down the following:

- **INTENDED CONSEQUENCES: 1ST ORDER IMPACT(S):** These are the positive, direct impacts that the innovation is/was designed to achieve.
- **POTENTIAL UNINTENDED CONSEQUENCES:** These could be positive or negative. For an existing innovation, these might be observations. For a new one, they're projections.
    - **2ND ORDER IMPACT(S):** Consequences of the 1ST ORDER IMPACT(S)
    - **3RD ORDER IMPACT(S):** Consequences of the 2ND ORDER IMPACT(S)

This tool also provides space for your team's ANALYSIS and IDEAS FOR MODIFiCATIONS.

HOW TO USE THIS TOOL

1. Start at the top of the tool and note down the OVERALL GOAL of the changemaking innovation.
2. Next, go to INNOVATION DESCRIPTION. Briefly describe the changemaking innovation and how it works.
3. Then go to the top row to the right of the INNOVATION DESCRIPTION. Note down the INTENDED CONSEQUENCES - 1ST ORDER IMPACT(S). Then consider the POTENTIAL UNINTENDED CONSEQUENCES. Note down what you believe might be some 2ND ORDER IMPACT(S) and 3RD ORDER IMPACT(S). Go to ANALYSIS and jot down any thoughts/ insights you might have based on the consequences.
4. Now go to IDEAS FOR MODIFICATIONS. Based on your analysis, how might you modify either the OVERALL GOAL and/or the INNOVATION DESCRIPTION?
5. Repeat steps 3 and 4 for additional consequences in the two rows below.
6. To conclude, go to NOW WHAT? and note down a few priority next steps based on what you've learned and/or new insights you've gained from using this tool.

CHANGEMAKER COACH | TOOL TIPS

- The title of this book reflects the importance of trying to create positive 2nd and 3rd order impacts.
- Use this tool to think of every "if this, then that" scenario you can think of. You might want to look at the well-being categories in T5.4 WELL-BEING MAP (p. 198) to help you think of all of the positive and/or negative ways that people might be impacted.
- This should help you put CT11 CREATE OPPORTUNITIES FOR CATALYTIC CONNECTIONS (p. 46) and CT12 SOLVE ONE PROBLEM TO ALSO SOLVE ANOTHER p. 48) into action.

CHANGEMAKING INNOVATION MINI-CASES	
V9	p. 359
V49	p. 367
V83	p. 374

CHANGEMAKING TRIMTABS	
CT11	p. 46
CT12	p. 48
CT17	p. 58

OVERALL GOAL	

INNOVATION DESCRIPTION	INTENDED CONSEQUENCES	POTENTIAL UNINTENDED CONSEQUENCES		ANALYSIS	IDEAS FOR MODIFICATIONS
	1ST ORDER IMPACT(S)	2ND ORDER IMPACT(S)	3RD ORDER IMPACT(S)		

NOW WHAT?	

TOOLS FOR TEAM-FOCUSED CONVERSATIONS | INNOVATION IDEATION + ANALYSIS WHITEBOARDS

TOOLKIT TOOLS REFLECTIONS

SCALE:
STRONGLY AGREE = 5, AGREE = 4, NOT SURE = 3, DISAGREE = 2, STRONGLY DISAGREE = 1

tinyurl.com/cctboxtoolsrflect

	CHANGEMAKING TOOLS								
REFLECTION STATEMENTS	T3.1	T3.2	T3.3	T3.4	T3.5	T3.6	T3.7	T3.8	T3.9
This tool is easy to understand.									
This tool is easy to use.									
This tool taught me/ us important new knowledge.									
This tool empowered new changemaking conversations.									
This tool helped to spark new ideas/ insights.									
This tool should be included in my/ our toolbox for the future.									
I/ we should share this tool with other changemakers.									

NOTES:

MODULE 02 | TOOLS FOR DISCOVERY + DIAGNOSIS CONVERSATIONS

NOTES:

GVK notes -

- Go to HOW TO CONDUCT PRIMARY + SECONDARY RESEARCH, HOW TO DESIGN CONSTRUCTIVE QUESTIONS, and HOW TO CRAFT A CONCISE PROBLEM STATEMENT (pg. 379)
- You don't just ask questions to get answers. Asking questions helps the person you're asking think about what the answer might be. How would they know if no one ever asked them? Asking good questions is a gift for others.
- Think of yourself as a waiter and the community (your team) as a table of clients. Always try to take something of value to the table, and always try to take away new knowledge/ insights/understanding. You should never be empty-handed.
- People don't prioritize their problems based on Maslow's Hierarchy of Needs. That's not how problem prioritization works.
- Complexity favors existing power holders. Complex healthcare, legal, political, and economic systems, etc. favor incumbent power holders. Because of this, complexity creates/ exacerbates inequities. Look for simplicity.

NOTES:

GVK notes -

- Know the difference between these terms. We confuse them all the time. This is one reason why problem-solving can feel paralyzing.
    - Issue - eg. Poverty
    - Effect/ Symptom - eg. Can't afford to pay for children's education
    - Problem - eg. Lack of income generation opportunities.
- ON SYSTEMS CHANGE: I think of changing MINDSETS as changing/ creating DEMAND. Offering new RESOURCES and/ or PROGRAMS is new SUPPLY. We fail when we create DEMAND but don't offer SUPPLY. Or when we create new SUPPLY without there being DEMAND. Make sure there's DEMAND and SUPPLY, or at least that you're working to empower equilibrium between the two.

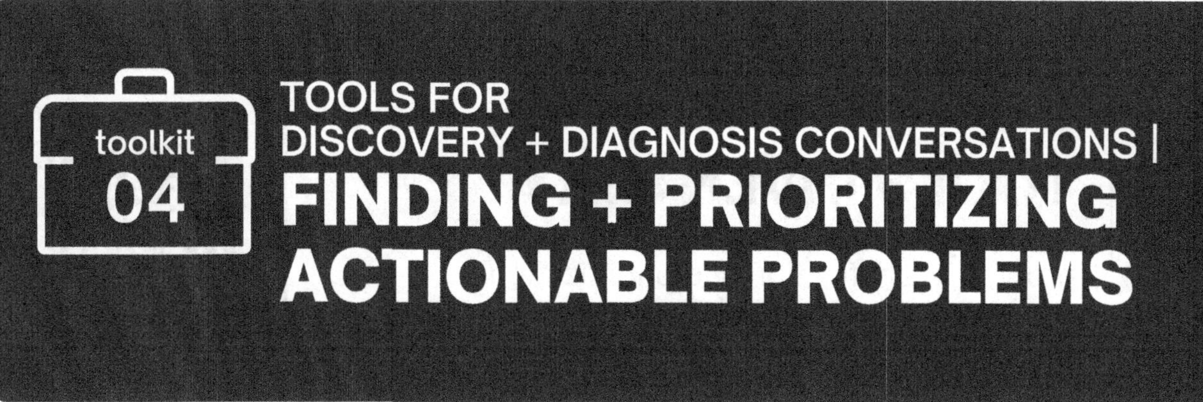

TOOLS FOR DISCOVERY + DIAGNOSIS CONVERSATIONS | FINDING + PRIORITIZING ACTIONABLE PROBLEMS

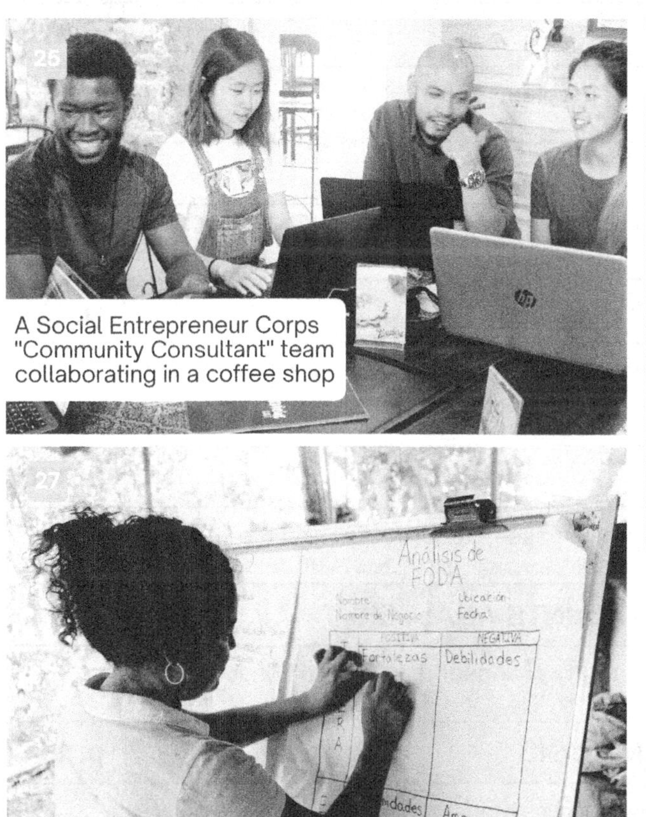

A Social Entrepreneur Corps "Community Consultant" team collaborating in a coffee shop

Entrepreneurs collaborating in Nicaragua

Factory well-being leadership teams collaborating to create women's health solutions in Port Said, Egypt

An entrepreneur and Social Entrepreneur Corps "Community Consultants" collaborating in Guatemala

NOTES:

GVK note -

- *When I try to solve a problem coming from my perspective, it can lead me to SYMPATHY. This often results in undignified design. The goal is to solve the problem from the community members' perspective. This is EMPATHY.*

toolkit 04

TOOLS FOR DISCOVERY + DIAGNOSIS CONVERSATIONS | FINDING + PRIORITIZING ACTIONABLE PROBLEMS

TOOLS INVENTORY

How might we equip ourselves with practical problem identification and prioritization methodologies and tools?

tinyurl.com/cctboxtools01

	T4.1 ROOT CAUSE ANALYSIS	p. 174

How might we work to understand the root cause(s) of problems?

	T4.2 PROBLEM TREE ANALYSIS	p. 176

How might we work to understand the both the root causes and negative effects of problems?

	T4.3 ICEBERG ANALYSIS	p. 178

How might we approach problem identification in a way that empowers us to potentially transform a system rather than simply react to an event?

	T4.4 SWOT ANALYSIS	p. 180

How might we gain insights by analyzing strengths, weaknesses, opportunities and threats?

	T4.5 PROBLEMS VS DESIGN CONSTRAINTS ANALYSIS	p. 182

How might we make sure we're prioritizing what's currently changeable instead of what isn't?

	T4.6 PROBLEM PRIORITIZATION ANALYSIS	p. 184

How might we prioritize problems based on frequency and severity?

NOTES:

TOOLS FOR DISCOVERY + DIAGNOSIS CONVERSATIONS | FINDING + PRIORITIZING ACTIONABLE PROBLEMS

TOOLKIT SCORECARD + PRIORITIZATION HELP

Score yourselves to help you decide which tool(s) you might want to prioritize for your changemaking conversations.

tinyurl.com/cctboxtoolsprior

SELF-CHECK STATEMENTS	HOW ARE WE DOING?	TOOL SUGGESTIONS
We make a habit of asking "WHY?" five times when we find problems.	0 1 2 3 4 5	T4.1
We're having in-depth conversations about both the root causes and effects of problems.	0 1 2 3 4 5	T4.2
We're working to get as in-depth as possible to really understand the mindsets causing problems.	0 1 2 3 4 5	T4.3
We're including all of the most important internal and external factors in our analysis.	0 1 2 3 4 5	T4.4
We're having conversations to make sure that we have an understanding, and are in agreement about, the things that we can change in the short term, and the things that we can't. We're not getting hung up on or paralyzed by the things we can't change.	0 1 2 3 4 5	T4.5
We're prioritizing problems through an analysis of both frequency and severity.	0 1 2 3 4 5	T4.6

NOTES:

50+ SPECIFIC APPLICATIONS

tinyurl.com/cctbpxapps

TOOLS FOR DISCOVERY + DIAGNOSIS CONVERSATIONS | FINDING + PRIORITIZING ACTIONABLE PROBLEMS

COLLABORATIVE CHANGEMAKING VOICES

Get into the mindset for this toolkit + include your voice in the conversation.

"If you don't understand, ask questions. If you're uncomfortable about asking questions, say you are uncomfortable about asking questions and then ask anyway."

CHIMAMANDA NGOZI ADICHIE
NIGERIAN AUTHOR | MACARTHUR FELLOW

"If I had an hour to solve a problem I'd spend 55 minutes thinking about the problem and 5 minutes thinking about solutions."

ALBERT EINSTEIN
THEORETICAL PHYSICIST

"The problem is not that there are problems. The problem is expecting otherwise and thinking that having problems is a problem."

THEODORE RUBIN
PSYCHIATRIST | AUTHOR

"Nothing in life is to be feared, it is only to be understood. Now is the time to understand more, so that we may fear less."

MARIE CURIE
PHYSICIST | CHEMIST
NOBEL PRIZE LAUREATE

"Look for what you notice but no one else sees."

RICK RUBIN
RECORD PRODUCER

"Amazing the things you find when you bother to search for them."

SACAGAWEA
LEWIS + CLARK EXPEDITION GUIDE

"A problem well stated is a problem half-solved."

CHARLES KETTERING
AMERICAN BUSINESSMAN

"It is better to solve one problem five different ways, than to solve five problems one way."

GEORGE POLYA
MATHEMATICIAN

"If you don't like something, change it. If you can't change it, change your attitude."

MAYA ANGELOU
AUTHOR | CIVIL RIGHTS ACTIVIST

T4.1

TOOLS FOR DISCOVERY + DIAGNOSIS CONVERSATIONS | FINDING + PRIORITIZING ACTIONABLE PROBLEMS

ROOT CAUSE ANALYSIS

How might we work to understand the root cause(s) of problems?

tinyurl.com/cctboxt41

ABOUT THIS TOOL

Whenever possible, it's best to solve problems at their root causes. One way to figure out root causes is through a technique called a Root Cause Analysis (RCA), also known as the "5 WHYs" questioning technique. This simple ROOT CAUSE ANALYSIS tool will help you and your team learn and apply this technique to your changemaking efforts.

As you work with this technique, keep in mind that asking WHY? five times is simply guidance. You may find a compelling and actionable root cause after asking WHY? only three times. Or you may need to ask WHY? seven times. In addition, most problems actually have many root causes. To uncover multiple root causes, use this tool multiple times with the same person and/or with multiple people.

Finally, although you may not be able to address the root cause itself, that doesn't mean you've failed. Of course, in an ideal world, we would focus all of our problem-solving energy on the deepest root causes. But often this isn't practically possible. Given this, your goal in using this questioning technique should be to find an actionable root cause and just get going. Focus on progress, not perfect. Don't get stuck in the paralysis of analysis. Get started. Action will lead to deeper understanding and more opportunities to effectuate positive change.

HOW TO USE THIS TOOL

1. Start by noting down THE PROBLEM/CHALLENGE at the top of the tool. Don't overthink it. Just write something down.
2. Now start the five WHYs process. Ask WHY? this problem exists. Note this down.
3. Next, use that response as a basis, and ask WHY? again. Note this down below the first WHY? Then repeat this three more times. Keep going if you feel like you need to.
4. To conclude, go to NOW WHAT? and note down a few priority next steps based on what you've learned and/or new insights you've gained from using this tool.

CHANGEMAKER COACH | TOOL TIPS

- Asking five WHYs should ideally become a habit for everyone on your team. It's an essential discovery/diagnosis technique.
- Use this technique with all of the other tools.
- You can also use this to question your own thoughts, ideas, and assumptions. Ask yourself WHY five times.

CHANGEMAKING INNOVATION MINI-CASES	
V35	p. 364
V71	p. 372
V85	p. 374

CHANGEMAKING TRIMTABS	
CT1	p. 26
CT3	p. 30
CT12	p. 48

THE PROBLEM/ CHALLENGE	
WHY?	
WHY?	
WHY?	
WHY?	
WHY?	

NOW WHAT?	

T4.2

TOOLS FOR DISCOVERY + DIAGNOSIS CONVERSATIONS | FINDING + PRIORITIZING ACTIONABLE PROBLEMS

PROBLEM TREE ANALYSIS

How might we work to understand both the root causes and negative effects of problems?

tinyurl.com/cctboxt42

ABOUT THIS TOOL

When you see a problem, one of the first things you should do is identify and analyze the root causes and negative effects of the problem. This helps you to decide where you might step in to address the problem. This PROBLEM TREE ANALYSIS tool will help you and your team do this in a simple and straightforward way.

There are three basic components to this tool. They are as follows:

- **THE PROBLEM:** This is the metaphorical trunk of the tree. Start here with the problem however it is that you're currently defining it.
- **THE CAUSES:** These are at the root level. Why does this problem exist? What's causing it? This is where you'll brainstorm and note down all of the causes you can think of. Use the 5 WHYs technique from the ROOT CAUSE ANALYSIS tool to do this.
- **THE EFFECTS/ SYMPTOMS:** These are at the branch level. When the problem occurs/ exists, what happens? What are the negative consequences? Capture everything you can think of here. Try to get to the consequences of consequences. Sometimes the second or third-order consequences are more important to understand than the direct consequences.

HOW TO USE THIS TOOL

1. Start by noting down THE PROBLEM in the middle of the tool. Don't overthink it. Just write something down.
2. Next, go to THE EFFECTS/ SYMPTOMS and note down as many as you can.
3. Then go to THE CAUSES and do the same.
4. To conclude, go to NOW WHAT? and note down a few priority next steps based on what you've learned and/or new insights you've gained from using this tool.

CHANGEMAKER COACH | TOOL TIPS

- This is an essential tool. I always use this when I'm facilitating, consulting, and/or teaching changemaking innovation. Apart from the explicit goal, this helps teams get into the spirit of brainstorming and "yes...and-ing."
- I prefer to have people draw this on a whiteboard whenever possible. Have people work in small teams. Make sure everyone has a marker.
- The "effects" part of this tool might help you with T3.9 CONSEQUENCES WHITEBOARD (p. 164)
- This is very helpful to use hand-in-hand with T10.1 PROBLEM SOLVING POSITIONING (p. 284). It can help you think about when and where you might want to/are able to intervene.

CHANGEMAKING INNOVATION MINI-CASES	
V49	p. 367
V72	p. 372
V86	p. 375

CHANGEMAKING TRIMTABS	
CT12	p. 48
CT16	p. 56
CT19	p. 62

THE EFFECTS/ SYMPTOMS						

THE PROBLEM		

THE CAUSES						

NOW WHAT?	

T4.3

TOOLS FOR DISCOVERY + DIAGNOSIS CONVERSATIONS | FINDING + PRIORITIZING ACTIONABLE PROBLEMS

tinyurl.com/cctboxt43

ICEBERG ANALYSIS

How might we approach problem identification in a way that empowers us to potentially transform a system rather than simply react to an event?

ABOUT THIS TOOL

Only 10 percent of the total mass of an iceberg is above the water and visible. The 90 percent that's underwater is what ocean currents act on, and what influences the iceberg's behavior. This is the same with problems. What's easily visible only tells you a small part of the story. If you want to understand what's really going on and influence behavior in a positive and proactive way, you need to do a deeper dive analysis. This ICEBERG ANALYSIS tool should help you and your team do this.

This tool is broken down into four levels to help you go deeper and deeper in your analysis. They are as follows:

- **THE PROBLEM/ EVENT:** This is what's happening or has just happened. This is at the visible level. We tend to REACT if we are only seeing what's going on at this level.
- **THE PATTERNS/ TRENDS:** Where do we see this problem/ event in other places as well? What's been going on over time? We can ANTICIPATE at this level.
- **THE UNDERLYING STRUCTURES:** What's influencing the patterns? What are the relationships among the parts? We're able to DESIGN once we can answer these questions.
- **THE MENTAL MODELS/ MINDSETS:** What values, beliefs, and assumptions do people hold about the system? What are the perceptions and perspectives? It's only when we have this level of understanding that we're able to TRANSFORM systems.

HOW TO USE THIS TOOL

1. First, what's THE PROBLEM/ EVENT that's causing pain, dissatisfaction, frustration, and/or failure in some way? Note this down as descriptively as possible at the top of the tool.
2. Next, note down any and all of THE PATTERNS/ TRENDS.
3. Third, note down your thoughts about THE UNDERLYING STRUCTURES. Why are THE PATTERNS/ TRENDS happening?
4. Now go to THE MENTAL MODELS/ MINDSETS. Is there some underlying thought pattern or understanding that's driving the situation? Is there a mindset that was or is behind the creation of THE UNDERLYING STRUCTURES? Note down your analysis/ thoughts.
5. To conclude, go to NOW WHAT? and note down a few priority next steps based on what you've learned and/or new insights you've gained from using this tool.

CHANGEMAKER COACH | TOOL TIPS

- It's hard to overstate how important it is to understand mindsets. Work as hard as you can to figure out the values, beliefs, and assumptions that drive behavior.
- T6.7 SYSTEM COMPONENTS MAP (p. 222) is another great tool to help you analyze mindsets.

CHANGEMAKING INNOVATION MINI-CASES	
V16	p. 361
V63	p. 370
V71	p. 372

CHANGEMAKING TRIMTABS	
CT1	p. 26
CT3	p. 30
CT21	p. 66

REACT	**THE PROBLEM/ EVENT**	
ANTICIPATE	**THE PATTERNS/ TRENDS**	
DESIGN	**THE UNDERLYING STRUCTURES**	
TRANSFORM	**THE MENTAL MODELS/ MINDSETS**	

NOW WHAT?	

T4.4

TOOLS FOR DISCOVERY + DIAGNOSIS CONVERSATIONS | FINDING + PRIORITIZING ACTIONABLE PROBLEMS

SWOT ANALYSIS

How might we gain insights by analyzing strengths, weaknesses, opportunities and threats?

tinyurl.com/cctboxt44

ABOUT THIS TOOL

SWOT is an acronym for STRENGTHS, WEAKNESSES, OPPORTUNITIES, and THREATS. A SWOT analysis is a broadly used technique for analyzing systems, organizations, projects, and products/services. This SWOT ANALYSIS tool should help you and your team apply this form of analysis to your changemaking efforts.

This SWOT ANALYSIS tool helps you to analyze the following:

INTERNAL FACTORS
- **STRENGTHS:** These are internal attributes that contribute to success.
- **WEAKNESSES:** These are internal characteristics that contribute to or may cause failure.

EXTERNAL FACTORS
- **OPPORTUNITIES:** These are external factors that can potentially be capitalized on to create greater success.
- **THREATS:** These are external factors that currently or could potentially jeopardize success.

CHANGEMAKER COACH | TOOL TIPS

This is a Swiss Army Knife tool that you can use to analyze just about anything. Analyze organizations, businesses, teams, communities, products, ideas...you name it.

HOW TO USE THIS TOOL

1. Start with INTERNAL FACTORS. Talk about and list STRENGTHS. What's working and why is it working? What are some of the key attributes and characteristics? Note these down. Make sure you zoom in and zoom out.
2. Next, go to WEAKNESSES. Note down what isn't working and what could be improved.
3. Now move to EXTERNAL FACTORS. Note down OPPORTUNITIES. For example, what might be new solutions, ideas, resources, approaches, collaborations, etc. that could potentially contribute to success?
4. After that, note down THREATS. These are externalities that are causing or might cause failure.
5. To conclude, go to NOW WHAT? and note down a few priority next steps based on what you've learned and/or new insights you've gained from using this tool.

CHANGEMAKING INNOVATION MINI-CASES	
V38	p. 365
V39	p. 365
V65	p. 370

CHANGEMAKING TRIMTABS	
CT5	p. 34
CT8	p. 40
CT20	p. 64

	STRENGTHS	WEAKNESSES
INTERNAL FACTORS		
	OPPORTUNITIES	**THREATS**
EXTERNAL FACTORS		

NOW WHAT?	

T4.5

TOOLS FOR DISCOVERY + DIAGNOSIS CONVERSATIONS | FINDING + PRIORITIZING ACTIONABLE PROBLEMS

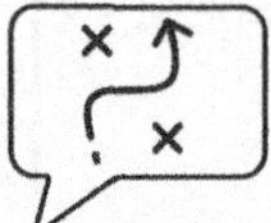

PROBLEMS VS DESIGN CONSTRAINTS ANALYSIS

How might we make sure we're prioritizing what's currently changeable instead of what isn't?

tinyurl.com/cctboxt45

ABOUT THIS TOOL

According to Harvard Business School professor and author Michael Porter, "The essence of strategy is choosing what not to do." This is easier said than done. One starting point for choosing what not to do is by analyzing and deciding what's currently changeable and what isn't. This ACTIONABLE PROBLEMS VS DESIGN CONSTRAINTS ANALYSIS tool should help you and your team avoid getting bogged down on things that can't be changed so that you can focus on what can.

This tool uses the following two key terms to help you and your team prioritize where to focus your changemaking efforts:

- **ACTIONABLE PROBLEMS:** These are things that can be changed within a reasonable amount of time given current/ projected systemic, time, and resource constraints.
- **DESIGN CONSTRAINTS:** These are things that can't be changed over the short/ medium term due to systemic, time, and/or resource constraints.

To note, don't look at DESIGN CONSTRAINTS as restraints. They're actually very helpful because they help you to better define boundaries. And clear boundaries spark the creativity that drives innovative thinking.

CHANGEMAKER COACH | TOOL TIPS

- I designed this tool out of a bit of frustration. I got tired of people talking in circles about things that weren't changeable under current circumstances.
- You might find that this works well with T5.5 JOURNEY MAP (p. 200) and T6.3 EQUITABLE ACCESS MAP (p. 214).

HOW TO USE THIS TOOL

1. Start at the top of the tool. What are you and/or the people you aspire to support trying to achieve? Note down THE GOAL.
2. Next, go to the CHALLENGES/ OBSTACLES header. From top to bottom, note down what's making achieving THE GOAL difficult.
3. Now analyze the first of the CHALLENGES/ OBSTACLES that you noted down. Go to the LEVEL OF EFFORT + RESOURCES REQUIRED TO SOLVE THE CHALLENGE/ OBSTACLE. Circle a number under RATING. "1" signifies very little effort, and "5" signifies a tremendous amount of effort. Under ANALYSIS note down why you chose this RATING.
4. Then go to CLASSIFICATION. Based on your RATING and ANALYSIS, would you classify this as an ACTIONABLE PROBLEM or DESIGN CONSTRAINT? Tick the appropriate box.
5. Repeat steps 3 and 4 for each of the CHALLENGES/ OBSTACLES that you noted down.
6. To conclude, go to NOW WHAT? and note down a few priority next steps based on what you've learned and/or new insights you've gained from using this tool.

CHANGEMAKING INNOVATION MINI-CASES	
V4	p. 358
V14	p. 360
V28	p. 363

CHANGEMAKING TRIMTABS	
CT6	p. 36
CT13	p. 50
CT19	p. 62

THE GOAL				

CHALLENGES/ OBSTACLES	**LEVEL OF EFFORT + RESOURCES REQUIRED TO SOLVE THE CHALLENGE/ OBSTACLE**		**CLASSIFICATION**	
	RATING	**ANALYSIS**	**ACTIONABLE PROBLEM**	**DESIGN CONSTRAINT**
	1 2 3 4 5		☐	☐
	1 2 3 4 5		☐	☐
	1 2 3 4 5		☐	☐
	1 2 3 4 5		☐	☐
	1 2 3 4 5		☐	☐
	1 2 3 4 5		☐	☐
	1 2 3 4 5		☐	☐

NOW WHAT?	

T4.6

TOOLS FOR DISCOVERY + DIAGNOSIS CONVERSATIONS | FINDING + PRIORITIZING ACTIONABLE PROBLEMS

PROBLEM PRIORITIZATION ANALYSIS

How might we prioritize problems based on frequency and severity?

tinyurl.com/cctboxt46

ABOUT THIS TOOL

When we're confronted with a lot of problems at once and are trying to figure out where to prioritize our problem-solving efforts, we tend to respond in one of two unhelpful ways. We feel overwhelmed and become paralyzed. Or we fall back on decision-making biases and focus on the wrong problem(s). Cognitive biases like confirmation bias, recency bias, and group thinking, lead us astray. This PROBLEM PRIORITIZATION ANALYSIS tool should help you and your team avoid these tendencies.

This tool helps you to analyze and prioritize problems based on the following two factors:

- **FREQUENCY:** How often do the problems happen?
- **SEVERITY:** How bad is the negative impact when the problems happen?

In particular, this tool helps you to avoid over-prioritizing either "Shark attacks" (low frequency/high negative impact) or nuisances (high frequency/low negative impact). And it helps you get to the business of having changemaking conversations about potential innovative solutions for the highest priority problems.

CHANGEMAKER COACH | TOOL TIPS

- This is great for helping you prioritize problems once you've diagnosed them with other tools. It keeps you focused on a "first things first" approach.
- This is a great one for teams/ community members to work on together using whiteboards.
- Take a look at T13.1 RESILIENCE ANALYSIS + STRATEGY (p. 332). You'll find some similarities.

HOW TO USE THIS TOOL

1. Start at the top of the tool. What are you and/or the people you aspire to support trying to achieve? Note down THE GOAL.
2. Next, under the PROBLEMS header, note down all of the current PROBLEMS that are getting in the way of achieving THE GOAL. There's space for five, but you may find that there are fewer or more.
3. Now, go to the PRIORITIZATION FORMULA header. Under the FREQUENCY header, for each of the PROBLEMS circle how often this is a problem. "1" signifies that this is very rarely a problem and "5" means that it's always a problem.
4. Next, do the same under the SEVERITY header. "1" means that the negative impact is very low when the problem happens, and "5" indicates a catastrophic impact.
5. After that, go to the PRIORITIZATION NUMBER header. For each of the PROBLEMS, multiply the FREQUENCY you've circled by the SEVERITY. Note down the product. The PROBLEMS with the higher numbers here are likely the higher priority problems and the best place to start.
6. Now go to the PROBLEMS with the highest numbers under PRIORITIZATION NUMBER. Note down IDEAS FOR SOLUTIONS for each of these.
7. To conclude, go to NOW WHAT? and note down a few priority next steps based on what you've learned and/or new insights you've gained from using this tool.

CHANGEMAKING INNOVATION MINI-CASES	
V13	p. 360
V26	p. 363
V38	p. 365

CHANGEMAKING TRIMTABS	
CT3	p. 30
CT12	p. 48
CT19	p. 62

THE GOAL	

	PRIORITIZATION FORMULA					
PROBLEMS	FREQUENCY	X	SEVERITY	=	PRIORITIZATION NUMBER	IDEAS FOR SOLUTIONS
	1 2 3 4 5	X	1 2 3 4 5	=		
	1 2 3 4 5	X	1 2 3 4 5	=		
	1 2 3 4 5	X	1 2 3 4 5	=		
	1 2 3 4 5	X	1 2 3 4 5	=		
	1 2 3 4 5	X	1 2 3 4 5	=		

NOW WHAT?	

TOOLS FOR DISCOVERY + DIAGNOSIS CONVERSATIONS | FINDING + PRIORITIZING ACTIONABLE PROBLEMS

TOOLKIT TOOLS REFLECTIONS

SCALE:
STRONGLY AGREE = 5, AGREE = 4, NOT SURE = 3, DISAGREE = 2, STRONGLY DISAGREE = 1

tinyurl.com/cctboxtoolsrflect

	CHANGEMAKING TOOLS					
REFLECTION STATEMENTS	**T4.1**	**T4.2**	**T4.3**	**T4.4**	**T4.5**	**T4.6**
This tool is easy to understand.						
This tool is easy to use.						
This tool taught me/ us important new knowledge.						
This tool empowered new changemaking conversations.						
This tool helped to spark new ideas/ insights.						
This tool should be included in my/ our toolbox for the future.						
I/ we should share this tool with other changemakers.						

NOTES:

TOOLS FOR DISCOVERY + DIAGNOSIS CONVERSATIONS | HUMAN-CENTERED MAPPING

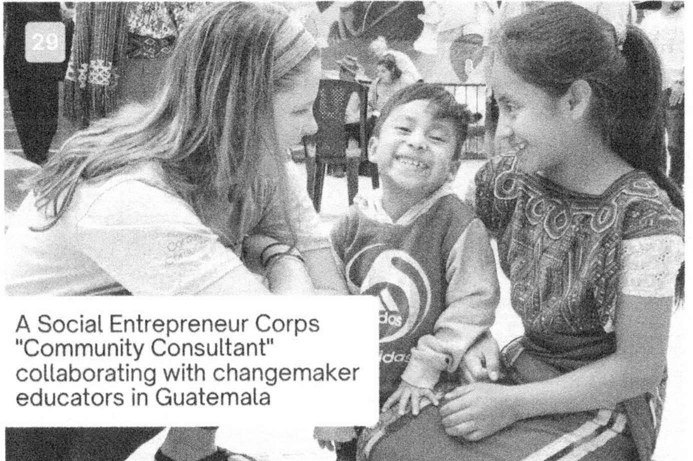

A Social Entrepreneur Corps "Community Consultant" collaborating with changemaker educators in Guatemala

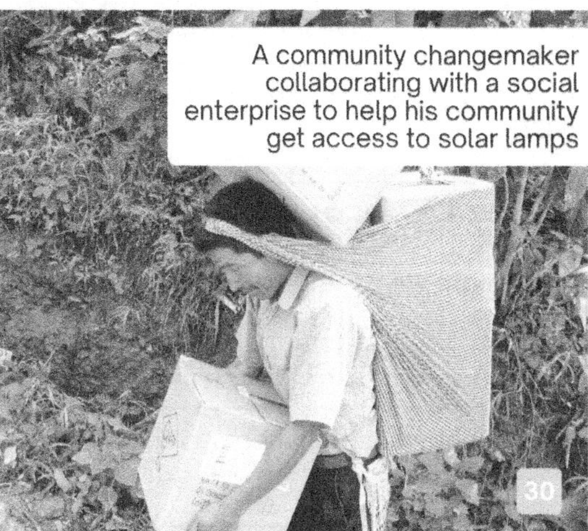

A community changemaker collaborating with a social enterprise to help his community get access to solar lamps

A Social Entrepreneur Corps "Community Consultant" team collaborating with community members in South Africa

Ashleigh G. collaborating with a community leader in Guatemala

NOTES:

GVK note -

- Avoid psychic numbing: This is psychological phenomenon that makes us feel indifferent to the suffering of large numbers of people. You need to connect with people and strengthen your empathy muscle continually. It atrophies quickly.

toolkit 05

TOOLS FOR DISCOVERY + DIAGNOSIS CONVERSATIONS | HUMAN-CENTERED MAPPING

TOOLS INVENTORY

How might we zoom in to understand the lives and perspectives of the people we aspire to support?

tinyurl.com/cctboxtools01

☐ T5.1 EMPATHY MAP — p. 192

How might we gain a deeper understanding of the lives and perspectives of the people we aspire to support?

☐ T5.2 PERSONA MAP — p. 194

How might we capture representative characteristics of the people we're hoping to support?

☐ T5.3 EMPOWERMENT MAP — p. 196

How might we better understand to what extent someone is relatively empowered and/or disempowered?

☐ T5.4 WELL-BEING MAP — p. 198

How might we focus our analysis holistically on well-being?

☐ T5.5 JOURNEY MAP — p. 200

How might we understand what obstacles are getting in the way as someone works towards achieving their goal?

☐ T5.6 DECISION MAKING BIASES MAP — p. 202

How might we understand what cognitive biases are influencing behavior?

NOTES:

GVK note -

- *Go to HOW TO HAVE EFFECTIVE CONVERSATIONS and HOW TO BE A KEEN OBSERVER (pg. 379)*

TOOLS FOR DISCOVERY + DIAGNOSIS CONVERSATIONS | HUMAN-CENTERED MAPPING

TOOLKIT SCORECARD + PRIORITIZATION HELP

Score yourselves to help you decide which tool(s) you might want to prioritize for your changemaking conversations.

tinyurl.com/cctboxtoolsprior

SELF-CHECK STATEMENTS	HOW ARE WE DOING?	TOOL SUGGESTIONS
We're having conversations with the people we hope to support so that we can better understand their lives from their perspectives.	0 1 2 3 4 5	T5.1
We're having conversations about the representative characteristics of the people we hope to support.	0 1 2 3 4 5	T5.2
We're talking about where and how people are relatively empowered and disempowered as they work to achieve their goals.	0 1 2 3 4 5	T5.3
We're having conversations focused on understanding all of the ways that someone may or may not be feeling a sense of well-being.	0 1 2 3 4 5	T5.4
We're having conversations with the people we hope to support so that we can understand the steps they have to take to achieve their goals. We're trying to understand which steps are the most difficult, and why they're difficult.	0 1 2 3 4 5	T5.5
We're trying to figure out where and how certain biases, if any, are currently affecting the situation.	0 1 2 3 4 5	T5.6

toolkit 05 TOOLS FOR DISCOVERY + DIAGNOSIS CONVERSATIONS | HUMAN-CENTERED MAPPING

COLLABORATIVE CHANGEMAKING VOICES

Get into the mindset for this toolkit + include your voice in the conversation.

"For me, empathy is an existential question...That is, it's imperative for us to overcome the challenges we face. Unless we can join forces and recognize each other's humanity, how can we do business together, let alone make progress on the increasingly complex and difficult problems in society?"

DANIEL LUBETZKY
FOUNDER + CEO - KIND SNACKS

"Only if we understand, will we care. Only if we care, will we help. Only if we help shall all be saved."

JANE GOODALL
PRIMATOLOGIST | ANTHROPOLOGIST

"All I was doing was trying to get home from work."

ROSA PARKS
CIVIL RIGHTS ACTIVIST

"Often it isn't the mountains ahead that wear you out, it's the little pebble in your shoe."

MUHAMMAD ALI
BOXER | ACTIVIST

"What would the world look like if we asked ourselves the following more often; are our actions helping others find a way to feel more free, more dignified, and more beautiful?"

JACQUELINE NOVOGRATZ
FOUNDER + CEO - ACUMEN

"Let each person tell the truth from his own experience."

FLORENCE NIGHTINGALE
FOUNDER OF MODERN NURSING

"The greatest compliment that was ever paid me was when one asked me what I thought, and attended to my answer."

HENRY DAVID THOREAU
AUTHOR | PHILOSOPHER

T5.1

TOOLS FOR DISCOVERY + DIAGNOSIS CONVERSATIONS | HUMAN-CENTERED MAPPING

toolkit 05

EMPATHY MAP

How might we gain a deeper understanding of the lives and perspectives of the people we aspire to support?

tinyurl.com/cctboxt51

ABOUT THIS TOOL

Changemaking is putting empathy into action. As such, you need to work as hard as possible to get to know and understand the people you aspire to support. Your goal should be to proactively overcome any preconceived ideas and biases you might have and to learn about people's lives from their perspectives. This EMPATHY MAP tool should help you and your team do this.

This tool uses the following four quadrants to note down as much as you're able to about THE PERSON/ GROUP you aspire to support:

WHAT ARE THEY...

- **SAYING + DOING:** Ask questions, listen, and observe.
- **SEEING:** Put yourself in their position as much as possible and look around.
- **HEARING:** Put yourself in their position as much as possible and listen. What are people saying? What noises are you hearing?
- **THINKING + FEELING:** Ask questions and listen. Use your imagination.

After you've worked through the four quadrants, try to distill PAIN POINTS. PAIN POINTS are what's getting in the way of someone achieving their goals.

To note, the goal isn't to note down "right" answers, but rather to capture as much relevant information as possible to gain a deeper level of understanding.

CHANGEMAKER COACH | TOOL TIPS

- This is an essential tool for human-centered design.
- You can also use this tool to help you consider what a more positive future might look like for the people you aspire to support. For example, you might ask, "If you were to achieve your goal, what would you be saying? What might you be doing? What would you be seeing, etc.?" Doing this might help you design success indicators.
- You'll certainly want to employ the 5 WHYs technique from T4.1 ROOT CAUSE ANALYSIS (p. 174) when using this tool.

HOW TO USE THIS TOOL

1. Start at the top of the tool. Note down any and all characteristics of THE PERSON/ GROUP that you're using this tool to better understand. Also, describe THE CONTEXT/ SITUATION. Are they trying to achieve something, but aren't able to? Are they living or working in certain conditions? What's going on in their environment that's important to note down? Try to paint a descriptive picture.
2. Next, go to the WHERE ARE THEY...header. Below this, in as much detail as possible, note down what THE PERSON/ GROUP is SAYING + DOING, SEEING, HEARING, and THINKING + FEELING as it relates to THE CONTEXT.
3. Now reflect on and consider what you've learned about THE PERSON/GROUP from their perspective. WHAT ARE THE MAIN PAIN POINTS? Note these down in the space provided.
4. To conclude, go to NOW WHAT? and note down a few priority next steps based on what you've learned and/or new insights you've gained from using this tool.

CHANGEMAKING INNOVATION MINI-CASES	
V17	p. 361
V44	p. 366
V54	p. 368

CHANGEMAKING TRIMTABS	
CT1	p. 26
CT13	p. 50
CT18	p. 60

THE PERSON/ GROUP	
THE CONTEXT/ SITUATION	

WHAT ARE THEY...

SAYING + DOING	SEEING	HEARING	THINKING + FEELING

WHAT ARE THE MAIN PAIN POINTS?

NOW WHAT?	

T5.2

TOOLS FOR DISCOVERY + DIAGNOSIS CONVERSATIONS | HUMAN-CENTERED MAPPING

PERSONA MAP

How might we capture representative characteristics of the people we're hoping to support?

tinyurl.com/cctboxt52

ABOUT THIS TOOL

Customer Personas are used in business to capture priority information about customers. They're representative portraits. Inspired by the Customer Persona, this PERSONA MAP tool will help you and your team create empathetic personas of the people you aspire to support.

Use this tool to note down the following with as much detail as possible:

- **PERSONA NAME:** Make up a descriptive and alliterative name like Motherly Maria or Sally Student. This technique makes the persona easy to remember and discuss.
- **GENDER IDENTIFICATION:** This is obviously from the persona's perspective, not yours.
- **AGE(RANGE):** Try to keep this as narrow a range as possible.
- **PLACE:** Where does your persona live and work?
- **FAMILY STATUS/ ROLE:** What's the persona's family situation?
- **EDUCATION SITUATION:** What's their past, current, and potential future situation? Include formal and informal education.
- **WORK SITUATION:** What's their past, current, and potential future situation? What exactly have they done? What do they do now? Where do they work and why?
- **FINANCIAL SITUATION:** What's their income, spending, savings, investment, rent, and/or debt situation? Why?
- **HOUSING/ TRANSPORTATION SITUATION:** What type of house or apartment do they live in? Do they have electricity, water, appliances, etc.? Why or why not? How do they get around from place to place? Do they have a preference?
- **HEALTH SITUATION:** How's their mental and physical health? How do they access healthcare services?
- **TECHNOLOGY ACCESS/ PREFERENCES:** What type of technology do they have access to, use, and/or prefer? Do they have a social media preference?
- **ASPIRATIONS/ GOALS:** What do they hope to achieve over the short, medium, and long term?
- **MOTIVATIONS:** What inspires and drives them?
- **OTHER:** What else is important?
- **A DAY IN THE LIFE:** Write down what this persona does throughout a typical day. Tell a story.
- **QUOTES:** What are some relevant things this persona says or might say?

HOW TO USE THIS TOOL

1. Start at the top of the tool. Note down the PERSONA NAME, GENDER IDENTIFICATION, AGE(RANGE), PLACE, and FAMILY STATUS/ ROLE. In addition, see if you can make a DRAWING OF THE PERSONA. Don't worry if you're not an artist.
2. Next, note down everything you know below. Start with EDUCATION SITUATION. Then work your way through the tool.
3. To conclude, go to NOW WHAT? and note down a few priority next steps based on what you've learned and/or new insights you've gained from using this tool.

CHANGEMAKER COACH | TOOL TIPS

- This is another "must-have" tool that should be used as early and often as possible.
- You'll likely want to create multiple personas.
- This is helpful for putting CT3 FOCUS ON THE WELL-BEING OF GIRLS + WOMEN (p. 30) in action.
- It's helpful to use this in conjunction with T5.4 WELL-BEING MAP (p. 198)
- This is helpful for defining innovators, early adopters, etc. for T8.4 DIFFUSION STRATEGY (p. 262)

CHANGEMAKING INNOVATION MINI-CASES		CHANGEMAKING TRIMTABS	
V21	p. 362	CT3	p. 30
V40	p. 365	CT14	p. 52
V83	p. 374	CT18	p. 60

DRAWING OF THE PERSONA	**PERSONA NAME**	
	GENDER IDENTIFICATION	
	AGE (RANGE)	
	PLACE	
	FAMILY STATUS/ ROLE	

EDUCATION SITUATION	**WORK SITUATION**	**FINANCIAL SITUATION**
HOUSING + TRANSPORTATION SITUATION	**HEALTH SITUATION**	**TECHNOLOGY ACCESS/ PREFERENCES**
ASPIRATIONS/ GOALS	**MOTIVATIONS**	**OTHER**

A DAY IN THE LIFE...	**QUOTES**

NOW WHAT?	

T5.3

TOOLS FOR DISCOVERY + DIAGNOSIS CONVERSATIONS | HUMAN-CENTERED MAPPING

EMPOWERMENT MAP

How might we better understand to what extent someone is relatively empowered and/or disempowered?

tinyurl.com/cctboxt53

ABOUT THIS TOOL

There's a goal that someone's trying to achieve, but they can't. Why can't they? It's probably because they're disempowered in some way. Your job as a changemaker is to play a value-added role in helping people to become (more) empowered to achieve their goals. This EMPOWERMENT MAP tool should help you and your team figure out where and how to do this.

This tool uses the "EMPOWERMENT AIR" formula to guide your conversations, decisions, and actions. The formula is as follows:

E (EMPOWERMENT) =
A (ABILITY) + I (INCENTIVES) + R (RESOURCES)

ABILITY consists of both the KNOWLEDGE and the SKILLS required. INCENTIVES are the intrinsic motivators and extrinsic drivers. And RESOURCES are the assets needed to achieve the goal.

In short, the necessary ABILITY, INCENTIVES, and RESOURCES must all be in place and "add up" for someone to be empowered to achieve their goal(s). Disempowerment results from a deficiency or gap in any one of these three components. Needless to say, both reality and perception matter.

Using this tool you should gain an understanding of where relative empowerment and disempowerment exist. Based on this, you'll be able to ideate and prioritize creative solutions that build on STRENGTHS and/or find ways to empathetically address WEAKNESSES.

HOW TO USE THIS TOOL

1. Start at the top of the tool. Note down THE PERSON/ GROUP. Then note down THE GOAL. This is what they're trying to achieve.
2. Next, go to the COMPONENTS header. Start with (A)BILITY - KNOWLEDGE. Go under the ANALYSIS header, and note down as many STRENGTHS as you're able to. This is a list of any existing (A)BILITY - KNOWLEDGE that's currently helping to empower THE PERSON/ GROUP to achieve THE GOAL. Then note down IDEAS FOR BUILDING ON STRENGTHS.
3. Repeat step 2 for each of the COMPONENTS. It's always best to take an asset frame and start with STRENGTHS.
4. Now go back up to (A)BILITY - KNOWLEDGE. Go under the ANALYSIS HEADER, and note down as many WEAKNESSES as you're able to. Where might gaps exist? What's needed? Then note down IDEAS FOR OVERCOMING WEAKNESSES.
5. Repeat step 4 for each of the COMPONENTS.
6. To conclude, go to NOW WHAT? and note down a few priority next steps based on what you've learned and/or new insights you've gained from using this tool.

CHANGEMAKER COACH | TOOL TIP

- This helps you start with an asset frame. Always start with people's aspirations and strengths.
- Use this to put CT4 HELP EMPOWER WOMEN AS LAST MILE PROFESSIONALS (p. 32) in action. I originally designed this to help figure out how to help the women entrepreneurs working with our MicroConsignment Model.
- T6.4 CAPITAL MIX MAP (p. 216) is similar but for communities/ systems. That said, you could use this tool for organizations, teams, etc.

CHANGEMAKING INNOVATION MINI-CASES	
V12	p. 360
V44	p. 366
V52	p. 368

CHANGEMAKING TRIMTABS	
CT3	p. 30
CT4	p. 32
CT6	p. 36

THE PERSON/ GROUP	
THE GOAL	

	ANALYSIS			
COMPONENTS	STRENGTHS	IDEAS FOR BUILDING ON STRENGTHS	WEAKNESSES	IDEAS FOR OVERCOMING WEAKNESSES
(A)BILITY - KNOWLEDGE				
(A)BILITY - SKILLS				
(I)NCENTIVES				
(R)ESOURCES				

NOW WHAT?	

T5.4

TOOLS FOR DISCOVERY + DIAGNOSIS CONVERSATIONS | HUMAN-CENTERED MAPPING

WELL-BEING MAP

How might we focus our analysis holistically on well-being?

tinyurl.com/cctboxt54

ABOUT THIS TOOL

Well-being can be defined as "being in a state of being comfortable, happy, and healthy." At its essence, helping people to improve their well-being is what changemaking is all about. In order to do this, it's important to identify and analyze all of the factors that are positively and negatively contributing to someone's well-being. This WELL-BEING MAP tool should help you and your team get started doing this.

This tool should help you and your team get an understanding of where you might help add value to avoid negative well-being and/ or reinforce positive well-being. It helps you gain a comprehensive understanding of someone's well-being by analyzing 12 factors.

CHANGEMAKER COACH | TOOL TIPS

- This tool works very well with individuals, teams, organizations, communities, etc.
- This should help you put CT 3 FOCUS ON THE WELL-BEING OF GIRLS + WOMEN (p. 30) in action.
- As you use this tool, be sure to work hard to understand how situations are interrelated. Keep in mind how one negative situation might affect another and cause a negative cascading effect. For example, if someone doesn't have savings, then that might mean they can't pay for education or health emergencies. Or if transportation is unreliable, a person might not be able to show up to their job on time. This might negatively affect their INCOME SITUATION. This can also work in a positive way. For example, a positive SOCIAL/ COMMUNITY SITUATION should positively affect someone's MENTAL HEALTH SITUATION.

HOW TO USE THIS TOOL

1. Start at the top of the tool. Note down THE PERSON/ GROUP.
2. Next, go to each of the factors that might be affecting the well-being of THE PERSON/ GROUP. Circle a well-being RATING for each. "0" is very negative and "5" is very positive. After circling a RATING, note down your ANALYSIS. Provide detail here. What's the situation? Why did you circle this RATING?
3. To conclude, go to NOW WHAT? and note down a few priority next steps based on what you've learned and/or new insights you've gained from using this tool.

CHANGEMAKING INNOVATION MINI-CASES	
V13	p. 360
V32	p. 364
V63	p. 370

CHANGEMAKING TRIMTABS	
CT3	p. 30
CT17	p. 58
CT19	p. 62

THE PERSON/ GROUP	

JOB SITUATION		INCOME SITUATION	
RATING	0 1 2 3 4 5	RATING	0 1 2 3 4 5
ANALYSIS		ANALYSIS	
CREDIT SITUATION		**SAVINGS SITUATION**	
RATING	0 1 2 3 4 5	RATING	0 1 2 3 4 5
ANALYSIS		ANALYSIS	
PHYSICAL HEALTH SITUATION		**MENTAL HEALTH SITUATION**	
RATING	0 1 2 3 4 5	RATING	0 1 2 3 4 5
ANALYSIS		ANALYSIS	
FAMILY SITUATION		**SOCIAL/ COMMUNITY SITUATION**	
RATING	0 1 2 3 4 5	RATING	0 1 2 3 4 5
ANALYSIS		ANALYSIS	
HOUSING SITUATION		**TRANSPORTATION SITUATION**	
RATING	0 1 2 3 4 5	RATING	0 1 2 3 4 5
ANALYSIS		ANALYSIS	
SECURITY SITUATION		**EDUCATION/ LEARNING SITUATION**	
RATING	0 1 2 3 4 5	RATING	0 1 2 3 4 5
ANALYSIS		ANALYSIS	

NOW WHAT?	

T5.5

TOOLS FOR DISCOVERY + DIAGNOSIS CONVERSATIONS | HUMAN-CENTERED MAPPING

JOURNEY MAP

How might we understand what obstacles are getting in the way as someone works towards achieving their goal?

tinyurl.com/cctboxt55

ABOUT THIS TOOL

What are all of the steps that someone needs to take to achieve their goal? Which ones are easy? Which ones are difficult? Which ones might be so difficult that they're getting in the way of success? This JOURNEY MAP tool should help you and your team figure all of this out.

Inspired by the commonly used Customer Journey Map, there are two different ways that you can use this tool. With both approaches, start with THE GOAL.

For the first approach, work backward from the last ACTIVITY required to achieve THE GOAL. For example, if THE GOAL is "To arrive at work safely and on time," the last ACTIVITY might be "Get off of the bus." Start there and then go back in time, step by step.

With the second approach, do the opposite. Decide a starting point and work forward to THE GOAL. Using the same example, with this approach you might want to start with "Get out of bed." and then go forward in time. There's no right approach. Just use the one that's most helpful given the current context.

CHANGEMAKER COACH | TOOL TIP

- It's helpful to break down the journey into as many small steps as possible. This helps you discover little things that might be getting in the way that no one has noticed.
- This is good to use in conjunction with T4.6 PROBLEM PRIORITIZATION ANALYSIS (p. 184) and T6.3 EQUITABLE ACCESS MAP (p. 214).
- You might also find this helpful for designing new journeys. What steps are required to achieve a goal?

HOW TO USE THIS TOOL

1. Start at the top of the tool. Note down THE GOAL. This is what the person/ group of people are trying to achieve.
2. Next, go to the JOURNEY header and note down the STEP # and ACTIVITY DESCRIPTION for each necessary step to achieve THE GOAL. As mentioned, there are two different ways to do this. If you want to work backward, start at the top with the last step. Note down the STEP # and ACTIVITY DESCRIPTION and work your way down the tool. Or, you can do the opposite. Go to the bottom of the tool. Note down fSTEP #"1" with its ACTIVITY DESCRIPTION and work your way up the tool towards THE GOAL. Use whichever approach is the easiest. To note, there are spaces for ten steps. Your JOURNEY might require fewer or more steps.
3. Now go under the ANALYSIS header to DIFFICULTY, and circle a number that represents how difficult it is to take each step. "0" means it's very easy and "5" means it's extremely difficult. Provide your reasoning under WHY THIS LEVEL OF DIFFICULTY?
4. After you've worked through the ANALYSIS for each step, note down IDEAS FOR SOLUTIONS. Prioritize your conversations on the most difficult steps.
5. To conclude, go to NOW WHAT? and note down a few priority next steps based on what you've learned and/or new insights you've gained from using this tool.

CHANGEMAKING INNOVATION MINI-CASES	
V67	p. 371
V69	p. 371
V85	p. 374

CHANGEMAKING TRIMTABS	
CT4	p. 32
CT9	p. 42
CT15	p. 54

THE GOAL	

JOURNEY		ANALYSIS		IDEAS FOR SOLUTIONS
STEP #	ACTIVITY DESCRIPTION	DIFFICULTY	WHY THIS LEVEL OF DIFFICULTY?	
		0 1 2 3 4 5		
		0 1 2 3 4 5		
		0 1 2 3 4 5		
		0 1 2 3 4 5		
		0 1 2 3 4 5		
		0 1 2 3 4 5		
		0 1 2 3 4 5		
		0 1 2 3 4 5		
		0 1 2 3 4 5		
		0 1 2 3 4 5		

NOW WHAT?	

T5.6

TOOLS FOR DISCOVERY + DIAGNOSIS CONVERSATIONS | HUMAN-CENTERED MAPPING

DECISION MAKING BIASES MAP

How might we understand what cognitive biases are influencing behavior?

tinyurl.com/cctboxt56

ABOUT THIS TOOL

We have all kinds of cognitive/ behavioral biases that influence how we think and what we do. As a changemaker, it's important to constantly be on the lookout for where and how these biases might be influencing people's behavior. This DECISION MAKING BIASES MAP tool should help you and your team identify some of the most common biases and ideate about potential responses.

Following is a list of the biases included in this tool:

- **AMBIGUITY (UNCERTAINTY) AVERSION:** We have a preference for known risks over unknown risks.
- **ANCHORING:** We rely heavily on one piece of information when making decisions.
- **AVAILABILITY HEURISTIC:** We have an overreliance on examples that immediately come to mind.
- **CHOICE OVERLOAD:** When confronted with too many choices, we get paralyzed and prefer to not choose at all, even if making a choice would lead to a better outcome.
- **CONFIRMATION BIAS:** We tend to look for and find information that confirms our assumptions/ beliefs.
- **DEFAULT EFFECT:** We tend to favor the default option.
- **ENDOWMENT EFFECT:** We place a higher value on objects we own than ones we don't.
- **FUNDAMENTAL ATTRIBUTION ERROR:** When bad things happen to others, we blame it on them. When bad things happen to us or those we're close to, we blame it on external factors.
- **HYPERBOLIC DISCOUNTING:** Given two similar rewards, we show a preference for one that arrives sooner rather than later.
- **LOSS AVERSION:** We prefer avoiding losses over acquiring gains.
- **RECENCY BIAS**: We overemphasize the importance of an event(s) that happened most recently.

HOW TO USE THIS TOOL

1. Start by describing THE CONTEXT at the top of the tool. What's the situation that you're analyzing?
2. Next, go to the DECISION MAKING BIASES header. Start with AMBIGUITY AVERSION and go under the ANALYSIS header. Work your way through DO WE SEE IT?, WHERE? and THE IMPACT.
3. Repeat step 2 for each of the DECISION MAKING BIASES.
4. Now, note down your IDEAS FOR RESPONSES. These inform your design decisions. Coming up with ideas here might take a bit of time and creativity.
5. To conclude, go to NOW WHAT? and note down a few priority next steps based on what you've learned and/or new insights you've gained from using this tool.

CHANGEMAKER COACH | TOOL TIPS

- I designed this tool to help you avoid some of the frustrations I've had over the years. These are some of the most frequent biases I've run into. We're not rational robots. Always keep that in mind.
- T11.4 MOTIVATIONS + CAPABILITIES STRATEGY (p. 304) and T11.6 NUDGE STRATEGY (p. 308) are two more tools that might help you understand/ change behavior in creative new ways.

CHANGEMAKING INNOVATION MINI-CASES		CHANGEMAKING TRIMTABS	
V61	p. 370	CT3	p. 30
V68	p. 371	CT14	p. 52
V72	p. 372	CT16	p. 56

THE CONTEXT				

	ANALYSIS			
DECISION MAKING BIASES	**DO WE SEE IT?**	**WHERE?**	**THE IMPACT**	**IDEAS FOR OUR RESPONSE**
AMBIGUITY AVERSION	YES NO			
ANCHORING	YES NO			
AVAILABILITY HEURISTIC	YES NO			
CHOICE OVERLOAD	YES NO			
CONFIRMATION BIAS	YES NO			
DEFAULT EFFECT	YES NO			
ENDOWMENT EFFECT	YES NO			
FUNDAMENTAL ATTRIBUTION ERROR	YES NO			
HYPERBOLIC DISCOUNTING	YES NO			
LOSS AVERSION	YES NO			
RECENCY BIAS	YES NO			

NOW WHAT?	

TOOLS FOR DISCOVERY + DIAGNOSIS CONVERSATIONS | HUMAN-CENTERED MAPPING

TOOLKIT TOOLS REFLECTIONS

SCALE:
STRONGLY AGREE = 5, AGREE = 4, NOT SURE = 3, DISAGREE = 2, STRONGLY DISAGREE = 1

tinyurl.com/cctboxtoolsrflect

	CHANGEMAKING TOOLS					
REFLECTION STATEMENTS	**T5.1**	**T5.2**	**T5.3**	**T5.4**	**T5.5**	**T5.6**
This tool is easy to understand.						
This tool is easy to use.						
This tool taught me/ us important new knowledge.						
This tool empowered new changemaking conversations.						
This tool helped to spark new ideas/ insights.						
This tool should be included in my/ our toolbox for the future.						
I/ we should share this tool with other changemakers.						

NOTES:

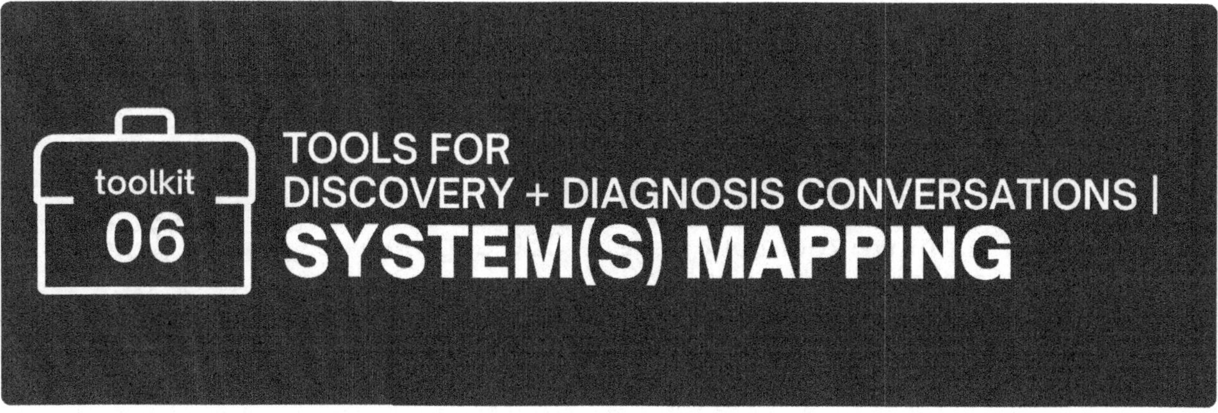

TOOLS FOR DISCOVERY + DIAGNOSIS CONVERSATIONS | SYSTEM(S) MAPPING

Changemaker educators collaborating at a retreat in New Mexico

Social Entrepreneur Corps "Community Consultants" collaborating with community members in the Dominican Republic

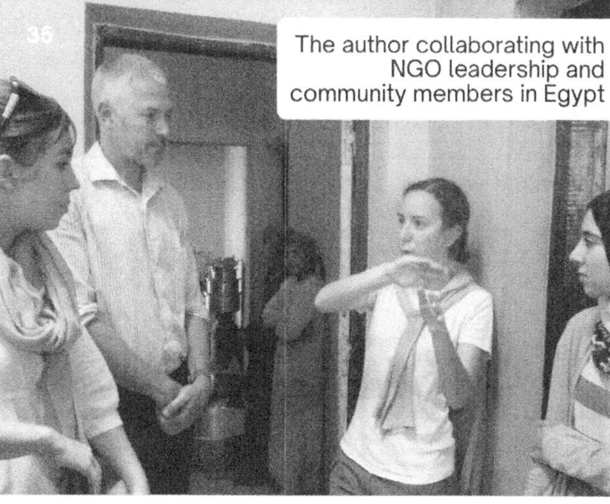

The author collaborating with NGO leadership and community members in Egypt

NOTES:

GVK note -
You can try to change the system from the inside or the outside. Whichever way, work to go from complain to contribute.

toolkit 06

TOOLS FOR DISCOVERY + DIAGNOSIS CONVERSATIONS | SYSTEM(S) MAPPING

TOOLS INVENTORY

How might we zoom out to get a 360 degree understanding of the context?

tinyurl.com/cctboxtools01

	Tool	Page
☐	**T6.1 BRIGHT SPOTS MAP**	**p. 210**

How might we analyze and amplify existing solutions for a pervasive community problem?

	Tool	Page
☐	**T6.2 CURRENT SOLUTIONS LANDSCAPE MAP**	**p. 212**

How might we analyze and learn from current solutions designed to solve the problem(s) we've identified?

	Tool	Page
☐	**T6.3 EQUITABLE ACCESS MAP**	**p. 214**

How might we analyze the specific ways that current solutions are and aren't creating access?

	Tool	Page
☐	**T6.4 CAPITAL MIX MAP**	**p. 216**

How might we identify community strengths that might be leveraged and/or weaknesses that might represent opportunities to provide support?

	Tool	Page
☐	**T6.5 SYSTEM STATUS MAP**	**p. 218**

How might we identify and analyze what's in a relatively stable, complicated, complex or chaotic status?

	Tool	Page
☐	**T6.6 SYSTEM FIVE R'S MAP**	**p. 220**

How might we gain an understanding of how resources, roles, relationships, and rules impact results?

	Tool	Page
☐	**T6.7 SYSTEM COMPONENTS MAP**	**p. 222**

How might we analyze five critical components of the system ranging from policies to mindsets?

	Tool	Page
☐	**T6.8 STAKEHOLDER POWER MAP**	**p. 224**

How might we analyze how different types of power are, could be, and should be distributed within the system?

	Tool	Page
☐	**T6.9 FIVE FORCES MAP**	**p. 226**

How might we analyze five critical forces that influence our work within the system?

	Tool	Page
☐	**T6.10 VUCA MAP**	**p. 228**

How might we analyze + account for volatility, uncertainty, complexity, and ambiguity within the system?

TOOLS FOR DISCOVERY + DIAGNOSIS CONVERSATIONS | SYSTEM(S) MAPPING

TOOLKIT SCORECARD + PRIORITIZATION HELP

Score yourselves to help you decide which tool(s) you might want to prioritize for your changemaking conversations.

tinyurl.com/cctboxtoolsprior

SELF-CHECK STATEMENTS	HOW ARE WE DOING?	TOOL SUGGESTIONS
We're trying to find and amplify solutions that community members have already designed within the current context.	0 1 2 3 4 5	T6.1
We've analyzed and gained insights from the existing landscape of solutions that are directly or indirectly addressing the problem(s).	0 1 2 3 4 5	T6.2
We're trying to understand the ways in which existing solutions are and aren't accessible to the community members we aspire to support.	0 1 2 3 4 5	T6.3
We're having conversations about current community assets so that we can leverage strengths and address weaknesses.	0 1 2 3 4 5	T6.4
We're having conversations about the status of different programs/ activities on a spectrum from stable to chaotic.	0 1 2 3 4 5	T6.5
We're having conversations about how the resources, roles, relationships and rules affect the desired results of the system.	0 1 2 3 4 5	T6.6
We're analyzing how all of the critical components of the system are creating positive and/or negative impact.	0 1 2 3 4 5	T6.7
We're talking about who holds, should hold and/or could hold power within the system.	0 1 2 3 4 5	T6.8
We're working to understand how forces such as competition, potential new entrants, supplier power and the potential for new opportunities are impacting the system.	0 1 2 3 4 5	T6.9
We're having conversations about where and how volatility, uncertainty, complexity and ambiguity are impacting the system.	0 1 2 3 4 5	T6.10

TOOLS FOR DISCOVERY + DIAGNOSIS CONVERSATIONS | SYSTEM(S) MAPPING

COLLABORATIVE CHANGEMAKING VOICES

Get into the mindset for this toolkit + include your voice in the conversation.

*"Once in a while, you get shown the light,
In the strangest of places if you look at it right."*

THE GRATEFUL DEAD

"A voice is a human gift; it should be cherished and used, to utter fully human speech as possible. Powerlessness and silence go together."

MARGARET ATWOOD
NOVELIST | POET | ACTIVIST

"If you want to find out about the road ahead, then ask about it from those coming back."

CHINESE PROVERB

"The most common way people give up their power is by thinking they don't have any."

ALICE WALKER
WRITER | POET | ACTIVIST

"Systems thinking is a discipline for seeing wholes. It is a framework for seeing interrelationships rather than things, for seeing 'patterns of change' rather than 'static snapshots.'"

PETER SENGE
SYSTEMS SCIENTIST | MIT LECTURER | FOUNDER OF SOCIETY FOR ORGANIZATIONAL LEARNING

"Always design a thing by considering it in its next larger context – a chair in a room, a room in a house, a house in an environment, an environment in a city plan."

ELIEL SAARINEN
FINISH AMERICAN ARCHITECT

"Whenever I run into a problem I can't solve, I always make it bigger. I can never solve it by trying to make it smaller, but if I make it big enough, I can begin to see the outlines of a solution."

DWIGHT D. EISENHOWER
34TH U.S. PRESIDENT

T6.1

TOOLS FOR DISCOVERY + DIAGNOSIS CONVERSATIONS | SYSTEM(S) MAPPING

BRIGHT SPOTS MAP

How might we analyze and amplify existing solutions that solve a pervasive community problem?

tinyurl.com/cctboxt61

ABOUT THIS TOOL

Your Plan A for problem-solving should be as follows: (1) Find outlier people in the system who've already solved the problem. These are what's known as "bright spots." (2) Figure out how they've solved the problem. Focus on finding the problem-solving behaviors that are replicable. (3) Share what you've learned with others who are dealing with the problem. Do this in a way that makes it as easy as possible for them to practice and adopt the replicable behaviors. This BRIGHT SPOTS MAP tool should help you and your team put Plan A into action.

This Plan A is based on what's known as a positive deviance (PD) approach for solving problems in complex systems. PD was first developed by Save the Children professionals Monique and Jerry Sternin when they were working to solve childhood nutrition problems in a Vietnamese community. They recognized there were community members who, in spite of the fact that they were working within the same constraints as everyone else, had already solved the nutrition problem. These bright spots, so to speak, could show the way forward for everyone else. The key was simply to analyze what made these bright spots successful and spotlight their uniquely successful behaviors/ strategies so that everyone else could see and copy them.

CHANGEMAKER COACH | TOOL TIPS

- Once you have a rough understanding of the problem, the first thing you should do is look for bright spots. And even if you can't find people who've figured out how to completely solve the problem, you'll likely find people who've partially solved it or who've solved certain aspects.
- This tool will help you put CT5 SPOTLIGHT BRIGHT SPOTS (p. 34) and CT6 OPTIMIZE COMMUNITY ABILITIES + ASSETS (p. 36) into practice.
- Use this with T6.2 CURRENT SOLUTIONS LANDSCAPE MAP (p. 212)

HOW TO USE THIS TOOL

1. Start at the top with a bit of a situational analysis. First, describe THE COMMUNITY. Next, note down THE PROBLEM, any and all of THE CAUSES OF THE PROBLEM, and THE EFFECTS OF THE PROBLEM.
2. Go to KEY IDENTIFIERS, and start under the BRIGHT SPOTS header with BRIGHT SPOT 1. Start by noting down a description of WHO IS IT? Then work your way down the rest of the question prompts.
3. Repeat step 2 for BRIGHT SPOT 2. To note, this tool includes space for you to analyze two BRIGHT SPOTS. You might find only one or possibly many more within THE COMMUNITY that you're analyzing,
4. To conclude, go to NOW WHAT? and note down a few priority next steps based on what you've learned and/or new insights you've gained from using this tool.

CHANGEMAKING INNOVATION MINI-CASES	
V37	p. 365
V41	p. 366
V71	p. 372

CHANGEMAKING TRIMTABS	
CT5	p. 34
CT6	p. 36
CT22	p. 68

THE COMMUNITY	
THE PROBLEM	
THE CAUSES OF THE PROBLEM	
THE EFFECTS OF THE PROBLEM	

	BRIGHT SPOTS	
KEY IDENTIFIERS	**BRIGHT SPOT 1**	**BRIGHT SPOT 2**
WHO IS IT?		
WHAT'S THE SOLUTION?		
HOW DO WE KNOW THE SOLUTION WORKS?		
WHAT'S UNIQUE ABOUT THE SOLUTION?		
WHAT RESOURCES ARE REQUIRED?		
WHAT'S REPLICABLE?		
WHY DON'T OTHERS KNOW THE SOLUTION?		
HOW CAN WE HELP OTHERS TO LEARN ABOUT THE SOLUTION?		
HOW CAN WE HELP OTHERS TO ADOPT THE SOLUTION?		

NOW WHAT?	

T6.2

TOOLS FOR DISCOVERY + DIAGNOSIS CONVERSATIONS | SYSTEM(S) MAPPING

CURRENT SOLUTIONS LANDSCAPE MAP

How might we analyze and learn from current solutions designed to solve the problem(s) we've identified?

tinyurl.com/cctboxt62

ABOUT THIS TOOL

Once you're at the point where you believe you have a basic understanding of the problem, it's time to research and analyze current solutions. Inspired by competitive analysis tools, this CURRENT SOLUTIONS LANDSCAPE MAP tool should help you and your team focus on gathering the most important information about existing solutions and solutions providers.

Amongst others, this tool serves three purposes. First, it's critical to know if there's a current solution that exists that's already effectively and efficiently solving the problem. If so, there's no reason for you to try to step in with a new solution. Focus your efforts on getting the current solution into the hands of the people you aspire to support.

Second, assuming there isn't already a great solution, analyzing the shortcomings of current solutions should help you figure out your potential value proposition.

And third, this tool should help you and your team consider what kind of relationships you could/ should try to form with current solutions providers.

CHANGEMAKER COACH | TOOL TIPS

- This tool is influenced by a competitive analysis that you might use in business. I've modified it because I don't want to assume there's competition. As well, from a community impact perspective, it's better to start out by viewing others organizations as potential collaborators.
- You might want to use this with T3.7 INNOVATION INSIGHTS + APPLICATIONS WHITEBOARD (p. 160)
- If you find an opportunity for collaboration you might want to use T8.2 COLLABORATOR COMPATIBILITY ANALYSIS (p. 258)

HOW TO USE THIS TOOL

1. Start by describing THE PROBLEM at the top of the tool. What's the overall problem that you're prioritizing and that organizations are currently trying to solve?
2. Next, go to the CURRENT SOLUTIONS LANDSCAPE header. Under this, there are three spaces to note down ORGANIZATION NAME. Note down the names of the organizations you're analyzing. You may only be analyzing one at the moment. That's fine.
3. Now go to the KEY INFORMATION header. Work your way down the question prompts for each of the organizations you're analyzing with this tool.
4. To conclude, go to NOW WHAT? and note down a few priority next steps based on what you've learned and/or new insights you've gained from using this tool.

CHANGEMAKING INNOVATION MINI-CASES		CHANGEMAKING TRIMTABS	
V52	p. 368	CT6	p. 36
V66	p. 371	CT16	p. 56
V80	p. 373	CT20	p. 64

THE PROBLEM	

KEY INFORMATION	CURRENT SOLUTIONS LANDSCAPE		
WHO'S THE LEADERSHIP + TEAM?			
WHERE ARE THEY LOCATED?			
WHAT'S THEIR HISTORY?			
WHO ARE THEY SPECIFICALLY HELPING?			
HOW MANY PEOPLE ARE THEY REACHING?			
WHAT'S THEIR SOLUTION?			
HOW DO THEY MEASURE SUCCESS?			
HOW DOES THEIR SOLUTION WORK?			
WHAT ARE SOME STRENGTHS OF THEIR SOLUTION?			
WHAT ARE SOME WEAKNESSES/ SHORTFALLS OF THEIR SOLUTION?			
WHAT OPPORTUNITIES EXIST?			
HOW MIGHT WE POTENTIALLY COLLABORATE WITH THIS ORGANIZATION?			
HOW MIGHT WE POTENTIALLY CO-EXIST OR COMPETE WITH THIS ORGANIZATION?			

NOW WHAT?	

T6.3

TOOLS FOR DISCOVERY + DIAGNOSIS CONVERSATIONS | SYSTEM(S) MAPPING

EQUITABLE ACCESS MAP

How might we analyze the specific ways that current solutions are and aren't creating access?

tinyurl.com/cctboxt63

ABOUT THIS TOOL

Your goal is to help empower people to have equitable access to solutions that will help them solve their problems and improve their lives. This requires taking context into account and recognizing that each person, group, and/or community lives and works in different circumstances, and in different ways. This EQUITABLE ACCESS MAP tool should help you and your team analyze if and where barriers to equitable access exist with current solutions, and brainstorm about ways to create more equitable access where needed.

This tool includes the following 14 factors to consider:

- **APPROPRIATENESS:** Is the solution age, gender, and culturally appropriate, for example?
- **ATTRACTIVENESS:** Nobody wants or deserves an ugly solution, even though it might work. Function and form matter.
- **AVAILABILITY:** If a solution isn't within reasonable reach, it may as well not exist.
- **AWARENESS:** If people aren't aware of the problem, let alone the solution, then it isn't accessible.
- **COMPLEXITY:** Increased complexity results in increased inaccessibility.
- **COST:** Is it too expensive or too cheap?
- **DEPENDABILITY:** Can you count on the solution consistently?
- **DESIGN:** Is it designed for the intended audience?
- **DURABILITY:** Does the solution last?
- **EASE OF ACQUISITION:** Do people have to "jump through too many hoops" to get access?
- **POWER/ CONTROL:** Who provides and can take away access?
- **QUALITY:** Everyone deserves quality.
- **SERVICE:** Is service required? Does after-service/ decent customer service exist?
- **TIME INVESTMENT REQUIRED:** There's only so much time in the day. The greater the time investment required, the more inaccessible.
- **OTHER:** What else should be considered?

HOW TO USE THIS TOOL

1. First, go to COMMUNITY DESCRIPTION and describe who the community is that's seeking equitable access to a solution.
2. Next, describe THE PROBLEM that current solutions are trying to solve.
3. Go to CURRENT SOLUTION #1, and write down the name and/or a description of a solution that's been designed to solve the problem. Do the same for CURRENT SOLUTION #2 if there are two solutions you're analyzing.
4. Now go to the ACCESS CONSIDERATIONS header and start with CURRENT SOLUTION #1. Work your way down the ACCESS CONSIDERATIONS. Circle a RATING from "0" to "5". "0" means it's failing and "5" means success. Under ANALYSIS, note down the reason you gave your RATING.
5. Repeat step 4 for CURRENT SOLUTION #2.
6. Now go to IDEAS FOR IMPROVEMENTS for each of the ACCESS CONSIDERATIONS. Consider the RATING and ANALYSIS for each. How might a solution create more equitable access for community members? Note down your ideas.
7. To conclude, go to NOW WHAT? and note down a few priority next steps based on what you've learned and/or new insights you've gained from using this tool.

CHANGEMAKER COACH | TOOL TIPS

- This tool can help you put CT4 HELP EMPOWER WOMEN AS LAST MILE PROFESSIONALS (p. 32) and CT13 RESTRUCTURE IT (p. 50) into practice.
- You might want to use this with T5.1 EMPATHY MAP (p. 192), PERSONA MAP (p. 194), and T11.1 KEYS TO INNOVATION ADOPTION (p. 298).
- This tool might also help you figure out T7.4 VALUE PROPOSITION BLUEPRINT (p. 244)

CHANGEMAKING INNOVATION MINI-CASES	
V18	p. 361
V67	p. 371
V69	p. 371

CHANGEMAKING TRIMTABS	
CT4	p. 32
CT13	p. 50
CT14	p. 52

COMMUNITY DESCRIPTION	
THE PROBLEM	

CURRENT SOLUTION #1	
CURRENT SOLUTION #2	

	CURRENT SOLUTION #1		**CURRENT SOLUTION #2**		**IDEAS FOR IMPROVEMENTS**
ACCESS CONSIDERATIONS	**RATING**	**ANALYSIS**	**RATING**	**ANALYSIS**	
APPROPRIATENESS	0 1 2 3 4 5		0 1 2 3 4 5		
ATTRACTIVENESS	0 1 2 3 4 5		0 1 2 3 4 5		
AVAILABILITY	0 1 2 3 4 5		0 1 2 3 4 5		
AWARENESS	0 1 2 3 4 5		0 1 2 3 4 5		
COMPLEXITY	0 1 2 3 4 5		0 1 2 3 4 5		
COST	0 1 2 3 4 5		0 1 2 3 4 5		
DEPENDABILITY	0 1 2 3 4 5		0 1 2 3 4 5		
DESIGN	0 1 2 3 4 5		0 1 2 3 4 5		
DURABILITY	0 1 2 3 4 5		0 1 2 3 4 5		
EASE OF ACQUISITION	0 1 2 3 4 5		0 1 2 3 4 5		
POWER/ CONTROL	0 1 2 3 4 5		0 1 2 3 4 5		
QUALITY	0 1 2 3 4 5		0 1 2 3 4 5		
SERVICE	0 1 2 3 4 5		0 1 2 3 4 5		
TIME INVESTMENT REQUIRED	0 1 2 3 4 5		0 1 2 3 4 5		
	0 1 2 3 4 5		0 1 2 3 4 5		

NOW WHAT?	

T6.4

TOOLS FOR DISCOVERY + DIAGNOSIS CONVERSATIONS | SYSTEM(S) MAPPING

CAPITAL MIX MAP

How might we identify community strengths that could be leveraged and/or weaknesses that might represent opportunities to provide support?

tinyurl.com/cctboxt64

ABOUT THIS TOOL

We fail when we take a myopic and/ or deficit view of the capital that exists in communities. We focus too much on financial capital. Or we brand communities as being "poor." Conversely, when we look at the capital in communities holistically and start with an asset frame, we're more likely to be successful at helping community members leverage strengths and overcome weaknesses. This CAPITAL MIX MAP tool should help you and your team do this.

This tool helps you analyze the following seven forms of capital:

- **SOCIAL:** These are the networks of relationships among people who live and/or work in a particular community including formal and informal groups that work together towards a specific purpose.
- **FINANCIAL:** These are the economic resources available or accessible.
- **HUMAN:** These are the people who can work on an issue or challenge.
- **PHYSICAL:** This includes things such as accessible raw materials, facilities, transportation, machinery, energy, supplies, local bodies of water, plants, animals, etc.
- **KNOWLEDGE:** This is oftentimes called intellectual capital. This includes knowledge about ideas, methods, and processes.
- **CULTURAL:** Cultural capital falls into three categories; institutionalized (education or specialized knowledge), embodied (personality, speech, skills), and objectified (clothes or other belongings).
- **EXPERIENTIAL:** These are skills and insights people have gained in work and life.

HOW TO USE THIS TOOL

1. First, go to COMMUNITY DESCRIPTION and describe the community you're analyzing.
2. Next, go to the CAPITALS header. Start with SOCIAL. Under the ANALYSIS header note down the CURRENT SITUATION, the STRENGHTS, and WEAKNESSES.
3. Repeat step 2 for each of the CAPITALS.
4. To conclude, go to NOW WHAT? and note down a few priority next steps based on what you've learned and/or new insights you've gained from using this tool.

CHANGEMAKER COACH | TOOL TIPS

- I designed this tool because too often people assume that a lack of financial capital is the problem and/or more financial capital is the solution. This is myopic.
- Social capital is first in this list because it's critically important for changemaking. Whenever possible, try to leverage existing social capital.
- This tool is particularly helpful for putting asset CT6 OPTIMIZE COMMUNITY ABILITIES + ASSETS (p. 36) into action.
- Use this with T5.3 EMPOWERMENT MAP (p. 196)

CHANGEMAKING INNOVATION MINI-CASES		CHANGEMAKING TRIMTABS	
V10	p. 359	CT1	p. 26
V37	p. 365	CT2	p. 28
V43	p. 366	CT6	p. 36

COMMUNITY DESCRIPTION	

	ANALYSIS		
CAPITALS	**CURRENT SITUATION**	**STRENGTHS**	**WEAKNESSES**
SOCIAL			
FINANCIAL			
HUMAN			
PHYSICAL			
KNOWLEDGE			
CULTURAL			
EXPERIENTIAL			

NOW WHAT?	

☐ **T6.5**

TOOLS FOR DISCOVERY + DIAGNOSIS CONVERSATIONS | SYSTEM(S) MAPPING

toolkit 06

SYSTEM STATUS MAP

How might we identify and analyze what's in a relatively stable, complicated, complex or chaotic status?

tinyurl.com/cctboxt65

ABOUT THIS TOOL

Your strategy for achieving goals should be driven by the status of the environment. For example, if your goal is to help people get vaccines, you should use one kind of strategy at the height of a pandemic and a different kind post-pandemic. Different status, different strategy. This SYSTEM STATUS MAP tool will help you and your team analyze if and how the strategy for achieving GOALS is in alignment with the status of the environment.

This tool is inspired by the work of Dave Snowden and his firm, The Cynefin Company, a leader in applying insights from Complex Adaptive Systems theory to management strategy. As a part of this work, Snowden and his team designed a framework to help people understand the STATUS of systems. This framework categorizes systems into the following four DOMAINS. With modifications, these DOMAINS are as follows:

- **STABLE:** The relationship between cause and effect is clear. If you do X, the result will be Y. Best practices exist.
- **COMPLICATED:** Within this DOMAIN you assess the facts, analyze, and apply the appropriate good practices. Expertise drives success. This is where engineers, surgeons, and lawyers work, for example.
- **COMPLEX:** Cause and effect can only be deduced in retrospect. There are no right answers, only better judgment calls. The only way to learn what works is through continuous ideation, testing, and reflection. This is where innovation is required.
- **CHAOTIC:** Cause and effect are unclear. The best response is to "stop the bleeding." Time is of the essence and knowledge is limited. Innovation is often required here as well.

HOW TO USE THIS TOOL

1. Start at the top of the tool and note down the SYSTEM DESCRIPTION. Think of the term system broadly. A system could be a national health care system, a supply chain, a community, an organization, a school, or a team, to name a few kinds of systems.
2. Next, go to the GOALS header. Below this, there are spaces for five GOALS. These are things that people are trying to achieve in the system. Note down one goal at the top and circle its PRIORITY. "1" means it's not important, and "5" means achieving it's critically important.
3. Now go to the STATUS ANALYSIS header and note down the CURRENT SITUATION DESCRIPTION for this goal. What's going on? How's the environment? Based on this, circle the DOMAIN. Is the current situation STABLE, COMPLICATED, COMPLEX, or CHAOTIC? To the right of this, note down the reason you circled the DOMAIN under DOMAIN RATIONALE.
4. As a last step for this goal, note down ACTION IDEAS. Given your STATUS ANALYSIS, should changes be made that will make it easier to achieve the goal? What might they be?
5. Repeat this process for additional GOALS.
6. To conclude, go to NOW WHAT? and note down a few priority next steps based on what you've learned and/or new insights you've gained from using this tool.

CHANGEMAKER COACH | TOOL TIP

I can't overstate the importance of having conversations about which domain you're currently operating in. It informs your expectations, your strategy, and how you measure success.

CHANGEMAKING INNOVATION MINI-CASES	
V12	p. 360
V43	p. 366
V64	p. 370

CHANGEMAKING TRIMTABS	
CT2	p. 28
CT14	p. 52
CT16	p. 56

SYSTEM DESCRIPTION	

	STATUS ANALYSIS			
GOALS	**CURRENT SITUATION DESCRIPTION**	**DOMAIN**	**DOMAIN RATIONALE**	**ACTION IDEAS**
		STABLE		
		COMPLICATED		
PRIORITY		COMPLEX		
1 2 3 4 5		CHAOTIC		
		STABLE		
		COMPLICATED		
PRIORITY		COMPLEX		
1 2 3 4 5		CHAOTIC		
		STABLE		
		COMPLICATED		
PRIORITY		COMPLEX		
1 2 3 4 5		CHAOTIC		
		STABLE		
		COMPLICATED		
PRIORITY		COMPLEX		
1 2 3 4 5		CHAOTIC		
		STABLE		
		COMPLICATED		
PRIORITY		COMPLEX		
1 2 3 4 5		CHAOTIC		

NOW WHAT?	

☐ **T6.6**

TOOLS FOR DISCOVERY + DIAGNOSIS CONVERSATIONS | SYSTEM(S) MAPPING

SYSTEM FIVE R'S MAP

How might we gain an understanding of of how resources, roles, relationships, and rules impact results?

tinyurl.com/cctboxt66

ABOUT THIS TOOL

Where are there strengths within the system? Where are there inadequacies? Which factors are contributing to positive results and which ones are causing negative ones? Where should you and your team intervene in the system with your changemaking innovation? This SYSTEM 5 R'S MAP tool should help you and your team have conversations about and answer these questions, amongst others.

This tool helps you understand and contemplate changes to systems by analyzing the following factors:

- **RESULTS:** What has the system been designed to achieve? What should it be achieving? You'll want to look at the DESIRED RESULTS, the ACTUAL POSITIVE RESULTS, and the ACTUAL NEGATIVE RESULTS.
- **RESOURCES:** What are the current RESOURCES being used to produce the DESIRED RESULTS? Are they sufficient? Are they the right ones? Are they increasing or decreasing? Are they reliable? Why and/or why not?
- **RELATIONSHIPS:** These are the interactions and connections in the system that might or might not be contributing to the DESIRED RESULTS. This includes formal and informal RELATIONSHIPS. How strong are they? Are they supportive? Are they conflictive? Are there missing RELATIONSHIPS. Why and/or why not?
- **ROLES:** These are both formal and informal. What ROLES are people currently performing that are or aren't contributing to the DESIRED RESULTS? What are the power dynamics? Are people in the right ROLES? Are there people who should have ROLES, but don't? Why and/or why not?
- **RULES:** This includes laws, policies, guidelines, norms, protocols, traditions, etc. What are they? Are the right RULES in place? Who establishes them? Does the system need more, fewer, or better ones? Why and/or why not?

HOW TO USE THIS TOOL

1. Start at the top of the tool and note down the SYSTEM DESCRIPTION. Think of the term system broadly. A system could be a national health care system, a supply chain, a community, an organization, a school, or a team, to name a few kinds of systems.
2. Next, go to RESULTS. Note down the DESIRED RESULTS, ACTUAL POSITIVE RESULTS, and ACTUAL NEGATIVE RESULTS.
3. Now go to the FACTORS INFLUENCING RESULTS header. Start with RESOURCES. Describe the CURRENT SITUATION. Then, under CONTRIBUTING FACTORS, note down how the RESOURCES CURRENT SITUATION might be contributing TO POSITIVE RESULTS and/or TO NEGATIVE RESULTS.
4. Zoom out for a moment and then jot down your thoughts about why this might be the case under ANALYSIS. Then, based on this, note down your IDEAS FOR CHANGES with regards to RESOURCES.
5. Repeat steps 3 and 4 for RELATIONSHIPS, ROLES, and RULES.
6. Finally, go to NOW WHAT? and note down a few priority next steps based on what you've learned and/ or new insights you've gained from using this tool.

CHANGEMAKER COACH | TOOL TIPS

- You might want to layer a T4.4 SWOT ANALYSIS (p. 180) on top of this tool to analyze each of the R's.
- Remember that these are complex adaptive systems. Don't get stuck looking at each of the R's in isolation. Zoom out and consider how one factor affects the others.

CHANGEMAKING INNOVATION MINI-CASES	
V28	p. 363
V32	p. 364
V37	p. 365

CHANGEMAKING TRIMTABS	
CT2	p. 28
CT19	p. 62
CT20	p. 64

SYSTEM DESCRIPTION					

RESULTS					
	DESIRED RESULTS				
	ACTUAL POSITIVE RESULTS				
	ACTUAL NEGATIVE RESULTS				

		CONTRIBUTING FACTORS			
FACTORS INFLUENCING RESULTS	**CURRENT SITUATION**	**TO POSITIVE RESULTS**	**TO NEGATIVE RESULTS**	**ANALYSIS**	**IDEAS FOR CHANGES**
RESOURCES					
RELATIONSHIPS					
ROLES					
RULES					

NOW WHAT?	

T6.7

TOOLS FOR DISCOVERY + DIAGNOSIS CONVERSATIONS | SYSTEM(S) MAPPING

SYSTEM COMPONENTS MAP

How might we analyze five critical components of the system ranging from policies to mindsets?

tinyurl.com/cctboxt67

ABOUT THIS TOOL

This tool is inspired by "The Water of Systems Change" by John Kania, Mark Kramer, and Peter Senge of FSG. This SYSTEM COMPONENTS MAP tool is designed to help you and your team analyze how the six different components of a system are and/ or aren't contributing to success, and to identify where to potentially prioritize interventions/ changes.

From top to bottom, explicit to implicit, simple to complex, the components included in this tool are as follows:

- **RESOURCES:** These are resources such as money, facilities, tools, people, knowledge, and information. What exists in the system? How are resources distributed and allocated?
- **POLICIES + RULES:** These are the government, institutional, and/or organizational policies, rules, and regulations that guide actions.
- **HABITS, PRACTICES + PROGRAMS:** This is what people do in planned and unplanned ways.
- **RELATIONSHIPS:** This is how people interact, communicate, live, and work within the system.
- **POWER DYNAMICS:** This is the distribution of decision-making power and authority, both formally and informally, between people/ organizations in the system.
- **MINDSETS/ PERSPECTIVES:** These are the deeply held beliefs, assumptions, and taken-for-granted ways of thinking that influence people's decisions and actions.

CHANGEMAKING INNOVATION MINI-CASES	
V37	p. 365
V71	p. 372
V82	p. 374

CHANGEMAKING TRIMTABS	
CT1	p. 26
CT12	p. 48
CT15	p. 54

HOW TO USE THIS TOOL

1. Start at the top of the tool and note down the SYSTEM DESCRIPTION. Think of the term system broadly. A system could be a national health care system, a supply chain, a community, an organization, a school, or a team, to name a few kinds of systems.
2. Next, go to the COMPONENTS OF THE SYSTEM header. Start with RESOURCES. Under ANALYSIS, describe the CURRENT SITUATION. Then note down the IDEAL SITUATION. What might the RESOURCES situation be in an ideal scenario?
3. Stay with RESOURCES, and note down your IDEAS FOR HOW TO GET FROM THE CURRENT SITUATION TO IDEAL SITUATION.
4. Repeat steps 2 and 3 for the remaining COMPONENTS OF THE SYSTEM.
5. Now zoom out. Go to the CURRENT PRIORITY header. Circle a number for each of the COMPONENTS OF THE SYSTEM. "1" means that addressing this component is a top priority, and "5" means it's a low priority.
6. To conclude, go to NOW WHAT? and note down a few priority next steps based on what you've learned and/or new insights you've gained from using this tool.

CHANGEMAKER COACH | TOOL TIPS

- This is my favorite tool for analyzing systems and trying to understand why things work and why they don't. In particular, it helps me to think of the first three components as "supply" and the last three as "demand." Typically, the easiest and quickest place to intervene is with supply. We provide new resources, create new programs, etc. However, when we do this without demand, we fail. This is one reason why programs don't sustain. Conversely, demand without supply leads to frustration, anger, etc. Your goal should be to find an equilibrium between supply and demand.
- This should help you consider mindsets so that you might put CT1 CHANGE THE NARRATIVE (p. 26) into practice.
- You might want to analyze each component through a T4.4 SWOT ANALYSIS (p. 180)

SYSTEM DESCRIPTION	

	ANALYSIS			
COMPONENTS OF OF THE SYSTEM	CURRENT SITUATION	IDEAL SITUATION	IDEAS FOR HOW TO GET FROM CURRENT TO IDEAL SITUATION	CURRENT PRIORITY
RESOURCES				1 2 3 4 5
POLICIES + RULES				1 2 3 4 5
HABITS, PRACTICES + PROGRAMS				1 2 3 4 5
RELATIONSHIPS				1 2 3 4 5
POWER DYNAMICS				1 2 3 4 5
MINDSETS/ PERSPECTIVES				1 2 3 4 5

NOW WHAT?	

T6.8

TOOLS FOR DISCOVERY + DIAGNOSIS CONVERSATIONS | SYSTEM(S) MAPPING

STAKEHOLDER POWER MAP

How might we analyze how different types of power are, could be, and should be distributed within the system?

tinyurl.com/cctboxt68

ABOUT THIS TOOL

A stakeholder is a person or entity that has an interest, concern, and/or involvement in the system you're analyzing. To understand how a system works, you need to know which stakeholders hold power and the forms of power they hold. It's also important to consider the form(s) of power stakeholders could potentially hold and/or leverage in the future. This STAKEHOLDER POWER MAP tool should help you and your team do this.

This tool includes the following eight forms of stakeholder power:

- **CHARISMATIC:** This is the ability to charm and persuade people with the power of personality.
- **COERCIVE:** This is a stakeholder's power to punish others for noncompliance.
- **EXPERT:** This is based on a stakeholder's levels of skill and knowledge.
- **INFORMATIONAL:** This results from a stakeholder's power to control the information that others might need.
- **LEGITIMATE:** A stakeholder has the formal power to make demands and to expect others to be compliant.
- **MORAL:** This is the degree to which a stakeholder, by virtue of their perceived moral stature, is able to persuade others to adopt a particular belief and/or take a particular course of action
- **REFERENT:** This is the result of a stakeholder's perceived attractiveness, worthiness, and right to others' respect.
- **REWARD:** This is a stakeholder's power to compensate another for compliance.

HOW TO USE THIS TOOL

1. Start at the top of the tool and note down the SYSTEM DESCRIPTION. Think of the term system broadly. A system could be a national health care system, a supply chain, a community, an organization, a school, or a team, to name a few kinds of systems.
2. Next, go to the FORMS OF POWER header. Start with CHARISMATIC. Under POWER ANALYSIS, note down who HAS THIS POWER + USES IT, HAS THIS POWER, BUT IT ISN'T RECOGNIZED, and DOESN'T HAVE THIS POWER, BUT SHOULD.
3. Repeat step 2 for each of the FORMS OF POWER.
4. To conclude, go to NOW WHAT? and note down a few priority next steps based on what you've learned and/or new insights you've gained from using this tool.

CHANGEMAKER COACH | TOOL TIPS

- Use this tool with T6.7 SYSTEM COMPONENTS MAP (p. 222) to analyze the types of power that people hold.
- This is a good tool to use with T1.1 OUR TEAM (p. 110) and T2.4 STAKEHOLDER POWER ENGAGEMENT CHECK-IN (p. 132).

CHANGEMAKING INNOVATION MINI-CASES	
V60	p. 369
V69	p. 371
V77	p. 373

CHANGEMAKING TRIMTABS	
CT1	p. 26
CT2	p. 28
CT4	p. 32

SYSTEM DESCRIPTION			
	POWER ANALYSIS		
FORMS OF POWER	**HAS THIS POWER + USES IT**	**HAS THIS POWER, BUT IT ISN'T RECOGNIZED**	**DOESN'T HAVE THIS POWER, BUT SHOULD**
CHARISMATIC			
COERCIVE			
EXPERT			
INFORMATIONAL			
LEGITIMATE			
MORAL			
REFERENT			
REWARD			

NOW WHAT?	

T6.9

TOOLS FOR DISCOVERY + DIAGNOSIS CONVERSATIONS | SYSTEM(S) MAPPING

FIVE FORCES MAP

How might we analyze five critical forces that influence our work within the system?

tinyurl.com/cctboxt69

ABOUT THIS TOOL

This tool is inspired by the "Five Forces" framework created by Harvard Business School professor Michael E. Porter. Since Porter first shared this framework over 40 years ago, it's become a standard way for businesses to analyze the competitive environment in industries. With slight modifications, it can also be a helpful way to analyze the forces in systems. This includes organization and community systems. This FIVE FORCES MAP tool should help you and your team analyze the forces impacting your system. .

The five forces included in this tool are as follows:

- **COMPETITION/ EXISTENCE OF SOLUTIONS PROVIDERS:** For example, are there currently organizations offering solutions to solve a problem that you've diagnosed? If so, how many are there? How strong and/or weak are they?
- **POTENTIAL OF NEW ENTRANTS:** For example, how easy or difficult is it for organizations to enter with new solutions? What are the barriers to entry? How high or low are they?
- **POWER OF SUPPLIERS/ PROVIDERS:** For example, how powerful are the organizations offering solutions? As well, how powerful are organizations supplying the inputs that are necessary for solutions? Why does this power exist?
- **POWER OF CONSUMERS/ USERS:** For example, how many consumers/ users are there? How much power do they have to choose between solutions? How much power do they have to influence prices?
- **THREAT OF SUBSTITUTES:** For example, are there substitutes? Do different products/ services or ways of doing things exist that solve the problem? What are they? What are their strengths and weaknesses?

HOW TO USE THIS TOOL

1. Start at the top of the tool and note down the SYSTEM DESCRIPTION. Think of the term system broadly. A system could be a national health care system, a supply chain, a community, an organization, a school, or a team, to name a few kinds of systems.
2. Next, note down the FOCUS AREA for this analysis. For example, this might be education services, banking, vision care, housing, healthcare services, ecotourism, cook stoves, etc.
3. Now go to the FIVE FORCES header. Start with COMPETITION/ EXISTENCE OF SOLUTIONS PROVIDERS. Under ANALYSIS, note down the CURRENT SITUATION and IMPACT ON THE SYSTEM.
4. Repeat step 3 for each of the FIVE FORCES.
5. To conclude, go to NOW WHAT? and note down a few priority next steps based on what you've learned and/or new insights you've gained from using this tool.

CHANGEMAKER COACH | TOOL TIPS

- This is helpful for analyzing how "receptive" a system/ community might be to new changemaking innovations.
- This works well with T6.3 EQUITABLE ACCESS MAP (p. 214) and T6.2 CURRENT SOLUTIONS LANDSCAPE MAP (p. 212).

CHANGEMAKING INNOVATION MINI-CASES		CHANGEMAKING TRIMTABS	
V30	p. 363	CT8	p. 40
V66	p. 371	CT13	p. 50
V81	p. 374	CT14	p. 52

SYSTEM DESCRIPTION	
FOCUS AREA	

	ANALYSIS	
FIVE FORCES	CURRENT SITUATION	IMPACT ON THE SYSTEM
COMPETITION/ EXISTENCE OF SOLUTIONS PROVIDERS		
POTENTIAL OF NEW ENTRANTS		
POWER OF SUPPLIERS/ PROVIDERS		
POWER OF CONSUMERS/ USERS		
THREAT OF/ OPPORTUNITY FOR NEW SOLUTIONS		

NOW WHAT?	

T6.10

TOOLS FOR DISCOVERY + DIAGNOSIS CONVERSATIONS | SYSTEM(S) MAPPING

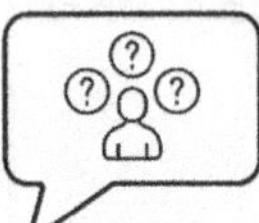

VUCA MAP

How might we analyze and account for volatility, uncertainty, complexity, and ambiguity within the system?

tinyurl.com/cctboxt610

ABOUT THIS TOOL

With the accelerating pace of change, we're increasingly surrounded by and working in VUCA (Volatility, Uncertainty, Complexity, and Ambiguity). VUCA can create unease and stress. It makes us reactive. It can be debilitating and negatively impact well-being. Given this, it's critical to identify where it exists, why it exists, who it's impacting, and how it's impacting the system. This VUCA MAP tool should help you and your team do this. It should also help you have conversations about mitigation and adaptation ideas.

Described in greater detail, the four components of VUCA are as follows:

- **(V)OLATILITY:** This is frequent, rapid, and significant change.
- **(U)NCERTAINTY:** Events and outcomes are unpredictable.
- **(C)OMPLEXITY:** Relationships are interrelated and difficult to understand. A change in one thing may cause an unintended change in another.
- **(A)MBIGUITY:** This is a lack of clarity and difficulty understanding exactly what's happening.

CHANGEMAKER COACH | TOOL TIPS

- You should find this helpful for analyzing any system, community, organization, team, etc. It should help you "turn over some stones" and discover some thoughts/ feelings that you didn't know were there.
- This might help you put CT19 BUILD A PRIORITIZATION ECOSYSTEM (p. 62) into practice.
- You might want to use this tool with T1.4 OUR COLLABORATIVE CULTURE (p. 116), T2.8 THREATS + REWARDS CHECK-IN (p. 140), T5.4 WELL-BEING MAP (p. 198), and T5.6 DECISION MAKING BIASES MAP (p. 202).

HOW TO USE THIS TOOL

1. Start at the top of the tool and note down the SYSTEM DESCRIPTION. Think of the term system broadly. A system could be a national health care system, a supply chain, a community, an organization, a school, or a team, to name a few kinds of systems.
2. Next, go to the VUCA FACTORS header. Start with (V)OLATILITY. Under ANALYSIS, note down WHERE WE SEE THIS, WHY THIS EXISTS, WHO THIS IMPACTS, and THE IMPACT.
3. Repeat step 2 for each of the VUCA FACTORS.
4. Now zoom out and discuss your ANALYSIS. Then note down IDEAS FOR MITIGATION AND/OR ADAPTATION for each of the VUCA FACTORS.
5. To conclude, go to NOW WHAT? and note down a few priority next steps based on what you've learned and/or new insights you've gained from using this tool.

CHANGEMAKING INNOVATION MINI-CASES		CHANGEMAKING TRIMTABS	
V43	p. 367	CT3	p. 30
V61	p. 367	CT9	p. 42
V68	p. 367	CT19	p. 62

SYSTEM DESCRIPTION	

	ANALYSIS				
VUCA FACTORS	WHERE WE SEE THIS	WHY THIS EXISTS	WHO THIS IMPACTS	THE IMPACT	IDEAS FOR MITIGATION AND/OR ADAPTATION
(V)OLATILITY					
(U)NCERTAINTY					
(C)OMPLEXITY					
(A)MBIGUITY					

NOW WHAT?	

TOOLS FOR DISCOVERY + DIAGNOSIS CONVERSATIONS | SYSTEM(S) MAPPING

TOOLKIT TOOLS REFLECTIONS

SCALE:
STRONGLY AGREE = 5, AGREE = 4, NOT SURE = 3, DISAGREE = 2, STRONGLY DISAGREE = 1

tinyurl.com/cclboxtoolsrflect

	CHANGEMAKING TOOLS									
REFLECTION STATEMENTS	T6.1	T6.2	T6.3	T6.4	T6.5	T6.6	T6.7	T6.8	T6.9	T6.10
This tool is easy to understand.										
This tool is easy to use.										
This tool taught me/ us important new knowledge.										
This tool empowered new changemaking conversations.										
This tool helped to spark new ideas/ insights.										
This tool should be included in my/ our toolbox for the future.										
I/ we should share this tool with other changemakers.										

NOTES:

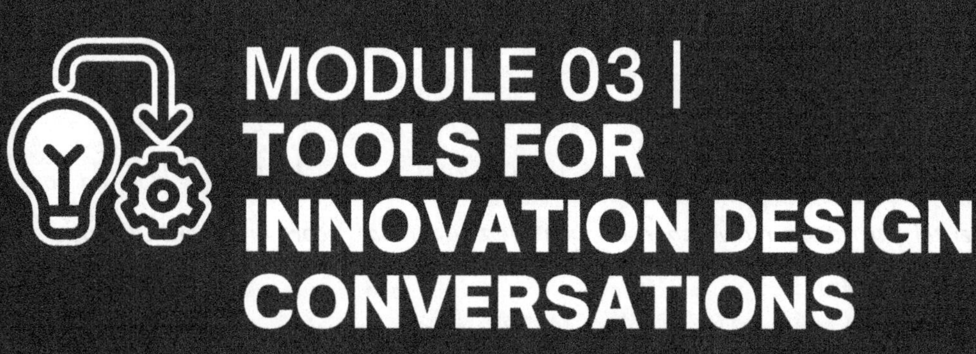

MODULE 03 | TOOLS FOR INNOVATION DESIGN CONVERSATIONS

NOTES:

GVK notes -

- Your goal is to create/ offer well-informed and dignified OPPORTUNITIES. Whether or not people decide to take advantage of opportunities is up to them.
- Avoid these two extremes -
    - HOBSON'S CHOICE: Only one thing is offered.
    - CHOICE OVERLOAD: Too many things are offered and it feels paralyzing.
- Try to design a "CURB CUT." This is when you design for the most vulnerable/ disadvantaged and it ends up benefitting everyone else. This originates from how sidewalk curb ramps were designed for people in wheelchairs. They ended up helping people with strollers, bikers, etc.

NOTES:

GVK notes -

- People need to feel a real sense of ownership for solutions. Think about it. How do you treat a rental car vs. your own car? Do you treat your bathroom differently than a gas station bathroom?
- We have KPIs for business. These are Key Performance Indicators. Wouldn't it be great if alongside them we also had CPIs: Community Performance Indicators?

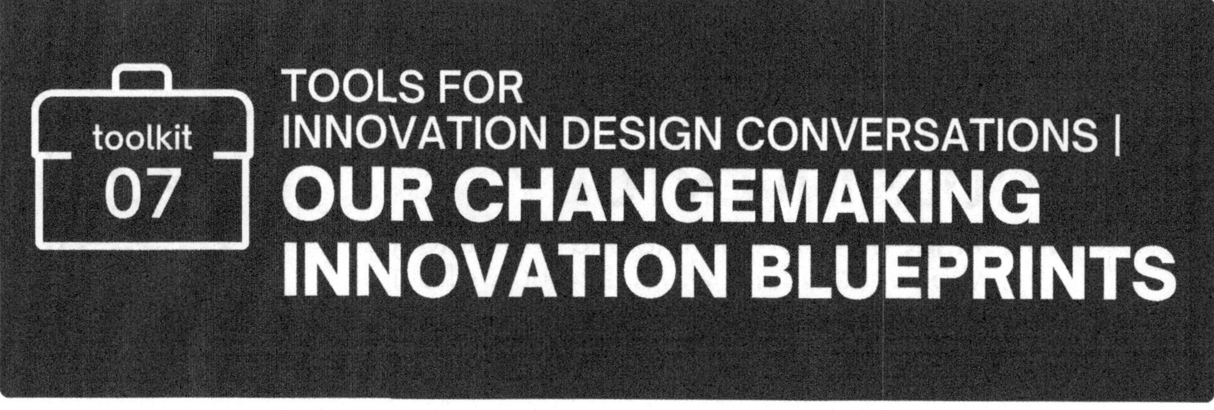

TOOLS FOR INNOVATION DESIGN CONVERSATIONS | OUR CHANGEMAKING INNOVATION BLUEPRINTS

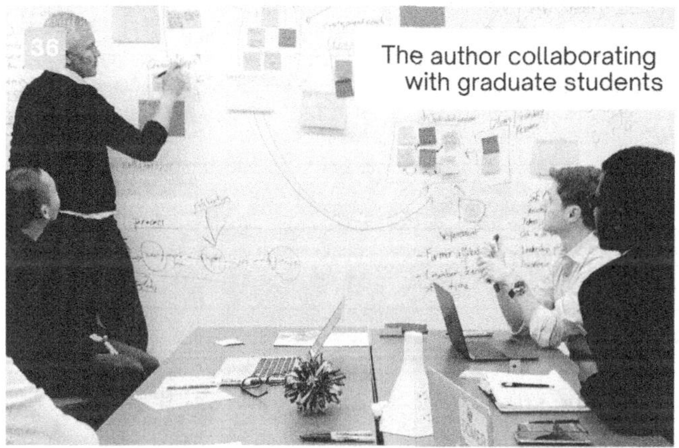

The author collaborating with graduate students

Lydia A. collaborating with teammates in Mexico

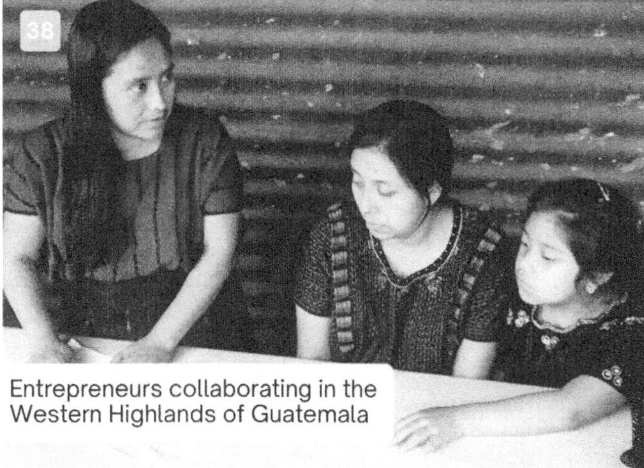

Entrepreneurs collaborating in the Western Highlands of Guatemala

Esperanza G. collaborating with changemaker educators in Nebaj, Guatemala

NOTES:

GVK note -

- *Go to HOW TO CRAFT A CONSTRUCTIVE OUTCOMES STATEMENT (pg. 379)*

TOOLS FOR INNOVATION DESIGN CONVERSATIONS | OUR CHANGEMAKING INNOVATION BLUEPRINTS

TOOLS INVENTORY

How might we clearly define and articulate the why, who, what, where, when, and how of our changemaking innovation?

tinyurl.com/cctboxtools01

☐	T7.1 LOGIC MODEL BLUEPRINT	p. 238

How might we describe the desired outcomes of our innovation and the model we've designed to achieve them?

☐	T7.2 DRIVER DIAGRAM BLUEPRINT	p. 240

How might we articulate the key drivers of our innovation design?

☐	T7.3 SUCCESS INDICATORS BLUEPRINT	p. 242

How might we design the most optimal ways to measure the success of our innovation over the short, medium and long term?

☐	T7.4 VALUE PROPOSITION BLUEPRINT	p. 244

How might we show how our innovation is delivering value?

☐	T7.5 NOVEL FEATURES + BENEFITS BLUEPRINT	p. 246

How might we specify the features that make our innovation uniquely beneficial?

☐	T7.6 INNOVATION DISTILLATION BLUEPRINT	p. 248

How might we distill the elements that make our innovation tick?

NOTES:

GVK notes -

- We value things very differently based on how they're offered to us. Offer me a "NY Yankees" T-shirt for free and I'll probably decline. Shoot it to me out of an air gun at a game and I'll dive over people to catch it.
- Measure (success indicators) what matters. And it matters when you measure it.

TOOLS FOR INNOVATION DESIGN CONVERSATIONS | OUR CHANGEMAKING INNOVATION BLUEPRINTS

TOOLKIT SCORECARD + PRIORITIZATION HELP

Score yourselves to help you decide which tool(s) you might want to prioritize for your changemaking conversations.

tinyurl.com/cctboxtoolsprior

SELF-CHECK STATEMENTS	HOW ARE WE DOING?	TOOL SUGGESTIONS
We can articulate our desired outcome(s), what the pathway is to get there, and how we'll measure success along the way.	0 1 2 3 4 5	T7.1
We feel confident we know and can share the key drivers of our innovation.	0 1 2 3 4 5	T7.2
We've discussed how we'll measure success and have chosen indicators that we believe are the most informative, inspirational, and practical.	0 1 2 3 4 5	T7.3
We've discussed and are confident about the value proposition of our changemaking innovation.	0 1 2 3 4 5	T7.4
We've had conversations about and have narrowed down the features and benefits that make our changemaking innovation unique.	0 1 2 3 4 5	T7.5
We've distilled and can share the most catalytic elements of our changemaking innovation.	0 1 2 3 4 5	T7.6

toolkit 07

TOOLS FOR INNOVATION DESIGN CONVERSATIONS |
OUR CHANGEMAKING INNOVATION BLUEPRINTS

COLLABORATIVE CHANGEMAKING VOICES

Get into the mindset for this toolkit + include your voice in the conversation.

"An innovation, to be effective, has to be simple and it has to be focused. It should do only one thing, otherwise, it confuses. If it is not simple, it won't work. Everything new runs into trouble; if complicated, it cannot be repaired or fixed. All effective innovations are breathtakingly simple. Indeed, the greatest praise an innovation can receive is for people to say: 'This is obvious. Why didn't I think of it?' Even the innovation that creates new uses and new markets should be directed toward a specific, clear, designed application. It should be focused on a specific need that it satisfies, on a specific end result that it produces."

PETER F. DRUCKER
MANAGEMENT CONSULTANT | EDUCATOR |
AUTHOR - *INNOVATION + ENTREPRENEURSHIP*

"Real change, enduring change, happens one step at a time."

RUTH BADER GINSBURG
SUPREME COURT JUSTICE

"Excellence is to do a common thing in an uncommon way. "

BOOKER T. WASHINGTON
EDUCATOR

"Most people overestimate what they can do in one year and underestimate what they can do in 10 years."

BILL GATES
CO-FOUNDER - MICROSOFT & BILL + MELINDA GATES FOUNDATION

"Build something 100 people love, not something 1 million people kind of like."

BRIAN CHESKY
CO-FOUNDER + CEO - AIRBNB

"The simpler you say it, the more eloquent it is."

AUGUST WILSON
PLAYWRIGHT

"People don't want to buy a quarter-inch drill. They want a quarter-inch hole."

THEODORE LEVITT
ECONOMIST

"Social entrepreneurs are not content just to give a fish or teach how to fish. They will not rest until they have revolutionized the fishing industry."

BILL DRAYTON
CEO - ASHOKA

T7.1

TOOLS FOR INNOVATION DESIGN CONVERSATIONS | OUR CHANGEMAKING INNOVATION BLUEPRINTS

toolkit 07

LOGIC MODEL BLUEPRINT

How might we describe the desired outcomes of our innovation and the model we've designed to achieve them?

tinyurl.com/cctboxt71

ABOUT THIS TOOL

Often referred to as a "theory of change," a logic model framework is an indispensable tool for changemakers. Although it may require some practice and deeper dive learning, building a logic model framework is well worth the time investment. This LOGIC MODEL BLUEPRINT tool will help you and your team do this for your changemaking innovation.

The components of this LOGIC MODEL BLUEPRINT are as follows:

- **COMMUNITY DESCRIPTION:** This is a summary description of the people whom you aspire to support with your changemaking innovation.
- **COMMUNITY SIZE:** This is the number of community members.
- **DESIRED OUTCOMES:** These are the benefits/ positive changes for community members during and/or after participating in changemaking innovation ACTIVITIES. These may be positive changes in behaviors, skills, knowledge, attitudes, values, conditions, etc.
- **SUCCESS INDICATORS:** These tell you if you're achieving your DESIRED OUTCOMES. These are typically numbers or percentages of the COMMUNITY SIZE.
- **MEASUREMENT TECHNIQUES:** These are how you collect information to understand your SUCCESS INDICATORS. This may include observation, surveys, tests, financial tracking, questionnaires, and the like.
- **INPUTS:** These are the resources required to implement the ACTIVITIES of the changemaking innovation.
- **ACTIVITIES:** These are what the innovation does with the INPUTS to produce the OUTPUTS that make the DESIRED OUTCOME possible.
- **OUTPUTS:** The INPUTS plus the ACTIVITIES create the OUTPUTS. These are usually measured in terms of the volume of work accomplished. Examples may be the number of classes taught, counseling sessions conducted, and educational materials distributed.

HOW TO USE THIS TOOL

1. Start at the top by filling out the COMMUNITY DESCRIPTION and COMMUNITY SIZE in as much detail as possible. Knowing the COMMUNITY SIZE is of particular importance for your SUCCESS INDICATORS, as you may define these by using a percentage.
2. Next, go to the COMPONENTS header and start with DATES. Under the TIME FRAME header to the right, note down how you'll define SHORT TERM, MEDIUM TERM, and LONG TERM. These could be specific DATES or expressed in months or years from now. Do this in whatever way is the easiest to understand/ follow.
3. Now, note down your DESIRED OUTCOME for each TIME FRAME. It's often helpful to use phrases such as "will have." For example, "X community will have become more economically stable." or "will have gained access to healthcare solutions."
4. After this, consider how you'll know if the DESIRED OUTCOME has been achieved. Go to SUCCESS INDICATORS and note down a quantifiable measurement. For example, "85% of the community" might be a way to express this. Make this achievable and ambitious. Note down your MEASUREMENT TECHNIQUE.
5. Next, note down the INPUTS, ACTIVITIES, and OUTPUTS for each TIME FRAME. Be specific.
6. To conclude, go to NOW WHAT? and note down a few priority next steps based on what you've learned and/or new insights you've gained from using this tool.

CHANGEMAKING INNOVATION MINI-CASES	
V2	p. 358
V15	p. 360
V18	p. 361

CHANGEMAKING TRIMTABS	
CT2	p. 28
CT4	p. 32
CT21	p. 66

COMMUNITY DESCRIPTION	
COMMUNITY SIZE	

	TIME FRAME		
COMPONENTS	**SHORT TERM**	**MEDIUM TERM**	**LONG TERM**
DATES			
DESIRED OUTCOME			
SUCCESS INDICATORS			
MEASUREMENT TECHNIQUE			
INPUTS			
ACTIVITIES			
OUTPUTS			

NOW WHAT?	

T7.2

TOOLS FOR INNOVATION DESIGN CONVERSATIONS | OUR CHANGEMAKING INNOVATION BLUEPRINTS

DRIVER DIAGRAM BLUEPRINT

How might we articulate the key drivers of our innovation design?

tinyurl.com/cctboxt72

ABOUT THIS TOOL

Creating a Driver Diagram helps you ensure that the relationships between activities and goals are aligned. It forces you to consider what's most important to achieve success within a specified time frame. This DRIVER DIAGRAM BLUEPRINT tool should help you and your team do this.

The key components of this tool are as follows:

- **AIM STATEMENT:** This is a clear, explicit statement of THE GOAL within a specific TIME FRAME. This also includes your SUCCESS INDICATOR, a statement about how you'll know if you've achieved THE GOAL.
- **PRIMARY DRIVERS:** These are sometimes referred to as "key drivers" and are components or factors that contribute directly to achieving the AIM STATEMENT.
- **SECONDARY DRIVERS:** These are actions, interventions, or lower-level components or factors necessary to achieve the PRIMARY DRIVERS.

CHANGEMAKER COACH | TOOL TIPS

- Use this to put CT21 DEFINE + SHARE THE BHAG (p. 66) into action.
- This tool is a somewhat abridged version of T7.1 LOGIC MODEL BLUEPRINT (p. 238).
- This is similar to T7.6 INNOVATION DISTILLATION BLUEPRINT (p. 248) in that both tools help you focus on defining the keys to success for your changemaking innovation.

HOW TO USE THIS TOOL

1. Start with the components of your AIM STATEMENT. Start by noting down THE GOAL. This is the positive change you hope to achieve. Next, note down the TIME FRAME. This is the time by which you hope to achieve THE GOAL. Then note down one or more SUCCESS INDICATOR(S). This is how you'll know if you've achieved THE GOAL.
2. Next, start at the top and note down the PRIMARY DRIVERS. There's space for four in this tool, although your changemaking innovation may have fewer or more. This is simply a guide.
3. Now note down the SECONDARY DRIVERS for each of your PRIMARY DRIVERS. There's space for three SECONDARY DRIVERS for each of the PRIMARY DRIVERS.
4. To conclude, go to NOW WHAT? and note down a few priority next steps based on what you've learned and/or new insights you've gained from using this tool.

CHANGEMAKING INNOVATION MINI-CASES	
V47	p. 367
V59	p. 369
V82	p. 374

CHANGEMAKING TRIMTABS	
CT9	p. 42
CT17	p. 58
CT21	p. 66

PRIMARY DRIVERS	SECONDARY DRIVERS

AIM STATEMENT

THE GOAL

TIME FRAME

SUCCESS INDICATOR(S)

NOW WHAT?

T7.3

TOOLS FOR INNOVATION DESIGN CONVERSATIONS | OUR CHANGEMAKING INNOVATION BLUEPRINTS

SUCCESS INDICATORS BLUEPRINT

How might we design the most optimal ways to measure the success of our innovation over the short, medium and long term?

tinyurl.com/cctboxl73

ABOUT THIS TOOL

Changemaking is an accretive process. Positive change builds over time. Short term positive changes lead to medium term positive changes that lead to long term positive changes. This SUCCESS INDICATORS BLUEPRINT tool should help you and your team design indicators for your changemaking innovation that reflect and respect this process.

This tool includes the following prompts to help guide your conversations:

- **SHORT TERM CHANGES:**
These are LEARNINGS + INSIGHTS that might include positive changes in AWARENESS, KNOWLEDGE, SKILLS, ATTITUDES, OPINIONS, ASPIRATIONS, and/or MOTIVATIONS.

- **MEDIUM TERM CHANGES:**
These are changes in WAYS OF DOING THINGS that might include positive changes in BEHAVIORS, PRACTICES, POLICIES, SOCIAL ACTION, and/or DECISION MAKING.

- **LONG TERM CHANGES:**
These are changes in CONDITIONS that might include positive changes in FAMILY, SOCIAL, OCCUPATIONAL, PHYSICAL, PSYCHOLOGICAL, ECONOMICAL, EDUCATIONAL, and/or ENVIRONMENTAL conditions.

HOW TO USE THIS TOOL

1. Start at the top of the tool and note down the INNOVATION DESCRIPTION.
2. Next, go to the SUCCESS INDICATOR CATEGORIES header. Start with the SHORT TERM CHANGES: LEARNINGS AND INSIGHTS, and go to AWARENESS. Now, under the ANALYSIS + DESIGN header, circle the RELEVANCE that increasing/ changing AWARENESS is for the innovation. It's either "N/A" (not applicable), LOW, MEDIUM, or HIGH. Then note down the CURRENT SITUATION and the DESIRED CHANGE in as much detail as possible.
3. Now consider how you'll know when someone has moved from the CURRENT SITUATION to the DESIRED CHANGE. Note down your ideas under SUCCESS INDICATOR.
4. Repeat steps 2 and 3 for each of the SUCCESS INDICATOR CATEGORIES. To note, there's no need to continue the ANALYSIS + DESIGN for any of these where you circle "N/A" under RELEVANCE.
5. To conclude, go to NOW WHAT? and note down a few priority next steps based on what you've learned and/or new insights you've gained from using this tool.

CHANGEMAKER COACH | TOOL TIPS

- Use this to put CT22 SHOW IT (p. 68) into practice. Show positive changes as much as possible. Showing motivates and inspires.
- This should be helpful for deciding your success indicators for T7.1 LOGIC MODEL BLUEPRINT (p. 238)

CHANGEMAKING INNOVATION MINI-CASES	
V30	p. 363
V48	p. 367
V84	p. 374

CHANGEMAKING TRIMTABS	
CT3	p. 30
CT18	p. 60
CT22	p. 68

INNOVATION DESCRIPTION	

		ANALYSIS + DESIGN			
	SUCCESS INDICATOR CATEGORIES	RELEVANCE	CURRENT SITUATION	DESIRED CHANGE	SUCCESS INDICATOR
SHORT TERM CHANGES: LEARNINGS + INSIGHTS	AWARENESS	N/A LOW MEDIUM HIGH			
	KNOWLEDGE	N/A LOW MEDIUM HIGH			
	SKILLS	N/A LOW MEDIUM HIGH			
	ATTITUDES	N/A LOW MEDIUM HIGH			
	OPINIONS	N/A LOW MEDIUM HIGH			
	MOTIVATIONS	N/A LOW MEDIUM HIGH			
MED TERM CHANGES: WAYS OF DOING THINGS	BEHAVIORS	N/A LOW MEDIUM HIGH			
	POLICIES	N/A LOW MEDIUM HIGH			
	SOCIAL ACTION	N/A LOW MEDIUM HIGH			
	DECISION MAKING	N/A LOW MEDIUM HIGH			
LONG TERM CHANGES: CONDITIONS	FAMILY	N/A LOW MEDIUM HIGH			
	SOCIAL	N/A LOW MEDIUM HIGH			
	OCCUPATIONAL	N/A LOW MEDIUM HIGH			
	PHYSICAL	N/A LOW MEDIUM HIGH			
	PSYCHOLOGICAL	N/A LOW MEDIUM HIGH			
	ECONOMIC	N/A LOW MEDIUM HIGH			
	EDUCATIONAL	N/A LOW MEDIUM HIGH			
	ENVIRONMENTAL	N/A LOW MEDIUM HIGH			

NOW WHAT?	

T7.4

TOOLS FOR INNOVATION DESIGN CONVERSATIONS | OUR CHANGEMAKING INNOVATION BLUEPRINTS

VALUE PROPOSITION BLUEPRINT

How might we show how our innovation is delivering value?

tinyurl.com/cctboxt74

ABOUT THIS TOOL

According to Clayton Christensen, author of The Innovator's Dilemma, "When we buy a product, we essentially 'hire' something to get a job done. If it does the job well, when we're confronted with the same job, we hire that same product again. And if the product does a crummy job, we 'fire' it and look around for something else we might hire to solve the problem." We hire products (innovations) to do two jobs; to relieve pains and satisfy wants. How well your changemaking innovation does these jobs is its value proposition. This VALUE PROPOSITION BLUEPRINT tool should help you and your team summarize why people should want to hire your changemaking innovation.

This tool is inspired by the "Value Proposition Canvas" that Dr. Alexander Osterwalder first developed. It uses the Jobs-to-be-done method. This involves moving away from needs, to focusing on the work someone wants to accomplish, the "job." The core components included in this tool are as follows:

SITUATIONAL ANALYSIS: This is an overview of the situation before someone has the opportunity to access your changemaking innovation.
THE JOB(S): What is the person trying to achieve? Following are three factors to consider for jobs:

- **FUNCTIONAL FACTORS:** These are the specific goals that someone is trying to achieve. This can be viewed through effectiveness and efficiency.
- **EMOTIONAL FACTORS:** This is how people want to feel while executing THE JOB(S).
- **SOCIAL FACTORS:** This is how someone feels they will be perceived by others while executing the job.

ANALYSIS: How well are current solutions achieving the THE JOB(S)? Analyze the factors.

- **PAIN POINTS:** These are all things that stop people from completing THE JOB(S).
- **WANTS:** Often referred to as gains, these include the positive experiences and desires that people hope to achieve through THE JOB(S)

INNOVATION VALUE PROPOSITION: This is a summary of how your changemaking innovation helps someone to accomplish THE JOB(S) in a better way.

INNOVATION DESCRIPTION: Describe your changemaking innovation in as much detail as possible.
FEATURES: These are the traits/ attributes that deliver value and differentiate your changemaking innovation.

- **PAIN RELIEVERS:** Which FEATURES alleviate the PAIN POINTS? How do they?
- **SATISFIERS:** Which FEATURES satisfy the WANTS? How do they?

HOW TO USE THIS TOOL

1. Start at the top of the tool. Note down any and all characteristics of THE PERSON/ GROUP.
2. Next, go to the SITUATIONAL ANALYSIS. Note down the JOB(S) that the PERSON/ GROUP is trying to achieve. Specify the FUNCTIONAL FACTORS, EMOTIONAL FACTORS, and SOCIAL FACTORS of THE JOB(S). Then go to the ANALYSIS and note down the PAIN POINTS and WANTS.
3. Now move to the INNOVATION VALUE PROPOSITION. Note down the INNOVATION DESCRIPTION. Below this, note down the FEATURES. These include the PAIN RELIEVERS and SATISFIERS. Make sure that the PAIN RELIEVERS address the PAIN POINTS and the SATISFIERS address the WANTS.
4. To conclude, go to NOW WHAT? and note down a few priority next steps based on what you've learned and/or new insights you've gained from using this tool

CHANGEMAKING INNOVATION MINI-CASES	
V5	p. 358
V23	p. 366
V81	p. 367

CHANGEMAKING TRIMTABS	
CT13	p. 38
CT19	p. 40
CT22	p. 50

THE PERSON/ GROUP		

SITUATIONAL ANALYSIS

THE JOB(S)		
FUNCTIONAL FACTORS	**EMOTIONAL FACTORS**	**SOCIAL FACTORS**

ANALYSIS

PAIN POINTS	**WANTS**

INNOVATION VALUE PROPOSITION

INNOVATION DESCRIPTION	

FEATURES

PAIN RELIEVERS	**SATISFIERS**

NOW WHAT?	

T7.5

TOOLS FOR INNOVATION DESIGN CONVERSATIONS | OUR CHANGEMAKING INNOVATION BLUEPRINTS

NOVEL FEATURES + BENEFITS BLUEPRINT

How might we specify the features that make our innovation uniquely beneficial?

tinyurl.com/cctboxt75

ABOUT THIS TOOL

Features are facts about products/ services. Benefits explain how features alleviate the pains, and improve the lives of people using products/ services. People are intrigued by features. They buy benefits. The more novel your features and benefits are in comparison to other options, the more attracted people will be to your changemaking innovation. This NOVEL FEATURES + BENEFITS BLUEPRINT tool should help you and your team clearly describe and prioritize your features and benefits.

Describing features is pretty straightforward. But at times, it can be frustratingly difficult to translate features into benefits. Fortunately, there's a little trick to help you do this. It's called the "So what?" trick. To do this, write down a feature and then ask yourself, "So what?" And then keep asking "So what?" to understand if the feature is truly of value and/or to understand all of the potential benefits that might resonate with people. For example, a feature for Spotify would be "Millions of songs are available through the app." That's a fact. So what? "Access to your favorite and new songs when and where you want them." So what? "No matter where you are or what you're doing, you can find music that fits your mood." Those are benefits.

CHANGEMAKER COACH | TOOL TIPS

- It's easy to fall into the trap of talking about features as opposed to benefits. People are most interested in knowing how your changemaking innovation will make their lives easier and better. Focus on benefits. What's the positive change from their perspective, not yours?
- This should be super helpful for all of the tools in TOOLBOX 10 - POSITIONING + MARKETING STRATEGIES (p. 293)
- This will help address the shortcomings you find using T6.3 EQUITABLE ACCESS MAP (p. 214)

HOW TO USE THIS TOOL

1. Start at the top of the tool. Note down your INNOVATION DESIRED OUTCOME. This is the positive change you hope the people you're supporting with your changemaking innovation can achieve. Below this note down your overall INNOVATION DESCRIPTION.
2. Next, go to the NOVEL FEATURES and BENEFITS headers. Note them down in no particular order.
3. Now, go through each of the NOVEL FEATURES and BENEFITS and rate their relative IMPORTANCE for achieving the INNOVATION DESIRED OUTCOME. Circle the number that reflects this. "1" is low and "5" is high.
4. To conclude, go to NOW WHAT? and note down a few priority next steps based on what you've learned and/or new insights you've gained from using this tool.

CHANGEMAKING INNOVATION MINI-CASES	
V3	p. 358
V20	p. 366
V84	p. 367

CHANGEMAKING TRIMTABS	
CT6	p. 38
CT8	p. 40
CT17	p. 50

INNOVATION DESIRED OUTCOME	
INNOVATION DESCRIPTION	

NOVEL FEATURES	BENEFITS	IMPORTANCE
		1 2 3 4 5
		1 2 3 4 5
		1 2 3 4 5
		1 2 3 4 5
		1 2 3 4 5
		1 2 3 4 5
		1 2 3 4 5
		1 2 3 4 5
		1 2 3 4 5
		1 2 3 4 5

NOW WHAT?	

T7.6

TOOLS FOR INNOVATION DESIGN CONVERSATIONS | OUR CHANGEMAKING INNOVATION BLUEPRINTS

toolkit 07

INNOVATION DISTILLATION BLUEPRINT

How might we distill the elements that make our innovation tick?

tinyurl.com/cctboxt76

ABOUT THIS TOOL

This INNOVATION DISTILLATION BLUEPRINT tool should help you and your team categorize the relative importance of the different elements of your changemaking innovation.

It's important to be passionate about your changemaking innovation. But it's dangerous to be passionate about every element of your changemaking innovation. This makes you less willing to adapt, and it makes it very difficult to scale. The fact of the matter is that there are likely many elements of your innovation that are NOT IMPORTANT. It doesn't matter very much if these change. There are a smaller number that are CONTEXTUALLY IMPORTANT. These are important given the current environment. And there are a precious few that are CRITICALLY IMPORTANT. These make your innovation "tick." These are the ones you should be passionate about.

Unfortunately, as changemakers, we often fail at scaling because we're precious. We put our metaphorical blood, sweat, and tears into creating all of the discrete elements of our innovations. As a natural result, we end up falling in love with all of the discrete elements. It's not just that we see the innovation as a whole as "our baby," we view all of the elements that make it up as our babies too. That's a problem. It leads us down the path of becoming overly rigid and prescriptive.

CHANGEMAKING INNOVATION MINI-CASES	
V50	p. 360
V59	p. 362
V66	p. 369

CHANGEMAKING TRIMTABS	
CT15	p. 34
CT19	p. 50
CT22	p. 54

HOW TO USE THIS TOOL

1. Start at the top of the tool. Note down your INNOVATION DESIRED OUTCOME. This is the positive change you hope the people you're supporting with your changemaking innovation can achieve. Below this note down your overall INNOVATION DESCRIPTION.
2. Next, go to the INNOVATION ELEMENTS header. Under this, list all of the key elements of your changemaking innovation.
3. After you've finished listing the INNOVATION ELEMENTS, go to the first one and circle it's IMPORTANCE FOR ACHIEVING THE DESIRED OUTCOME. Circle whether it's NOT IMPORTANT, CONTEXTUALLY IMPORTANT, or CRITICALLY IMPORTANT. Note down your REASONING for your decisions.
4. Repeat step 3 for each of your INNOVATION ELEMENTS.
5. To conclude, go to NOW WHAT? and note down a few priority next steps based on what you've learned and/or new insights you've gained from using this tool.

CHANGEMAKER COACH | TOOL TIPS

- Always try to keep in mind that very few people will want to read a text-heavy document/book about your changemaking innovation. In order to both engage with people, and to scale, you need to distill and share what really makes it tick. This tool is a forcing mechanism to help you figure this out.
- Use this tool to put CT15 CONFRONT COMPLEXITY WITH SIMPLICITY (p. 54) into action.
- This should be of particular help for T10.4 MARKETING MIX STRATEGY (p. 290) and T12.2 STICKY MESSAGING STRATEGY (p. 318).

INNOVATION DESIRED OUTCOME	
INNOVATION DESCRIPTION	

INNOVATION ELEMENTS	**IMPORTANCE FOR ACHIEVING THE DESIRED OUTCOME**			**REASONING**
	NOT IMPORTANT	CONTEXTUALLY IMPORTANT	CRITICALLY IMPORTANT	
	NOT IMPORTANT	CONTEXTUALLY IMPORTANT	CRITICALLY IMPORTANT	
	NOT IMPORTANT	CONTEXTUALLY IMPORTANT	CRITICALLY IMPORTANT	
	NOT IMPORTANT	CONTEXTUALLY IMPORTANT	CRITICALLY IMPORTANT	
	NOT IMPORTANT	CONTEXTUALLY IMPORTANT	CRITICALLY IMPORTANT	
	NOT IMPORTANT	CONTEXTUALLY IMPORTANT	CRITICALLY IMPORTANT	
	NOT IMPORTANT	CONTEXTUALLY IMPORTANT	CRITICALLY IMPORTANT	
	NOT IMPORTANT	CONTEXTUALLY IMPORTANT	CRITICALLY IMPORTANT	
	NOT IMPORTANT	CONTEXTUALLY IMPORTANT	CRITICALLY IMPORTANT	
	NOT IMPORTANT	CONTEXTUALLY IMPORTANT	CRITICALLY IMPORTANT	

NOW WHAT?	

TOOLS FOR INNOVATION DESIGN CONVERSATIONS | OUR CHANGEMAKING INNOVATION BLUEPRINTS

TOOLKIT TOOLS REFLECTIONS

SCALE:
STRONGLY AGREE = 5, AGREE = 4, NOT SURE = 3, DISAGREE = 2, STRONGLY DISAGREE = 1

tinyurl.com/cctboxtoolsrflect

	CHANGEMAKING TOOLS					
REFLECTION STATEMENTS	**T7.1**	**T7.2**	**T7.3**	**T7.4**	**T7.5**	**T7.6**
This tool is easy to understand.						
This tool is easy to use.						
This tool taught me/ us important new knowledge.						
This tool empowered new changemaking conversations.						
This tool helped to spark new ideas/ insights.						
This tool should be included in my/ our toolbox for the future.						
I/ we should share this tool with other changemakers.						

NOTES:

TOOLS FOR INNOVATION DESIGN CONVERSATIONS | LAUNCH + SCALING STRATEGIES

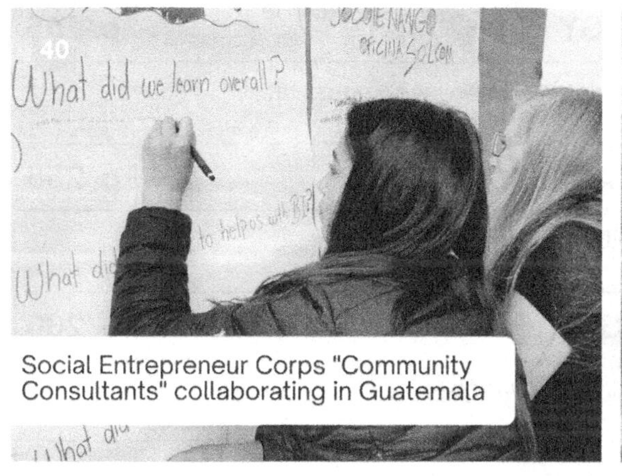

40 Social Entrepreneur Corps "Community Consultants" collaborating in Guatemala

41 Community members collaborating to design appropriate technology solutions

42 Miguel B. collaborating with MicroConsignment Model entrepreneurs

43 David W. and Kim A. collaborating with Worker Well-being Champions in Bangkok

NOTES:

toolkit 08 TOOLS FOR INNOVATION DESIGN CONVERSATIONS | LAUNCH + SCALING STRATEGIES

TOOLS INVENTORY

How might we figure out the where to start and how to distribute and scale our changemaking innovation?

tinyurl.com/cctboxtools01

NOTES:

GVK notes -

- When you're first launching, you might want to work with an established organization to create what I call "adjacent credibility."
- Two important concepts with the word "ocean" in them -
  - BLUE OCEAN: A new market with very little competition or barriers to entry.
  - Don't try to "Boil the Ocean": Trying to do an impossible task or project. It can often mean you're trying to do too much, too fast.

Need help, ideas or guidance? Go to CHANGEMAKER COACH "ADVICE/ ASK ME ANYTHING" on page 378.

TOOLS FOR INNOVATION DESIGN CONVERSATIONS |
LAUNCH + SCALING STRATEGIES

toolkit 08

TOOLKIT SCORECARD + PRIORITIZATION HELP

Score yourselves to help you decide which tool(s) you might want to prioritize for your changemaking conversations.

tinyurl.com/cctboxtoolsprior

SELF-CHECK STATEMENTS	HOW ARE WE DOING?	TOOL SUGGESTIONS
We've analyzed and have a good feel for the overall size and characteristics of the "market." We've had conversations about where and how we should launch our changemaking innovation.	0 1 2 3 4 5	T8.1
We're discussing and analyzing the compatibility of potential collaborations.	0 1 2 3 4 5	T8.2
We're discussing all of the potential distribution channels for our innovation so that we decide which ones are the most effective, efficient, and scalable	0 1 2 3 4 5	T8.3
We've discussed who the innovators and early adopters might be for our changemaking innovation.	0 1 2 3 4 5	T8.4

NOTES:

GVK notes -

- *How are you going to achieve "hockey stick" growth/ scale?*
- *Remember there are two ways to scale -*
    - *Scale BROAD: Try to reach a growing number of people*
    - *Scale DEEP: Offer more and more opportunities to the same people*

TOOLS FOR INNOVATION DESIGN CONVERSATIONS | LAUNCH + SCALING STRATEGIES

COLLABORATIVE CHANGEMAKING VOICES

Get into the mindset for this toolkit + include your voice in the conversation.

"Action is the antidote to despair."

JOAN BAEZ
SINGER | SONGWRITER | ACTIVIST

"Opportunity is missed by most people because it is dressed in overalls and looks like work."

THOMAS EDISON
INVENTOR

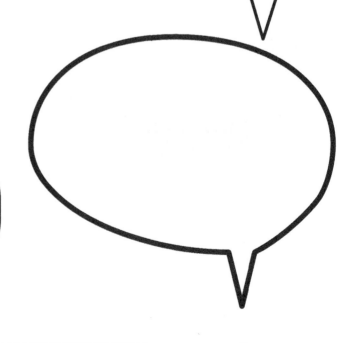

"Change moves at the speed of trust."

STEPHEN COVEY
AUTHOR - *THE SEVEN HABITS OF HIGHLY EFFECTIVE PEOPLE*

"When I'm playing, I'm never through. It's unfinished. I like to find a place to leave for someone else to finish it."

MILES DAVIS
JAZZ MUSICIAN

"If you can't fly, then run. If you can't run, then walk. If you can't walk, then crawl. But whatever you do, you have to keep moving forward."

MARTIN LUTHER KING JR.
NOBEL PEACE PRIZE LAUREATE

"I get angry about things and then I go to work."

TONI MORRISON
AUTHOR | NOBEL PRIZE LAUREATE

"Is there anyone so wise as to learn by the experience of others?"

VOLTAIRE
FRENCH WRITER

"The most difficult thing is the decision to act, the rest is merely tenacity."

AMELIA EARHART
AVIATOR

T8.1

TOOLS FOR INNOVATION DESIGN CONVERSATIONS | LAUNCH + SCALING STRATEGIES

toolkit 08

MARKET SIZE ANALYSIS + STRATEGY

How might we both define the size of the opportunity and decide where we should start?

tinyurl.com/cctboxt81

ABOUT THIS TOOL

In the business start-up community, a "funnel" approach is a popular way of defining market size and launch markets. This approach can be helpful for every kind of organization. You start by defining the total global size of your potential market and then work your way down to a definition of your launch market. This MARKET SIZE ANALYSIS + DESIGN tool should help you and your team apply this approach to your changemaking efforts.

From biggest to smallest and most aspirational to most actionable, the four market sizes used in this tool are as follows:

- **TAM (Total Addressable (Available) Market):** How big is the largest market? This is the entirety of the market for your innovation. This is everyone worldwide who could benefit from your innovation. Although it's not realistic that you'd ever reach all of these people, this is a good place to start. Start here and work your way down.
- **SAM (Service (Serviceable) Addressable Market):** How big is the market you could actually reach? This is the proportion of the TAM that you're potentially able to actually serve with your innovation. This would be a long-term goal and assumes you'll have the resources you need.
- **SOM (Service Obtainable Market):** What's the market you could reach with current resources? This is what's attainable over the medium term. This might be over the next six months, a year, or two years. This is what you might use as a basis for projections.
- **LAM (Launch Addressable Market):** Who are the best people to reach right now? This is the market where you'll test and validate your innovation to make informed modifications and improvements.

HOW TO USE THIS TOOL

1. Start at the MARKETS header at the TAM (TOTAL ADDRESSABLE MARKET). Under the ANALYSIS + DESIGN header, note down the DESCRIPTION in as much detail as possible. Then note down the LOCATION. For your TAM this will likely be global. Then note down the SIZE. Define the SIZE in a way that's most fitting for your changemaking innovation. This might be the number of people, sales, or units, for example.
2. Next, follow the same process for your SAM, SOM, and LAM.
3. To conclude, go to NOW WHAT? and note down a few priority next steps based on what you've learned and/or new insights you've gained from using this tool.

CHANGEMAKER COACH | TOOL TIPS

- I've included this in the design tools module, however I'd encourage you to also use this during your discovery and diagnosis work to help you define the size of the problem/ opportunity.
- This should help put CT21 DEFINE + SHARE THE BHAG (p. 66) into action.
- Note that the LAM (Launch Addressable Market) in this tool is likely the same as the INNOVATORS and EARLY ADOPTERS referred to in T8.4 DIFFUSION STRATEGY DESIGN (p. 262)
- You'll likely want to use this with T5.2 PERSONA MAP (p. 194).

CHANGEMAKING INNOVATION MINI-CASES	
V17	p. 361
V59	p. 369
V65	p. 370

CHANGEMAKING TRIMTABS	
CT8	p. 40
CT13	p. 50
CT21	p. 66

	ANALYSIS + DESIGN		
MARKETS	**DESCRIPTION**	**LOCATION**	**SIZE**
TAM (TOTAL ADDRESSABLE MARKET)			
SAM (SERVICE ADDRESSABLE MARKET)			
SOM (SERVICE OBTAINABLE MARKET)			
LAM (LAUNCH ADDRESSABLE MARKET)			

NOW WHAT?	

T8.2

TOOLS FOR INNOVATION DESIGN CONVERSATIONS | LAUNCH + SCALING STRATEGIES

COLLABORATOR COMPATIBILITY ANALYSIS

How might we analyze our compatibility with potential collaborators?

linyurl.com/cclboxl82

ABOUT THIS TOOL

A dating app is a kind of collaborator compatibility analysis. You analyze characteristics about someone, decide whether or not you think you're compatible, and then swipe right or swipe left. This COLLABORATOR COMPATIBILITY ANALYSIS tool should help you and your team decide which way you should swipe when contemplating collaboration with organizations.

Collaborating with other organizations can be a fantastic way to help get your changemaking innovation to the people who can most benefit from it. You should always be seeking out collaborators. It can be a great way to create leverage where everyone optimizes the use of their limited time, knowledge, power, and resources. It might help with awareness building, marketing, scaling distribution, or sales, for example. It might make sense to collaborate with the government, schools, libraries, nonprofits, or businesses, for example. However, before you dive into any collaboration, it's important to step back and analyze your compatibility. Because once you do start collaborating, if things go sideways, the negative impact can be brutal.

CHANGEMAKER COACH | TOOL TIPS
• This tool should help you put CT10 BUILD PURPOSE-DRIVEN TEAMS + TEAMS OF TEAMS (p. 44) and CT20 BUILD A MUTUALLY SYMBIOTIC ECOSYSTEM (p. 64) into action. • You might want to use this with T7.2 DRIVER DIAGRAM BLUEPRINT (p. 240) to help you figure out alignment. • Once you've created a formal collaboration, you might want to divide and conquer roles using T2.2 RACI STRUCTURE CHECK-IN (p. 128).

HOW TO USE THIS TOOL

1. Start by going to the DECISION MAKING CRITERIA header. Go to OVERALL VISION. Under DESCRIPTION note down the OVERALL VISION for OUR TEAM and the POTENTIAL COLLABORATOR.

2. Next, go to ANALYSIS. Is the OVERALL VISION for OUR TEAM and the POTENTIAL COLLABORATOR compatible? Circle HIGH, MEDIUM, or LOW under PERCEIVED COMPATIBILITY. Then note down your REASON FOR PERCEIVED COMPATIBILITY .

3. Repeat this process for all of the DECISION MAKING CRITERIA.

4. To conclude, go to NOW WHAT? and note down a few priority next steps based on what you've learned and/or new insights you've gained from using this tool.

CHANGEMAKING INNOVATION MINI-CASES		CHANGEMAKING TRIMTABS	
V19	p. 361	CT9	p. 42
V70	p. 371	CT10	p. 44
V82	p. 374	CT20	p. 64

DECISION MAKING CRITERIA	DESCRIPTION		ANALYSIS	
	OUR TEAM	POTENTIAL COLLABORATOR	PERCEIVED COMPATIBILITY	REASON FOR PERCEIVED COMPATIBILITY
OVERALL VISION			HIGH MEDIUM LOW	
REASON FOR POTENTIAL COLLABORATION			HIGH MEDIUM LOW	
PRIMARY CONSTITUENTS			HIGH MEDIUM LOW	
PROBLEM BEING SOLVED			HIGH MEDIUM LOW	
CURRENT SOLUTION OFFERINGS			HIGH MEDIUM LOW	
GEOGRAPHIC FOCUS			HIGH MEDIUM LOW	
CURRENT CHANNELS BEING LEVERAGED			HIGH MEDIUM LOW	
LEADERSHIP + ORG CULTURE			HIGH MEDIUM LOW	
ORG CAPACITY			HIGH MEDIUM LOW	
EXTERNAL INCENTIVES			HIGH MEDIUM LOW	
INTERNAL INCENTIVES			HIGH MEDIUM LOW	
EXISTING COLLABORATIONS			HIGH MEDIUM LOW	
SENSE OF URGENCY ABOUT THIS COLLABORATION			HIGH MEDIUM LOW	

NOW WHAT?	

☐ **T8.3**

TOOLS FOR INNOVATION DESIGN CONVERSATIONS | LAUNCH + SCALING STRATEGIES

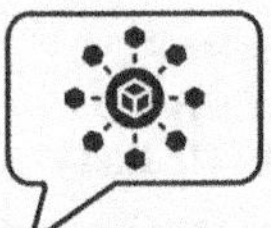

DISTRIBUTION CHANNEL STRATEGY

How might we define how we'll distribute our changemaking innovation?

tinyurl.com/cctboxt83

ABOUT THIS TOOL

According to Reid Hoffman, co-founder of LinkedIn, "Having a great idea for a product is important, but having a great idea for product distribution is even more important." This DISTRIBUTION CHANNEL STRATEGY tool should help you and your team decide which distribution channels might be best to get your changemaking innovation into the hands of the people you aspire to support.

This tool includes the following 15 distribution channels (Technically speaking, these are a mix of distribution and marketing channels. Keep in mind that the goal is to have robust changemaking conversations. Don't get tripped up by semantics.):

- **AFFILIATES:** Think of affiliate marketing. An example is putting Amazon hyperlinks on a website and getting paid a commission when people click through and buy books.
- **BRANCHES:** These are owned by the organization. Examples are Starbucks, Walgreens, and Apple stores.
- **CHAPTERS:** These are usually associated with nonprofit organizations/ associations and have members.
- **FRANCHISING:** This has a franchisor and franchisees. The franchisor grants franchisees proprietary business knowledge, processes, and trademarks, and allows it to sell a product/service under the franchisor's name.
- **GOVERNMENT:** These are often partnerships where the focus is community well-being. This channel is critical in post-disaster situations.
- **INFLUENCERS/ AMBASSADORS:** These are people in your niche/ industry with sway over your target audience. They transfer credibility.
- **LICENSING:** This is when one party signs an agreement to use and/or earn revenue from the name/IP/property of the owner. An example is a musician licensing a song for a movie.
- **MICRO-ENTREPRENEURS/ COMMUNITY PROFESSIONALS:** These are people who might go from town to town or door-to-door offering/selling products/services. Examples are Avon Ladies and community health workers.
- **NETWORKING:** This might be at conferences, through associations, via social media, etc.
- **NON PROFITS (NGO'S):** Nonprofits have specific audiences. They've typically engendered trust in the communities.
- **RETAIL STORES:** These are brick-and-mortar and sell directly to customers.
- **SCHOOLS:** These might include traditional and non-traditional.
- **SOCIAL MEDIA:** This is Instagram, Facebook, TikTok, LinkedIn etc.
- **WEBSITES:** This would be through an organization's or third-party website.
- **WHOLESALERS:** These organizations purchase in bulk and then distribute through other channels.

HOW TO USE THIS TOOL

1. Go to the CHANNELS header. Start with AFFILIATES. Note down your DESIGN IDEAS for how to use AFFILIATES. Then do an ANALYSIS of the ADVANTAGES and DISADVANTAGES. Based on this ANALYSIS, go to RATINGS and circle a number from "0" to "5" under FIT WITH DESIRED OUTCOME, FIT WITH CURRENT ORG. CAPACITY, and OVERALL RATING. "0" is "extremely weak", and "5" is "extremely strong."
2. Repeat this process for all CHANNELS.
3. To conclude, go to NOW WHAT? and note down a few priority next steps based on what you've learned and/or new insights you've gained from using this tool.

CHANGEMAKING INNOVATION MINI-CASES	
V45	p. 366
V61	p. 370
V75	p. 372

CHANGEMAKING TRIMTABS	
CT4	p. 32
CT5	p. 34
CT8	p. 40

CHANNELS	DESIGN IDEAS	ANALYSIS		RATINGS		
		ADVANTAGES	DISADVANTAGES	FIT WITH DESIRED OUTCOME	FIT WITH CURRENT ORG. CAPACITY	OVERALL RATING
AFFILIATES				0 1 2 3 4 5	0 1 2 3 4 5	0 1 2 3 4 5
BRANCHES				0 1 2 3 4 5	0 1 2 3 4 5	0 1 2 3 4 5
CHAPTERS				0 1 2 3 4 5	0 1 2 3 4 5	0 1 2 3 4 5
FRANCHISING				0 1 2 3 4 5	0 1 2 3 4 5	0 1 2 3 4 5
GOVERNMENT				0 1 2 3 4 5	0 1 2 3 4 5	0 1 2 3 4 5
INFLUENCERS/ AMBASSADORS				0 1 2 3 4 5	0 1 2 3 4 5	0 1 2 3 4 5
LICENSING				0 1 2 3 4 5	0 1 2 3 4 5	0 1 2 3 4 5
MICRO-ENTREPRENEURS/ COMMUNITY PROFESSIONALS				0 1 2 3 4 5	0 1 2 3 4 5	0 1 2 3 4 5
NETWORKING				1 1 2 3 4 5	1 1 2 3 4 5	1 1 2 3 4 5
NON PROFITS (NGO'S)				0 1 2 3 4 5	0 1 2 3 4 5	0 1 2 3 4 5
RETAIL STORES				0 1 2 3 4 5	0 1 2 3 4 5	0 1 2 3 4 5
SCHOOLS				0 1 2 3 4 5	0 1 2 3 4 5	0 1 2 3 4 5
SOCIAL MEDIA				0 1 2 3 4 5	0 1 2 3 4 5	0 1 2 3 4 5
WEBSITE				0 1 2 3 4 5	0 1 2 3 4 5	0 1 2 3 4 5
WHOLESALERS				0 1 2 3 4 5	0 1 2 3 4 5	0 1 2 3 4 5

NOW WHAT?	

T8.4

TOOLS FOR INNOVATION DESIGN CONVERSATIONS | LAUNCH + SCALING STRATEGIES

toolkit 08

DIFFUSION STRATEGY

How might we define who the most likely adopters of our innovation will be when we launch?

tinyurl.com/cctboxt84

ABOUT THIS TOOL

Don't spend your limited time and resources trying to convince skeptics to adopt your changemaking innovation, even if supporting them is your ultimate goal. Start by engaging with the people most likely to want what you're offering. Get them on board and then shine a spotlight on their successful experiences to get others on board. This DIFFUSION STRATEGY tool will help you and your team to do this.

This tool is inspired by the "Diffusion of Innovation Theory (DOI)" developed by Everett Rogers in 1962. This theory explains how, why, and at what rate innovations spread. According to Rogers, a population can be segmented into the following five adopter categories:

- **INNOVATORS (2.5%):** Innovators are willing to take risks. They're great for helping you test your changemaking innovation ideas.
- **EARLY ADOPTERS (13.5%):** These people have the highest degree of opinion leadership among the other adopter categories. They are key influencers. Work with them to help you spread the word.
- **EARLY MAJORITY (34%):** These people start skeptical. Your goal is to get to this category. Research shows that there can be a "chasm" that exists between EARLY ADOPTERS and this category. Your challenge is to bridge that chasm.
- **LATE MAJORITY (34%):** These people are highly skeptical. People in this category will adopt an innovation after the average member of society.
- **LAGGARDS (16%):** People in this category are the last to adopt an innovation. They're averse to change and may never adopt.

This tool helps you focus your efforts on defining INNOVATORS and EARLY ADOPTERS. It also includes space to ideate about spotlighting their experiences to reach everyone else.

HOW TO USE THIS TOOL

1. Start at the top by noting down the GOALS OF OUR CHANGEMAKING INNOVATION, the OVERALL TARGET POPULATION DESCRIPTION, and the SIZE OF THE TOTAL POPULATION.
2. Next, go to the DEFINING QUESTIONS header and INNOVATORS (2.5%) under the ADOPTER CATEGORIES header. Work your way down the DEFINING QUESTIONS prompts.
3. Do the same for the EARLY ADOPTERS(13.5%).
4. To conclude, go to NOW WHAT? and note down a few priority next steps based on what you've learned and/or new insights you've gained from using this tool.

CHANGEMAKER COACH | TOOL TIPS

- If you find yourself focused on convincing skeptics about the value of your changemaking innovation, you're going about it the wrong way. We all fall into this trap. Beware! Use this tool to avoid this.
- When considering how to get innovators on board, you should call on T11.1 KEYS TO INNOVATION ADOPTION (p. 298)
- You'll likely want to compliment this tool with T5.2 PERSONA MAP (p. 194), T7.5 NOVEL FEATURES + BENEFITS BLUEPRINT (p. 246), and T12.3 COMMUNICATION CHANNEL STRATEGY (p. 320), to name a few.

CHANGEMAKING INNOVATION MINI-CASES	
V20	p. 361
V23	p. 362
V55	p. 368

CHANGEMAKING TRIMTABS	
CT5	p. 34
CT8	p. 40
CT21	p. 66

GOALS OF OUR CHANGEMAKING INNOVATION	
OVERALL TARGET POPULATION DESCRIPTION	
SIZE OF THE TOTAL POPULATION	

	ADOPTER CATEGORIES	
DEFINING QUESTIONS	**INNOVATORS (2.5%)**	**EARLY ADOPTERS (13.5%)**
WHO ARE THEY?		
WHERE ARE THEY?		
WHAT'S THE TOTAL SIZE?		
WHAT ARE THEIR CURRENT PRACTICES?		
WHAT ARE THEIR ASPIRATIONS?		
WHAT ARE THEIR PAIN POINTS?		
WHY DO WE BELIEVE THEY'RE IN THIS CATEGORY?		
WHAT ARE THE BEST WAYS TO REACH THEM?		
WHAT DO THEY EXPECT/ REQUIRE?		
HOW CAN WE INSPIRE/ EMPOWER THEM TO EVANGELIZE?		

NOW WHAT?	

TOOLS FOR INNOVATION DESIGN CONVERSATIONS | LAUNCH + SCALING STRATEGIES

TOOLKIT TOOLS REFLECTIONS

SCALE:
STRONGLY AGREE = 5, AGREE = 4, NOT SURE = 3, DISAGREE = 2, STRONGLY DISAGREE = 1

tinyurl.com/cctboxtoolsrflect

	CHANGEMAKING TOOLS			
REFLECTION STATEMENTS	T8.1	T8.2	T8.3	T8.4
This tool is easy to understand.				
This tool is easy to use.				
This tool taught me/ us important new knowledge.				
This tool empowered new changemaking conversations.				
This tool helped to spark new ideas/ insights.				
This tool should be included in my/ our toolbox for the future.				
I/ we should share this tool with other changemakers.				

NOTES:

TOOLS FOR INNOVATION DESIGN CONVERSATIONS | SPECIAL: PEOPLE-FOR-PEOPLE STRATEGIES

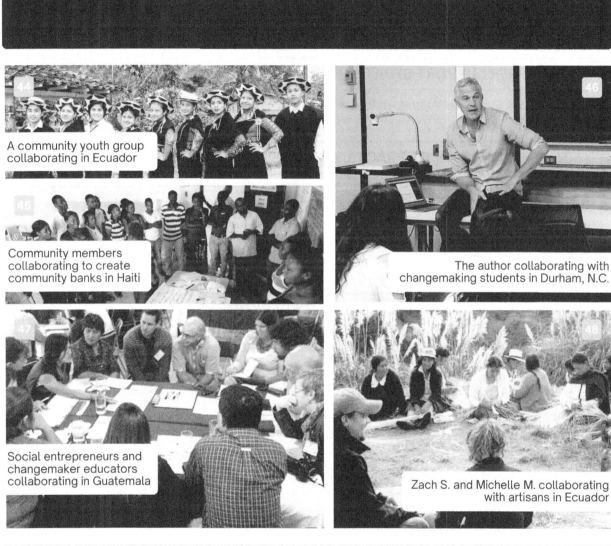

A community youth group collaborating in Ecuador

Community members collaborating to create community banks in Haiti

The author collaborating with changemaking students in Durham, N.C.

Social entrepreneurs and changemaker educators collaborating in Guatemala

Zach S. and Michelle M. collaborating with artisans in Ecuador

NOTES:

Need help, ideas or guidance? Go to CHANGEMAKER COACH "ADVICE/ ASK ME ANYTHING" on page 378.

toolkit 09

TOOLS FOR INNOVATION DESIGN CONVERSATIONS |
SPECIAL: PEOPLE-FOR-PEOPLE STRATEGIES

TOOLS INVENTORY

How might we start to create strategies that help people support and empower each other?

tinyurl.com/cctboxtools01

NOTES:

GVK notes -

- Never underestimate the power of JOY!!!
- Can you create NON ZERO SUM OPPORTUNITIES? These are win-wins. Everyone benefits from working/ spending time with each other.

TOOLS FOR INNOVATION DESIGN CONVERSATIONS | SPECIAL: PEOPLE-FOR-PEOPLE STRATEGIES

TOOLKIT SCORECARD + PRIORITIZATION HELP

Score yourselves to help you decide which tool(s) you might want to prioritize for your changemaking conversations.

tinyurl.com/cctboxtoolsprior

SELF-CHECK STATEMENTS	HOW ARE WE DOING?	TOOL SUGGESTIONS
We're having strategic conversations about how we can help people dealing with the same challenges come together to support and empower each other.	0 1 2 3 4 5	T9.1
We're talking about how we can help people who have the same goal(s) come together as a community of practice.	0 1 2 3 4 5	T9.2
We're having conversations about how we can help design a mutual aid strategy.	0 1 2 3 4 5	T9.3
We're having strategic conversations about how we can help like-minded organizations work together to solve a mutually agreed upon big, systemic problem.	0 1 2 3 4 5	T9.4

NOTES:

collaborativechangemaking.com
for updates, new resources, to report problems, share your ideas, provide feedback, etc.

youtube.com/@collaborativechangemaking
for HOW-TO videos, extra CHANGEMAKING INNOVATION MINI-CASES, etc.

toolkit 09

TOOLS FOR INNOVATION DESIGN CONVERSATIONS |
SPECIAL: PEOPLE-FOR-PEOPLE STRATEGIES

COLLABORATIVE CHANGEMAKING VOICES

Get into the mindset for this toolkit + include your voice in the conversation.

"Find a group of people who challenge and inspire you, spend a lot of time with them, and it will change your life."

AMY POEHLER
COMEDIAN | WRITER

"Look, if I were alone in the world, I would have the right to choose despair, solitude and self-fulfillment. But I am not alone."

ELIE WIESEL
AUTHOR| HOLOCAUST SURVIVOR
NOBEL PEACE PRIZE LAUREATE

"Alone we can do so little; together we can do so much."

HELEN KELLER
DISABILITY RIGHTS ADVOCATE

"When people are depending on us, we end up finding strength we didn't know we had."

ADAM GRANT
PROFESSOR | AUTHOR - *GIVE + TAKE*

"No one has ever become poor by giving."

ANNE FRANK
DIARIST

"In a world where there is so much to be done, I felt strongly impressed that there must be something for me to do."

DOROTHEA DIX
AUTHOR | TEACHER | REFORMER

"Trust others and they will trust you."

GUY KAWASAKI
AUTHOR | VENTURE CAPITALIST

"A neighbor is a far better and cheaper alternative to government services."

JENNIFER PAHLKA
FOUNDER - CODE FOR AMERICA

"The fight is never about grapes or lettuce, it is always about people."

CESAR CHAVEZ
LABOR LEADER | CIVIL RIGHTS ACTIVIST

T9.1

TOOLS FOR INNOVATION DESIGN CONVERSATIONS | SPECIAL: PEOPLE-FOR-PEOPLE STRATEGIES

PEER SUPPORT STRATEGY DESIGN

How might we start to design a structure focused on empowering people with similar challenges to help each other?

tinyurl.com/cctboxt91

ABOUT THIS TOOL

Peers are people who either are having or have had the same or similar experiences. When peers support peers, transformational changemaking becomes possible. This PEER SUPPORT STRATEGY DESIGN tool should help you and your team get started designing a strategy to bring peers together to support each other to create positive change.

There are two common approaches that changemakers take when designing peer support strategies. These are by no means mutually exclusive. One approach is what's known as a "near-peer" strategy. This typically prioritizes prevention. People who've experienced a challenge help people who are either experiencing or are at risk of experiencing the same challenge. This looks like a mentor/mentee relationship.

The other approach often prioritizes emotional support. This is a "peer-to-peer" strategy. People confronting the same challenge come together to support and empower each other. Regardless of your approach, you'll likely want to start by specifying the following:

- **THE SHARED EXPERIENCE:** What experience brings peers together? What's the motivation?
- **PEER DESCRIPTION(S):** Describe the peers.
- **FIRST ORDER DESIRED IMPACT(S):** What are the desired immediate, direct impacts?
- **FIRST ORDER IMPACT INDICATOR(S):** How will you know you've achieved them?
- **SECOND ORDER DESIRED IMPACT(S):** What are some knock-on positive impacts? You may not know these until you get going.
- **SECOND ORDER IMPACT INDICATOR(S):** How will you know you've achieved them?

KEY CONSIDERATIONS

- **WHAT'S THE ACTIVITY?:** How will peers come together? Meeting? Dinner? Walking?
- **WHERE WILL THE ACTIVITY TAKE PLACE?**
- **HOW WILL PEERS LEARN ABOUT/ BE INVITED TO THE ACTIVITY?**
- **HOW FREQUENTLY WILL THE ACTIVITY BE SCHEDULED?**
- **HOW WILL THE ACTIVITY BE STRUCTURED?:** What are the logistics? How will it work
- **WHAT ARE KEY ROLES + RESPONSIBILITIES?:** Who does what?
- **WHAT ARE IMPORTANT GUIDELINES/ POLICIES?**
- **HOW WILL PEERS PROVIDE FEEDBACK?:** How will you learn about people's feelings and opinions so that you can make modifications to emphasize and/or improve the design?

HOW TO USE THIS TOOL

1. First, go to the top of the tool and note down everything from THE SHARED EXPERIENCE to the SECOND ORDER IMPACT INDICATOR(S).
2. Next, go to the KEY CONSIDERATIONS header. Start with WHAT'S THE ACTIVITY? Under the PEER ACTIVITY STRUCTURE DESIGN header note down your DESIGN IDEAS and WHY?
3. Repeat this for each of the KEY CONSIDERATIONS.
4. To conclude, go to NOW WHAT? and note down a few priority next steps based on what you've learned and/or new insights you've gained from using this tool.

CHANGEMAKER COACH | TOOL TIPS

- This is great for CT9 BUILD PEER-FOR-PEER FRAMEWORKS (p.42) and CT17 FORTIFY EVERYDAY ACTIVITIES (p. 58).
- While not listed below, this might help you put CT11 CREATE OPPORTUNITIES FOR CATALYTIC CONNECTIONS (p. 46) into action.
- Use T1.4 OUR COLLABORATIVE CULTURE (p. 116), T5.4 WELL-BEING MAP (p. 198), and T12.5 TOUCHPOINT STRATEGY (p. 324) to help implement this tool.

CHANGEMAKING INNOVATION MINI-CASES	
V58	p. 369
V73	p. 372
V74	p. 372

CHANGEMAKING TRIMTABS	
CT9	p. 42
CT17	p. 58
CT20	p. 64

THE SHARED EXPERIENCE		
PEER DESCRIPTION(S)		
FIRST ORDER DESIRED IMPACT(S)		
FIRST ORDER IMPACT INDICATOR(S)		
SECOND ORDER DESIRED IMPACT(S)		
SECOND ORDER IMPACT INDICATOR(S)		

	PEER ACTIVITY STRUCTURE DESIGN	
KEY CONSIDERATIONS	**DESIGN IDEAS**	**WHY?**
WHAT'S THE ACTIVITY?		
WHERE WILL THE ACTIVITY TAKE PLACE?		
HOW WILL PEERS LEARN ABOUT/ BE INVITED TO THE ACTIVITY?		
HOW FREQUENTLY WILL THE ACTIVITY BE SCHEDULED?		
HOW WILL THE ACTIVITY BE STRUCTURED?		
WHAT ARE KEY ROLES + RESPONSIBILITIES?		
WHAT ARE IMPORTANT GUIDELINES/ POLICIES?		
HOW WILL PEERS PROVIDE FEEDBACK?		

NOW WHAT?	

T9.2

TOOLS FOR INNOVATION DESIGN CONVERSATIONS | SPECIAL: PEOPLE-FOR-PEOPLE STRATEGIES

COMMUNITY OF PRACTICE STRATEGY DESIGN

How might we start to design a means for people to share what's working, what isn't, and to learn from each other?

tinyurl.com/cctboxl92

ABOUT THIS TOOL

The World Bank Group (WBG) defines communities of practice (CoPs) as "Gatherings of individuals motivated by the desire to cross organizational boundaries, to relate to one another, and to build a body of actionable knowledge through coordination and collaboration." Communities of practice are indispensable for changemaking success. This COMMUNITY OF PRACTICE STRATEGY DESIGN tool will help you and your team get started designing a community of practice.

This tool should help you and your team define the following:

- **CoP NAME:** Name your Community of Practice
- **CoP MEMBERS:** Describe the members. Who will be invited/ included?
- **THE CoP'S PURPOSE:** Why are you forming this CoP?
- **CONVENING STRATEGY:** How will everyone come together? Zoom? Meetings? Dinner?
- **CoP MEMBERS' KNOWLEDGE, LESSONS LEARNED + INSIGHTS:**
  - **INTERNAL SHARING STRATEGY:** How will you share within the CoP?
  - **DOCUMENTATION STRATEGY:** How will information be captured?
  - **EXTERNAL DISSEMINATION STRATEGY:** What will be shared outside of the CoP? How?
- **CoP MEMBER NAMES:** This might be people, teams, and/or organizations.
- **CoP MEMBERS' KNOWLEDGE, LESSONS LEARNED + INSIGHTS:**
  - **SHARING GOAL(S):** What do they want to share? What are PRIORITY #1 and PRIORITY #2?
  - **LEARNING GOAL(S):** What do they want/ need to learn? What are PRIORITY #1 and PRIORITY #2?

HOW TO USE THIS TOOL

1. First, go to the top of the tool and note down everything from CoP NAME to the EXTERNAL DISSEMINATION STRATEGY.
2. Next, go to the CoP MEMBER NAMES header. There's space for five names. Your CoP might have fewer or more members.
3. Go to the first name and note down their SHARING GOALS and LEARNING GOALS. Prioritize them.
4. Repeat step three for each of the CoP MEMBER NAMES.
5. To conclude, go to NOW WHAT? and note down a few priority next steps based on what you've learned and/or new insights you've gained from using this tool.

CHANGEMAKER COACH | TOOL TIPS

- This should help you put CT2 LEAD WITH COMMUNITY VOICE + CHOICE (p. 28) into action.
- Use T1.1 OUR TEAM (p. 110), T1.2 OUR WHY (p. 112), T4.6 PROBLEM PRIORITIZATION ANALYSIS (p.184), and T5.3 EMPOWERMENT MAP (p. 196) to help implement this tool.

CHANGEMAKING INNOVATION MINI-CASES		CHANGEMAKING TRIMTABS	
V15	p. 360	CT2	p. 28
V56	p. 369	CT9	p. 42
V79	p. 373	CT10	p. 44

CoP NAME		
CoP MEMBERS		
THE CoP's PURPOSE		
CONVENING STRATEGY		
CoP MEMBERS' KNOWLEDGE, LESSONS LEARNED +INSIGHTS	INTERNAL SHARING STRATEGY	
	DOCUMENTATION STRATEGY	
	EXTERNAL DISSEMINATION STRATEGY	

CoP MEMBER NAMES	CoP KNOWLEDGE, LESSONS LEARNED + INSIGHTS			
	SHARING GOAL(S)		LEARNING GOAL(S)	
	PRIORITY #1	PRIORITY #2	PRIORITY #1	PRIORITY #2

NOW WHAT?	

T9.3

TOOLS FOR INNOVATION DESIGN CONVERSATIONS | SPECIAL: PEOPLE-FOR-PEOPLE STRATEGIES

toolkit 09

MUTUAL AID STRATEGY DESIGN

How might we start to design a means for community members to exchange and share resources?

tinyurl.com/cctboxt93

ABOUT THIS TOOL

Mutual aid is solidarity-based support where communities unite against a common struggle. Mutual aid was indispensable for communities around the world during the Covid-19 pandemic. People shared food etc. with each other and looked after the needs of their most vulnerable neighbors. This MUTUAL AID STRATEGY DESIGN tool should help you and your team get started creating a mutual aide strategy for yourselves and/ or with a community.

To note, mutual aid is different from traditional charity. Charity usually features a hierarchical structure, requirements, and one-way relationships between givers and recipients. In a mutual aid model, everyone is viewed as equal and there are no contracts or conditions. Mutual aid groups are volunteer-run, decentralized, and driven by the priority needs of community members.

This tool should help you and your team get started by defining the following:

- **THE MUTUAL AID COMMUNITY DESCRIPTION:** Describe the community.
- **PRIORITY PURPOSE(S):** Why is the mutual aid community being created?
- **PARTICIPANT'S PROFILES #1, #2, #3:** Describe the characteristics of participants. For example, this might include supermarkets, elderly people, nonprofits, restaurants, etc.
- **EXCHANGE/ SHARING PLACES:** Where will people exchange goods/ services?

KEY COMPONENTS:
For each participant note down the following;

- **PRIMARY ROLE:** How are they contributing and/or benefitting?
- **EXPECTATIONS:** What do they expect from this mutual aid community?
- **PRIORITY NEEDS:** What's their most important need (DESCRIPTION) and how often do they need it (FREQUENCY)?
- **ADDITIONAL NEEDS:** What's a lower priority need (DESCRIPTION) and how often do they need it (FREQUENCY)?
- **PRIMARY CONTRIBUTIONS:** What's their most important contribution (DESCRIPTION) and how often do they contribute it (FREQUENCY)?
- **ADDITIONAL CONTRIBUTIONS:** What's a lower priority contribution (DESCRIPTION) and how often do they contribute it (FREQUENCY)?

To note, you shouldn't expect everyone to have needs and be a contributor. That's fine.

HOW TO USE THIS TOOL

1. First, go to the top of the tool and note down everything from THE MUTUAL AID COMMUNITY DESCRIPTION to the EXCHANGE/ SHARING SPACES. There's space for three participant profiles. Your community might have fewer or more.
2. Next, go to the KEY COMPONENTS header. Start with PRIMARY ROLE. Under the PARTICIPANTS header, note this down for each participant.
3. Repeat this for each of the KEY COMPONENTS.
4. To conclude, go to NOW WHAT? and note down a few priority next steps based on what you've learned and/or new insights you've gained from using this tool.

CHANGEMAKER COACH | TOOL TIPS

- Although not listed below, this might help you with CT6 OPTIMIZE COMMUNITY ABILITIES + ASSETS (p. 36),
- Great for CT10 BUILD PURPOSE-DRIVEN TEAMS + TEAMS OF TEAM (p. 44), and CT20 BUILD A MUTUALLY SYMBIOTIC ECOSYSTEM (p. 64).
- Use T3.1 PROXIMITY WHITEBOARD (p. 148), T5.2 PERSONA MAP (p. 194), T5.5 JOURNEY MAP (p. 200), and T6.3 EQUITABLE ACCESS MAP (p. 214) to help implement this tool.

CHANGEMAKING INNOVATION MINI-CASES	
V55	p. 368
V64	p. 370
	p. 367

CHANGEMAKING TRIMTABS	
CT9	p. 42
CT10	p. 44
CT20	p. 64

THE MUTUAL AID COMMUNITY DESCRIPTION	
PRIORITY PURPOSE(S)	

PARTICIPANT PROFILE #1	
PARTICIPANT PROFILE #2	
PARTICIPANT PROFILE #3	

EXCHANGE/ SHARING PLACES	

	PARTICIPANTS		
KEY COMPONENTS	**PARTICIPANT #1**	**PARTICIPANT #2**	**PARTICIPANT #3**
PRIMARY ROLE			
EXPECTATIONS			
PRIORITY NEEDS			
DESCRIPTION			
FREQUENCY			
ADDITIONAL NEEDS			
DESCRIPTION			
FREQUENCY			
PRIMARY CONTRIBUTIONS			
DESCRIPTION			
FREQUENCY			
ADDITIONAL CONTRIBUTIONS			
DESCRIPTION			
FREQUENCY			

NOW WHAT?	

T9.4

TOOLS FOR INNOVATION DESIGN CONVERSATIONS | SPECIAL: PEOPLE-FOR-PEOPLE STRATEGIES

toolkit 09

COLLECTIVE IMPACT STRATEGY DESIGN

How might we start to design a means for organizations with similar missions to work together to solve big problems?

tinyurl.com/cctboxt94

ABOUT THIS TOOL

Collective impact brings people and/ or organizations together to achieve large-scale, measurable social change. It's a "whole is greater than the sum of its parts" strategy for changemaking. Partners align, learn from each other, and integrate their actions to achieve systems change. This COLLECTIVE IMPACT STRATEGY DESIGN tool should help you and your team start creating a collective impact community.

This tool should help you define the following:

- **THE NAME OF THE COLLECTIVE IMPACT INITIATIVE:** An attention-grabbing and uniting name is important.
- **OVERALL GOAL:** What's the Big, Hairy, Audacious Goal (BHAG)?
- **THE PROBLEM:** Describe the big problem you're trying to solve. Be specific.
- **GENERAL STRATEGY DESCRIPTION:** In a few sentences, how will this work?
- **PARTNERS - KEY COMPONENTS:**
    - **PARTNER NAME:** These might be individuals, for-profits, nonprofits, government institutions, etc.
    - **PRIMARY ROLE:** Why are they a partner in this effort? What's their contribution?

For each partner, you'll want to note down their individual and SHARED KEY PERFORMANCE INDICATORS(KPI'S) over the SHORT TERM, MEDIUM TERM, and LONG TERM. How will they measure their success?

You'll also want to agree on the DATA COLLECTION STRATEGY and the top three PRIORITY ACTIVITIES for each of the PARTNERS individually and on a SHARED basis. Then consider the COMMUNICATION STRATEGY, including preferred CHANNELS, the PRIORITY MESSAGING, and the FREQUENCY of communication.

In addition, what will be the DEDICATED INFRASTRUCTURE/ CAPITAL CONTRIBUTION for each of the PARTNERS and on a SHARED basis be over the SHORT TERM, MEDIUM TERM, and LONG TERM? And what will everyone's DEDICATED TIME be individually and SHARED?

HOW TO USE THIS TOOL

1. First, go to the top of the tool and note down everything from THE NAME OF THE COLLECTIVE IMPACT INITIATIVE to the GENERAL STRATEGY DESCRIPTION.
2. Next, go to the KEY COMPONENTS header. Go to PARTNER NAME. Then go to the PARTNERS header to the right and note down the names PARTNER 1, PARTNER 2, and PARTNER 3. There's space for three PARTNERS. You'll likely have more.
3. Then work your way down the tool for each of the KEY COMPONENTS for each PARTNER and on a SHARED basis where relevant.
4. To conclude, go to NOW WHAT? and note down a few priority next steps based on what you've learned and/or new insights you've gained from using this tool.

CHANGEMAKER COACH | TOOL TIPS

- This should help put CT10 BUILD PURPOSE-DRIVEN TEAMS + TEAMS OF TEAM (p. 44), CT19 BUILD A PRIORITIZATION ECOSYSTEM (p. 62), and CT21 DEFINE + SHARE THE BHAG (p. 66) into action.
- You might want to use T6.6 SYSTEM 5 R'S MAP (p. 220) before starting with this tool.
- Use T1.2 OUR WHY (p. 112), T2.7 KANBAN CHECK-IN (p. 138), T7.1 LOGIC MODEL BLUEPRINT (p. 238), and T8.2 COLLABORATOR COMPATIBILITY ANALYSIS (p. 258) to help implement this tool.

CHANGEMAKING INNOVATION MINI-CASES	
V43	p. 366
V68	p. 371
V70	p. 371

CHANGEMAKING TRIMTABS	
CT10	p. 44
CT19	p. 62
CT21	p. 66

THE NAME OF COLLECTIVE IMPACT INITIATIVE	
OVERALL GOAL(S)	
THE PROBLEM	
GENERAL STRATEGY DESCRIPTION	

	PARTNERS			
KEY COMPONENTS	PARTNER 1	PARTNER 2	PARTNER 3	SHARED
PARTNER NAME				N/A
PRIMARY ROLE(S)				N/A
KEY PERFORMANCE INDICATORS (KPI'S)				
SHORT TERM				
MEDIUM TERM				
LONG TERM				
DATA COLLECTION STRATEGY				
PRIORITY ACTIVITIES				
1				
2				
3				
COMMUNICATION STRATEGIES				
CHANNELS				
PRIORITY MESSAGING				
FREQUENCY				
DEDICATED INFRASTRUCTURE/ CAPITAL CONTRIBUTIONS				
SHORT TERM				
MEDIUM TERM				
LONG TERM				
DEDICATED TIME				

NOW WHAT?	

TOOLS FOR INNOVATION DESIGN CONVERSATIONS | SPECIAL: PEOPLE-FOR-PEOPLE STRATEGIES

TOOLKIT TOOLS REFLECTIONS

SCALE:
STRONGLY AGREE = 5, AGREE = 4, NOT SURE = 3, DISAGREE = 2, STRONGLY DISAGREE = 1

tinyurl.com/cctboxtoolsrflect

	CHANGEMAKING TOOLS			
REFLECTION STATEMENTS	T9.1	T9.2	T9.3	T9.4
This tool is easy to understand.				
This tool is easy to use.				
This tool taught me/ us important new knowledge.				
This tool empowered new changemaking conversations.				
This tool helped to spark new ideas/ insights.				
This tool should be included in my/ our toolbox for the future.				
I/ we should share this tool with other changemakers.				

NOTES:

toolkit 10

TOOLS FOR INNOVATION DESIGN CONVERSATIONS | POSITIONING + MARKETING STRATEGIES

49

MicroConsignment Model entrepreneurs collaborating with communities in Haiti

50

Ricardo G. collaborating with community members in Guatemala

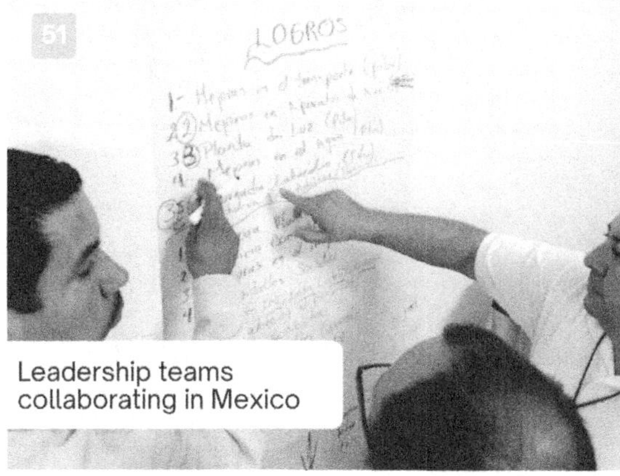

51

Leadership teams collaborating in Mexico

52

Olivia Z. collaborating with the leaders of a local social enterprise in Haiti

NOTES:

toolkit 10 TOOLS FOR INNOVATION DESIGN CONVERSATIONS | POSITIONING + MARKETING STRATEGIES

TOOLS INVENTORY

How might we decide and market the unique positioning of our innovation?

tinyurl.com/cctboxtools01

NOTES:

GVK note -

- There's a difference between "cheap" and "inexpensive." It's in the eye of the beholder.

TOOLS FOR INNOVATION DESIGN CONVERSATIONS |
POSITIONING + MARKETING STRATEGIES

TOOLKIT SCORECARD + PRIORITIZATION HELP

Score yourselves to help you decide which tool(s) you might want to prioritize for your changemaking conversations.

tinyurl.com/cctboxtoolsprior

SELF-CHECK STATEMENTS	HOW ARE WE DOING?	TOOL SUGGESTIONS
We're having conversations about whether our innovation should intervene before or after the problem happens, given the current context.	0 1 2 3 4 5	T10.1
We're having conversations about which two attributes of our innovation create unique positioning.	0 1 2 3 4 5	T10.2
We're having conversations about our overall branding strategy.	0 1 2 3 4 5	T10.3
We've had conversations about how our product, price, place and promotion strategies all work together.	0 1 2 3 4 5	T10.4

TOOLS FOR INNOVATION DESIGN CONVERSATIONS | POSITIONING + MARKETING STRATEGIES

COLLABORATIVE CHANGEMAKING VOICES

Get into the mindset for this toolkit + include your voice in the conversation.

"Pretend that every single person you meet has a sign around his or her neck that says, 'Make me feel important.' Not only will you succeed in sales, you will succeed in life."

MARY KAY ASH
FOUNDER - MARY KAY COSMETICS

"Don't find customers for your products, find products for your customers."

SETH GODIN
AUTHOR - *TRIBES*

"We cannot direct the wind, but we can adjust the sails."

DOLLY PARTON
SINGER-SONGWRITER | ACTRESS | BUSINESS WOMAN

"In differentiation, not in uniformity, lies the path of progress."
LOUIS D. BRANDEIS
SUPREME COURT JUSTICE
"Plant a good seed in the right spot and it will grow without further coaxing."
BJ FOGG
SOCIAL SCIENTIST | AUTHOR | PROFESSOR
"The aim of marketing is to know and understand the customer so well that the product or service fits him and sells itself."
PETER F. DRUCKER
MANAGEMENT CONSULTANT | AUTHOR
"People don't buy what you do, they buy why you do it."
SIMON SINEK
AUTHOR - START WITH WHY: HOW GREAT LEADERS INSPIRE EVERYONE TO TAKE ACTION

☐ **T10.1**

TOOLS FOR INNOVATION DESIGN CONVERSATIONS | POSITIONING + MARKETING STRATEGIES

toolkit 10

PROBLEM-SOLVING POSITIONING

How might we decide when our innovation should intervene?

tinyurl.com/cctboxt101

ABOUT THIS TOOL

Where should you step in with your changemaking innovation? Ideally, you'd step in before problems ever happen to eliminate them. Unfortunately, oftentimes this isn't feasible. And sometimes, even when it is feasible, it isn't the most practical approach. Different contexts require different problem-solving approaches. This PROBLEM-SOLVING POSITIONING tool should help you and your team design with this in mind.

Following are six problem-solving approaches broken down into two broad categories:

CATEGORY 1 - STOP THE PROBLEM:

- **ELIMINATE IT:** An example is efforts to eliminate polio and other diseases.
- **PREVENT IT:** An example is preventing drunk driving.
- **REDUCE IT:** This is an effective solution for problems that simply cannot be eliminated, such as food waste.

CATEGORY 2-DEAL WITH THE PROBLEM:

- **TREAT IT:** In this case, we repair the damage that's been caused. An example is drug treatment programs.
- **TOLERATE IT:** In this case, the effects of the problem are simply put up with. This often means doing nothing, for better or worse.
- **REDIRECT IT:** The problem is deflected. Sometimes the problem will simply be redefined as not being a problem anymore. Reimagining graffiti as street art is an example.

CHANGEMAKER COACH | TOOL TIPS

- Note that solving a problem in one way isn't inherently better than another. It's contextual. Your goal should be to design the best way(s) given current circumstances. And as these circumstances change, your problem-solving approach might change as well.
- This should help you put CT2 LEAD WITH COMMUNITY VOICE + CHOICE (p. 28) into action.
- Use this tool with T4.2 PROBLEM TREE ANALYSIS (p. 176), T5.5 JOURNEY MAP (p. 200), and T6.5 SYSTEM STATUS MAP (p. 218).

HOW TO USE THIS TOOL

1. Start at the top of the tool by describing THE PROBLEM.
2. Next, go to the PROBLEM-SOLVING APPROACH header. First, go to ELIMINATE IT. To the right, look under the CURRENT SOLUTION(S) header to the DESCRIPTION. Note down if and how CURRENT SOLUTION(S) are working to eliminate THE PROBLEM, and then include your ANALYSIS. How are they doing? What's working and what isn't?
3. Repeat step 2 for each PROBLEM-SOLVING APPROACH.
4. Now start with ELIMINATE IT again, and go to the OUR INNOVATION header. Note down your DESIGN IDEAS, and how feasible you think they are on a FEASIBILITY RATING scale from "0" to "5." Then note down your REASON FOR FEASIBILITY RATING.
5. Repeat step 3 for each PROBLEM-SOLVING APPROACH.
6. To conclude, go to NOW WHAT? and note down a few priority next steps based on what you've learned and/or new insights you've gained from using this tool.

CHANGEMAKING INNOVATION MINI-CASES		CHANGEMAKING TRIMTABS	
V21	p. 362	CT2	p. 28
V33	p. 364	CT12	p. 48
V72	p. 372	CT15	p. 54

THE PROBLEM	

		CURRENT SOLUTION(S)		OUR INNOVATION		
	PROBLEM SOLVING APPROACH	DESCRIPTION	ANALYSIS	DESIGN IDEAS	FEASIBILITY RATING	REASON FOR FEASIBILITY RATING
STOP THE PROBLEM	ELIMINATE IT				0 1 2 3 4 5	
	PREVENT IT				0 1 2 3 4 5	
	REDUCE IT				0 1 2 3 4 5	
DEAL WITH THE PROBLEM	TREAT IT				0 1 2 3 4 5	
	TOLERATE IT				0 1 2 3 4 5	
	REDIRECT IT				0 1 2 3 4 5	

NOW WHAT?	

T10.2

TOOLS FOR INNOVATION DESIGN CONVERSATIONS | POSITIONING + MARKETING STRATEGIES

toolkit 10

TWO ATTRIBUTES POSITIONING

How might we design our innovation to be uniquely positioned based on two attributes?

tinyurl.com/cctboxt102

ABOUT THIS TOOL

In the words of Harvard Business School professor Michael Porter, "Strategy is about setting yourself apart from the competition. It's not a matter of being better at what you do - it's a matter of being different at what you do." Whether you're in the private or social sector, you need to differentiate what you're offering. You need to find a unique position that attracts and satisfies the people you aspire to support. This TWO ATTRIBUTES POSITIONING tool should help you and your team figure out a unique position for your changemaking innovation.

A straightforward way to find an attractive position is through a three-step process. First, learn the attributes (features, benefits, qualities, etc.) that people want the most. Next, analyze if and to what extent existing solutions are delivering those attributes. And third, based on this analysis, look for a unique position for your innovation compared to existing solutions. Following is a list of some attributes that you might find helpful for working with this tool:

- **ACCESSIBILITY**: High vs. low
- **ATTRACTIVENESS:** Very vs. not very
- **COMPATIBILITY:** High vs. low
- **COMPLEXITY:** Complex vs. simple
- **CONVENIENCE:** Convenient vs. inconvenient
- **EFFORT REQUIRED:** A lot vs. a little
- **IMPACT:** High vs. low
- **JOY:** Fun vs. boring
- **KNOWLEDGE REQUIRED:** A lot vs. a little
- **PRICE:** High vs. low
- **PRODUCTIVITY:** High vs. low
- **QUALITY:** High vs. low
- **SIZE:** Big vs. small
- **SPEED:** Fast vs. slow
- **SUSTAINABILITY:** High vs. low
- **TIME REQUIRED:** A lot vs. a little
- **USABILITY:** Difficult vs. easy

HOW TO USE THIS TOOL

1. Start at the top of the tool. Go to OUR INNOVATION. Next to "A:" note down the name of your innovation.
2. Next, go to CURRENT SOLUTIONS. From "B:" to "E:" note down the names of the solutions that you're plotting on the grid with OUR INNOVATION.
3. Now go to the top of the Y-Axis to ATTRIBUTE CATEGORY #1. Note down the attribute. For example, you might write "Price - High." Then go to the bottom of the Y-Axis, and note down the opposite extreme for ATTRIBUTE CATEGORY #1. Using the same example this might be "Price - Low."
4. Go to the X-Axis and repeat this process for ATTRIBUTE CATEGORY #2. For example, on the left, you might note "Quality - High," and on the right you might write "Quality - Low."
5. Now go ahead and plot where the CURRENT SOLUTIONS should be. Write "B", "C", and so forth on the grid.
6. Once you've done this, plot where "A" (OUR INNOVATION) could/ should be to achieve noticeable differentiation.
7. To conclude, go to NOW WHAT? and note down a few priority next steps based on what you've learned and/or new insights you've gained from using this tool.

CHANGEMAKER COACH | TOOL TIPS

- I'd recommend iterating/ toggling with different attributes. Be creative!
- Maybe use T6.3 EQUITABLE ACCESS MAP (p. 214) to help you figure out which attributes to prioritize.

CHANGEMAKING INNOVATION MINI-CASES	
V17	p. 361
V46	p. 367
V57	p. 369

CHANGEMAKING TRIMTABS	
CT7	p. 38
CT8	p. 40
CT22	p. 68

OUR INNOVATION	**A:**	
CURRENT SOLUTIONS	**B:**	
	C:	
	D:	
	E:	

ATTRIBUTE CATEGORY #1

ATTRIBUTE CATEGORY #2

X AXIS (HORIZONTAL)

ATTRIBUTE CATEGORY #2

Y AXIS (VERTICAL)

ATTRIBUTE CATEGORY #1

NOW WHAT?	

T10.3

TOOLS FOR INNOVATION DESIGN CONVERSATIONS | POSITIONING + MARKETING STRATEGIES

toolkit 10

BRAND STRATEGY

How might we keep key considerations in mind as we design our brand?

tinyurl.com/cctboxt103

ABOUT THIS TOOL

Your brand is the world's perception of you. In the words of best-selling author and marketing strategist Seth Godin, "Every interaction, in any form, is branding." This BRAND DESIGN tool should help you and your team capture key brand components in one place and keep some of the most important considerations in mind.

The key branding components in this tool are as follows:

- **BRAND NAME:** Your organization and/or changemaking innovation's name
- **BRAND DESIGN:** Your logo
- **BRAND VALUES:** The key principles that guide you
- **BRAND PROMISE:** The commitment made to the people you hope to support
- **BRAND MESSAGING:** How your brand communicates its unique value proposition/ personality
- **BRAND EXPERIENCE:** The perception people have when interacting with your organization and/or changemaking innovation

The BRANDING CONSIDERATIONS included in this tool are as follows:

- **ALIGNED:** Is your brand aligned with the desired outcome of your innovation?
- **AUTHENTIC:** Is it true to who you are and what you care about?
- **CONSISTENT:** Is there a continuous throughline?
- **CREDIBLE:** Is it believable and substantial?
- **DIFFERENTIATED:** Does it stand out? Is it unique?
- **DIGESTIBLE:** Can it be captured and understood quickly? Is it simple?
- **EXTENDABLE:** Does it work across innovations? Does it work for different media? Does it work both internally and externally?
- **RELEVANT:** Does it feel right? Is it relatable to the intended audience?
- **RESONANT:** Is it evocative emotionally?
- **SUSTAINABLE:** Will it last? Will it help you grow and scale?

HOW TO USE THIS TOOL

1. Start at the top of the tool and note down everything from your BRAND NAME to the BRAND EXPERIENCE you hope to create.
2. Next, go to the BRANDING CONSIDERATIONS header. Start with ALIGNED. Note down your DESIGN STRATEGY and rate how strong you believe it is under STRENGTH. Circle a number from "1" to "5." "1" means it's very weak, and "5" means you believe it's very strong. Based on this analysis, note down any IDEAS FOR MODIFICATIONS AND/OR IMPROVEMENTS to your DESIGN STRATEGY.
3. Repeat step 2 for each of the BRANDING CONSIDERATIONS.
4. To conclude, go to NOW WHAT? and note down a few priority next steps based on what you've learned and/or new insights you've gained from using this tool.

CHANGEMAKER COACH | TOOL TIPS

- Needless to say, branding decisions are complex, and there isn't enough space on this tool to capture everything. My goal in designing this tool was to help you and your team have conversations about the most important considerations.
- This should help you put CT1 CHANGE THE NARRATIVE (p. 26) into action.
- Your responses to the prompts in this tool will be driven by what you might learn using T1.2 OUR WHY (p. 112), T1.3 OUR CORE VALUES (p. 114), T3.6 DESIGN PRINCIPLES WHITEBOARD (p. 158), and T7.4 VALUE PROPOSITION BLUEPRINT (p. 244), for example.

CHANGEMAKING INNOVATION MINI-CASES	
V74	p. 372
V80	p. 373
V81	p. 374

CHANGEMAKING TRIMTABS	
CT1	p. 26
CT8	p. 40
CT14	p. 52

BRAND NAME	
BRAND IDENTITY	
BRAND VALUES	
BRAND PROMISE	
BRAND MESSAGING	
BRAND EXPERIENCE	

BRANDING CONSIDERATIONS	DESIGN STRATEGY	STRENGTH	IDEAS FOR MODIFICATIONS AND/ OR IMPROVEMENTS
ALIGNED		1 2 3 4 5	
AUTHENTIC		1 2 3 4 5	
CONNECTED		1 2 3 4 5	
CONSISTENT		1 2 3 4 5	
CREDIBLE		1 2 3 4 5	
DIFFERENTIATED		1 2 3 4 5	
DIGESTIBLE		1 2 3 4 5	
EXTENDABLE		1 2 3 4 5	
RELEVANT		1 2 3 4 5	
RESONANT		1 2 3 4 5	
SUSTAINABLE		1 2 3 4 5	

NOW WHAT?	

T10.4

TOOLS FOR INNOVATION DESIGN CONVERSATIONS | POSITIONING + MARKETING STRATEGIES

MARKETING MIX STRATEGY

How might we define our product, promotion, place, and price?

tinyurl.com/cctboxt104

ABOUT THIS TOOL

Your marketing mix is your product (service), price, place, and promotion. These are known as the "4 P's" of marketing." They're the core components of your marketing strategy. They should fit together like pieces of a puzzle. This MARKETING MIX DESIGN tool should help you and your team zoom in on each of these P's, and zoom out to assess how well they're aligned.

This tool is both one of the simplest to use and one of the most important to include in your team's toolbox. Following is a summary description of the 4 P's:

- **PRODUCT/ SERVICE:** This is what you're offering. This is your changemaking innovation. It may include products, services, and/or "people for people" strategies. Here you'll want to describe things such as features, benefits, packaging, services, guarantees, styles, etc.
- **PROMOTION:** This is the messaging and communication used to make the product known, and to persuade people to want to acquire it. Examples are community campaigns, advertising, public relations, direct selling, and sales promotions.
- **PLACE:** This can be either a physical location(s) and/ or a distribution channel(s).
- **PRICE:** This is the cost to acquire your product. Every product has a cost. Here you should describe not only the monetary amount but any other less explicit costs that someone is required to "pay" for acquiring your product. You should also describe the terms. For example, will people have to pay 100% upfront or can they pay over time?

HOW TO USE THIS TOOL

1. Start by describing your PRODUCT in as much detail as possible.
2. Next, note down the PROMOTION, PLACE, and PRICE. There's no need to do this in any particular order. As you work through this be as specific as possible, and keep an eye out for any misalignment between the 4 P's.
3. To conclude, go to NOW WHAT? and note down a few priority next steps based on what you've learned and/or new insights you've gained from using this tool.

CHANGEMAKER COACH | TOOL TIPS

- Given its comprehensive nature, I thought about putting this tool in TOOLKIT 07: OUR CHANGEMAKING BLUEPRINTS, but I decided it might be more useful in this toolkit.
- You might also want to use this to analyze current solutions.
- This should help put CT22 SHOW IT (p. 68) into action.
- Following are examples of tools that will help you with this tool: T7.5 NOVEL FEATURES + BENEFITS BLUEPRINT(p. 246), T11.2 PRICING FOR ADOPTION STRATEGY (p. 300), and T12.2 STICKY MESSAGING STRATEGY (p. 318).

CHANGEMAKING INNOVATION MINI-CASES	
V5	p. 358
V75	p. 372
V81	p. 374

CHANGEMAKING TRIMTABS	
CT8	p. 40
CT13	p. 50
CT14	p. 52

PRODUCT	PROMOTION
PLACE	**PRICE**

NOW WHAT?	

TOOLS FOR INNOVATION DESIGN CONVERSATIONS | POSITIONING + MARKETING STRATEGIES

TOOLKIT TOOLS REFLECTIONS

SCALE:
STRONGLY AGREE = 5, AGREE = 4, NOT SURE = 3, DISAGREE = 2, STRONGLY DISAGREE = 1

tinyurl.com/cctboxtoolsrflect

REFLECTION STATEMENTS	CHANGEMAKING TOOLS			
	T10.1	T10.2	T10.3	T10.4
This tool is easy to understand.				
This tool is easy to use.				
This tool taught me/ us important new knowledge.				
This tool empowered new changemaking conversations.				
This tool helped to spark new ideas/ insights.				
This tool should be included in my/ our toolbox for the future.				
I/ we should share this tool with other changemakers.				

NOTES:

TOOLS FOR INNOVATION DESIGN CONVERSATIONS | GETTING TO ADOPTION STRATEGIES

Tim T. collaborating with community members in Guatemala

Leadership teams collaborating in Colombia

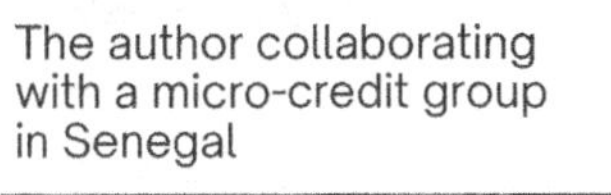

The author collaborating with a micro-credit group in Senegal

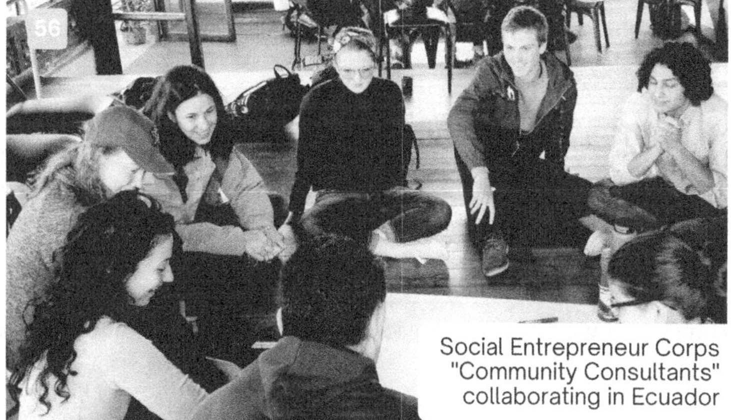

Social Entrepreneur Corps "Community Consultants" collaborating in Ecuador

NOTES:

GVK note -

- I love BJ Fogg's formula - B=MAP. To spark a behavior change, you need MOTIVATION, ABILITY + a PROMPT.

toolkit 11 TOOLS FOR INNOVATION DESIGN CONVERSATIONS | GETTING TO ADOPTION STRATEGIES

TOOLS INVENTORY

How might we design strategies that focus on influencing and empowering user adoption?

tinyurl.com/cctboxtools01

NOTES:

GVK notes -

- *Can you create a JND? This is a JUST NOTICEABLE DIFFERENCE.*
- *Help people feel and see early/ easy wins. It's important for motivation.*

TOOLS FOR INNOVATION DESIGN CONVERSATIONS | GETTING TO ADOPTION STRATEGIES

TOOLKIT SCORECARD + PRIORITIZATION HELP

Score yourselves to help you decide which tool(s) you might want to prioritize for your changemaking conversations.

tinyurl.com/cctboxtoolsprior

SELF-CHECK STATEMENTS	HOW ARE WE DOING?	TOOL SUGGESTIONS
We're having conversations about how well our changemaking innovation "passes" the five keys to innovation adoption.	0 1 2 3 4 5	T11.1
We've considered a broad variety of pricing models, and have chosen the one that's the most compelling given the context.	0 1 2 3 4 5	T11.2
We're working to prioritize the most important factors for great user experience.	0 1 2 3 4 5	T11.3
We're having conversations about where and how individual, social, and structural factors are influencing people's motivations and capabilities so that we factor this into our design.	0 1 2 3 4 5	T11.4
We're working to include the right mix of intrinsic and extrinsic incentives in the design of our changemaking innovation.	0 1 2 3 4 5	T11.5
We're talking about how we might include behavioral nudge strategies in our design.	0 1 2 3 4 5	T11.6

TOOLS FOR INNOVATION DESIGN CONVERSATIONS | GETTING TO ADOPTION STRATEGIES

COLLABORATIVE CHANGEMAKING VOICES

Get into the mindset for this toolkit + include your voice in the conversation.

"My greatest challenge has been to change the mindset of people. Mindsets play strange tricks on us. We see things the way our minds have instructed our eyes to see."

MUHAMMAD YUNUS
FOUNDER - GRAMEEN BANK |
NOBEL PEACE PRIZE LAUREATE

"You've got to start from customer experience and work backward."

STEVE JOBS
CO-FOUNDER - APPLE

"Design isn't finished until somebody is using it."

BRENDA LAUREL, PHD
VIDEO GAME/ INTERACTIVE DESIGNER

"The only way on Earth to influence other people is to talk about what they want and show them how to get it."

DALE CARNEGIE
AUTHOR | SELF-HELP GURU

"I think there is a profound and enduring beauty in simplicity; in clarity, in efficiency. True simplicity is derived from so much more than just the absence of clutter and ornamentation. It's about bringing order to complexity."

JONY IVE
FORMER CHIEF DESIGN OFFICER - APPLE

"The emotional tail wags the rational dog."

JONATHAN HAIDT
SOCIAL PSYCHOLOGIST | AUTHOR | EDUCATOR

"Just as no building lacks an architecture, so no choice lacks a context."

RICHARD H. THALER
AUTHOR - *NUDGE: IMPROVING DECISIONS ABOUT HEALTH, WEALTH, AND HAPPINESS*

T11.1

TOOLS FOR INNOVATION DESIGN CONVERSATIONS | GETTING TO ADOPTION STRATEGIES

KEYS TO INNOVATION ADOPTION

How might we design our innovation in alignment with the five keys to adoption?

tinyurl.com/cclboxt111

ABOUT THIS TOOL

If the people you aspire to support don't adopt your innovation, if they don't actually use it, then it may as well not exist. This KEYS TO INNOVATION ADOPTION tool will help you and your team analyze how likely people are to adopt your innovation and make design modifications accordingly.

This tool is based on the work of Everett Rogers, who was a communication theorist, sociologist, and is the father of the "Diffusion of Innovation (DOI) Theory." He identified five characteristics that an innovation must have to achieve adoption. They are as follows:

- **RELATIVE ADVANTAGE:** This is how improved an innovation is compared to other options (even doing nothing) or to the previous generation. Is it a better user experience in some way?
- **COMPATIBILITY:** This is how well an innovation assimilates into a person's work/ life. The innovation should "meet people where they are."
- **SIMPLICITY:** If the solution is too difficult to understand or use, people will be unlikely to adopt it. It has to be simple. And only simple scales.
- **TRIALABILITY:** This is the degree to which an innovation can be experimented with before requiring a full commitment. Can the user take the innovation for a "road test" in some way before making a final purchase decision?
- **OBSERVABILITY:** This is the extent to which the expected positive impact/ change resulting from the use of the innovation is felt and/or is visible.

To note, it may not be possible for your changemaking innovation to be strong in all of these areas. If so, try compensating with other characteristics.

HOW TO USE THIS TOOL

1. Start by going to the KEYS TO ADOPTION header. First, go to RELATIVE ADVANTAGE.
2. Under the ANALYSIS header, answer HOW IS OUR INNOVATION ACHIEVING THIS? Rate the STRENGTH of your response by circling a number between 1 and 5. "1" signifies you might need to make some big changes, and "5" means your innovation is very strong.
3. Repeat step 2 for each of the KEYS TO ADOPTION.
4. Next, based on your ANALYSIS, note down your IDEAS FOR EMPHASIS AND/OR IMPROVEMENTS for each of the KEYS TO ADOPTION.
5. To conclude, go to NOW WHAT? and note down a few priority next steps based on what you've learned and/or new insights you've gained from using this tool.

CHANGEMAKER COACH | TOOL TIPS

- This is one of my top go-to tools for discovery/ diagnosis and design. In fact, whenever I'm trying to figure out why a product/ service/ program isn't working, I intuitively start by analyzing these five keys to adoption.
- This should help you put CT13 RESTRUCTURE IT (p. 50) and CT15 CONFRONT COMPLEXITY WITH SIMPLICITY (p. 54)(not included below) into practice.
- You might want to use this with T3.4 SWEET SPOT WHITEBOARD (p. 154).
- This goes hand-in-hand with T8.4 DIFFUSION STRATEGY (p. 262).

CHANGEMAKING INNOVATION MINI-CASES	
V5	p. 358
V30	p. 363
V58	p. 369

CHANGEMAKING TRIMTABS	
CT4	p. 32
CT13	p. 50
CT17	p. 58

	ANALYSIS		
KEYS TO ADOPTION	**HOW IS OUR INNOVATION ACHIEVING THIS?**	**STRENGTH**	**IDEAS FOR EMPHASIS AND/ OR IMPROVEMENT**
RELATIVE ADVANTAGE		1 2 3 4 5	
COMPATIBILITY		1 2 3 4 5	
SIMPLICITY		1 2 3 4 5	
TRIALABILITY		1 2 3 4 5	
OBSERVABILITY		1 2 3 4 5	

NOW WHAT?	

T11.2

TOOLS FOR INNOVATION DESIGN CONVERSATIONS | GETTING TO ADOPTION STRATEGIES

toolkit 11

PRICING FOR ADOPTION STRATEGY

How might we decide and define the most compelling pricing strategy given the context?

tinyurl.com/cctboxt111

ABOUT THIS TOOL

The main goal for your pricing strategy should be user adoption. This PRICING FOR ADOPTION STRATEGY tool should help you and your team consider which pricing strategies might be the best to achieve this goal.

This tool includes the following 15 common pricing strategies:

- **FREE (DONATION):** There's no charge for the product/ service.
- **IN-KIND:** Use a good or service as payment instead of cash.
- **FREEMIUM:** This is popular with software. Offer free plans to gain new users and then charge extra for additional/ premium features.
- **SUBSIDY:** Only ask people to pay for a portion of the actual cost.
- **CROSS SUBSIDY/ BUY ONE GIVE ONE (B1G1):** Use a portion of the revenues from sales of a product to people who can afford to pay for it as a way to donate/ subsidize the same kind of product for those who can't afford to pay.
- **CONSIGNMENT:** This is useful for sellers. Sellers only pay for the product after they've sold it.
- **PAY-AS-YOU-GO (PAYGO)/ METERING:** This has become popular to create access to solar energy. People only pay for what they use. There's a meter that tracks usage.
- **TRY BEFORE YOU BUY:** Test the product/ service for a predetermined amount of time and then either return it or purchase it.
- **LAYAWAY:** Pay a deposit to "hold" the product until full payment can be made.
- **CREDIT:** Access a product/ service and then pay over time with an interest payment added
- **RENT/ LEASE:** Regular payments to an owner over a predetermined amount of time for the right to use something
- **SUBSCRIPTION:** Commonly used with creative content like Netflix, magazines, etc. with monthly or annual payments.
- **BUNDLED:** This is payment for a variety of products/ services with one payment. This is used in healthcare.
- **PIGGYBACK:** This is adding a lower-cost product onto a higher-cost product.
- **FULL PRICE (100% AT TIME OF PURCHASE:):** This is for people who can afford to pay upfront and all at once.

HOW TO USE THIS TOOL

1. Start at the top and describe the DESIRED USER(S) and anticipated PAYER for your product/ service. These are usually the same. Examples where they might be different would be when an organization is purchasing something for its employees, or when a parent buys something for her child. Below this, describe your PRODUCT/ SERVICE INNOVATION.
2. Next, go to the PRICING STRATEGY header. For each strategy, note down your DESIGN IDEAS and then an analysis of the ADVANTAGES and DISADVANTAGES for the DESIRED USER/ PAYER and the PROVIDER/ SELLER. Based on this analysis, circle a POTENTIAL FOR ADOPTION RATING. "0" means that the PRICING STRATEGY will almost certainly not lead to adoption, and "5" means that it will.
3. To conclude, go to NOW WHAT? and note down a few priority next steps based on what you've learned and/or new insights you've gained from using this tool.

CHANGEMAKER COACH | TOOL TIPS

- Use this tool to help put CT14 MAKE PRICING THE ONRAMP (p. 52) into action.
- This should help you with T3.5 FOUR FITS WHITEBOARD (p. 156) and T10.4 MARKETING MIX STRATEGY (p. 290).

CHANGEMAKING INNOVATION MINI-CASES	
V29	p. 363
V81	p. 374
V85	p. 374

CHANGEMAKING TRIMTABS	
CT8	p. 40
CT13	p. 50
CT14	p. 52

DESIRED USER(S)		PAYER	
PRODUCT/ SERVICE INNOVATION			

PRICING STRATEGY	DESIGN IDEAS	ADVANTAGES		DISADVANTAGES		POTENTIAL FOR ADOPTION RATING
		DESIRED USER/ PAYER	PROVIDER/ SELLER	DESIRED USER/ PAYER	PROVIDER/ SELLER	
ZERO (FREE/ DONATION)						0 1 2 3 4 5
IN-KIND						0 1 2 3 4 5
FREEMIUM						0 1 2 3 4 5
SUBSIDY						0 1 2 3 4 5
CROSS SUBSIDY (BUY ONE GIVE ONE - B1G1)						0 1 2 3 4 5
CONSIGNMENT						0 1 2 3 4 5
PAY-AS-YOU-GO (PAYGO)/ METERING						0 1 2 3 4 5
TRY BEFORE YOU BUY						0 1 2 3 4 5
LAYAWAY						0 1 2 3 4 5
CREDIT						0 1 2 3 4 5
LICENSE						0 1 2 3 4 5
SUBSCRIPTION						0 1 2 3 4 5
BUNDLED						0 1 2 3 4 5
PIGGYBACK						0 1 2 3 4 5
MARKET PRICE (100% AT TIME OF PURCHASE)						0 1 2 3 4 5

NOW WHAT?	

T11.3

TOOLS FOR INNOVATION DESIGN CONVERSATIONS | GETTING TO ADOPTION STRATEGIES

USER EXPERIENCE STRATEGY

How might we design our innovation keeping critical factors for successful user experience in mind?

tinyurl.com/cctboxt111

ABOUT THIS TOOL

According to management guru Peter F. Drucker, "Customers pay only for what is of use to them and gives them value." Value is the benefit someone receives relative to what they pay. Value is created through user experience. This USER EXPERIENCE STRATEGY tool will help you and your team design your changemaking innovation to create value for the people you hope to support.

The design of this tool is inspired by the work of Peter Morville, a pioneer in information architecture and user experience. He advocates that user experience design must address six key factors to create value. In alphabetical order, they are as follows:

- **ACCESSIBILITY:** Can the innovation be accessed by users with a full range of abilities?
- **CREDIBILITY:** Does the user trust that the innovation will perform as promised for an extended amount of time?
- **DESIRABILITY:** Are the branding and the aesthetics desirable to the target audience?
- **FINDABILITY:** Is it easy for users to find the innovation and all of the features that make it beneficial?
- **USABILITY:** Can users effectively and efficiently achieve their desired outcome with the innovation?
- **USEFULNESS:** Can it be used for the practical purpose it was intended for and/or for multiple purposes?

HOW TO USE THIS TOOL

1. Start at the top of the tool. Describe OUR INNOVATION and the DESIRED USER.
2. Next, go to the KEY SUCCESS FACTORS header. Start with ACCESSIBILITY. Work through the ANALYSIS by answering HOW IS OUR INNOVATION ACHIEVING THIS? and HOW IS THIS SPECIFICALLY VALUABLE FOR THE USER? Then rate the STRENGTH of your responses. "1" means "very weak," and "5" means "very strong."
3. Repeat step 2 for each of the KEY SUCCESS FACTORS.
4. Now go back to ACCESSIBILITY and, based on your ANALYSIS, note down IDEAS FOR EMPHASIS AND/OR IMPROVEMENTS.
5. Repeat step 4 for each of the KEY SUCCESS FACTORS.
6. To conclude, go to NOW WHAT? and note down a few priority next steps based on what you've learned and/or new insights you've gained from using this tool.

CHANGEMAKER COACH | TOOL TIPS

- This is great for putting CT13 RESTRUCTURE IT (p. 50) and CT14 MAKE PRICING THE ONRAMP (p. 52) (not listed below) into practice.
- You might want to use this with T3.4 SWEET SPOT WHITEBOARD (p. 154), T5.5 JOURNEY MAP (p. 200), T10.2 TWO ATTRIBUTES POSITIONING (p. 286), and T12.5 TOUCHPOINT STRATEGY (p. 324).

CHANGEMAKING INNOVATION MINI-CASES	
V1	p. 358
V18	p. 361
V81	p. 374

CHANGEMAKING TRIMTABS	
CT8	p. 40
CT13	p. 50
CT22	p. 68

OUR INNOVATION	
DESIRED USER	

	ANALYSIS			
KEY SUCCESS FACTORS	**HOW IS OUR INNOVATION ACHIEVING THIS?**	**HOW IS THIS SPECIFICALLY VALUABLE FOR THE USER?**	**STRENGTH**	**IDEAS FOR EMPHASIS AND/ OR IMPROVEMENTS**
ACCESSIBILTY			1 2 3 4 5	
CREDIBILITY			1 2 3 4 5	
DESIRABILITY			1 2 3 4 5	
FINDABILITY			1 2 3 4 5	
USABILITY			1 2 3 4 5	
USEFULNESS			1 2 3 4 5	

NOW WHAT?	

☐ T11.4

TOOLS FOR INNOVATION DESIGN CONVERSATIONS | GETTING TO ADOPTION STRATEGIES

MOTIVATORS + CAPABILITIES STRATEGY

How might we design our innovation accounting for the personal, social, and structural factors that influence motivations and capabilities?

tinyurl.com/cctboxt111

ABOUT THIS TOOL

Inspired by the book ***Influencer: The Power to Change Anything***, this tool should help you design strategies to influence positive behavior change. Changemakers are in the positive behavior change business. And a key to being successful in this business is understanding and increasing people's motivation and capabilities. This MOTIVATORS + CAPABILITIES STRATEGY tool should help you and your team do this.

Research shows that before we decide to do anything, we consciously or subconsciously ask ourselves two questions from a PERSONAL, SOCIAL, and STRUCTURAL perspective; "Is it worth it?"(Motivation) and "Can I do it?"(Capability). If the answer is "No" to either of these questions, we don't move forward. As a changemaker, your goal is to help people get to "Yes." This tool includes the following prompts to help you increase people's motivation and capabilities so that they can get to "Yes.":

PERSONAL

- **SOURCES OF MOTIVATION:** What are these? Does the person actually want to do it? Is there intrinsic motivation?
- **CAPABILITIES:** Does the person have the requisite knowledge and skills?

SOCIAL

- **SOURCES OF MOTIVATION:** Are other people/ team members encouraging the desired behavior? Is there positive or negative peer pressure at play?
- **CAPABILITIES:** Do others provide the necessary support, tools, and/or resources? Is there strength in numbers?

STRUCTURAL

- **SOURCES OF MOTIVATION:** Does the environment encourage the desired behavior? Are the right rewards and/or incentives in existence?
- **CAPABILITY:** Does the environment empower or hinder success? Are there aspects of the environment that are acting as obstacles?

HOW TO USE THIS TOOL

1. Start by noting down THE DESIRED BEHAVIOR. For example, this might be "Wash hands," "Drink filtered water," "Go to school every day," "Be entrepreneurial," Eat healthy meals," "Be a more empathetic leader," etc.
2. Next, go to PERSONAL and SOURCES OF MOTIVATION. Note down WHAT'S HELPING? These are the current PERSONAL SOURCES OF MOTIVATION that are contributing to THE DESIRED BEHAVIOR. Then note down WHAT'S HURTING? Are there any SOURCES OF MOTIVATION or demotivation that are getting in the way? Then note down WHAT'S MISSING? Next, review what you've written and then note your team's (RE)DESIGN IDEAS. How might you design or redesign a/your changemaking innovation based on your analysis of PERSONAL SOURCES OF MOTIVATION?
3. After this, go through this same process for the other five boxes in the tool.
4. To conclude, go to NOW WHAT? and note down the most important short-term action items/next steps based upon your learnings and insights from using this tool.

CHANGEMAKER COACH | TOOL TIPS

- This is one of my favorites. Invest some time with this tool. Influencing behavior is difficult no matter what. It's especially difficult when we look at motivation and capabilities too narrowly. We tend to fall prey to this. This tool forces you to look at all six sources of motivation and capability.
- Pay special attention to the social sources of motivation and capabilities. These are often overlooked, despite being the most influential.
- I struggled to decide where to put this tool. It's a great tool for both diagnosis and design.

CHANGEMAKING INNOVATION MINI-CASES	
V37	p. 365
V53	p. 368
V82	p. 374

CHANGEMAKING TRIMTABS	
CT9	p. 42
CT13	p. 50
CT16	p. 56

THE DESIRED BEHAVIOR	

	SOURCES OF MOTIVATION		CAPABILITIES	
PERSONAL	WHAT'S HELPING? WHAT'S HURTING? WHAT'S MISSING?	(RE)DESIGN IDEAS	WHAT'S HELPING? WHAT'S HURTING? WHAT'S MISSING?	(RE)DESIGN IDEAS
SOCIAL	WHAT'S HELPING? WHAT'S HURTING? WHAT'S MISSING?	(RE)DESIGN IDEAS	WHAT'S HELPING? WHAT'S HURTING? WHAT'S MISSING?	(RE)DESIGN IDEAS
STRUCTURAL	WHAT'S HELPING? WHAT'S HURTING? WHAT'S MISSING?	(RE)DESIGN IDEAS	WHAT'S HELPING? WHAT'S HURTING? WHAT'S MISSING?	(RE)DESIGN IDEAS

NOW WHAT?	

☐ T11.5

TOOLS FOR INNOVATION DESIGN CONVERSATIONS | GETTING TO ADOPTION STRATEGIES

INCENTIVIZATION STRATEGY

How might we include the most influenctial intrinsic and extrinsic incentives in our design?

tinyurl.com/cctboxt111

ABOUT THIS TOOL

In the words of Charlie Munger, former Vice-Chairman of Berkshire Hathaway, "Show me the incentives, and I'll show you the outcome." It's incentives that move people to make decisions and take action. And there's no one-size-fits-all incentive. People are typically moved by a mix of intrinsic motivators, extrinsic drivers, and organizational/societal factors. Figuring out the right mix requires analysis and thoughtfulness. This INCENTIVIZATION STRATEGY tool should help you and your team have conversations about the mix of incentives that might work best for your changemaking efforts.

It's helpful to put incentives in the three following categories when you're considering their relevance for your changemaking efforts:

- **PERSONAL INTRINSIC:** These are personal motivations driven by a felt need and/or desire. This is where you should start. Three examples in this category are LOVE, SELF ACTUALIZATION, and MORAL MOTIVATIONS.
- **PERSONAL EXTRINSIC:** These affect the personal, but come from the outside. One or more of these are often necessary, but insufficient and/or unsustainable without other types of incentives in place. Three examples in this category are CAREER ADVANCEMENT, INCREASED EARNINGS, and AVOIDING PUNISHMENT.
- **ORGANIZATIONAL/ SOCIETAL:** These incentives tend to be less personal, and more general in nature. Three examples in this category are RESPONDING TO A CRISIS, FOLLOWING A POLITICAL PARTY, and COMPLIANCE WITH A RULE/REGULATION.

HOW TO USE THIS TOOL

1. Start by going to the INCENTIVES header. Review all of the INCENTIVES included in this tool.
2. Next, go to RELEVANCE FOR OUR DESIGN for each of the INCENTIVES and circle a number. "0" means that it's not relevant and "5" means that the INCENTIVE is extremely relevant.
3. Once you've done this, start with the INCENTIVES with the highest RELEVANCE FOR OUR DESIGN. Work your way from high to low and note down OUR DESIGN FEATURE IDEAS to incorporate the incentive in your changemaking innovation design.
4. To conclude, go to NOW WHAT? and note down a few priority next steps based on what you've learned and/or new insights you've gained from using this tool.

CHANGEMAKER COACH | TOOL TIPS

- We tend to start with extrinsic incentives. This is probably because they're more visible, easier to understand, more concrete, and more universal in nature. Don't! My strong suggestion would be to first work to understand and design for intrinsic motivations.
- Examples of other tools that touch on incentives/ motivation are T1.1 OUR WHY (p. 112), T3.1 PROXIMITY ANALYSIS (p. 148), T5.3 EMPOWERMENT MAP (p. 196), T7.3 SUCCESS INDICATORS BLUEPRINT (p. 242), and T11.2 PRICING FOR ADOPTION STRATEGY (p. 300).

CHANGEMAKING INNOVATION MINI-CASES		CHANGEMAKING TRIMTABS	
V55	p. 368	CT18	p. 60
V61	p. 370	CT19	p. 62
V76	p. 373	CT22	p. 68

	INCENTIVES	RELEVANCE FOR OUR DESIGN	OUR DESIGN FEATURE IDEAS
PERSONAL INTRINSIC	LOVE	0 1 2 3 4 5	
	SELF- ACTUALIZATION	0 1 2 3 4 5	
	SENSE OF PURPOSE	0 1 2 3 4 5	
	BEING A ROLE MODEL AND/ OR MENTOR	0 1 2 3 4 5	
	FUN/ JOY	0 1 2 3 4 5	
	SENSE OF COMMUNITY	0 1 2 3 4 5	
	INCREASED HAPPINESS	0 1 2 3 4 5	
	BETTER PHYSICAL/ MENTAL HEALTH	0 1 2 3 4 5	
	A SENSE OF MORALITY/ PERSONAL OBLIGATION	0 1 2 3 4 5	
	SENSE OF SECURITY	0 1 2 3 4 5	
	FRIENDSHIP/ FAMILY	0 1 2 3 4 5	
		0 1 2 3 4 5	
PERSONAL EXTRINSIC	CAREER ADVANCEMENT	0 1 2 3 4 5	
	AWARDS OR RECOGNITION	0 1 2 3 4 5	
	INCREASED EARNINGS	0 1 2 3 4 5	
	AVOIDING PUNISHMENT	0 1 2 3 4 5	
		0 1 2 3 4 5	
ORGANIZATIONAL/ SOCIETAL	FOLLOWING A MOVEMENT	0 1 2 3 4 5	
	FOLLOWING A POLITICAL PARTY	0 1 2 3 4 5	
	RESPONSE TO A CRISIS	0 1 2 3 4 5	
	GOALS + OBJECTIVES	0 1 2 3 4 5	
	INCREASED TRANSPARENCY	0 1 2 3 4 5	
	ADHERENCE TO A POLICY	0 1 2 3 4 5	
	COMPLIANCE WITH A RULE/ REGULATION	0 1 2 3 4 5	
		0 1 2 3 4 5	

NOW WHAT?	

T11.6

TOOLS FOR INNOVATION DESIGN CONVERSATIONS | GETTING TO ADOPTION STRATEGIES

NUDGE STRATEGY

How might we include nudges in our innovation design?

tinyurl.com/cctboxt111

ABOUT THIS TOOL

The concept of nudges comes from the book ***Nudge: Improving Decisions About Health, Wealth, and Happiness***, written by Nobel Prize-winning economist Richard Thaler and scholar Cass Sunstein. A nudge is an aspect of the choice architecture (the way in which choices are presented to decision-makers) that's designed to change someone's behavior. Nudges do this without eliminating options or significantly changing economic incentives. Nudges are small, often incredibly powerful, ways to influence behavior. This NUDGE STRATEGY tool should help you and your team include nudges in your changemaking innovation.

Ten common nudge strategies included in this tool are as follows:

- **CHANGE THE LOCATION:** An example is a lunchroom in schools where small changes in positioning affect what students choose. Studies show moving salad bars to high-traffic areas and placing fruit baskets next to registers results in students selecting healthier foods.
- **CHANGE THE SIZE:** An example is using smaller plates to reduce food consumption and food waste. Research shows that even a small reduction can have a significant impact.
- **CREATE RAPID FEEDBACK:** One example is radar speed signs. Research shows that these reduce driver speeds. For every decrease of even one mph in speed, accident rates drop 5%
- **DO THE UNEXPECTED:** For example, in a tube station in London, the manager had his nine-year-old daughter record escalator safety announcements. People didn't expect a girl's voice. Injuries fell by two-thirds.
- **MAKE IT CONCRETE:** These are often used to reduce consumption. For example, for toilets with one button for a large flush and another for a small flush, people still often push the large button unnecessarily. When the text "5 liters" and "1 liter" are written on the buttons, people push the smaller button more often.
- **MAKE IT EASIER:** For example, a medicine bottle that reads "Take one pill after breakfast." works better than "Take once a day."
- **MAKE IT FUN/ USE HUMOR:** For example, in Stockholm, Sweden, "piano stairs" were installed in a subway station next to an escalator to encourage people to use the stairs. Each step of the staircase was painted like a piano key and produced a different sound when it was stepped on. Studies showed that 66% more commuters took the stairs.
- **REVERSE THE DEFAULT:** For example, in the U.S., the default option for employees at companies was to opt-out of 401(k) retirement savings plans. The nudge was to enroll workers automatically, but offer the right to opt-out to anyone who didn't want to participate. One study suggested that this more than doubled retirement plan participation.
- **USE DIFFERENT SENSES:** Examples are the small bumps on the sides of highways that make a noise and make you feel when you're going off the road. Another is a McDonald's restaurant that used classical music in their restaurants to reduce loitering by teens.
- **USE SOCIAL COMPARISONS:** Home Energy Reports (HERs) are an example. HERs provide information about a household's energy usage and how it compares with neighbors' usage. HERs also show estimated financial savings from a list of suggested conservation steps. These have been shown to create energy savings of up to 6%.

HOW TO USE THIS TOOL

1. Start at the top of the tool. Note down THE BEHAVIOUR WE WANT TO ENCOURAGE, THE CURRENT SITUATION, and CURRENT SHORTCOMINGS.
2. Next, go to the NUDGING STRATEGIES header. For each one, try to come up with a NUDGE DESIGN IDEA(S) that might help you achieve THE BEHAVIOUR WE WANT TO ENCOURAGE.
3. To conclude, go to NOW WHAT? and note down a few priority next steps based on what you've learned and/or new insights you've gained from using this tool.

CHANGEMAKING INNOVATION MINI-CASES	
V23	p. 362
V36	p. 365
V81	p. 374

CHANGEMAKING TRIMTABS	
CT7	p. 38
CT15	p. 54
CT22	p. 68

THE BEHAVIOUR WE WANT TO ENCOURAGE	
THE CURRENT SITUATION	
CURRENT SHORTCOMINGS	

NUDGING STRATEGIES	NUDGE DESIGN IDEA(S)
CHANGE THE LOCATION	
CHANGE THE SIZE	
CREATE RAPID FEEDBACK	
DO THE UNEXPECTED	
MAKE IT CONCRETE	
MAKE IT EASIER	
MAKE IT FUN/ USE HUMOR	
REVERSE THE DEFAULT	
USE DIFFERENT SENSES	
USE SOCIAL COMPARISONS	

NOW WHAT?	

TOOLS FOR INNOVATION DESIGN CONVERSATIONS |
GETTING TO ADOPTION STRATEGIES

TOOLKIT TOOLS REFLECTIONS

SCALE:
STRONGLY AGREE = 5, AGREE = 4, NOT SURE = 3, DISAGREE = 2, STRONGLY DISAGREE = 1

tinyurl.com/cctboxtoolsrflect

	CHANGEMAKING TOOLS					
REFLECTION STATEMENTS	**T11.1**	**T11.2**	**T11.3**	**T11.4**	**T11.5**	**T11.6**
This tool is easy to understand.						
This tool is easy to use.						
This tool taught me/ us important new knowledge.						
This tool empowered new changemaking conversations.						
This tool helped to spark new ideas/ insights.						
This tool should be included in my/ our toolbox for the future.						
I/ we should share this tool with other changemakers.						

NOTES:

TOOLS FOR INNOVATION DESIGN CONVERSATIONS | MESSAGING + COMMUNICATION STRATEGIES

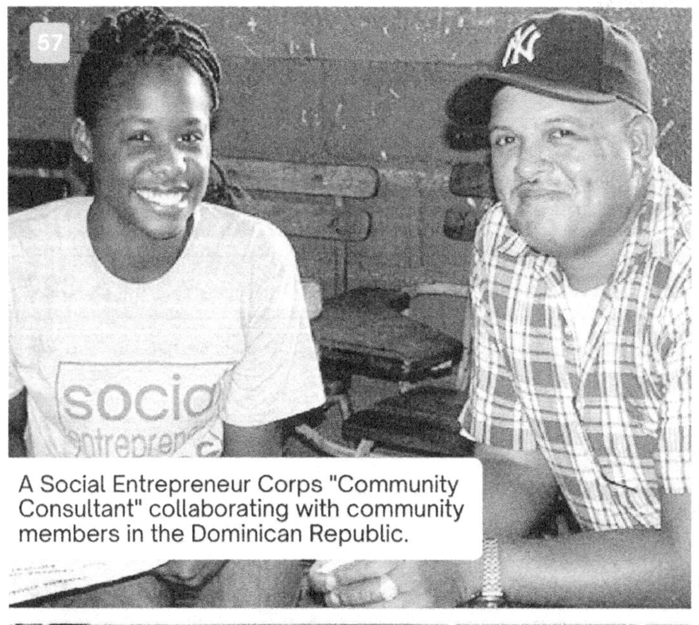

A Social Entrepreneur Corps "Community Consultant" collaborating with community members in the Dominican Republic.

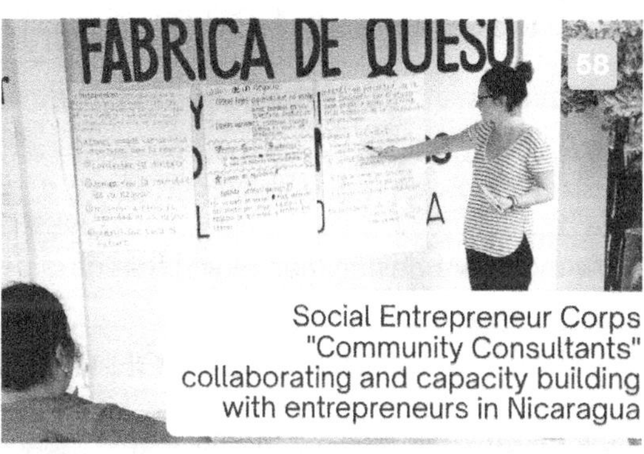

Social Entrepreneur Corps "Community Consultants" collaborating and capacity building with entrepreneurs in Nicaragua

Entrepreneurs collaborating to provide vision solutions

The author collaborating with a corporate leadership team in Mexico

Marta V. collaborating with radio station leadership in Ecuador

NOTES:

GVK note -

- *Go to HOW TO GIVE AN EFFECTIVE PRESENTATION (pg. 380)*

toolkit 12

TOOLS FOR INNOVATION DESIGN CONVERSATIONS | MESSAGING + COMMUNICATION STRATEGIES

TOOLS INVENTORY

How might we design messaging and communication that's effective, efficient and responsive?

tinyurl.com/cctboxtools01

NOTES:

GVK notes -

- How many floors is your elevator pitch? Do you know?
- Spend a good amount of time on EXPOSITION. This is the first part of a story arc that offers background information about the main characters and the circumstances. You need people to understand and care. Exposition helps create empathy.

TOOLS FOR INNOVATION DESIGN CONVERSATIONS | MESSAGING + COMMUNICATION STRATEGIES

TOOLKIT SCORECARD + PRIORITIZATION HELP

Score yourselves to help you decide which tool(s) you might want to prioritize for your changemaking conversations.

tinyurl.com/cctboxtoolsprior

SELF-CHECK STATEMENTS	HOW ARE WE DOING?	TOOL SUGGESTIONS
We feel confident about telling our changemaking innovation story to team members, collaborators, supporters, and/or investors/ donors.	0 1 2 3 4 5	T12.1
We're talking about how we can make our messaging attract attention and be sticky.	0 1 2 3 4 5	T12.2
We're discussing which communication channels might be the most effective and efficient for reaching our target audience.	0 1 2 3 4 5	T12.3
We're having conversations about how we're building feedback strategies.	0 1 2 3 4 5	T12.4
We've working to include the right number and kind of touchpoints.	0 1 2 3 4 5	T12.5

toolkit 12

TOOLS FOR INNOVATION DESIGN CONVERSATIONS | MESSAGING + COMMUNICATION STRATEGIES

COLLABORATIVE CHANGEMAKING VOICES

Get into the mindset for this toolkit + include your voice in the conversation.

"When you listen, you learn. You absorb like a sponge and your life becomes so much better than when you are just trying to be listened to all the time."

STEVEN SPIELBERG
FILMMAKER

"Storytelling offers the opportunity to talk with your audience, not at them."

LAURA HOLLOWAY
FOUNDER - THE STORYTELLER AGENCY

"The most basic way to get someone's attention is this: Break a pattern."

CHIP HEATH
AUTHOR | PROFESSOR

"The most important thing in your story is going to be intention and obstacle...What does this character want and what's standing in the way of getting it?"

AARON SORKIN
SCREENWRITER

"Well told stories help turn moments of great crisis into moments of new beginnings."

MARSHALL GANZ
HARVARD LECTURER | AUTHOR

"I've learned that people will forget what you said, people will forget what you did, but people will never forget how you made them feel."

MAYA ANGELOU
AUTHOR | ACTIVIST

"True intuitive expertise is learned from prolonged experience with good feedback on mistakes."

DANIEL KAHNEMAN
NOBEL PRIZE ECONOMIST
AUTHOR - *THINKING, FAST AND SLOW*

T12.1

TOOLS FOR INNOVATION DESIGN CONVERSATIONS | MESSAGING + COMMUNICATION STRATEGIES

INNOVATION STORY STRATEGY

How might we capture the story of our innovation in the most concise and compelling way?

tinyurl.com/cctboxt121

ABOUT THIS TOOL

You have to be able to tell the story of your changemaking innovation in a logical, concise, and compelling way. This is critical for giving pitches, talking to potential partners, onboarding teammates, building websites, designing marketing, filling out funding applications, etc. This INNOVATION STORY STRATEGY tool should help you and your team capture the most important information you'll need for telling your changemaking innovation's story.

The question prompts in this tool are categorized and listed in the order that you might use for a pitch. They are as follows:

ABOUT OUR TEAM
- **WHAT'S OUR BRAND?:** Design and name
- **WHAT'S OUR VISION?:** Aspirations for impact on the world
- **WHO'S ON OUR TEAM?:** Names, roles, and descriptions
- **WHAT ARE OUR CORE VALUES?:** List of three to ten

ABOUT THE PROBLEM
- **WHAT'S THE PROBLEM?:** A very specific problem
- **WHO'S MOST AFFECTED BY THE PROBLEM?:** Persona of people who acutely feel the problem
- **WHAT ARE THE NEGATIVE CONSEQUENCES OF THE PROBLEM?:** Short, medium, and long-term negative impacts
- **HOW BIG IS THE PROBLEM?:** The scale
- **WHY'S IT CRITICAL THAT WE WORK TO SOLVE THE PROBLEM NOW?:** The urgent need
- **WHAT'S THE CURRENT SITUATION?:** A landscape/industry/competitive analysis

ABOUT OUR SOLUTION
- **WHAT'S OUR SOLUTION?:** A description with features and benefits
- **HOW DOES OUR SOLUTION WORK?:** The steps/process/customer journey
- **WHAT MAKES OUR SOLUTION INNOVATIVE?:** Differentiating characteristics/ attributes
- **WHAT'S THE MARKETING MIX FOR OUR SOLUTION?:** Product, price, place + promotion strategies
- **WHO WILL ADOPT OUR SOLUTION + WHY?:** Personas of innovators/early adopters and rationale
- **HOW WILL WE GET STARTED?:** Lunch strategy
- **HOW WILL WE SCALE/ GROW?:** Scaling strategy
- **HOW WILL WE DEFINE SUCCESS?:** The short, medium + long-term success indicators
- **WHAT ARE THE COST/ REVENUE CONSIDERATIONS?:** The key drivers
- **WHAT ARE OUR PROJECTIONS?:** Projected sources of funds, break-even point, revenues + expenses, etc.
- **WHAT DO WE NEED TO BE SUCCESSFUL?:** Resources, time, knowledge, etc.
- **WHAT ARE OUR NEXT STEPS?:** Now, next month, three months, six months, etc.

HOW TO USE THIS TOOL

1. Start at the top of the tool. Note down your TARGET AUDIENCE and your CALL TO ACTION. It's important to know who your innovation story is for, and what you want them to do once they've heard it.
2. Next, work through each of the question prompts in the tool.
3. To conclude, go to NOW WHAT? and note down a few priority next steps based on what you've learned and/or new insights you've gained from using this tool.

CHANGEMAKING INNOVATION MINI-CASES	
V20	p. 361
V29	p. 363
V52	p. 368

CHANGEMAKING TRIMTABS	
CT5	p. 34
CT10	p. 44
CT21	p. 66

TARGET AUDIENCE	
CALL TO ACTION	

ABOUT OUR TEAM	
WHAT'S OUR BRAND?	
WHAT'S OUR VISION?	
WHO'S ON OUR TEAM?	
ABOUT THE PROBLEM	
WHAT'S THE PROBLEM?	
WHO'S MOST AFFECTED BY THE PROBLEM?	
WHAT ARE THE NEGATIVE CONSEQUENCES OF THE PROBLEM?	
HOW BIG IS THE PROBLEM?	
WHY'S IT CRITICAL THAT WE WORK TO SOLVE THIS PROBLEM NOW?	
WHAT'S THE CURRENT SITUATION?	
ABOUT OUR SOLUTION	
WHAT'S OUR SOLUTION?	
HOW DOES OUR SOLUTION WORK?	
WHAT MAKES OUR SOLUTION INNOVATIVE?	
WHAT'S THE MARKETING MIX FOR OUR SOLUTION?	
WHO WILL ADOPT OUR SOLUTION + WHY?	
HOW WILL WE GET STARTED?	
HOW WILL WE SCALE/ GROW?	
HOW WILL WE DEFINE SUCCESS?	
WHAT ARE THE COST/ REVENUE CONSIDERATIONS?	
WHAT ARE OUR PROJECTIONS?	
WHAT DO WE NEED TO BE SUCCESSFUL?	
WHAT ARE OUR NEXT STEPS?	

NOW WHAT?	

TOOLS FOR INNOVATION DESIGN CONVERSATIONS | MESSAGING + COMMUNICATION STRATEGIES

STICKY MESSAGING STRATEGY

How might we design messaging that gets people's attention and sticks?

tinyurl.com/cctboxt122

ABOUT THIS TOOL

This tool is inspired by Chip and Dan Heath's book ***Made to Stick: Why Some Ideas Survive and Others Die.*** In the book, the Heath brothers share what they've found to be the keys to creating sticky messaging. When messaging's sticky, people take notice. Sticky messaging is understandable, interesting, and memorable. This STICKY MESSAGING STRATEGY tool will help you and your team design sticky messaging for your changemaking innovation.

Following are the six characteristics included in this tool that make messages "sticky."

- **SIMPLE:** What's at the heart of the idea/concept? This should be your core message.
- **SURPRISING:** Create messaging that's unexpected and grabs people's attention. Be unique and differentiate yourself in surprising ways. Break patterns.
- **TANGIBLE:** Make sure your messaging speaks to something concrete. It shouldn't be abstract or theoretical. Make messaging easily understood and remembered.
- **CREDIBLE:** Convey that you know what you're talking about and that you're believable. Be aspirational, but grounded in reality.
- **EMOTIONAL:** People make decisions with their hearts, not their heads. Appeal to emotions.
- **STORIFIED:** Tell stories. Build a narrative. If you're hoping that someone will remember your messaging, stories beat lists of facts every day of the week.

HOW TO USE THIS TOOL

1. Start at the top of the tool. Describe your TARGET AUDIENCE.
2. Next, go to the STICKINESS ATTRIBUTES header. Start with SIMPLE. Note down your DESIGN STRATEGY to make your messaging SIMPLE. Then work through the ANALYSIS. Give your response a RATING. "1" means "very weak", and "5" signifies "very strong." Next, answer WHY THIS RATING?
3. Repeat step 2 for each of the STICKINESS ATTRIBUTES.
4. Now go back to SIMPLE and, based on your ANALYSIS, note down IDEAS TO CREATE MORE STICKINESS.
5. Repeat step 4 for each of the STICKINESS ATTRIBUTES.
6. To conclude, go to NOW WHAT? and note down a few priority next steps based on what you've learned and/or new insights you've gained from using this tool.

CHANGEMAKER COACH | TOOL TIPS

- This should help you put CT16 DO THE OPPOSITE (p. 56) into practice.
- You might want to use this with T3.4 SWEET SPOT WHITEBOARD (p. 154), T10.4 MARKETING MIX STRATEGY (p. 290), and T11.6 NUDGE STRATEGY (p. 308).

CHANGEMAKING INNOVATION MINI-CASES		CHANGEMAKING TRIMTABS	
V5	p. 358	CT13	p. 50
V7	p. 359	CT16	p. 56
V31	p. 364	CT22	p. 68

TARGET AUDIENCE	

		ANALYSIS		
STICKINESS ATTRIBUTES	DESIGN STRATEGY	RATING	WHY THIS RATING?	IDEAS TO CREATE MORE STICKINESS
SIMPLE		1 2 3 4 5		
SURPRISING		1 2 3 4 5		
TANGIBLE		1 2 3 4 5		
CREDIBLE		1 2 3 4 5		
EMOTIONAL		1 2 3 4 5		
STORIFIED		1 2 3 4 5		

NOW WHAT?	

T12.3

TOOLS FOR INNOVATION DESIGN CONVERSATIONS | MESSAGING + COMMUNICATION STRATEGIES

toolkit 12

COMMUNICATION CHANNEL STRATEGY

How might we prioritize communication channels based on both the target audience and purpose of the message?

tinyurl.com/cctboxt123

ABOUT THIS TOOL

Effective and efficient communication requires defining your TARGET AUDIENCE and selecting the right COMMUNICATION CHANNEL based on the PURPOSE OF THE COMMUNICATION. This COMMUNICATION STRATEGY DESIGN tool should help you and your team work through this process.

This tool includes 20 different common COMMUNICATION CHANNELs. They're listed on a spectrum from BROADCAST (good for reaching a lot of people at once) to NARROWCAST (good for very targeted and personalized communication). The PURPOSE OF THE COMMUNICATION should be the driving factor when deciding which COMMUNICATION CHANNEL to use. Following are five purposes that you might want to consider when using this tool:

- **Create awareness:** Help people become aware of a problem, new information, a program, an event, an opportunity, a solution, etc.
- **Share knowledge:** Help people learn something new in greater depth than simple awareness.
- **Call to action:** Motivate someone to do something.
- **Gather feedback:** Inspire people to share ideas, opinions, and/or evaluations.
- **Encourage referral:** Activate people to share positive opinions about your changemaking innovation with others who might benefit.

HOW TO USE THIS TOOL

1. Start at the top of the tool. Describe your TARGET AUDIENCE.
2. Next, go to the PURPOSE OF COMMUNICATION header. Under this header there are spaces for five communication purposes. Start by noting down PURPOSE 1.
3. Now go to the COMMUNICATION CHANNEL header. Work your way down the communication channels, and rate each one for PURPOSE 1 on a scale of "0" to "5". "0" means that this would be a very poor COMMUNICATION CHANNEL for PURPOSE 1. And "5" means it would be ideal.
4. Assuming you have another PURPOSE OF COMMUNICATION, repeat this process for PURPOSE 2. Then do the same for PURPOSE 3, etc.
5. To conclude, go to NOW WHAT? and note down a few priority next steps based on what you've learned and/or new insights you've gained from using this tool.

CHANGEMAKER COACH | TOOL TIPS

- Changemaking innovation success requires "meeting people where they are" and specificity. This tool should help you with this.
- This tool should help you put CT21 DEFINE + SHARE THE BHAG (p. 66) (not listed below) in practice.
- You might want to use this tool with T8.4 DIFFUSION STRATEGY (p. 262) and T10.4 MARKETING MIX STRATEGY (p. 290).

CHANGEMAKING INNOVATION MINI-CASES	
V16	p. 361
V56	p. 369
V70	p. 371

CHANGEMAKING TRIMTABS	
CT11	p. 46
CT18	p. 60
CT22	p. 68

TARGET AUDIENCE	

	COMMUNICATION CHANNEL	**PURPOSE OF THE COMMUNICATION**				
NARROWCAST	IN-PERSON (ONE-ON-ONE)	0 1 2 3 4 5	0 1 2 3 4 5	0 1 2 3 4 5	0 1 2 3 4 5	0 1 2 3 4 5
	PHONE CALL	0 1 2 3 4 5	0 1 2 3 4 5	0 1 2 3 4 5	0 1 2 3 4 5	0 1 2 3 4 5
	TEXT MESSAGE	0 1 2 3 4 5	0 1 2 3 4 5	0 1 2 3 4 5	0 1 2 3 4 5	0 1 2 3 4 5
	WHATSAPP/ DM	0 1 2 3 4 5	0 1 2 3 4 5	0 1 2 3 4 5	0 1 2 3 4 5	0 1 2 3 4 5
	LETTER	0 1 2 3 4 5	0 1 2 3 4 5	0 1 2 3 4 5	0 1 2 3 4 5	0 1 2 3 4 5
	EMAIL/IN MAIL	0 1 2 3 4 5	0 1 2 3 4 5	0 1 2 3 4 5	0 1 2 3 4 5	0 1 2 3 4 5
	IN-PERSON/ VIRTUAL (MEETING)	0 1 2 3 4 5	0 1 2 3 4 5	0 1 2 3 4 5	0 1 2 3 4 5	0 1 2 3 4 5
	IN-PERSON/VIRTUAL (INFO SESSION)	0 1 2 3 4 5	0 1 2 3 4 5	0 1 2 3 4 5	0 1 2 3 4 5	0 1 2 3 4 5
	IN-PERSON/ VIRTUAL (CAMPAIGN/DEMO/ WORKSHOP)	0 1 2 3 4 5	0 1 2 3 4 5	0 1 2 3 4 5	0 1 2 3 4 5	0 1 2 3 4 5
	IN-PERSON/ VIRTUAL (EVENT)	0 1 2 3 4 5	0 1 2 3 4 5	0 1 2 3 4 5	0 1 2 3 4 5	0 1 2 3 4 5
	NEWSLETTER (ELECTRONIC)	0 1 2 3 4 5	0 1 2 3 4 5	0 1 2 3 4 5	0 1 2 3 4 5	0 1 2 3 4 5
	NEWSLETTER (PAPER)	0 1 2 3 4 5	0 1 2 3 4 5	0 1 2 3 4 5	0 1 2 3 4 5	0 1 2 3 4 5
	SOCIAL MEDIA (LINKEDIN, TIK TOK ETC.)	0 1 2 3 4 5	0 1 2 3 4 5	0 1 2 3 4 5	0 1 2 3 4 5	0 1 2 3 4 5
	MEGAPHONE	0 1 2 3 4 5	0 1 2 3 4 5	0 1 2 3 4 5	0 1 2 3 4 5	0 1 2 3 4 5
	WEBSITE	0 1 2 3 4 5	0 1 2 3 4 5	0 1 2 3 4 5	0 1 2 3 4 5	0 1 2 3 4 5
	PODCAST	0 1 2 3 4 5	0 1 2 3 4 5	0 1 2 3 4 5	0 1 2 3 4 5	0 1 2 3 4 5
	POSTER/ FLYER	0 1 2 3 4 5	0 1 2 3 4 5	0 1 2 3 4 5	0 1 2 3 4 5	0 1 2 3 4 5
	YOUTUBE	0 1 2 3 4 5	0 1 2 3 4 5	0 1 2 3 4 5	0 1 2 3 4 5	0 1 2 3 4 5
	RADIO	0 1 2 3 4 5	0 1 2 3 4 5	0 1 2 3 4 5	0 1 2 3 4 5	0 1 2 3 4 5
BROADCAST	TV/ STREAMER	0 1 2 3 4 5	0 1 2 3 4 5	0 1 2 3 4 5	0 1 2 3 4 5	0 1 2 3 4 5

(BROADCAST <------ ------> NARROWCAST)

NOW WHAT?	

T12.4

TOOLS FOR INNOVATION DESIGN CONVERSATIONS | MESSAGING + COMMUNICATION STRATEGIES

toolkit 12

FEEDBACK PROCESS STRATEGY

How might we build feedback loops into the design of our innovation?

tinyurl.com/cctboxt124

ABOUT THIS TOOL

According to Ken Blanchard, the author of ***One Minute Manager***, "Feedback is the breakfast of champions." This is especially true when working in complex environments where continuous learning and pivoting are required. Use this FEEDBACK PROCESS STRATEGY tool to help you and your team address all key components necessary for getting actionable, quality, and timely feedback.

When using this tool, once you've defined your TARGET AUDIENCE and LEARNING GOALS (why you want/ need feedback), some of the KEY DECISIONS you'll need to make are as follows:

- **LOCATION OF COLLECTION:** Where will people leave feedback and where will you collect it? In boxes? Online forms?
- **TIMING OF COLLECTION:** When are the most helpful times to solicit feedback?
- **FREQUENCY OF COLLECTION:** How often will you collect feedback?
- **COMMUNICATION CHANNELS:** What are the best ways to communicate with your TARGET AUDIENCE?
- **HOW TO CREATE A SENSE OF SAFETY:** How will you make people feel that they can be honest and open?
- **INCENTIVES/ MOTIVATIONS FOR SHARING:** Why will people share? What's in it for them?
- **FREQUENCY OF ANALYSIS:** How often will you analyze the feedback?
- **ANALYSIS- PARTICIPANTS:** Who will analyze the feedback?
- **DURATION OF ANALYSIS:** How long will it take to analyze the feedback? Do it quickly.
- **RECOMMENDATION CRITERIA:** How will you turn feedback into recommendations for changes?
- **RECOMMENDATION DESIGN-PARTICIPANTS:** Who will design the recommendations?
- **RECOMMENDATION COMMUNICATION STRATEGY:** How will you communicate the recommendations to your TARGET AUDIENCE?
- **IMPLEMENTATION CRITERIA:** How will you decide what to put into action?

HOW TO USE THIS TOOL

1. Start at the top of the tool. Describe your TARGET AUDIENCE. Then note down your LEARNING GOALS. What do you hope to learn from feedback?
2. Next, go to the KEY DECISIONS header. Start with LOCATION OF COLLECTION. Under the DESIGN header note down your IDEAS and WHY?
3. Repeat step 2 for each of the KEY DECISIONS.
4. To conclude, go to NOW WHAT? and note down a few priority next steps based on what you've learned and/or new insights you've gained from using this tool.

CHANGEMAKER COACH | TOOL TIP

- Build feedback loops/ mechanisms into everything you do. In my experience, five good practices to keep in mind are -
  - Account for power dynamics.
  - Embed feedback loops in your innovation. It shouldn't be an "add-on" or something extra.
  - Keep it super simple.
  - Make it continuous. That's the only way to recognize patterns.
  - Respond quickly to show people that their feedback is valued.
- Remember that good feedback should be a component of your marketing content.

CHANGEMAKING INNOVATION MINI-CASES	
V60	p. 369
V63	p. 370
V66	p. 371

CHANGEMAKING TRIMTABS	
CT9	p. 42
CT10	p. 44
CT19	p. 62

TARGET AUDIENCE		
LEARNING GOALS		
	DESIGN	
KEY DECISIONS	**IDEAS**	**WHY?**
LOCATION OF COLLECTION		
TIMING OF COLLECTION		
FREQUENCY OF COLLECTION		
COMMUNICATION CHANNELS		
HOW TO CREATE A SENSE OF SAFETY		
INCENTIVES/ MOTIVATIONS FOR SHARING		
FREQUENCY OF ANALYSIS		
ANALYSIS - PARTICIPANTS		
DURATION OF ANALYSIS		
RECOMMENDATION CRITERIA		
RECOMMENDATION DESIGN - PARTICIPANTS		
RECOMMENDATION COMMUNICATION STRATEGY		
IMPLEMENTATION CRITERIA		

NOW WHAT?	

T12.5

TOOLS FOR INNOVATION DESIGN CONVERSATIONS | MESSAGING + COMMUNICATION STRATEGIES

toolkit 12

TOUCHPOINT STRATEGY

How might we define a robust touchpoint strategy for each critical phase of interaction?

tinyurl.com/cctboxt125

ABOUT THIS TOOL

Successful changemaking is created through relationships. And relationships are built on touchpoints. A touchpoint is any time you're in contact with the people you aspire to support. This TOUCHPOINT STRATEGY tool should help you and your team design a thoughtful and comprehensive touchpoint strategy.

As a general rule, the more quality touchpoints you have, the better the relationship. The touchpoints included in this tool are as follows:

- **PRE-DECISION PHASE**
  - **AWARENESS:** This is making people aware of your product/ service as a solution to a specific pain point or problem.
  - **CONSIDERATION:** This is people considering your solution as opposed to others.
- **DECISION PHASE:** This is when a person makes a decision to "buy" your changemaking innovation.
- **POST-DECISION PHASE:**
  - **RETENTION:** Retention refers to the ability to retain customers/ users over time. It involves ensuring that people continue to find value in the product/ service and remain satisfied with their overall experience.
  - **ADVOCACY**: Advocacy means turning satisfied customers/ users into advocates who promote to others.

HOW TO USE THIS TOOL

1. Start at the top of the tool. Describe your TARGET AUDIENCE.
2. Next, go to the STRATEGY IDEAS header. Start with PRIORITY 1. Note down GOALS and DESIGN IDEAS for all of the relevant TOUCHPOINT PHASES.
3. Repeat step 2 for PRIORITY 2 and PRIORITY 3.
4. To conclude, go to NOW WHAT? and note down a few priority next steps based on what you've learned and/or new insights you've gained from using this tool.

CHANGEMAKER COACH | TOOL TIP

- Designing a well-thought-out and robust touchpoint strategy is important no matter what kind of product/ service innovation you're designing.
- You might want to change the wording, but this is a particularly helpful tool to use with all of the TOOLKIT 09: SPECIAL - PEOPLE-FOR-PEOPLE STRATEGIES.

CHANGEMAKING INNOVATION MINI-CASES		CHANGEMAKING TRIMTABS	
V5	p. 358	CT4	p. 32
V73	p. 372	CT8	p. 40
V85	p. 374	CT11	p. 46

TARGET AUDIENCE	

STRATEGY IDEAS		TOUCHPOINT PHASES				
		PRE-DECISION		DECISION	POST-DECISION	
		AWARENESS	CONSIDERATION		RETENTION	ADVOCACY
PRIORITY 1	GOAL(S)					
	DESIGN IDEAS					
PRIORITY 2	GOAL(S)					
	DESIGN IDEAS					
PRIORITY 3	GOAL(S)					
	DESIGN IDEAS					

NOW WHAT?	

TOOLS FOR INNOVATION DESIGN CONVERSATIONS | MESSAGING + COMMUNICATION STRATEGIES

TOOLKIT TOOLS REFLECTIONS

SCALE:
STRONGLY AGREE = 5, AGREE = 4, NOT SURE = 3, DISAGREE = 2, STRONGLY DISAGREE = 1

tinyurl.com/cctboxtoolsrflect

	CHANGEMAKING TOOLS				
REFLECTION STATEMENTS	**T12.1**	**T12.2**	**T12.3**	**T12.4**	**T12.5**
This tool is easy to understand.					
This tool is easy to use.					
This tool taught me/ us important new knowledge.					
This tool empowered new changemaking conversations.					
This tool helped to spark new ideas/ insights.					
This tool should be included in my/ our toolbox for the future.					
I/ we should share this tool with other changemakers.					

NOTES:

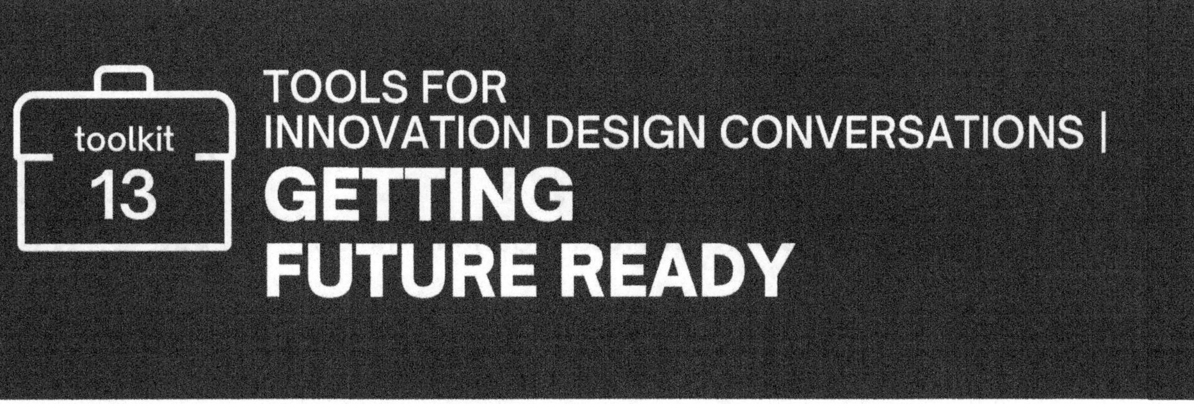

TOOLS FOR INNOVATION DESIGN CONVERSATIONS | GETTING FUTURE READY

Women collaborating in rural Guatemala to help design marketing strategies for solar lamps

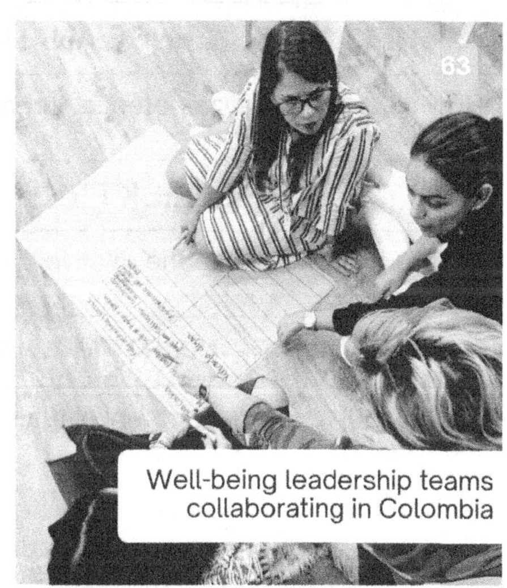

Well-being leadership teams collaborating in Colombia

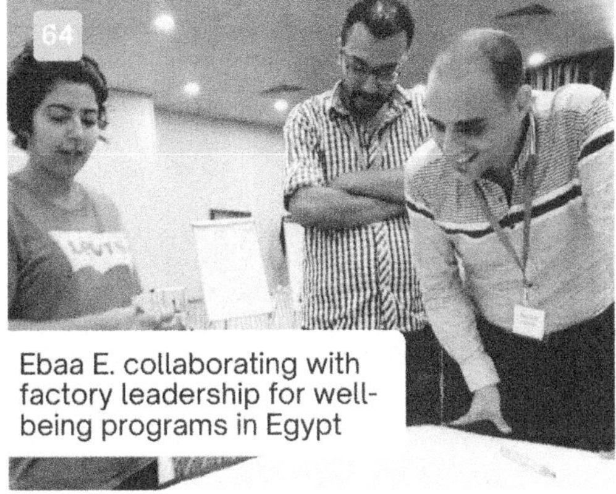

Ebaa E. collaborating with factory leadership for well-being programs in Egypt

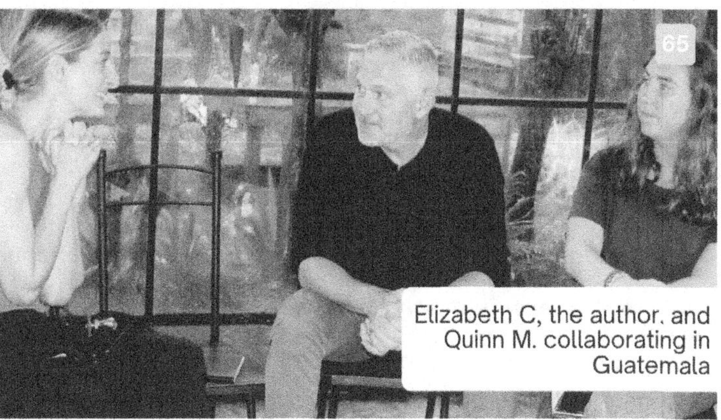

Elizabeth C, the author, and Quinn M. collaborating in Guatemala

NOTES:

toolkit 13 TOOLS FOR INNOVATION DESIGN CONVERSATIONS | GETTING FUTURE READY

TOOLS INVENTORY

How might we design with future contingencies in mind?

tinyurl.com/cctboxtools01

NOTES:

GVK notes -

- Try to create HOMEOSTASIS. This is a self-regulating process to help maintain internal stability while adjusting to changing external conditions.
- Beware that sometimes efficiency is the enemy of resilience. Build in a bit of redundancy. Think of all of the efficient supply chains that broke down during Covid-19.

TOOLS FOR INNOVATION DESIGN CONVERSATIONS | GETTING FUTURE READY

toolkit 13

TOOLKIT SCORECARD + PRIORITIZATION HELP

Score yourselves to help you decide which tool(s) you might want to prioritize for your changemaking conversations.

tinyurl.com/cctboxtoolsprior

SELF-CHECK STATEMENTS	HOW ARE WE DOING?	TOOL SUGGESTIONS
We're having conversations about potential threats and how we should design keeping them in mind.	0 1 2 3 4 5	13.1
We've created risk statements and are designing contingency plans.	0 1 2 3 4 5	13.2
We're discussing what might potentially cause our innovation to fail in the future and are designing ways to either avoid or mitigate these causes.	0 1 2 3 4 5	13.3

NOTES:

Need help, ideas or guidance? Go to CHANGEMAKER COACH "ADVICE/ ASK ME ANYTHING" on page 378.

TOOLS FOR INNOVATION DESIGN CONVERSATIONS | GETTING FUTURE READY

COLLABORATIVE CHANGEMAKING VOICES

Get into the mindset for this toolkit + include your voice in the conversation.

"Security is mostly a superstition. Life is either a daring adventure or nothing."

HELEN KELLER
AUTHOR | DISABILITY RIGHTS ADVOCATE

"You can't let your failures define you. You have to let your failures teach you."

BARACK OBAMA
34TH U.S. PRESIDENT

"I skate to where the puck is going, not to where it's been."

WAYNE GRETZKY
RETIRED PROFESSIONAL ICE HOCKEY PLAYER

"Nothing is absolute. Everything changes, everything moves, everything revolves, everything flies and goes away."

FRIDA KAHLO
PAINTER

"Life is 10% what happens to me and 90% of how I react to it."

CHARLES SWINDOLL
PASTOR | AUTHOR | EDUCATOR

"The quality I look for most is optimism: especially optimism in the face of reverses and apparent defeat. Optimism is true moral courage."

ERNEST SHACKLETON
ANTARCTIC EXPLORER

"There is nothing so stable as change."

BOB DYLAN
SINGER | SONGWRITER

"Progress always involves risks. You can't steal second base and keep your foot on first."

FREDERICK B. WILCOX
AMERICAN BUSINESSMAN

"Resilience is very different than being numb. Resilience means you experience, you feel, you fail, you hurt. You fall. But, you keep going."

YASMIN MOGAHED
EDUCATOR | MOTIVATIONAL SPEAKER

T13.1

TOOLS FOR INNOVATION DESIGN CONVERSATIONS | GETTING FUTURE READY

RESILIENCE ANALYSIS + STRATEGY

How might we analyze potential threats and build resilience strategies into the design of our innovation?

tinyurl.com/cctboxt131

ABOUT THIS TOOL

Resilience is the capacity to stay true to a purpose, maintain integrity, and bounce back when confronted with threatening circumstances. As Andrew Zolli and Ann Marie Healy write in ***Resilience: Why Things Bounce Back***, "If we cannot control the volatile tides of change, we can learn to build better boats....Resilience must continually be refreshed and recommitted to. Every effort at resilience buys us not certainty, but another day, another chance." In other words, the capacity for resilience must be built continuously. This RESILIENCE ANALYSIS + STRATEGY tool should support you and your team with your continuous resilience capacity-building efforts.

This tool helps you analyze and respond to the following twelve THREAT CATEGORIES:

- **COMPETITIVE:** These threats might be existing competitors or new entrants and include new models, substitutes, pricing, etc.
- **ENVIRONMENTAL:** These might include climate threats, earthquakes, floods, etc.
- **FINANCIAL:** These might include funding shortages, interest rate changes, inflation, theft, etc.
- **HEALTH:** These might include threats to the physical and/or mental health of team members and/or key stakeholders.
- **HUMAN CAPACITY:** These might include the loss of team members, a lack of necessary knowledge/skills, attrition, etc.
- **LEADERSHIP:** These might include a leader leaving, etc.
- **PARTNERSHIP:** These might include either the loss or a reduction in participation by a key buyer, seller, etc.
- **POLITICAL:** These might be at a local, national, and/or global level.
- **REGULATORY:** These might be changes in rules, laws, etc.
- **SECURITY:** These might be physical, structural, financial, etc.
- **SUPPLY CHAIN:** These might be breakdowns, reliability issues, etc.
- **TECHNOLOGICAL:** These might be failures, emergent technologies, etc.

HOW TO USE THIS TOOL

1. Start by going to the THREAT CATEGORY header. Go to COMPETITIVE and work your way across the tool under the THREAT ANALYSIS header. Note down your DESCRIPTION of the COMPETITIVE threat.
2. Next, under the LIKELIHOOD header, circle how likely it is for this COMPETITIVE threat to happen. "1" signifies that it's extremely unlikely, and "5" means that it's a near certainty.
3. Then do the same under the NEGATIVE CONSEQUENCES header. "1" means that the negative consequences are very low, and "5" indicates catastrophic consequences.
4. Now multiply the LIKELIHOOD you've circled by the NEGATIVE CONSEQUENCES. Note down the product under PRIORITY LEVEL.
5. Repeat this process for each THREAT CATEGORY.
6. Once you've worked your way through each THREAT CATEGORY, start with the threats with the highest number under PRIORITY LEVEL, and note down your RESILIENCE STRATEGY IDEAS.
7. To conclude, go to NOW WHAT? and note down a few priority next steps based on what you've learned and/or new insights you've gained from using this tool.

CHANGEMAKER COACH | TOOL TIP

Apart from using this tool to analyze your changemaking innovation, this is helpful for building resilience in communities, organizations, teams, etc.

CHANGEMAKING INNOVATION MINI-CASES		CHANGEMAKING TRIMTABS	
V2	p. 358	CT2	p. 28
V9	p. 359	CT3	p. 30
V32	p. 364	CT4	p. 32

THREAT CATEGORY	THREAT ANALYSIS						RESILIENCE STRATEGY IDEAS
	DESCRIPTION	LIKELIHOOD	X	NEGATIVE CONSEQUENCES	=	PRIORITY LEVEL	
COMPETITIVE		1 2 3 4 5	X	1 2 3 4 5	=		
ENVIRONMENTAL		1 2 3 4 5	X	1 2 3 4 5	=		
FINANCIAL		1 2 3 4 5	X	1 2 3 4 5	=		
HEALTH		1 2 3 4 5	X	1 2 3 4 5	=		
HUMAN CAPACITY		1 2 3 4 5	X	1 2 3 4 5	=		
LEADERSHIP		1 2 3 4 5	X	1 2 3 4 5	=		
PARTNERSHIP		1 2 3 4 5	X	1 2 3 4 5	=		
POLITICAL		1 2 3 4 5	X	1 2 3 4 5	=		
REGULATORY		1 2 3 4 5	X	1 2 3 4 5	=		
SECURITY		1 2 3 4 5	X	1 2 3 4 5	=		
SUPPLY CHAIN		1 2 3 4 5	X	1 2 3 4 5	=		
TECHNOLOGICAL		1 2 3 4 5	X	1 2 3 4 5	=		

NOW WHAT?	

☐ T13.2

TOOLS FOR INNOVATION DESIGN CONVERSATIONS | GETTING FUTURE READY

toolkit 13

NASA RISK PRIORITIZATION ANALYSIS

How might we analyze the relative likelihood and consequences of risks?

tinyurl.com/cctboxt132

ABOUT THIS TOOL

Who better to look to for a great risk management tool than NASA?! Inspired by the NASA Risk Matrix this NASA RISK PRIORITIZATION ANALYSIS TOOL should help you and your team determine the level of risk associated with potential situations and to decide how to react.

This tool includes the following components:

- **THE RISK:** This is what you're analyzing.
- **THE RISK STATEMENT:** Use the following template:

  "Assuming that [CONDITION], there is a likelihood of [DEPARTURE] adversely impacting [ASSET], thereby leading to [CONSEQUENCE]."

  - [CONDITION] = The situation that's causing concern/ anxiety.
  - [DEPARTURE] = The undesired potential change from the original plan made more likely as a result of the [CONDITION].
  - [ASSET] = What's affected by **THE RISK** you identified?
  - [CONSEQUENCE] = The potential negative impact THE RISK can have on THE ASSET.
- **THE RISK MATRIX:** Plot THE RISK using two factors.
  - **LIKELIHOOD:** This is how likely the potential [DEPARTURE] is to happen.
  - **CONSEQUENCE:** This is the negative impact of the [DEPARTURE].

After you've determined where THE RISK should be positioned in the matrix, NASA recommends the following:

- **LOWEST RISK:** Monitor these and re-assess them regularly.
- **LOW RISK:** Perform extra research to better understand these and devise a mitigation plan.
- **MEDIUM RISK:** In addition to a mitigation plan, continually monitor, and assign resources.
- **HIGH RISK:** Prioritize these and inform all relevant stakeholders.
- **HIGHEST RISK:** Consider changing the original concept to account for these.

HOW TO USE THIS TOOL

1. Start by describing THE RISK.
2. Next, note down your RISK STATEMENT.
3. Now go to the risk matrix and plot where you believe THE RISK should be taking into account the LIKLIHOOD and CONSEQUENCE.
4. To conclude, go to NOW WHAT? and note down a few priority next steps based on what you've learned and/or new insights you've gained from using this tool.

CHANGEMAKING INNOVATION MINI-CASES		CHANGEMAKING TRIMTABS	
V11	p. 360	CT11	p. 46
V25	p. 362	CT12	p. 48
V28	p. 363	CT19	p. 62

THE RISK				
THE RISK STATEMENT	**ASSUMING THAT**		**THERE'S A POSSIBILITY OF**	
	ADVERSELY IMPACTING		**, THEREBY LEADING TO**	

LIKELIHOOD						
	5 = NEAR CERTAINTY					
	4 = HIGHLY LIKELY					
	3 = LIKELY					
	2 = NOT VERY LIKELY					
	1 = NOT LIKELY					
		1 = MINIMAL	**2 = MINOR**	**3 = MEDIUM**	**4 = MAJOR**	**5 = FATAL**
		CONSEQUENCE				

NOW WHAT?	

☐ **T13.3**

TOOLS FOR INNOVATION DESIGN CONVERSATIONS | GETTING FUTURE READY

PRE-MORTEM ANALYSIS

How might we analyze potential future causes and consequences of failure and so that we can design with them in mind?

tinyurl.com/cctboxt133

ABOUT THIS TOOL

Post-mortem conversations focus on reflection and learning. During post-mortem conversations, teams focus on the past. They reflect on what worked, what didn't, and what could have worked better. Pre-mortem conversations focus on prevention. They employ a prospective hindsight approach. Prospective hindsight is when you imagine that an event has happened at some point in the future and analyze why it might have happened. This PRE-MORTEM ANALYSIS tool should help you and your team use prospective hindsight to imagine a future when your changemaking innovation has failed so that you can make design modifications to prevent it from failing.

The pre-mortem is a risk assessment method first developed by research psychologist Gary Klein Ph.D. In Klein's words, "The pre-mortem technique is a sneaky way to get people to do contrarian, devil's advocate thinking, without encountering resistance." Following are some advantages of pre-mortem conversations:

- They create safe spaces and permission for people to talk about problems/ risks.
- Team members don't feel uncomfortable raising concerns.
- They spark out-of-the-box thinking.
- They encourage dissenting opinions and help teams avoid "groupthink."
- They help teams identify decision-making biases.
- They help you avoid overconfidence.

CHANGEMAKER COACH | TOOL TIPS

- Ideally, you and your team should be conducting a PRE-MORTEM ANALYSIS for every project.
- The good thing is, when you plan for surprises, they aren't surprises.
- You might want to use T6.10 VUCA MAP (p. 230) along with this tool.

HOW TO USE THIS TOOL

1. First, go to the FAILURE CATEGORY PROMPTS header. Scan below and decide which of the prompts you'd like to begin with.
2. Once you've decided on a prompt, work across the tool. Start by noting down the FAILURE SCENARIO DESCRIPTION. What's the potential failure in the future of the prompt you're discussing?
3. Next, note down your ANALYSIS of the ROOT CAUSE OF THE FAILURE(S) and the CONSEQUENCE(S) OF THE FAILURE. These are what you imagine they might be based on the current design of your changemaking innovation.
4. Then zoom out and have a conversation about REDESIGN IDEAS based on your ANALYSIS.
5. Repeat this process for all of the FAILURE CATEGORY PROMPTS that you're discussing. There's a space for you to add one of your own.
6. To conclude, go to NOW WHAT? and note down a few priority next steps based on what you've learned and/or new insights you've gained from using this tool.

CHANGEMAKING INNOVATION MINI-CASES	
V15	p. 360
V39	p. 365
V49	p. 367

CHANGEMAKING TRIMTABS	
CT14	p. 52
CT15	p. 54
CT21	p. 66

FAILURE CATEGORY PROMPTS	FAILURE SCENARIO	ANALYSIS		REDESIGN IDEAS
		ROOT CAUSE OF FAILURE(S)	CONSEQUENCE(S) OF FAILURE	
HUMAN RESOURCES				
DISTRIBUTION				
MARKET SELECTION				
PRICING				
PROMOTION				
QUALITY				
USER EXPERIENCE				

NOW WHAT?	

TOOLS FOR INNOVATION DESIGN CONVERSATIONS | GETTING FUTURE READY

TOOLKIT TOOLS REFLECTIONS

SCALE:
STRONGLY AGREE = 5, AGREE = 4, NOT SURE = 3, DISAGREE = 2, STRONGLY DISAGREE = 1

tinyurl.com/cctboxtoolsrflect

	CHANGEMAKING TOOLS		
REFLECTION STATEMENTS	T13.1	T13.2	T13.3
This tool is easy to understand.			
This tool is easy to use.			
This tool taught me/ us important new knowledge.			
This tool empowered new changemaking conversations.			
This tool helped to spark new ideas/ insights.			
This tool should be included in my/ our toolbox for the future.			
I/ we should share this tool with other changemakers.			

NOTES:

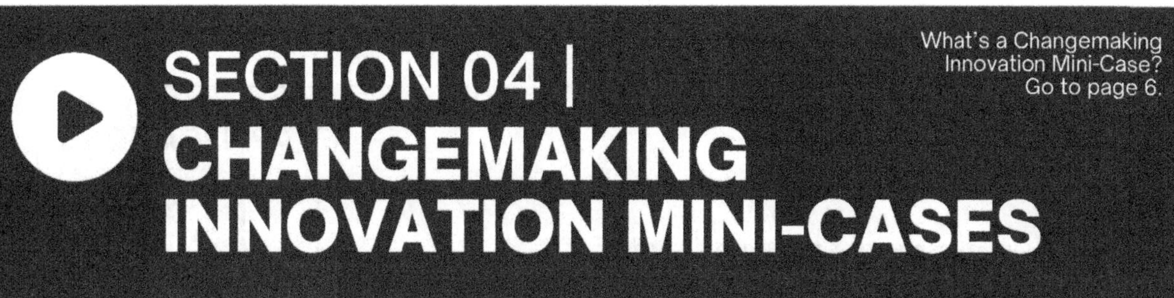

SECTION 04 | CHANGEMAKING INNOVATION MINI-CASES

What's a Changemaking Innovation Mini-Case? Go to page 6.

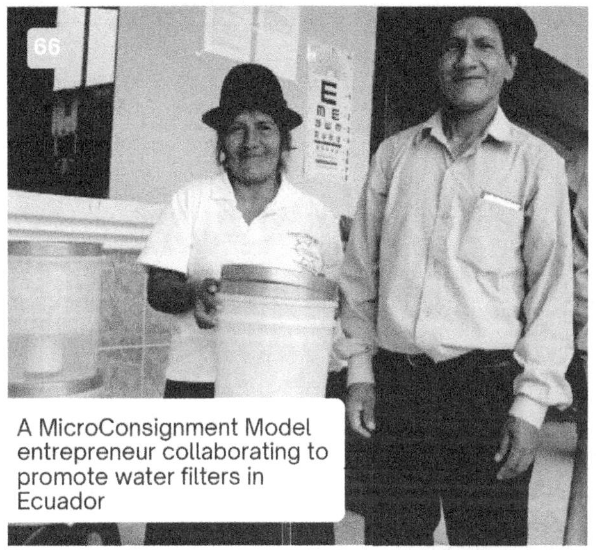

A MicroConsignment Model entrepreneur collaborating to promote water filters in Ecuador

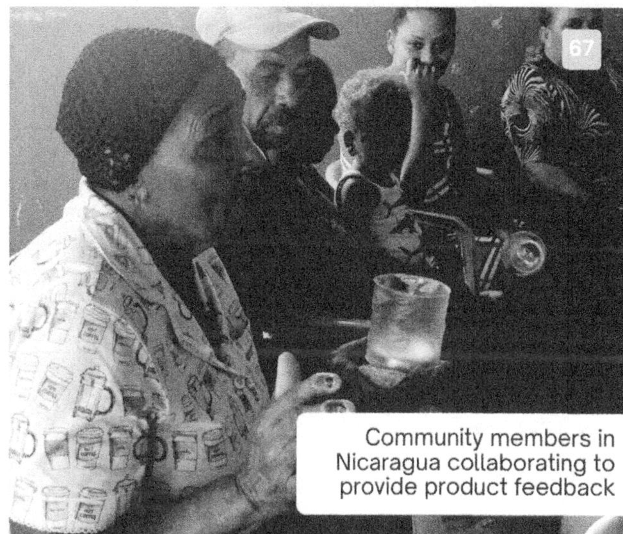

Community members in Nicaragua collaborating to provide product feedback

The author collaborating with vision care professionals and families in Haiti

A MicroConsignment Model entrepreneur collaborating with community members in Guatemala

NOTES:

NOTES:

50+ SPECIFIC APPLICATIONS
tinyurl.com/cctbpxapps

GVK notes -

- Share these with family and friends!
- Check out where you see EMPATHY, EQUITY, + EMPOWERMENT in each of these videos.
- Watch one video a day for 3 months. I gotta think that will make in impact.

collaborativechangemaking.com
for updates, new resources, to report problems, share your ideas, provide feedback, etc.

youtube.com/@collaborativechangemaking
for HOW-TO videos, extra CHANGEMAKING INNOVATION MINI-CASES, etc.

CHANGEMAKING INNOVATION MINI-CASES SECTION OVERVIEW

What's a Changemaking Innovation Mini-Case? Go to page 6.

HOW THE CHANGEMAKING INNOVATION MINI-CASES WORK

Go here to learn how to use the Changemaking Innovation Mini-Cases. This includes the following:

- **THE CHANGEMAKING INNOVATION MINI-CASE FORMAT**
- **SCAFFOLDING CHANGEMAKING INNOVATION MINI-CASES**
- **CHANGEMAKING CONVERSATION WORKSHEET**

INVENTORY SEARCH OPTIONS

Go here to find the the Changemaking Innovation Mini-Case(s) you're looking for. They've been curated in the following ways:

- **SEARCH BY: KEY CHANGEMAKING CHARACTERISTICS**
- **SEARCH BY: SUSTAINABLE DEVELOPMENT GOALS (SDG'S)**
- **SEARCH BY: SPECIAL PLAYLISTS**
  - PLAYLIST 1 | ASHOKA FELLOWS
  - PLAYLIST 2 | WOMEN'S HEALTH-FOCUSED
  - PLAYLIST 3 | WORKPLACE IMPACT
  - PLAYLIST 4 | BUILDING NEW BRIDGES
  - PLAYLIST 5 | FOOD + MEALS
  - PLAYLIST 6 | GROWING THINGS
  - PLAYLIST 7 | USING PLAY + EXERCISE
- **SEARCH BY: YOUR OWN PLAYLISTS** (CREATE YOUR OWN)

THE 90 CHANGEMAKING INNOVATION MINI-CASES

Go here for the full inventory of Changemaking Innovation Mini-Cases in alphabetical order by country name.

NOTES:

HOW THE CHANGEMAKING INNOVATION MINI-CASES WORK

What's a Changemaking Innovation Mini-Case? Go to page 6.

THE CHANGEMAKING INNOVATION MINI-CASE FORMAT

① ② ③

☐ V81 — UNITED STATES

④ **FOCUSING ON INNOVATION** (7.5 minutes)

tinyurl.com/cctboxv81 ⑥

⑤ Learn the origin story of Warby Parker from the four co-founders who came up with the idea after one of them lost his glasses. This comprehensive interview dives into everything that makes Warby Parker unique, including their branding, pricing, their "buy one, give one" program, and their customer experience approach.

Good for teaching, learning + practicing CT12, CT13, CT14, T3.6, T7.4, T12.5

⑦

① **TRACKING BOX:** This is for keeping track of the mini-case videos you've watched/ used. Just tick this box or maybe fill in a "rating" number. Use this box however works best for you.

② **CHANGEMAKING TOOL IDENTIFIER:** This is used throughout the toolbox.

③ **COUNTRY MAP + COUNTRY:** This tells you where the the changemaking is happening in the mini-case.

④ **CHANGEMAKING VIDEO MINI-CASE TITLE with APPROX. VIDEO LENGTH**

⑤ **CHANGEMAKING VIDEO MINI-CASE BRIEF DESCRIPTION**

⑥ **LINK + QR CODE:** These take you to the Changemaking Innovation Mini-Case.

⑦ **Good for teaching, learning + practicing:** This includes suggestions for three Changemaking Trimtabs **(CT)** and three Changemaking Tools **(T)**. These are not all-inclusive.

The Changemaking Trimtabs: This means this Changemaking Innovation Mini-Case does a great job of showing these in action. For example, the Warby Parker mini-case above shows "CT 12: SOLVE ONE KIND OF PROBLEM TO SOLVE ANOTHER" in action. Warby Parker solves the problem of affordability for customers in the US, and then through their "buy one give one" program, they also solve the problems of access and affordability for people in developing world countries. Use these for GUIDANCE: SCAFFOLDING CHANGEMAKING INNOVATION MINI-CASES on page 343.

The Changemaking Tools: This Changemaking Innovation Mini-Case should be helpful for teaching/ practicing these suggested Changemaking Tools, amongst many others. For example, the Warby Parker mini-case above should be helpful for practicing "T3.6 DESIGN PRINCIPLES WHITEBOARD." Go learn about this Changemaking Tool, and then watch the mini-case noting down how Warby Parker's social enterprise model is empathetic, trusting, dignified, etc. Use these for GUIDANCE: SCAFFOLDING CHANGEMAKING INNOVATION MINI-CASES on page 343.

SCAFFOLDING CHANGEMAKING INNOVATION MINI-CASES

Go to page 10 to see the Learning Pyramid that informed this design.

This is guidance for scaffolding Changemaking Innovation Mini-Cases with Changemaking Trimtabs and Changemaking Tools. Use this for facilitation/ teaching with teams, in class, in communities, on Zoom calls, etc. Modify this guidance based on your own goals and constraints.

GET STARTED

1. **CHOOSE ONE OF THE 90 CHANGEMAKING INNOVATION MINI-CASES**

OPTION 1: USING CHANGEMAKING TRIMTABS

2. **LECTURE/ READING:**
Choose two to three of the Changemaking Trimtabs from "Good for teaching, learning + practicing...." Teach and/or have participants read the BRIEF CHANGEMAKING TRIMTAB DESCRIPTION + QUOTE for each of the Changemaking Trimtabs. This might be an exercise you have participants do before the meeting/ class.

3. **AUDIO/ VISUAL + DEMONSTRATION:**
Have the participants watch the Changemaking Innovation Mini-Case.

4. **DISCUSSION/ TEACH OTHERS:**
As a group and/or in small groups, discuss how the changemakers in the videos are putting the Changemaking Trimtabs into action.

5. **APPLY:**
Break up into existing teams or small groups. Have participants discuss how they might put what they've learned/ new insights into action in their own real projects, ventures, etc.

OPTION 2: USING CHANGEMAKING TOOLS

2. **LECTURE/ READING:**
Choose one of the Changemaking Tools from "Good for teaching, learning + practicing...." Teach and/or have participants read the DESCRIPTION, INSTRUCTION + RESOURCES PAGE and review the CHANGEMAKING CONVERSATION WORKSHEET for the Changemaking Tool. This might be an exercise you have participants do before the meeting/ class.

3. **AUDIO/ VISUAL + DEMONSTRATION:**
Have the participants watch the Changemaking Innovation Mini-Case.

4. **DISCUSSION/ TEACH OTHERS:**
As a group and/or in small groups, discuss insights about the changemaking innovation in the video through the lens of the Changemaking Tool.

5. **APPLY:**
Break up into existing teams or small groups. Have participants discuss how they might put what they've learned/ new insights into action in their own real projects, ventures, etc.

NOTES:

tinyurl.com/cctboxmctemplate

CHANGEMAKING CONVERSATION WORKSHEET

Use the Changemaking Innovation Mini-Cases standalone.

The Changemaking Innovation Mini-Cases are great resources for educational and collaborative conversations with your class, team, community, etc. They're a "snackable" and inspiring means for learning new approaches/ strategies and gaining new insights. Use the following worksheet to guide these conversations. It includes spaces for up to three mini-cases. Make photocopies or go to the link/ QR code above if you're online.

	CHANGEMAKING INNOVATION MINI-CASES		
ANALYSIS + REFLECTION PROMPTS	ID + TITLE	ID + TITLE	ID + TITLE
THE PEOPLE: Who does this innovation support/ empower?			
THE PLACE: Where are the people? Where's the problem?			
THE PROBLEM(S): What's problem? What's the cause? What are the effects?			
THE SOLUTION - THE CHANGEMAKING INNOVATION			
WHO: Who's engaged in solving the problem?			
HOW: How are they solving the problem?			
WHY: Why does this changemaking innovation seem to work?			
REFLECTIONS			
REFLECTION #1: What did we like about this mini-case? Why?			
REFLECTION #2: What are some new/ helpful things that we've learned?			
REFLECTION #3: What new perspectives/ insights have we gained?			

APPLICATION IDEATION: How might we apply learnings/ new insights to our own changemaking efforts?	

NOW WHAT?	

INVENTORY SEARCH OPTIONS

tinyurl.com/cctboxmcinv

SEARCH BY KEY CHANGEMAKING CHARACTERISTICS pp. 346 - 348

Search for Changemaking Innovation Mini-Cases that are women-led. Search for social enterprises. And search by the PRIMARY WHY. There are four PRIMARY WHY's. Changemaking Innovation Mini-Cases are either primarily focused on creating access to a product/ service, bringing people together to support each other, changemaker education, or the environment/climate/animals.

SEARCH BY SUSTAINABLE DEVELOPMENT GOALS (SDG'S) pp. 349 - 351

Search for Changemaking Innovation Mini-Cases categorized by "Primary/ Driving SDG" and "Additional Impacted SDG's."

SEARCH BY SPECIAL PLAYLISTS pp. 352 - 354

PLAYLIST 1 | ASHOKA FELLOWS (31 VIDEOS) p. 352

These are changemaking innovations designed/ led by Ashoka Fellows. Ashoka Fellows are recognized as leading social entrepreneurs (changemakers). Ashoka (www.ashoka.org) is the organization that coined the terms "social entrepreneur" and "changemaker." I had the good fortune of being selected as an Ashoka Fellow in 2008. Because of this, I've had a unique window into the work of some truly wonderful changemakers. You'll find 31 of them here. (Note: The Ashoka Fellow isn't necessarily featured in the video.)

SEARCH BY YOUR OWN PLAYLISTS pp. 355 - 356

Note down your own personal favorites and create playlists for future reference.

SEARCH BY KEY CHANGEMAKING CHARACTERISTICS

LEGEND	HOW MANY?
WOMAN/ WOMEN-LED	44
SOCIAL ENTERPRISE (PROFIT + PURPOSE)	39
THE PRIMARY WHY: THIS IS THE DRIVING GOAL, BUT MAY NOT BE THE ONLY GOAL.	
TO CREATE ACCESS TO A PRODUCT AND/OR SERVICE INNOVATION	37
TO BRING PEOPLE TOGETHER TO SUPPORT/ EMPOWER EACH OTHER	23
TO IMPROVE/ SHIFT PARADIGM OF EDUCATION OUTCOMES/ CHANGEMAKER EDUCATION	15
TO PROTECT/HONOR THE PLANET (ENVIRONMENT, CLIMATE, ANIMALS ETC.)	15

						THE PRIMARY WHY			
▶		MINI-CASE TITLE	COUNTRY	[Woman/Women-led]	[Social enterprise]	[Access]	[Together]	[Education]	[Planet]
☐	V1	CLEAN CLOTHES + CONVERSATIONS	AUSTRALIA			●			
☐	V2	DESIGNING FOR CHANGE	AUSTRALIA	●	●	●			
☐	V3	SOLVING THE ARSENIC PROBLEM	BANGLADESH		●	●			
☐	V4	FOUR EYED CATTLE	BOTSWANA						●
☐	V5	PURIFYING WATER WITH THE SUN	BRAZIL	●	●	●			
☐	V6	MEDIATING CHANGE	BURUNDI	●			●		
☐	V7	WHERE BABIES DO THE TEACHING	CANADA	●				●	
☐	V8	CHILD-CENTERED EDUCATION	COLOMBIA	●				●	
☐	V9	GROW YOUR OWN RAINFOREST	ECUADOR						●
☐	V10	MUSHROOM GARAGES	FRANCE		●				●
☐	V11	THE ALCHEMY OF COMPOSTING	FRANCE	●	●				●
☐	V12	MICROCONSIGNMENT FOR THE LAST MILE	GUATEMALA	●	●	●			
☐	V13	SANITATION TO SOIL	HAITI	●	●	●			
☐	V14	FROM FOREST FIRES TO FUEL	INDIA		●	●			
☐	V15	MOVING KNOWLEDGE INSTEAD OF PATIENTS	INDIA			●			
☐	V16	THEY CALL HIM POOP GUY	INDIA			●			
☐	V17	DESIGNED "WITH", NOT "FOR"	INDIA	●	●	●			
☐	V18	A VISION FOR IMPACT	INDIA	●	●	●			
☐	V19	REEF STARS TO THE RESCUE	INDONESIA						●
☐	V20	HARVESTING RAINWATER	INDONESIA		●	●			

				THE PRIMARY WHY					
		MINI-CASE TITLE	COUNTRY						
☐	V21	BUDDY BENCHES	IRELAND					●	
☐	V22	ULTIMATE PEACEMAKING	ISRAEL					●	
☐	V23	FREE BEER FOR CYCLING	ITALY						●
☐	V24	VIOLENCE INTERRUPTER	JAMAICA				●		
☐	V25	FROM WASTE TO WALKWAYS	KENYA	●	●				●
☐	V26	A CUSTOMER-FOCUSED APPROACH	KENYA		●	●			
☐	V27	MICROGRIDS IN ACTION	KENYA		●	●			
☐	V28	PIPING THROUGH PROBLEMS	KENYA		●	●			
☐	V29	CLEAN COOKING ATM'S	KENYA		●	●			
☐	V30	POO POWER	KENYA		●	●			
☐	V31	GIVING CHOICE FOR A CHANGE	KENYA			●			
☐	V32	A COOPERATIVE FUTURE	MADAGASCAR	●	●	●			
☐	V33	HEROES OF E-WASTE	MALAYSIA		●				●
☐	V34	LITERALLY A SCHOOL BUS	MEXICO	●				●	
☐	V35	COMMUNITY-OWNED EDUCATION	NATIVE AMERICAN					●	
☐	V36	NAMING + FAMING	NEPAL				●		
☐	V37	WE'LL SOLVE IT OURSELVES!	NIGERIA	●			●		
☐	V38	CROWD FARMING	NIGERIA		●	●			
☐	V39	HYDROPONIC SHIPPING CONTAINERS	NIGERIA	●	●	●			
☐	V40	EMPOWERING WOMEN-LED TELEMEDICINE	PAKISTAN	●		●			
☐	V41	A STOPLIGHT FOR POVERTY ALLEVIATION	PARAGUAY	●		●			
☐	V42	PROFESSIONALIZING WASTE PICKERS	PERU	●	●	●			
☐	V43	A COMMUNITY-LED RECOVERY	PUERTO RICO, USA	●			●		
☐	V44	STORIES OF CHANGE	REFUGEE CAMPS				●		
☐	V45	LIGHTING UP LIVES + LIVELIHOODS	RWANDA	●	●	●			
☐	V46	WRITING A BOOK A DAY	SOUTH AFRICA					●	
☐	V47	BLACK MAMBAS PREVENTING POACHING	SOUTH AFRICA	●					●
☐	V48	LIVING WITH MANDATORY FRIENDS	SWEDEN				●		
☐	V49	VEGGIES FOR EDUCATION	TANZANIA					●	
☐	V50	HANDS-ON LEADERSHIP + EMPATHY	THAILAND					●	
☐	V51	3D PRINTING SURPRISES + SMILES	TURKEY				●		
☐	V52	FROM PATIENT TO HEALER	UGANDA	●			●		
☐	V53	SANITARY PADS FOR EDUCATION	UGANDA		●			●	
☐	V54	COOKING EMPATHY	UNITED KINGDOM	●			●		
☐	V55	POWERED BY OLD BAGELS	UNITED KINGDOM	●	●				●

						THE PRIMARY WHY			
		MINI-CASE TITLE	COUNTRY						
☐	V56	CHANGING NARRATIVES ABOUT BLACK MEN	UNITED STATES				●		
☐	V57	PATIENT CAPITAL	UNITED STATES	●	●	●			
☐	V58	DINNER TOGETHER FOR LOSS	UNITED STATES	●			●		
☐	V59	PLAY WITH PURPOSE	UNITED STATES	●				●	
☐	V60	WORKER-LED PRIORITIZATION	UNITED STATES	●	●		●		
☐	V61	FITNESS FUELED SECOND CHANCES	UNITED STATES		●	●			
☐	V62	BUZZING WITH BOOKS	UNITED STATES					●	
☐	V63	WELCOMING COMMUNITIES	UNITED STATES				●		
☐	V64	EXCHANGING PEANUT BUTTER FOR PRODUCE	UNITED STATES				●		
☐	V65	A SCRAPPY SOCIAL ENTERPRISE	UNITED STATES	●	●				●
☐	V66	TRUST-BASED LENDING	UNITED STATES			●			
☐	V67	HUMANIZING HEALTHCARE	UNITED STATES	●		●			
☐	V68	GETTING TO ZERO HOMELESSNESS	UNITED STATES	●		●			
☐	V69	THE CITIZENS JUSTICE LEAGUE	UNITED STATES	●			●		
☐	V70	TRUCKERS FIGHTING TRAFFICKING	UNITED STATES	●			●		
☐	V71	SOLUTIONS JOURNALISM	UNITED STATES	●		●			
☐	V72	BATTLING CASH BAIL	UNITED STATES	●			●		
☐	V73	SURROUNDING STUDENTS WITH SUPPORT	UNITED STATES	●				●	
☐	V74	WALKING FOR TRANSFORMATION	UNITED STATES	●			●		
☐	V75	GIRLS FINDING THEIR PACE	UNITED STATES	●				●	
☐	V76	HIP HOP THERAPY	UNITED STATES				●		
☐	V77	ADVANCING EMPLOYEE OWNERSHIP	UNITED STATES	●	●	●			
☐	V78	FUTURE READY EDUCATION	UNITED STATES	●				●	
☐	V79	A CIVIC JOURNALISM HUB	UNITED STATES	●			●		
☐	V80	BITE-SIZED CHANGEMAKING	UNITED STATES	●	●				●
☐	V81	FOCUSING ON INNOVATION	UNITED STATES		●	●			
☐	V82	TURNING BUILDINGS INTO TESLAS	UNITED STATES		●				●
☐	V83	CROSS SUBSIDIZING HEALTHY MEALS	UNITED STATES		●	●			
☐	V84	EMPOWERING OPPORTUNITY IN APPALACHIA	UNITED STATES		●	●			
☐	V85	CODING FOR CHANGE	UNITED STATES	●		●			
☐	V86	3D OCEAN FARMING	UNITED STATES		●				●
☐	V87	ABOUT THE HOW, NOT THE COW	UNITED STATES		●				●
☐	V88	BUSINESS FOR A BETTER WORLD	UNITED STATES		●		●		
☐	V89	INTERGENERATIONAL IMPACT	UNITED STATES				●		
☐	V90	PEDAL POWER	ZAMBIA	●	●	●			

SEARCH BY SUSTAINABLE DEVELOPMENT GOALS (SDG'S)

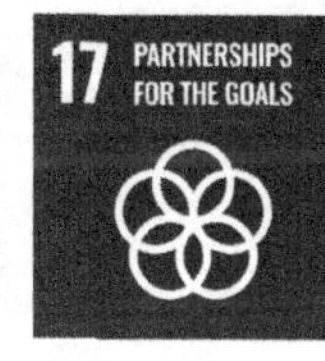

◉ = THE PRIMARY/ DRIVING SDG

✓ = ADDITIONAL IMPACTED SDG'S

Note: GOAL 17 is not included below.

	SUSTAINABLE DEVELOPMENT GOALS (SDG'S)															
▶	1	2	3	4	5	6	7	8	9	10	11	12	13	14	15	16
V1			◉			✓					✓		✓			
V2				✓				◉	✓	✓						
V3			✓			◉		✓			✓		✓			
V4	✓							✓							◉	
V5	✓		✓			◉		✓			✓	✓	✓			
V6					✓			✓		✓						◉
V7			✓	◉												✓
V8				◉						✓						✓
V9												✓	✓		◉	
V10								✓	✓		◉	✓				
V11							◉	✓	✓		✓	✓	✓		✓	
V12	◉		✓	✓	✓	✓	✓	✓		✓			✓			
V13	✓		✓			◉		✓	✓		✓	✓	✓			
V14							◉	✓	✓				✓		✓	
V15			◉	✓	✓			✓	✓	✓	✓					
V16			✓	✓		◉			✓	✓	✓				✓	
V17	✓		✓		✓		◉	✓			✓	✓	✓			
V18	✓		◉	✓	✓			✓		✓						

	SUSTAINABLE DEVELOPMENT GOALS (SDG'S)															
▶	01	02	03	04	05	06	07	08	09	10	11	12	13	14	15	16
V19								✓						●		
V20	✓		✓			●			✓	✓	✓	✓			✓	
V21			✓	●												✓
V22			✓	✓						✓						●
V23			✓						✓		●	✓	✓			
V24			✓								●					✓
V25								✓	✓		✓	●	✓		✓	
V26	✓	✓	✓	✓				●	✓			✓			✓	
V27	✓			✓			●	✓	✓		✓	✓	✓			
V28	✓		✓			●				✓	✓				✓	
V29	✓		✓				●	✓	✓		✓	✓	✓		✓	
V30	✓		✓				●	✓	✓			✓	✓		✓	
V31	●				✓			✓		✓						
V32	✓		✓	✓	✓			●	✓	✓						
V33			✓					✓	✓		✓	●	✓		✓	
V34				●					✓	✓						✓
V35			✓	●						✓						✓
V36										✓	●					✓
V37			●		✓					✓	✓					
V38	✓	✓	✓	✓	✓			●	✓	✓	✓					
V39	✓		✓		✓			●	✓	✓	✓	✓				
V40			●	✓	✓			✓	✓	✓	✓					
V41	●	✓	✓	✓	✓			✓	✓	✓	✓					
V42	✓		✓		✓			✓	✓	✓	●	✓				
V43	✓		✓		✓				✓	✓	●	✓				
V44			●	✓	✓					✓						✓
V45	✓		✓	✓	✓		✓	●	✓	✓	✓		✓			
V46				●						✓						
V47					✓			✓		✓					●	
V48			●								✓					
V49	✓	●	✓	✓						✓		✓			✓	
V50	✓	✓	✓	●	✓	✓	✓	✓		✓						✓
V51			✓								●					
V52			●	✓	✓					✓						
V53	✓		●	✓	✓			✓	✓							
V54			✓					✓		●	✓					✓

	SUSTAINABLE DEVELOPMENT GOALS (SDG'S)															
	01	02	03	04	05	06	07	08	09	10	11	12	13	14	15	16
V55	✓	✓	✓					✓			✓	◉				
V56			✓		✓			✓		◉	✓					✓
V57	◉	✓			✓			✓	✓	✓	✓					
V58			◉													
V59			✓	◉	✓											✓
V60			✓	✓	✓			◉	✓	✓	✓					✓
V61	✓		✓					◉		✓						
V62			✓	◉												
V63			✓		✓					◉	✓					✓
V64	✓	✓	◉					✓		✓	✓	✓				
V65								✓	✓			◉				
V66	✓		✓	✓	✓			◉	✓	✓			◉			
V67	✓		◉	✓	✓			✓	✓							
V68	✓	✓	✓						✓	✓	◉					
V69			✓	✓	✓					✓	✓					◉
V70			✓		✓				✓							◉
V71			✓	◉	✓			✓								✓
V72	✓		✓							✓						◉
V73			✓	◉						✓						
V74			◉	✓	✓					✓						
V75			✓	◉	✓					✓						
V76			◉	✓						✓						
V77					✓			◉	✓	✓						
V78			✓	◉	✓					✓	✓					
V79			✓	✓	✓			✓		✓						◉
V80			✓					✓				◉				
V81			◉	✓				✓		✓						
V82			✓				✓	✓	✓	✓	◉		✓			
V83		✓	◉					✓		✓	✓	✓				
V84	✓		✓	✓				◉	✓	✓	✓	✓	✓			
V85	◉	✓	✓	✓	✓			✓		✓						
V86								✓			✓	✓	✓	◉		
V87								✓			✓	◉	✓			
V88								◉	✓		✓	✓				
V89			✓	✓				◉	✓							
V90			✓						✓		◉					✓

SEARCH BY SPECIAL PLAYLISTS

PLAYLIST 1 | ASHOKA FELLOWS

▶	FIRST NAME	LAST NAME	ORGANIZATION	YEAR SELECTED
V15	SANJEEV	AURORA, MD	PROJECT ECHO	2009
V16	SWAPNIL	CHATURVEDI	SAMAGRA	2014
V75	MOLLY	BARKER	GIRLS ON THE RUN	2008
V71	DAVID	BORNSTEIN	SOLUTIONS JOURNALISM NETWORK	2016
V8	VICKY	COLBERT	ESCUELA NUEVA	2003
V53	ERIC	DAWSON	PEACE FIRST	2007
V84	BRANDON	DENNISON	COALFIELD DEVELOPMENT	2018
V74	MORGAN	DIXON	GIRLTREK	2014
V58	LENNON	FLOWERS	THE DINNER PARTY	2016
V89	MARC	FREEDMAN	COGENERATE	2005
V7	MARY	GORDON	ROOTS OF EMPATHY	2002
V68	ROSANNE	HAGGERTY	COMMUNITY SOLUTIONS	2007
V40	ASHER	HASAN	NAYA JAVEEN	2011
V73	SARAH	HEMMINGER	THREAD	2013
V79	DARRLY	HOLLIDAY	CITY BUREAU	2021
V69	RAJ	JAYADEV	De-Bug/ACJP	2014
V18	JORDAN	KASSALOW	VISION SPRING	2010
V13	SASHA	KRAMER	SOIL	2015
V77	ALISON	LINGANE	PROJECT EQUITY	2019
V63	DAVID	LUBELL	WELCOMING AMERICA	2012
V45	KATHERINE	LUCY	SOLAR SISTER	2012
V60	MICHELLE	MILLER	COWORKER	2019
V76	DANA	MORTENSON	WORLD SAVVY	2011
V85	JENNIFER	PAHLKA	CODE FOR AMERICA	2012
V70	KENDIS	PARIS	TRUCKERS AGAINST TRAFFICKING	2013
V42	ALBINA	RUIZ	CIUDAD SALUDABLE	1996
V56	TRABIAN	SHORTERS	BEME	2015
V86	BREN	SMITH	GREENWAVE	2015
V24	GARY	SLUTKIN	CEASE FIRE	2009
V12	GREG	VAN KIRK	COMMUNITY ENTERPRISE SOLUTIONS	2008
V59	JILL	VIALET	PLAYWORKS	2004

PLAYLIST 2 | WOMEN'S HEALTH-FOCUSED

▶	CHANGEMAKING INNOVATION MINI-CASE	COUNTRY
V16	THEY CALL HIM POOP GUY	INDIA
V17	DESIGNED "WITH", NOT "FOR"	INDIA
V37	WE'LL SOLVE IT OURSELVES!	NIGERIA
V40	EMPOWERING WOMEN-LED TELEMEDICINE	PAKISTAN
V52	FROM PATIENT TO HEALER	UGANDA
V53	SANITARY PADS FOR EDUCATION	UGANDA
V58	DINNER TOGETHER FOR LOSS	UNITED STATES
V67	HUMANIZING HEALTHCARE	UNITED STATES
V74	WALKING FOR TRANSFORMATION	UNITED STATES

PLAYLIST 3 | WORKPLACE IMPACT

▶	CHANGEMAKING INNOVATION MINI-CASE	COUNTRY
V2	DESIGNING FOR CHANGE	AUSTRALIA
V36	NAMING + FAMING	NEPAL
V60	WORKER-LED PRIORITIZATION	UNITED STATES
V77	ADVANCING EMPLOYEE OWNERSHIP	UNITED STATES
V79	A CIVIC JOURNALISM HUB	UNITED STATES
V81	FOCUSING ON INNOVATION	UNITED STATES
V84	EMPOWERING OPPORTUNITY IN APPALACHIA	UNITED STATES
V88	BUSINESS FOR A BETTER WORLD	UNITED STATES

PLAYLIST 4 | BUILDING NEW BRIDGES

▶	CHANGEMAKING INNOVATION MINI-CASE	COUNTRY
V6	MEDIATING CHANGE	BURUNDI
V24	VIOLENCE INTERRUPTER	JAMAICA
V54	COOKING EMPATHY	UNITED KINGDOM
V63	WELCOMING COMMUNITIES	UNITED STATES
V73	SURROUNDING STUDENTS WITH SUPPORT	UNITED STATES
V89	INTERGENERATIONAL IMPACT	UNITED STATES

PLAYLIST 5 | FOOD + MEALS

▶	CHANGEMAKING INNOVATION MINI-CASE	COUNTRY
V49	VEGGIES FOR EDUCATION	TANZANIA
V54	COOKING EMPATHY	UNITED KINGDOM
V55	POWERED BY OLD BAGELS	UNITED KINGDOM
V58	DINNER TOGETHER FOR LOSS	UNITED STATES
V64	EXCHANGING PEANUT BUTTER FOR PRODUCE	UNITED STATES
V83	CROSS SUBSIDIZING HEALTHY MEALS	UNITED STATES

PLAYLIST 6 | GROWING THINGS

▶	CHANGEMAKING INNOVATION MINI-CASE	COUNTRY
V9	GROW YOUR OWN RAINFOREST	ECUADOR
V10	MUSHROOM GARAGES	FRANCE
V19	REEF STARS TO THE RESCUE	INDONESIA
V11	THE ALCHEMY OF COMPOSTING	FRANCE
V13	SANITATION TO SOIL	HAITI
V26	A CUSTOMER-FOCUSED APPROACH	KENYA
V38	CROWD FARMING	NIGERIA
V39	HYDROPONIC SHIPPING CONTAINERS	NIGERIA
V49	VEGGIES FOR EDUCATION	TANZANIA
V86	3D OCEAN FARMING	UNITED STATES
V87	ABOUT THE HOW, NOT THE COW	UNITED STATES

PLAYLIST 7 | USING PLAY + EXERCISE

▶	CHANGEMAKING INNOVATION MINI-CASE	COUNTRY
V22	ULTIMATE PEACEMAKING	ISRAEL
V23	FREE BEER FOR CYCLING	ITALY
V59	PLAY WITH PURPOSE	UNITED STATES
V61	FITNESS FUELED SECOND CHANCES	UNITED STATES
V74	WALKING FOR TRANSFORMATION	UNITED STATES
V75	GIRLS FINDING THEIR PACE	UNITED STATES

SEARCH BY YOUR PERSONAL PLAYLISTS

tinyurl.com/cctboxyours

	INNOVATION MINI-CASE TITLE	PLAYLIST NAME
V		
V		
V		
V		
V		
V		
V		
V		
V		
V		
V		
V		
V		
V		
V		
V		
V		
V		
V		
V		
V		
V		
V		

	INNOVATION MINI-CASE TITLE	PLAYLIST NAME
V		
V		
V		
V		
V		
V		
V		
V		
V		
V		
V		
V		
V		
V		
V		
V		
V		
V		
V		
V		
V		
V		
V		
V		
V		
V		
V		

What's a Changemaking
Innovation Mini-Case?
Go to page 6.

THE 90 CHANGEMAKING INNOVATION MINI-CASES

Note: The country is the country where the changemaking is happening in the Changemaking Innovation Mini-Case video. Many of the organizations featured are headquartered in different countries and/or work in multiple countries.

NOTES:

50+ SPECIFIC APPLICATIONS

tinyurl.com/cctbpxapps

☐ **V1**  **AUSTRALIA**

CLEAN CLOTHES + CONVERSATIONS

tinyurl.com/cctboxv1

(2 minutes)

Orange Sky Laundry is a mobile laundry service for people experiencing homelessness. It was started in 2014 by young changemakers Nicholas Marchesi and Lucas Patchett. But it's about more than clean clothes. It's about creating conditions for community conversations and engagement.

Good for teaching, learning + practicing CT11, CT15, CT17, T2.6, T3.8, T11.3

☐ **V2**  **AUSTRALIA**

DESIGNING FOR CHANGE

tinyurl.com/cctboxv2

(4.5 minutes)

Learn about how Melanie Perkins, the co-founder of Canva, leads with the attitude that she's serving her team, not the boss of her team. She started the online design platform company after becoming frustrated with how hard existing solutions were to use. Canva's goals are to be easy and broadly accessible.

Good for teaching, learning + practicing CT11, CT14, CT16, T1.4, T3.6, T7.1

☐ **V3**  **BANGLADESH**

SOLVING THE ARSENIC PROBLEM

tinyurl.com/cctboxv3

(4 minutes)

In Bangladesh, roughly 20 million people are at risk from arsenic poisoning. This situation has been referred to as "the biggest mass poisoning in human history." Learn about Drinkwell. They've created a social enterprise solution that's using technology to provide access to clean water, to save lives and to scale.

Good for teaching, learning + practicing CT13, CT18, CT21, T4.2, T5.1, T7.5

☐ **V4**  **BOTSWANA**

FOUR EYED CATTLE

tinyurl.com/cctboxv4

(2 minutes)

In Botswana, lions have been attacking and killing cattle. Now farmers are experimenting by painting eyes on the rumps of their cattle. The research says it's working.

Good for teaching, learning + practicing CT13, CT15, CT16, T4.5, T11.6, T13.2

☐ **V5** 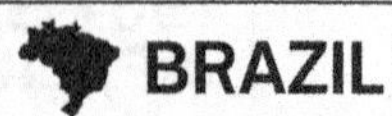 **BRAZIL**

PURIFYING WATER WITH THE SUN

tinyurl.com/cctboxv5

(3 minutes)

Learn about how young social entrepreneur Ana Luisa Santo has created a social enterprise that helps families get access to clean water for the first time. She's mixing ingenuity, empathy and the power of the sun to help people live healthier lives.

Good for teaching, learning + practicing CT4, CT13, CT22, T7.4, T10.4, T11.1

☐ **V6**

MEDIATING CHANGE

(4 minutes)

Learn about how hundreds of women mediators throughout Burundi are leading conflict resolution efforts. They're solving problems within families and communities. As a result, these women gain respect, increased stature, and are changing gender perceptions of community leaders.

Good for teaching, learning + practicing CT4, CT9, CT10, T1.1, T1.5, T6.8

☐ **V7**

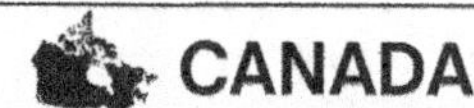

WHERE BABIES DO THE TEACHING

(4 minutes)

Naomi isn't exactly your average teacher. She's only seven months old. Her empathy superpower is at the heart of an inspired and innovative program designed by Roots of Empathy. This innovation has been proven to increase empathy and reduce bullying in schools.

Good for teaching, learning + practicing CT6, CT7, CT11, T5.1, T5.2, T12.2

☐ **V8**

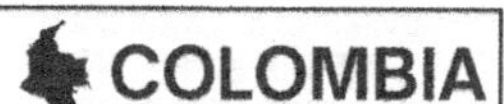

CHILD-CENTERED EDUCATION

tinyurl.com/cctboxv8

(3 minutes)

Fundación Escuela Nueva is an organization in Colombia founded on the belief that sustainable development and democracy stem from children being educated to become future citizens. It uses a powerful child-centered and collaborative approach that's been designed for resource constrained schools.

Good for teaching, learning + practicing CT13, CT16, CT21, T1.2, T3.6, T7.1

☐ **V9**

GROW YOUR OWN RAINFOREST

tinyurl.com/cctboxv9

(5 minutes)

Meet Omar Tello from Ecuador. He's spent the last 40 years recreating a patch of pristine forest that had previously been cleared and used for farmland. Now he's working with an organization trying to incentivize others to combat deforestation by growing their own forests.

Good for teaching, learning + practicing CT5, CT13, CT14, T3.9, T4.2, T13.1

☐ **V10**

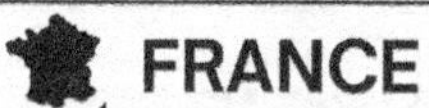

MUSHROOM GARAGES

(2.5 minutes)

What do you do with a useless car park in your city? Transportation habits have changed over time, and Paris has too many underground parking lots. Now they're helping entrepreneurs leverage these spaces to do all sorts of things, including growing mushrooms.

Good for teaching, learning + practicing CT6, CT7, CT12, T3.5, T6.4, T8.1

V11 - V15

V11 — FRANCE

tinyurl.com/cctboxv11

THE ALCHEMY OF COMPOSTING

(3.5 minutes)

Learn about a social enterprise outside of Paris that turns food waste into compost that's then sold to farmers. Les Alchimistes uses special industrial composters and employs a team of cyclist entrepreneurs who pick up the food waste from restaurants.

Good for teaching, learning + practicing CT8, CT12, CT20, T2.4, T7.1, T8.3

V12

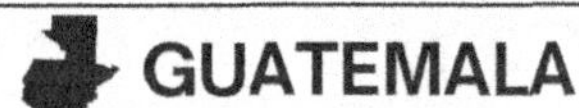

GUATEMALA

tinyurl.com/cctboxv12

MICROCONSIGNMENT FOR THE LAST MILE

(5.5 minutes)

Learn about how the MicroConsignment Model is creating access to vital technologies in last mile communities. Using a consignment strategy, first-time, women social entrepreneurs are empowered to start and lead their own micro ventures offering clean cookstoves, eye glasses, solar lamps, and water filters.

Good for teaching, learning + practicing CT4, CT16, CT19, T3.3, T5.3, T6.5

V13 — HAITI

tinyurl.com/cctboxv13

SANITATION TO SOIL

(4 minutes)

Learn about a social enterprise in Haiti called Soil. Soil is simultaneously offering people dignified economical sanitation solutions, helping the environment, organically restoring soil fertility, and creating new job opportunities for local entrepreneurs.

Good for teaching, learning + practicing CT8, CT12, CT20, T1.1, T3.3, T5.4

V14

INDIA

tinyurl.com/cctboxv14

FROM FOREST FIRES TO FUEL

(5 minutes)

Learn about an innovative couple in India who moved to a rural community for a relaxed life, and ended up discovering a new power source; the resin in pine needles. They're creating electricity for their community and helping to prevent forest fires at the same time.

Good for teaching, learning + practicing CT6, CT8, CT12, T2.2, T4.5, T6.1

V15

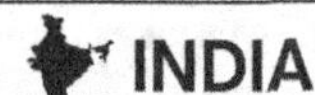

INDIA

tinyurl.com/cctboxv15

MOVING KNOWLEDGE INSTEAD OF PATIENTS

(7.25 minutes)

Project ECHO, a telehealth organization, is moving medical knowledge to remote areas so that patients don't have to travel long distances. They're upskilling existing health systems by building communities of practice, applying proven adult learning techniques, and by using simple video technology.

Good for teaching, learning + practicing CT6, CT9, CT19, T2.4, T5.3, T9.2

☐ **V16**  **INDIA**

THEY CALL HIM POOP GUY

tinyurl.com/cctboxv16

(2 minutes)

In an area of India where roughly 60% of people have very limited access to toilets, there's a man they call the "Poop Guy" who's making change. Learn about how Swapnil Chaturvedi is working in urban slums to provide dignified sanitation services for all.

Good for teaching, learning + practicing CT1, CT3, CT18, T4.3, T6.7, T12.3

☐ **V17** 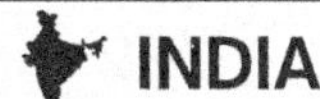 **INDIA**

DESIGNED "WITH", NOT "FOR"

tinyurl.com/cctboxv17

(2 minutes)

Learn a bit about Greenway Grameen in India. This social enterprise has created an efficient cookstove to replace the traditional mud stoves. They've done so by focusing on a user-centric approach that engages local women throughout the design process.

Good for teaching, learning + practicing CT2, CT3, CT13, T5.1, T8.1, T10.2

☐ **V18** 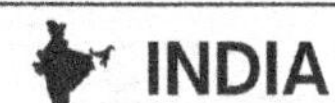 **INDIA**

A VISION FOR IMPACT

tinyurl.com/cctboxv18

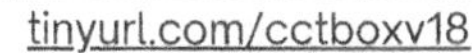

(5.5 minutes)

Watch this Skoll Foundation video to learn about how optometrist Jordan Kassalow became inspired to help people get access to glasses and founded VisionSpring. This is an example of how old technology, coupled with innovative new distribution approaches, can catalyze incredible change.

Good for teaching, learning + practicing CT4, CT12, CT18, T6.3, T7.1, T11.3

☐ **V19**  **INDONESIA**

REEF STARS TO THE RESCUE

tinyurl.com/cctboxv19

(2 minutes)

Learn about how coral reefs have been restored in Indonesia as part of a collaboration between local groups, The Nature Conservancy and the pet brand, Sheba. They're showing how restoring a natural ecosystem starts with a changemaking ecosystem.

Good for teaching, learning + practicing CT13, CT15, CT22, T1.2, T4.5, T8.2

☐ **V20**  **INDONESIA**

HARVESTING RAINWATER

tinyurl.com/cctboxv20

(6 minutes)

For far too many people, accessing clean water can be difficult and expensive. But this doesn't have to be the case. Learn about a pastor in an Indonesian village who inspires people to make use of the most dependable water supply that literally falls from the sky.

Good for teaching, learning + practicing CT2, CT6, CT13, T7.5, T8.4, T12.1

V21 - V25

☐ V21

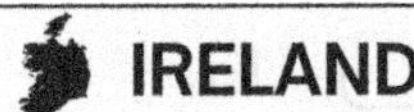

IRELAND

BUDDY BENCHES

tinyurl.com/cctboxv21

(1.5 minutes)

Buddy Benches were invented to combat loneliness and bullying in schools. Accompanied with simple instruction and capacity building, they're proving popular in Irish schools.

Good for teaching, learning + practicing CT9, CT15, CT21, T3.9, T4.2, T5.2

☐ V22

ISRAEL

ULTIMATE PEACEMAKING

tinyurl.com/cctboxv22

(4.5 minutes)

Learn about an organization that's using ultimate frisbee as a way to bring Israeli and Palestinian youth together. These neighbors are meeting each other for the very first time. They're creating empathy, building relationships, and learning conflict resolution through play.

Good for teaching, learning + practicing CT7, CT15, CT17, T4.3, T7.3, T8.4

☐ V23

ITALY

FREE BEER FOR CYCLING

tinyurl.com/cctboxv23

(3 minutes)

An urban planner in Bologna is fighting pollution by designing creative new incentive schemes. Learn about a program called "Bella Mossa" (Good Job). People use an app and earn points for things like beer and ice cream by riding bicycles, walking, and taking public transportation.

Good for teaching, learning + practicing CT14, CT20, CT22, T7.4, T8.4, T11.6

☐ V24

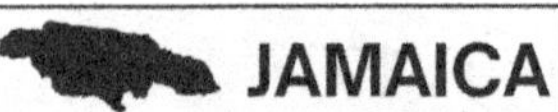

JAMAICA

VIOLENCE INTERRUPTER

tinyurl.com/cctboxv24

(3 minutes)

Violence interruption is a community-based approach to reducing violence by empowering near peers as conflict mediators in their own communities. Learn about how Ruben Robinson is working as a violence interrupter in his Jamaican community to create a better life for himself, his daughter, and his neighbors.

Good for teaching, learning + practicing CT6, CT9, CT18, T1.2, T1.5, T2.4

☐ V25

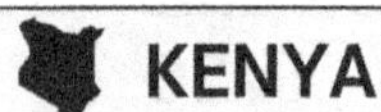

KENYA

FROM WASTE TO WALKWAYS

tinyurl.com/cctboxv25

(2.5 minutes)

Nairobi, Kenya generates roughly 500 metric tons of plastic waste per day. Only a fraction of that is recycled. Learn about how Kenyan entrepreneur Nzambi Matee started a social enterprise to turn this "trash into cash." Her organization converts plastic waste into high-quality building products.

Good for teaching, learning + practicing CT8, CT12, CT13, T3.4, T3.6, T12.1

▢ V26

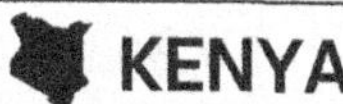

KENYA

A CUSTOMER-FOCUSED APPROACH

tinyurl.com/cctboxv26

(3.5 minutes)

One Acre Fund works with smallholder farmers providing them with holistic access to the financing and training they need to grow more food and earn more money. Instead of taking a charity approach, they invest in farmers and look at them as valued-customers, not beneficiaries.

Good for teaching, learning + practicing CT1, CT5, CT21, T1.2, T4.6, T5.3

▢ V27

KENYA

MICROGRIDS IN ACTION

tinyurl.com/cctboxv27

(4 minutes)

80% of rural African communities don't have access to electricity through their national grid. Learn about how RVE.SOL is working with communities to install solar microgrids. Community members can now use appliances, students can study longer, and businesses can stay open longer.

Good for teaching, learning + practicing CT12, CT13, CT20, T3.1, T3.4, T3.9

▢ V28

KENYA

PIPING THROUGH PROBLEMS

tinyurl.com/cctboxv28

(4 minutes)

Learn about how Kennedy Odede solved the problems of broken pipes and the power of water cartels to provide affordable and clean water to his community. By reimagining how the water distribution system works, Shofco, his organization, has been able to create the impact that eluded previous efforts.

Good for teaching, learning + practicing CT12, CT13, CT15, T4.5, T6.6, T13.2

▢ V29

KENYA

CLEAN COOKING ATM'S

tinyurl.com/cctboxv29

(3 minutes)

Throughout Kenya, people have traditionally cooked using charcoal or wood. In addition to other negative effects, this impacts health and the environment. Now Koko, a social enterprise, is installing machines that work like ATM's and dispense clean cooking fuel in increments and at prices that people can afford.

Good for teaching, learning + practicing CT13, CT14, CT20, T7.1, T8.4, T11.2

▢ V30

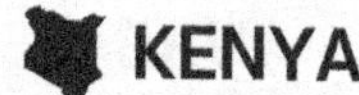

KENYA

POO POWER

tinyurl.com/cctboxv30

(4 minutes)

Sanivation, a social enterprise in Kenya, is making fuel out of human feces. When combined with sawdust and rose waste, a sludge is produced and transformed into coal briquettes. These briquettes are effective, efficient, and produce just a third of the emissions of traditional cooking methods.

Good for teaching, learning + practicing CT7, CT8, CT20, T6.9, T7.3, T8.4

V31 - V35

V31  KENYA

GIVING CHOICE FOR A CHANGE

tinyurl.com/cctboxv31

(4.25 minutes)

Eunice was one of a few hundred entrepreneurs who received $1,125 as part of a GiveDirectly COVID-19 relief program focused on entrepreneurs. This dignified donation was provided to Eunice with no strings attached and gave her the power to prioritize. Learn about its impact.

Good for teaching, learning + practicing CT2, CT14, CT16, T5.1, T5.2, T5.4

V32  MADAGSCAR

A COOPERATIVE FUTURE

tinyurl.com/cctboxv32

(3.5 minutes)

In Madagascar, USAID and McCormick & Co helped local communities create farming cooperatives for vanilla production. These cooperatives offer opportunities for more certainty and income. Learn about how this community-driven approach for farmers is making profound change.

Good for teaching, learning + practicing CT9, CT10, CT18, T5.4, T6.4, T13.1

V33  MALAYSIA

HEROES OF E-WASTE

tinyurl.com/cctboxv33

(6 minutes)

The world creates approximately 50 million tons of electronic waste each year, mostly from personal consumer electronics. Learn about how Egyptian-Finnish entrepreneurs Mo El-Fatatry and Nahed Bedir Eletribi launched an e-waste recycling platform for households powered by "champions."

Good for teaching, learning + practicing CT8, CT10, CT14, T1.2, T2.4, T10.1

V34  MEXICO

LITERALLY A SCHOOL BUS

tinyurl.com/cctboxv34

(3 minutes)

Learn about how an organization called Yes We Can converted a bus into a mobile classroom. They create a safe and dynamic educational environment for migrant children who have no other opportunities while they wait for rulings on their asylum status.

Good for teaching, learning + practicing CT7, CT13, CT15, T2.1, T3.2, T3.6

V35  NATIVE AMERICAN COMMUNITIES

COMMUNITY-OWNED EDUCATION

tinyurl.com/cctboxv35

(4.5 minutes)

Schools run by outside agencies that serve Native American students have a history of failure. In 2006, the Native American Community Academy (NACA) launched as a community-led charter school. Recently, over 90 percent of the graduating class was accepted into college.

Good for teaching, learning + practicing CT2, CT7, CT18, T1.2, T2.4, T3.6

☐ V36

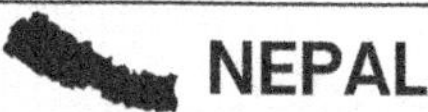 NEPAL

NAMING + FAMING

tinyurl.com/cctboxv36

(3 minutes)

Learn about how a show in Nepal called "Integrity Idol" is helping government efforts to fight corruption. Instead of "naming and shaming" corrupt government workers, this innovative program "names and fames" the most honest, hard working officials.

Good for teaching, learning + practicing CT5, CT16, CT22, T3.2, T8.3, T11.4

☐ V37

NIGERIA

WE'LL SOLVE IT OURSELVES!

tinyurl.com/cctboxv37

(3 minutes)

Learn about how a group of women in a rural community in Nigeria worked together to address infant mortality. They got fed up waiting for the government, and came up with a simple, elegant solution. Ironically, the government is now working to scale their solution throughout the country.

Good for teaching, learning + practicing CT5, CT10, CT15, T6.1, T6.7, T7.2

☐ V38

 NIGERIA

CROWD FARMING

tinyurl.com/cctboxv38

(3 minutes)

Learn about how Farmcrowdy, an agritech social enterprise in Lagos, Nigeria, is connecting young urban investors with rural farmers to help them scale. Farmers get what they need, investors earn returns, and prices are kept reasonable for local consumers. A simple app helps bring everyone together.

Good for teaching, learning + practicing CT11, CT20, CT21, T3.1, T3.9, T6.3

☐ V39

 NIGERIA

HYDROPONIC SHIPPING CONTAINERS

tinyurl.com/cctboxv39

(2 minutes)

Learn about how entrepreneur Angel Adelaja has built and is scaling the first farm in Africa using discarded shipping containers. She's using hydroponics to grow vegetables and create jobs for local women.

Good for teaching, learning + practicing CT3, CT7, CT13, T2.8, T4.4, T5.3

☐ V40

 PAKISTAN

EMPOWERING WOMEN-LED TELEMEDICINE

tinyurl.com/cctboxv40

(4 minutes)

60% of medical graduates in Pakistan are women. However, only 25% of these women are currently able to contribute to the healthcare workforce. Learn about DoctHERs, which aims to change this by matching the underutilized capacity of female doctors to unmet needs via technology such as telemedicine.

Good for teaching, learning + practicing CT3, CT4, CT6, T1.2, T5.2, T11.4

☐ **V41** 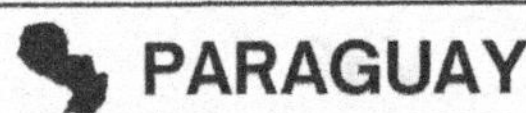 **PARAGUAY**

tinyurl.com/cctboxv41

A STOPLIGHT FOR POVERTY ALLEVIATION

(5.5 minutes)

Learn about a visual tool developed by Fundacion Paraguaya that helps community members identify and prioritize their own challenges and strengths. Using this information, communities become better equipped to focus their efforts and lift themselves out of poverty.

Good for teaching, learning + practicing CT2, CT5, CT19, T2.4, T3.1, T6.1

☐ **V42**  **PERU**

tinyurl.com/cctboxv42

PROFESSIONALIZING WASTE PICKERS

(7.5 minutes)

Pucallpa was in danger of drowning in garbage because, like many other cities in the world, it had no organized waste disposal system. Thanks to Albina Ruiz, that changed. She founded Ciudad Saludable, which means "Healthy City," and has turned the waste problem into an entrepreneurial success story.

Good for teaching, learning + practicing CT6, CT8, CT12, T3.2, T3.6, T7.1

☐ **V43** **PUERTO RICO, UNITED STATES**

tinyurl.com/cctboxv43

A COMMUNITY-LED RECOVERY

(5.5 minutes)

Learn about a nonprofit that created a participatory model that helps communities recover from disasters such as Hurricane Maria in 2017. They believe that projects are more likely to succeed and promote long term engagement when there's community prioritization and ownership.

Good for teaching, learning + practicing CT2, CT6, CT10, T1.4, T6.5, T6.10

☐ **V44** **REFUGEE COMMUNITIES**

tinyurl.com/cctboxv44

STORIES OF CHANGE

(4.5 minutes)

#MeWe Intl. works with refugees and vulnerable communities. Its methodology leverages communications skills-building and narrative interventions as tools for psychological well-being, leadership development, and community building.

Good for teaching, learning + practicing CT1, CT9, CT15, T1.2, T5.2, T6.6

☐ **V45**  **RWANDA**

tinyurl.com/cctboxv45

LIGHTING UP LIVES + LIVELIHOODS

(3 minutes)

Learn about the work of Solar Sister, an organization that's building networks of women entrepreneurs throughout several African countries. These women provide light and hope to community members whilst earning a compelling living that helps them support their own families.

Good for teaching, learning + practicing CT4, CT10, CT13, T5.3, T8.5, T11.3

☐ V46

WRITING A BOOK A DAY

tinyurl.com/cctboxv46

(3 minutes)

An organization in South Africa holds hackathons to write children's books in a day. Learn about how Book Dash is trying to tackle low levels of child literacy by having teams write and distribute books that are fun to read and culturally relevant.

Good for teaching, learning + practicing CT6, CT10, CT13, T1.1, T2.6, T3.8

☐ V47

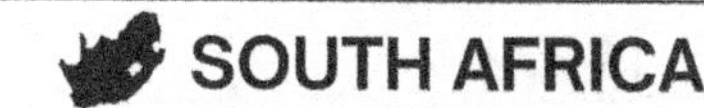

BLACK MAMBAS PREVENTING POACHING

tinyurl.com/cctboxv47

(5.5 minutes)

The Black Mambas is an unarmed group that's effectively preventing poaching. These are all young women who come from local communities. They're saving wildlife through empowerment, education, and by creating bonds with local communities.

Good for teaching, learning + practicing CT4, CT6, CT12, T1.2, T6.6, T7.2

☐ V48

SWEDEN

LIVING WITH MANDATORY FRIENDS

tinyurl.com/cctboxv48

(4 minutes)

Loneliness is a problem for both young people and senior citizens in Sweden. Many people live alone. Learn about how a city council is working to change this. They've built apartment buildings for people under 25 and pensioners that have one important rule. Tenants are required to spend two hours together per week.

Good for teaching, learning + practicing CT11, CT18, CT20, T4.1, T5.4, T7.3

☐ V49

VEGGIES FOR EDUCATION

tinyurl.com/cctboxv49

(3.5 minutes)

For The O'Brien School, gardening is a way to get kids in school and keep them coming. Most students come from the Maasai tribe. Droughts have made their traditional diet challenging. After teaching vegetable gardening and cooking at school, students are bringing what they've learned home.

Good for teaching, learning + practicing CT2, CT12, CT13, T4.2, T5.1, T6.4

☐ V50

THAILAND

HANDS-ON LEADERSHIP + EMPATHY

tinyurl.com/cctboxv50

(5.5 minutes)

Learn about the Bamboo School in rural Thailand. Here students have direct control over their learning and focus on coursework that prioritizes leadership and empathy. The hands-on curriculum includes gardening, community service, entrepreneurship, and much more.

Good for teaching, learning + practicing CT2, CT7, CT10, T5.4, T7.1, T7.6

V51

TURKEY

3D PRINTING SURPRISES + SMILES

tinyurl.com/cctboxv51

(4 minutes)

Near Istanbul's historic Istiklal Street, a group of local artists is working to improve the city's public spaces and bring smiles to residents' faces. Learn about Onaranlar Kulubu, an organization that's focused on building community by using street art as an inspiration.

Good for teaching, learning + practicing CT7, CT10, CT18, T3.1, T4.5, T5.4

V52

UGANDA

FROM PATIENT TO HEALER

tinyurl.com/cctboxv52

(4.5 minutes)

Learn about a program that's designed a methodology to help women battle depression and mental health issues. In a country where there are only 40 psychiatrists, women who join the program participate in group therapy sessions facilitated by other women who've been through the program themselves.

Good for teaching, learning + practicing CT4, CT6, CT9, T5.4, T7.1, T9.1

V53

UGANDA

SANITARY PADS FOR EDUCATION

tinyurl.com/cctboxv53

(6 minutes)

One in ten girls in Sub-Saharan Africa misses school during her menstrual cycle. Walter is a young entrepreneur supported by Peace First who's training young women to make sanitary pads to help solve this problem. Learn about how he's creating jobs and helping young women continue with their education.

Good for teaching, learning + practicing CT3, CT4, CT12, T3.1, T3.5, T11.2

V54

UNITED KINGDOM

COOKING EMPATHY

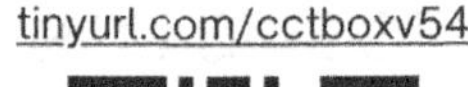

tinyurl.com/cctboxv54

(5 minutes)

Learn how Migrateful, a UK-based organization, is helping to bring people together and creating job opportunities through cooking. Recent immigrants teach recipes from their home countries, learn new skills to help them assimilate, and create community with other immigrants and participants.

Good for teaching, learning + practicing CT11, CT17, CT18, T2.8, T5.1, T9.1

V55

UNITED KINGDOM

POWERED BY OLD BAGELS

tinyurl.com/cctboxv55

(4.5 minutes)

Olio, a social enterprise in London, recruits "food waste heroes" to gather excess food from restaurants and redistribute it within their neighborhoods. The Olio app helps reduce food waste and helps everyone, from students to the elderly, save money. It also helps people feel more connected to their communities.

Good for teaching, learning + practicing CT2, CT8, CT20, T8.4, T9.3, T11.5

▢ V56 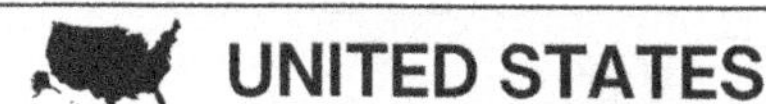 UNITED STATES

CHANGING THE NARRATIVE ABOUT BLACK MEN

tinyurl.com/cctboxv56

(3 minutes)

BMe Community is working to change the narrative about Black men in the United States and to accelerate their efforts as catalysts for community building and social change. BMe does this by connecting Black male leaders with each other and with key influencers across industries and sectors.

Good for teaching, learning + practicing CT1, CT5, CT9, T1.3, T7.2, T9.2

▢ V57 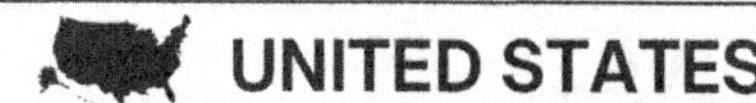 UNITED STATES

PATIENT CAPITAL

tinyurl.com/cctboxv57

(5 minutes)

Acumen, founded by Jacqueline Novogratz in 2001, believes in and supports using the power of entrepreneurship to build a world where everyone has the opportunity to live with dignity. Acumen uses "Patient Capital" to bridge the gap between market-based investing approaches and philanthropy.

Good for teaching, learning + practicing CT7, CT13, CT14, T1.2, T4.2, T10.2

▢ V58 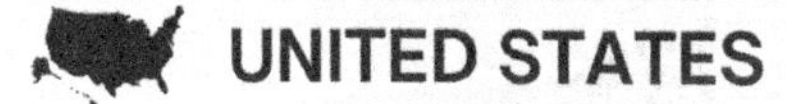 UNITED STATES

DINNER TOGETHER FOR LOSS

tinyurl.com/cctboxv58

(4.5 minutes)

Learn about The Dinner Party. Young adults come together over dinner to help each other talk about and deal with loss and grief. What started as an idea between friends has grown rapidly and proved to be incredibly resilient during the Covid 19 pandemic.

Good for teaching, learning + practicing CT2, CT9, CT17, T1.4, T8.5, T9.1

▢ V59 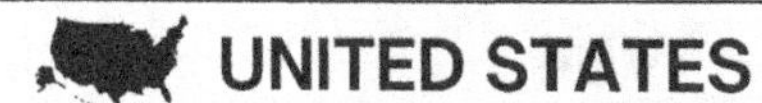 UNITED STATES

PLAY WITH PURPOSE

tinyurl.com/cctboxv59

(3 minutes)

Learn about Playworks, an organization that helps kids stay active and build life skills through play. Playworks focuses on creating safe, healthy, inclusive and respectful conditions so that children can be their best selves and engage positively with their peers and adults.

Good for teaching, learning + practicing CT7, CT12, CT17, T7.2, T7.6, T8.3

▢ V60 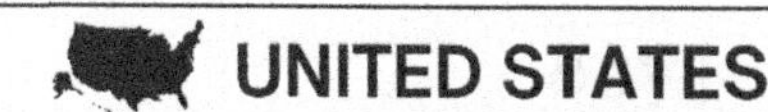 UNITED STATES

WORKER-LED PRIORITIZATION

tinyurl.com/cctboxv60

(3.5 minutes)

Learn about Coworker.org, which provides support for workplace well-being and organizing. They've created a simple technology platform to help workers run campaigns, build digital communities of like-minded workers, and to decide for themselves about their own workplace improvement priorities.

Good for teaching, learning + practicing CT2, CT10, CT19, T2.4, T6.8, T12.4

☐ **V61** 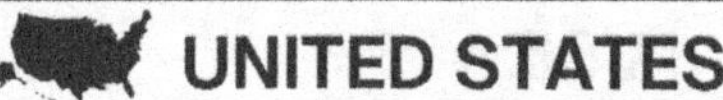 **UNITED STATES**

FITNESS FUELED SECOND CHANCES

(3 minutes)

tinyurl.com/cctboxv61

Learn about an organization that helps formerly incarcerated individuals transition into jobs in the fitness industry as personal trainers. Started by Hector Guadalupe, A Second U Foundation is transforming a way to cope into a way to earn a dignified living.

Good for teaching, learning + practicing CT2, CT7, CT9, T5.1, T6.10, T8.3

☐ **V62**  **UNITED STATES**

BUZZING WITH BOOKS

(2 minutes)

tinyurl.com/cctboxv62

Barbers at a Berks County, Pennsylvania, barbershop are giving children haircuts and confidence boosters. These changemaking barbers offer children $3 to read books aloud during their haircuts. It's a creative way to leverage an everyday activity into something more impactful.

Good for teaching, learning + practicing CT6, CT7, CT17, T1.3, T1.5, T7.3

☐ **V63**  **UNITED STATES**

WELCOMING COMMUNITIES

(4.5 minutes)

tinyurl.com/cctboxv63

Welcoming America has created a community-driven way for US towns with fast-growing immigrant populations to build mutual respect and understanding. They help to organize empathetic environments where people come together to talk about their histories, cultures, hopes, and challenges.

Good for teaching, learning + practicing CT2, CT11, CT21, T4.1, T5.2, T8.2

☐ **V64**  **UNITED STATES**

EXCHANGING PEANUT BUTTER FOR PRODUCE

(3.5 minutes)

tinyurl.com/cctboxv64

Learn about how mutual aid strategies were being used to help solve problems of food insecurity in Massachusetts during Covid-19. People shared vital information and resources with neighbors and strangers. And it all started with bananas.

Good for teaching, learning + practicing CT2, CT6, CT20, T6.4, T6.5, T9.3

☐ **V65**  **UNITED STATES**

A SCRAPPY SOCIAL ENTERPRISE

(5.5 minutes)

tinyurl.com/cctboxv65

Learn about how FABSCRAP, a Brooklyn based social enterprise, is working with fashion brands to recycle and reuse their excess fabric. They collect, consolidate and store fabric that then gets repurposed/ sold through a variety of different channels to everyone from artists, to students to designers.

Good for teaching, learning + practicing CT8, CT12, CT13, T3.4, T6.9, T12.2

☐ V66  UNITED STATES

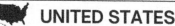

TRUST-BASED LENDING

tinyurl.com/cctboxv66

(3.5 minutes)

Steve Wanta, the co-founder and CEO of Just, talks about making microfinance work in the US through a macro and micro approach. Learn about how Just invests in women entrepreneurs to help them grow their businesses, build resilience, and create more joy.

Good for teaching, learning + practicing CT1, CT3, CT13, T1.2, T2.4, T7.6

☐ V67  UNITED STATES

HUMANIZING HEALTHCARE

tinyurl.com/cctboxv67

(4 minutes)

Magdalena, a patient at Loma Linda University Health's Diabetes Treatment Center, was depressed and immobile. Learn how a community health worker connected with her, learned about her specific challenges, and helped her navigate the complexities of the healthcare system.

Good for teaching, learning + practicing CT4, CT6, CT19, T6.6, T10.1, T12.5

☐ V68  UNITED STATES

GETTING TO ZERO HOMELESSNESS

tinyurl.com/cctboxv68

(3 minutes)

Rosanne Haggerty of Community Solutions shares how a holistic, command-center approach is solving the problem of homelessness city by city. Community Solutions use of "by-name", real-time information equips communities to match resources to the specific needs of individuals.

Good for teaching, learning + practicing CT1, CT10, CT19, T6.10, T8.2, T9.4

☐ V69  UNITED STATES

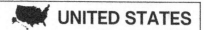

THE CITIZENS JUSTICE LEAGUE

tinyurl.com/cctboxv69

(5 minutes)

In the US, 80% of defendants are represented by public defenders. Often overloaded with huge caseloads, these lawyers don't have the time or resources they need. Learn about "participatory defense," a methodology designed by Raj Jayadev that empowers families as legal defense teams for their loved ones.

Good for teaching, learning + practicing CT2, CT10, CT15, T5.2, T6.3, T6.8

☐ V70  UNITED STATES

TRUCKERS FIGHTING TRAFFICKING

tinyurl.com/cctboxv70

(3 minutes)

Learn about how the Michigan State Police is teaming up with Truckers Against Trafficking (TAT). TAT teaches truck drivers and freight haulers how to identify and report signs of human trafficking, a pervasive, yet often very hidden problem at truck stops.

Good for teaching, learning + practicing CT2, CT19, CT20, T8.2, T9.4, T12.3

V71 - V75

☐ V71  UNITED STATES

SOLUTIONS JOURNALISM

tinyurl.com/cctboxv71

(4 minutes)

David Bornstein, Tina Rosenberg, and their colleagues at Solutions Journalism Network work with journalists to help build their capacity to produce rigorous reporting about solutions, not just problems. They aspire to "rebalance the news" and help people get access to "the whole story."

Good for teaching, learning + practicing CT1, CT5, CT16, T3.1, T4.3, T6.1

☐ V72  UNITED STATES

BATTLING CASH BAIL

tinyurl.com/cctboxv72

(3 minutes)

Learn about the work of The Bail Project. This is a dedicated group of advocates and activists who are working to eliminate cash bail. Many people within the movement have been personally impacted by the criminal legal system.

Good for teaching, learning + practicing CT13, CT15, CT21, T5.6, T6.7, T10.1

☐ V73  UNITED STATES

SURROUNDING STUDENTS WITH SUPPORT

tinyurl.com/cctboxv73

(3 minutes)

Thread supports students in Baltimore who are facing the most significant opportunity and achievement gaps. Thread's focus is to surround students with a cohesive "family" of volunteers who stick with participants "no matter what." This creates deep, long lasting, and trusting relationships.

Good for teaching, learning + practicing CT10, CT11, CT19, T4.2, T9.1, T12.5

☐ V74  UNITED STATES

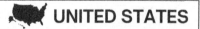

WALKING FOR TRANSFORMATION

tinyurl.com/cctboxv74

(3 minutes)

GirlTrek believes that walking 30 minutes a day is a radical act of self-love. But it's more than a walking group for Black women. GirlTrek is a campaign to heal intergenerational trauma, fight systemic racism, and transform Black lives.

Good for teaching, learning + practicing CT3, CT9, CT17, T3.9, T9.1, T10.3

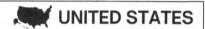

☐ V75  UNITED STATES

GIRLS FINDING THEIR PACE

tinyurl.com/cctboxv75

(2 minutes)

Learn about Girls on the Run (GOTR). GOTR is a physical activity-based positive youth development program whose desired outcome is to help girls be joyful, healthy, and confident. GOTR creatively leverages running to help girls develop essential life and leadership skills.

Good for teaching, learning + practicing CT3, CT11, CT17, T1.2, T3.1, T7.3

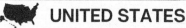

☐ V76  UNITED STATES

HIP HOP THERAPY

tinyurl.com/cctboxv76

(2.5 minutes)

Tomás Alvarez is a social entrepreneur making mental health and wellness services more accessible, useful, and meaningful for youth of color. His innovative approach integrates pop culture with proven therapy models.

Good for teaching, learning + practicing CT6, CT7, CT17, T4.1, T5.2, T5.4

☐ V77  UNITED STATES

ADVANCING EMPLOYEE OWNERSHIP

tinyurl.com/cctboxv77

(4 minutes)

Learn about how Project Equity is leading an employee ownership movement. Their goal is to raise awareness about employee ownership as an exit strategy for current business owners, and as an approach for increasing employee engagement and well-being.

Good for teaching, learning + practicing CT2, CT12, CT21, T6.7, T6.8, T7.4

☐ V78  UNITED STATES

FUTURE READY EDUCATION

tinyurl.com/cctboxv78

(3.5 minutes)

World Savvy believes that students learn best when they're engaged in relevant and important issues that impact their communities and the world. World Savvy partners with schools and districts to integrate global competence in K-12 teaching, learning, and culture.

Good for teaching, learning + practicing CT7, CT10, CT17, T1.3, T3.6, T7.6

☐ V79  UNITED STATES

A CIVIC JOURNALISM LAB

tinyurl.com/cctboxv79

(3 minutes)

Founded in 2015, City Bureau is an organization based in the South Side of Chicago. It's a non-profit newsroom that aspires to produce civic journalism that brings journalists and communities together in a collaborative spirit. The goal is to produce media that's impactful, equitable, and responsive to the public.

Good for teaching, learning + practicing CT11, CT19, CT20, T1.4, T2.5, T9.2

☐ V80  UNITED STATES

BITE-SIZED CHANGEMAKING

tinyurl.com/cctboxv80

(3 minutes)

One billion plastic toothpaste tubes are thrown away every year. Learn about how Lindsay McCormick started Bite Toothpaste to help reduce plastic pollution and provide a chemical-free brushing solution. Bite achieves this through the use of a refillable, recyclable glass container and a subscription model.

Good for teaching, learning + practicing CT7, CT12, CT13, T4.4, T5.5, T12.2

V81 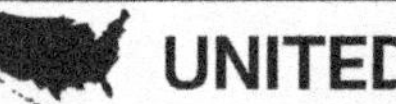 UNITED STATES

FOCUSING ON INNOVATION

tinyurl.com/cctboxv81

(7.5 minutes)

Learn the origin story of Warby Parker from the four co-founders who came up with the idea after one of them lost his glasses. This comprehensive interview dives into everything that makes Warby Parker unique, including their branding, pricing, their "buy one, give one" program, and their customer experience approach.

Good for teaching, learning + practicing CT7, CT13, CT14, T3.6, T7.4, T12.5

V82  UNITED STATES

TURNING BUILDINGS INTO TESLAS

tinyurl.com/cctboxv82

(7 minutes)

If every building in the US became electric and stopped burning oil and gas, the result would be a 30% reduction in greenhouse gas emissions. Learn how Donnel Baird, CEO and founder of BlocPower, has built a social enterprise that's using creative financing and partnering with a growing number of cities across the US.

Good for teaching, learning + practicing CT12, CT14, CT20, T3.4, T7.2, T8.2

V83  UNITED STATES

CROSS SUBSIDIZING HEALTHY MEALS

tinyurl.com/cctboxv83

(5.5 minutes)

Learn about Everytable, a start-up founded in Los Angeles whose goal is to make healthy, fresh, and delicious food affordable for everyone, regardless of where they live. This social enterprise uses a creative pricing model and works to meet people "where they are" culturally, economically, and geographically.

Good for teaching, learning + practicing CT2, CT13, CT14, T3.9, T8.1, T11.2

V84  UNITED STATES

EMPOWERING OPPORTUNITY IN COAL COUNTRY

tinyurl.com/cctboxv84

(4 minutes)

Learn about how Brandon Dennison started Coalfield Development to help empower aspiring entrepreneurs in Appalachia create a diversified economy. He's designed a unique model that helps to incubate and grow social enterprises through mixing work, professional education, and personal development.

Good for teaching, learning + practicing CT1, CT7, CT8, T3.1, T7.4, T9.2

V85  UNITED STATES

CODING FOR CHANGE

tinyurl.com/cctboxv85

(5.5 minutes)

Learn about an organization that's using a human-centered approach to help make government at all levels work well for everyone. Founded by Jennifer Pahlka, Code for America works with citizens and critical stakeholders to help government programs realize their potential.

Good for teaching, learning + practicing CT6, CT10, CT13, T4.2, T6.3, T11.1

☐ V86

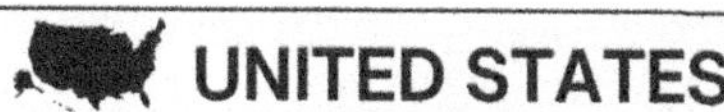

3D OCEAN FARMING

tinyurl.com/cctboxv86

(3.5 minutes)

Learn about how Bren Smith, a lifelong commercial fisherman, went on a personal search for sustainability and started GreenWave. GreenWave's 3D ocean farming model empowers fishermen to both grow food, and to be change agents for restoring, instead of depleting, local ecosystems.

Good for teaching, learning + practicing CT7, CT8, CT15, T4.2, T8.1, T10.2

☐ V87

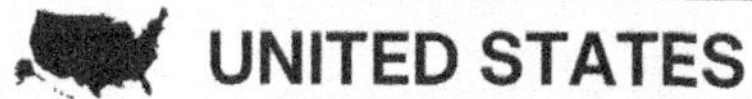

ABOUT THE HOW, NOT THE COW

tinyurl.com/cctboxv87

(4 minutes)

Learn about how Gabe Brown, a pioneer in regenerative agriculture, decided to work with nature, instead of against her. He uses techniques that mimic nature and has built economic resilience by creating 17 enterprises on his ranch.

Good for teaching, learning + practicing CT1, CT8, CT16, T3.9, T4.2, T11.3

☐ V88

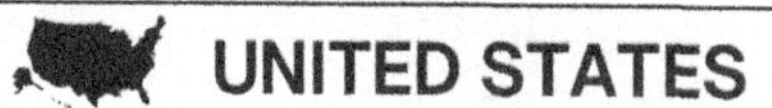

BUSINESS FOR A BETTER WORLD

tinyurl.com/cctboxv88

(2.5 minutes)

Learn about the B Corps movement, led by B Lab & Sistema B, that's working to transform the global economy to benefit people, communities, and the planet. The focus is to enable companies to improve their social and environmental impact through adopting new standards and tools.

Good for teaching, learning + practicing CT5, CT10, CT13, T8.2, T8.4, T10.3

☐ V89

INTERGENERATIONAL IMPACT

tinyurl.com/cctboxv89

(3 minutes)

Learn about how CoGenerate (formerly Encore.org) works to create a better future for younger generations through mobilizing the passions, skills, investment and wisdom of the growing older population. CoGenerate helps empower older adults to innovate and help young people in ways that create value for everyone involved.

Good for teaching, learning + practicing CT6, CT9, CT20, T1.1, T5.2, T9.1

☐ V90

PEDAL POWER

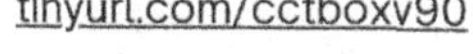

(5.5 minutes)

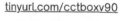

Sometimes adding just one piece to the changemaking puzzle can be truly catalytic. Learn about how an entrepreneur in Zambia created a social enterprise to help rural women entrepreneurs get access to bicycles for the first time by using a creative, smartphone-based pricing strategy.

Good for teaching, learning + practicing CT3, CT13, CT21, T4.1, T5.5, T11.2

NOTES:

collaborativechangemaking.com
for updates, new resources, to report problems, share your ideas, provide feedback, etc.

youtube.com/@collaborativechangemaking
for HOW-TO videos, extra CHANGEMAKING INNOVATION MINI-CASES, etc.

SECTION 05 | CHANGEMAKER COACH

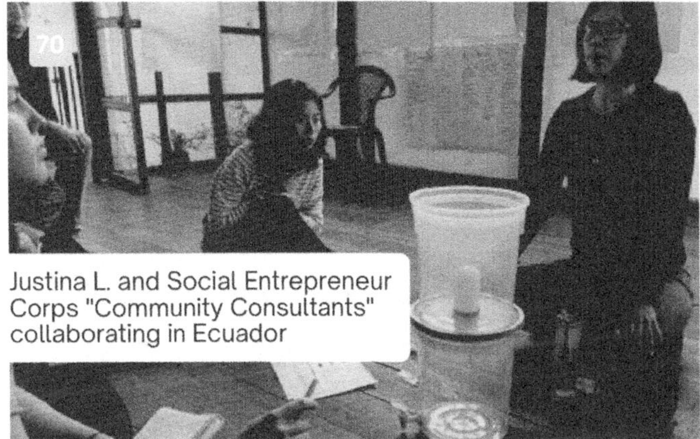

70

Justina L. and Social Entrepreneur Corps "Community Consultants" collaborating in Ecuador

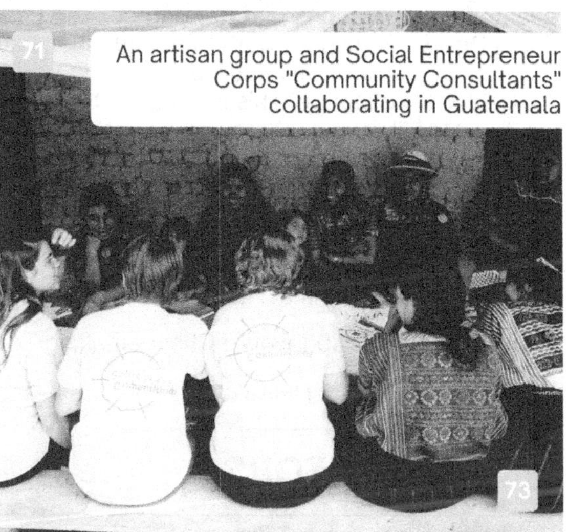

71

An artisan group and Social Entrepreneur Corps "Community Consultants" collaborating in Guatemala

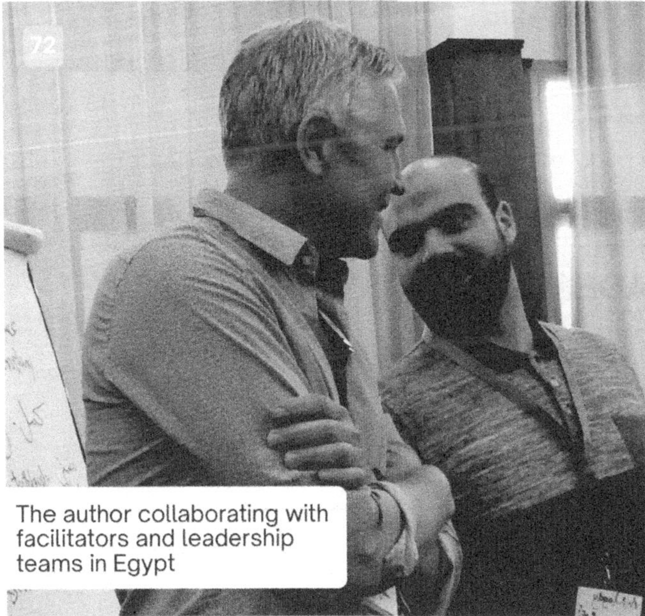

72

The author collaborating with facilitators and leadership teams in Egypt

73

Brett S. and the author collaborating in Guatemala

NOTES:

tinyurl.com/cctboxcoachama
ADVICE + ASK
ME ANYTHING (AMA)

I'd love to help you with specific questions you might have about how to use this toolbox. Below are examples of questions that I've categorized under headers by user type. Go to the link/ QR code above to find a Google Document with these questions and my responses. You'll also see more questions and answers and additional headers such as FOUNDATION LEADERS, FACILITATORS, STUDENTS, and PARENTS, for example. This list will continue to grow. And at the top of the Google Document, you'll find a link to a Google Form where you can ask your own questions. Don't hesitate to ask me anything.

GENERAL QUESTIONS

Which of the Changemaking Trimtabs are the most catalytic from your perspective? Why?

What are your top 10 favorite Changemaking Tools and why?

Which Changemaking Innovation Mini-Cases do you find are the comprehensive for learning/ insights?

EDUCATORS

How could I structure a 12-week course using this toolbox?

Which Changemaking Tools do you believe are the best/ easiest to integrate into other courses?

How would you build a course focused on the SDG's?

ORGANIZATION/ TEAM LEADERS

How might Employee Resource Groups (ERG's) use this toolbox?

How would you recommend using this for onboarding new team members?

How would you use this toolbox for team building either in-person or remotely?

(SOCIAL) ENTREPRENEURS

Which of the Changemaking Trimtabs do really wish you had known when you first started your journey?

Wearing your social entrepreneur hat, what are your top 10 favorite Changemaking Video Mini-Cases?

COMMUNITY IMPACT PROFESSIONALS/ VOLUNTEERS

Which of the Changemaking Trimtabs do you believe are the most critical to incorporate?

Which Changemaking Tools would recommend for high school students doing community service work?

Choosing from this entire toolbox, what do you wish you had when you were a Peace Corps Volunteer?

tinyurl.com/cctboxhowtos

PRIORITY HOW-TO'S FOR CHANGEMAKERS

In my experience, I've found that there are some really important foundational things that every changemaker should know how to do. On this page and the next, you'll find the titles of what I believe are fourteen PRIORITY HOW-TO'S FOR CHANGEMAKERS. I've categorized these under thematic hashtags. The link/ QR code above will take you to a Google Folder with PDF's for each of these.

#COMMUNITY ENGAGEMENT

- [ ] HOW TO **HAVE EFFECTIVE CONVERSATIONS**
- [ ] HOW TO **BE A KEEN OBSERVER**

#IDEATING TOGETHER

- [ ] HOW TO **BRAINSTORM EFFECTIVELY**
- [ ] HOW TO **FACILITATE GROUP CONVERSATIONS**
- [ ] HOW TO **DESIGN TEAM REFLECTIONS**

#DISCOVERY

- [ ] HOW TO **CONDUCT PRIMARY + SECONDARY RESEARCH**
- [ ] HOW TO **DESIGN CONSTRUCTIVE QUESTIONS**

#CRAFTING GUIDING STATEMENTS

- [ ] HOW TO **CRAFT A CONCISE PROBLEM STATEMENT**
- [ ] HOW TO **CRAFT AN INSPIRING VISION STATEMENT**
- [ ] HOW TO **CRAFT A CONSTRUCTIVE OUTCOMES STATEMENT**

#CHANGEMAKING LEADERSHIP

- [ ] HOW TO **PRACTICE SERVANT LEADERSHIP**
- [ ] HOW TO **LEAD CHANGE**

#SHARING + VETTING YOUR INNOVATION

- [ ] HOW TO **TEST YOUR INNOVATION CONCEPTS**
- [ ] HOW TO **GIVE AN EFFECTIVE PRESENTATION**

NOTES:

collaborativechangemaking.com
for updates, new resources, to report problems, share your ideas, provide feedback, etc.

youtube.com/@collaborativechangemaking
for HOW-TO videos, extra CHANGEMAKING INNOVATION MINI-CASES, etc.

RECOMMENDED RESOURCES FOR CHANGEMAKERS

tinyurl.com/cctboxrecres

I've curated lists of what I believe are some of the most helpful resources for changemakers in all stages, all fields, and of all ages. These are practical resources that you should find inspirational, informational and insightful. I've included summary lists in this toolbox. The link/ QR code above will take you to a Google Sheet with the complete lists. I'll update/ add to these periodically. To note, I'm definitely missing some great resources. Please don't hesitate to email me to point out omissions and/or recommendations. I'll add them to the Google Sheets.

CHANGEMAKING "GO-TO'S" TO BOOKMARK

These are resources that I visit and use frequently for a variety of different reasons. For example, the ideas for many of the tools came from *Harvard Business Review* and *Stanford Social Innovation Review* articles, amongst others listed below. And a good number of the Changemaking Innovation Mini-Cases came from using Solutions Journalism Network's indispensable StoryTracker ®. I'd recommend that you explore these ASAP! My short descriptions certainly don't do these websites justice.

☐ **ELLEN MACARTHUR FOUNDATION**	ellenmacarthurfoundation.org	A one-stop website for all things related to building circular economies
☐ **ENGINEERING FOR CHANGE**	engineeringforchange.org	Vast library of engineering/ technology solutions, articles and trend analysis etc.
☐ **FEEDBACK LABS**	feedbacklabs.org	Resources, tools, insights and tips about building feedback loops
☐ **HARVARD BUSINESS REVIEW**	hbr.org	Articles with ideas and advice on strategy, innovation and leadership from business and management experts
☐ **IDEO.ORG**	ideo.org	The go-to place for all things human-centered design
☐ **NESS LABS**	nesslabs.com	Articles focused on science-based strategies for creativity and productivity. Access to a supportive learning community
☐ **NEXT BILLION**	nextbillion.net	Original guest-written articles, events and a jobs board related to the opportunities/ challenges of doing business in low- and middle-income countries
☐ **PLAYWORKS** (V59)	playworks.org	A games library, tool, tips and more focused on ways to use play as an educator
☐ **SOLUTIONS JOURNALISM NETWORK** (V71)	solutionsjournalism.org	A curated database of rigorous reporting on responses to social problems with nearly 15,000 stories produced by journalists and news outlets covering 190 countries (as of 3/31/23)
☐ **STANFORD SOCIAL INNOVATION REVIEW**	ssir.org	Articles that cover cross-sector solutions to global problems written by and for social change leaders from around the world and from all sectors

THE CHANGEMAKER'S BOOKSHELF

These are books that are either on my bookshelf, or that I need put on my bookshelf. I've included everything from textbooks, to how-to books, to narratives. Many of the books in this summary list are from friends and people that I've worked with and truly admire. Don't forget to use the link/ QR code on the previous page to go to the Google Sheet with the more expansive list. And don't forget to send me titles that I should add.

☐ **AMERICA'S PATH FORWARD** Conversations with Social Innovators on the Power of Communities Everywhere	Konstanze Frischen + Michael Zakaras (Editors)
☐ **BECOMING A CHANGEMAKER** An Actionable, Inclusive Guide to Leading Positive Change at Any Level	Alex Budak
☐ **THE BLUE SWEATER** Bridging the Gap Between Rich and Poor in an Interconnected World	Jacqueline Novogratz
☐ **CHANGEMAKER PLAYBOOK** The New Physics of Leadership in a World of Explosive Change	Henry F. DeSio Jr.
☐ **CYNEFIN®** (T6.5) Weaving Sensemaking into the Fabric of our World	David Snowden + Friends
☐ **DARE TO MATTER** Your Path to Making a Difference Now	Jordan Kassalow + Jennifer Krause
☐ **FACILITATOR'S GUIDE TO PARTICIPATORY DECISION MAKING**	Sam Kaner with Lenny Lind, Catherine Toldi, Sarah Fisk + Duane Berger
☐ **IMPACT WITH INTEGRITY** Repair the World Without Breaking Yourself	Becky Margiotta
☐ **INFLUENCER** (T11.4) The New Science of Leading Change	Joseph Grenny, Kerry Patterson, David Maxfield, Ron McMillan + Al Switzler
☐ **INTERNATIONAL MODELS OF CHANGEMAKER EDUCATION** Programs, Methods, and Design	Viviana Alexandrowicz + Paul M. Rogers (Editors)
☐ **PATTERNS OF ENTREPRENEURSHIP MANAGEMENT**	Jack McGourty + Jack M. Kaplan
☐ **RECODING AMERICA** (V85) Why Government Is Failing in the Digital Age and How We Can Do Better	Jennifer Pahlko
☐ **RIPPLING** How Social Entrepreneurs Spread Innovation Throughout the World	Beverly Schwartz
☐ **SOCIAL ENTREPRENEURSHIP** What Everyone Needs to Know	David Bornstein + Susan Davis
☐ **THINKING, FAST + SLOW**	Daniel Khaneman
☐ **UNDERSTANDING SOCIAL ENTREPRENEURSHIP** The Relentless Pursuit of Mission in and Ever Changing World	Jill Kickul and Thomas S. Lyons
☐ **WHO OWNS POVERTY?** (V41)	Martin Burt

CHANGEMAKING ORGANIZATIONS, NETWORKS + COMMUNITIES

This list includes a wide variety organizations. Most of these organizations offer many different opportunities and ways to engage. Instead of writing my own inadequate description, I've used their taglines. Contact me if you'd like specific recommendations.

☐ **ACUMEN** (V57)	acumen.org	Changing the way the world tackles poverty
☐ **AMANI INSTITUTE**	amaniinstitute.org	A world where people go to work to make a difference
☐ **ASHOKA**	ashoka.org	Everyone a changemaker
☐ **B LAB**	bcorporation.net	Make business a force for good
☐ **BMe COMMUNITY** (V56)	bmecommunity.org	Build Black L.O.V.E. without stigmatizing Black people
☐ **CHANGEMAKERS**	changemakers.com	A place to connect with people who are transforming our world for the good of all. There are thousands of us. We are all ages.
☐ **CHANGE X**	changex.org	Proven ideas and funding for your community
☐ **DO SOMETHING**	dosomething.org	Fueling young people to change the world..
☐ **ECHOING GREEN**	echoinggreen.org	Supporting bold ideas and extraordinary leaders
☐ **ENACTUS**	enactus.org	Engaging next gen of entrepreneurial leaders to use innovation + business principles to improve the world
☐ **GLOBAL IMPACT INVESTING NETWORK (GIIN)**	thegiin.org	We are dedicated to increasing impact investing's scale and effectiveness around the world.
☐ **IMPACT HUB**	impacthub.net	To build a more just and sustainable society
☐ **NATIONAL PEACE CORPS ASSOC.**	peacecorpsconnect.org	Helping Peace Corps + Returned Peace Corps Volunteers
☐ **NET IMPACT**	netimpact.org	Inspiring and equipping new leaders building a just and sustainable world
☐ **OPPORTUNITY COLLABORATION**	ocimpact.com	A global network of leaders dedicated to building sustainable solutions to poverty and injustice
☐ **PEACE FIRST** (V53)	peacefirst.org	Let's create a better world together
☐ **SKOLL FOUNDATION**	skoll.org	Social entrepreneurs driving large-scale change
☐ **SOCAP GLOBAL**	socapglobal.com	Unlock the power of markets for impact
☐ **SOCIAL ENTERPRISE GREENHOUSE**	segreenhouse.org	Creates and nurtures inclusive entrepreneurial ecosystems that foster just, equitable and resilient communities.
☐ **SOLUTIONS JOURNALISM NETWORK** (V71)	solutionsjournalism.org	Transforming news is critical to building a more equitable and sustainable world.
☐ **THE SPACESHIP ACADEMY**	thespaceship.org	Prepare for impact.
☐ **STARTINGBLOC**	startingbloc.org	Shifting the culture of leadership
☐ **VILLAGE CAPITAL**	villcap.com	Democratizing entrepreneurship
☐ **THE WEAVING LAB**	weavinglab.org	System change for a better world

YOUR FAVORITE CHANGEMAKING RESOURCES

tinyurl.com/cctboxyours

RESOURCE NAME	WHY IT'S A FAVORITE	WHERE TO FIND IT

SECTION 06 | CHOOSE YOUR DONATION DESTINATION

Photos of the Centro Explorativo in La Pista, Guatemala

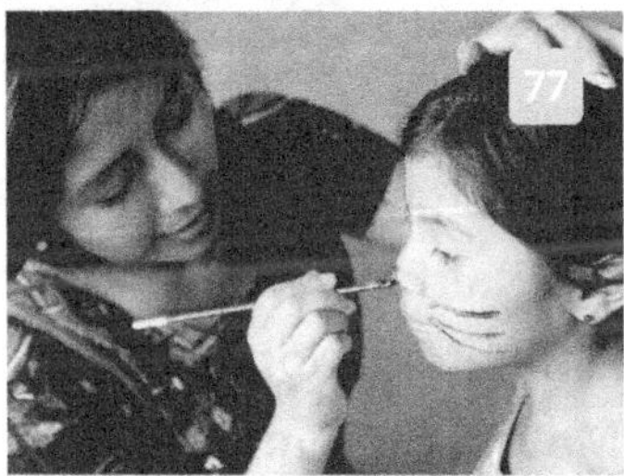

NOTES:

15% 15% of the sales price of this book will be reinvested in the kind of changemaking that made this resource possible in the first place.

1/2 Half will be donated to The Centro Explorativo (the "Centro") in La Pista, Guatemala. The Centro's an education and exploration center that I helped start roughly 20 years ago using profits from my first social entrepreneurial venture, El Descanso Restaurant. It's owned and managed by a local association. The photos on the previous page are from the Centro. You can visit the Centro at elcentroexplorativo.org. Don't hesitate to make your own contribution as well!

1/2 For the other half, I'm trying something out and am asking for your help. Below, you'll find a list of some fantastic organizations doing really important work. These are organizations that are in some way dear to family/ friends who've been especially supportive of my efforts creating this toolbox. If you have a moment, I'd ask you to use the link/ QR code above to go to a Google Form and designate which of these organizations you'd like to receive the 7.5% contribution. Donations that aren't designated will be allocated to these organizations on a rotating basis. To note, this allocation methodology and/or list of organizations included may change. Check the Google Form for changes.

All Grow Association	en.allgrowromania.org
American Cancer Society	cancer.org (in honor of Mary Van Kirk)
Girls on the Run (Central Maryland)	gotrcentralmd.org
Habitat for Humanity (Morris County, NJ)	morrishabitat.org (in honor of Philip Van Kirk)
Holt International	holtinternational.org
MeWe International	meweintl.org
L.I.F.E	lifemiamioh.com
National Peace Corps Assoc.	peacecorpsconnect.org
Queen City Book Bank	queencitybookbank.org
Per Scholas	perscholas.org
Save the Syrian Children	savethesyrianchildren.org
Solutions Journalism Network	solutionsjournalism.org
UN Foundation	unfoundation.org
Vision Spring	visionspring.org
World Savvy	worldsavvy.org

NOTES:

SECTION 07 | GRATITUDE

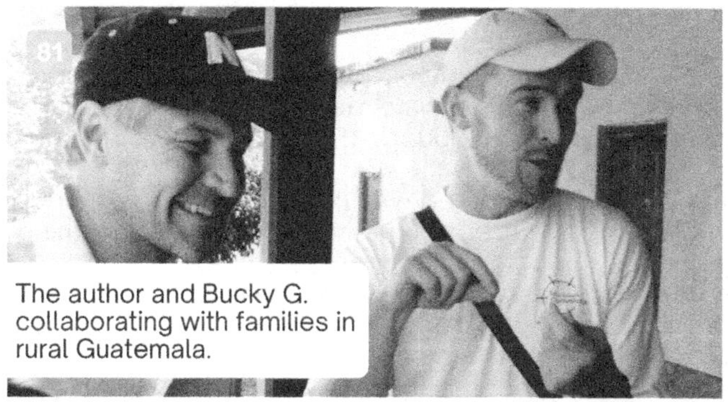

The author and Bucky G. collaborating with families in rural Guatemala.

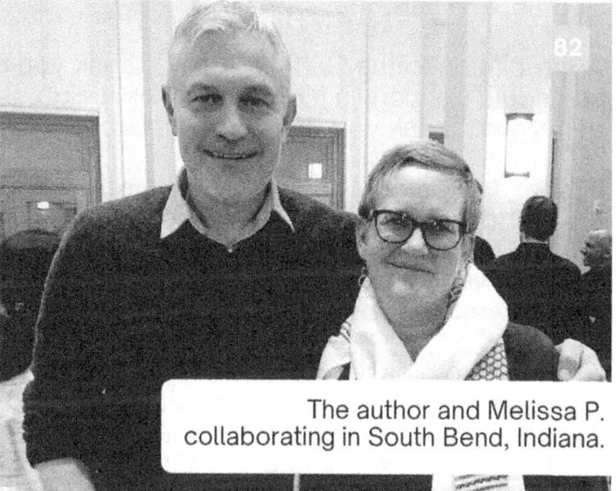

The author and Melissa P. collaborating in South Bend, Indiana.

Juana X. collaborating with artisans in Solola, Guatemala.

The author collaborating with Antonio V. and local agronomists in Haiti.

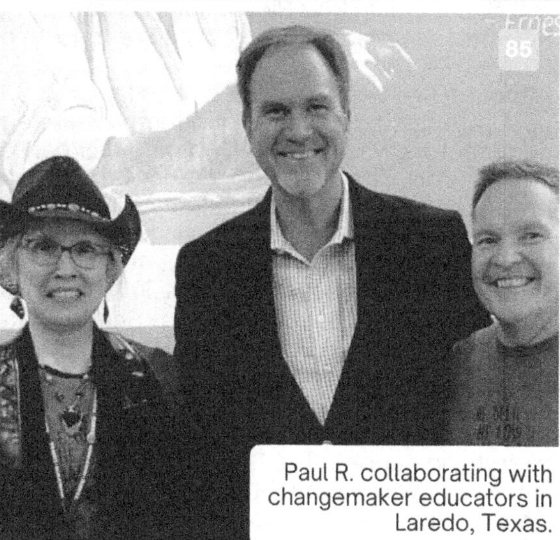

Paul R. collaborating with changemaker educators in Laredo, Texas.

NOTES:

***"I wish I was as fortunate, as fortunate as me."* - EDDIE VEDDER | PEARL JAM**

This book is a product of my changemaking journey. I've been fortunate to collaborate with, learn from, and be supported by so many incredible people during this journey. It's obviously impossible to acknowledge everyone. Forgive any omissions.

Biggest possible thank you Ali, EvaLuna, and Hudson for your love, patience, understanding, and overall awesomeness. I'm so blessed and I know it. And thank you Blu and Lucy for hanging out with me while I wrote and walking around with me while I was pacing and thinking.

Mary and Phil Van Kirk always had my back and were my biggest cheerleaders. That was huge. I love you and miss you. Thank you Larisa as well for all of the encouragement and support. And to Davor, Vedran, and Elle.

Appreciation to the Gartner family. Thank you Bette and Fritz (Miss you buddy!) for watching Hudson so I could go work in the coffee shop. Leigh, Susan, and Liz, you've always been so supportive and generous. Thank you. Alex, Gabby, Lucas, Emma, Sydney and Max. You rock!

First and foremost I have to acknowledge all of the people I've worked with in communities around the world who will likely never see this. I never studied social entrepreneurship or design, or anything related to community impact. More than anyone else, it's the community members I've aspired to support who've been my teachers. Thank you for your kindness, your openness, your care, and for sharing your wisdom.

I've been so blessed to have to opportunity to work with and become friends with so many people who I admire to no end. In particular, I'd like to give a shout-out to some of these OG's! Thank you Bucky Glickley, Miguel Brito, Maria Luz Giambartolomei, Madalina Bouros, Luke Burchell, Neil Blumenthal, David Bornstein, Brett Smith, Chris Adkins, Melissa Paulsen, Paul Rogers, Jordan Kassalow, Tim Trusz, Ashleigh Glickley, Graham MacMillan, Peter Eliassen, Beck Pryor, Holley Gaskill, Jeff Snell, Albina Ruiz Rios, Paula Cardenau, Dana Mortenson, Bob Dillman, Larry Lunt, Jill Vialet, Lynn Roberts, and Martin Burt. You inspire me. I'm not worthy.

Although I've been working on this for over 20 years in some way, shape, or form, I started with the concrete design probably about four years ago. I'd like to acknowledge all of the friends, colleagues, and mentors who helped me during this part of this journey. They gave me feedback, ideas, opinions, and support. They were generous with their time and asked for nothing in return. In no particular order, thank you Alanna Hughes, Andy Coravos, Ivan Cestero, Sara Webb, Jeff Hittner, Colleen Sheehy, Molly Babbington, Kevin Kushman, Rick Emanuel, Arathi Ravier, Mary Claire Mandeville, Kathryn Werner, Beth McNamee, Alli O'Connell, Ciara Post, Becky O'Neill, Sarah Connell, Katie Brickwood, Elizabeth Mays, Mohsin Mohi Ud Din, Lindsay Siegel, Jane Dimyan-Ehrenfeld, Marta Verani, Olivia Zeydlar, Mike Duchen, Mike Sherry, Natalia Ruiz, Joe O'Connor, Carmi Margalit, Mark Tucci, Ashna Ram, Rachel Botos, John Hoeppner, Alan Harlem, and Michelle Mullins. A special acknowledgment and huge thanks to Quinn McKenna!

It's the Turismo Ixil (El Descanso), Soluciones Comunitarias, and Centro Explorative teams that made everything happen. They lead the continuous learning process. These are the leading community innovators who've taught me over the years. Thank you to Ricardo Tomas Guzman Cedillo, Yoli Garcia, Alma Santos, Teodolinda Herrera Cifuentes, Antonio Vixama, Juana Xoch Ibate, Jose Xoch Ibate, MartaLida Garcia Sitan, Virgilio Velasco Raymundo, Ana Vargas Bautista, Petrona Olivia Brito Perez, Catarina Perez de Paz, Maria Terraza Cobo, Juana Raymundo Brito, Maria Matom Luis, Juan Esquivel Ramirez Raymundo, Wilson Osiel Villatoro, Domingo Jeampol, Felipe Bernal Cuchil, Felipe Brito Cedillo, Ana Everilda Sánchez Ceto, Lesvia Maria Ceto de León, Emilio Velasco Raymundo, Vilma Alma Santos, Julio Victor Xol Coy, Rosa Raymundo Brito, Elisabeth Cuyuch Sanches, and María Cedillo Brito. Gratitude to Clara Luz Cho de Montezuma. I can still hear your voice saying, "Gregorio."

Huge shout out to CE Solutions/ Social Entrepreneur Corps/ CareerX leaders and participants. You always brought your heart and put communities first. You turned crazy new ideas into practical community impact. I regret not being the leader you always deserved. Thank you Conor Powell, Ruairi Nolan, Lydia Walker, Richard Sawyer, Jo Wignall, Willa Fouts, Kathleen Walsh Moschella, Alyssa Mercedes Hopun, Dan Malin, Justina Loh, Estela Aragon, Michelle Burkowitz Sultan, Megan Curran, Carrie Magnuson, Jessica Jones, Meg Capshew, Nina Karambelas, Anna Moccia-Field, Lia Hulit, Krissy Werner, Nikki Brand, Katie Sierra, Santa Letonia, Izzy Peer, Tanja Gibbons, Michael Gibbons, Zach Smith, Ricky Bogert, Mark Kurzrok, Brad Mattan, Sarah Spinetti, Aude Mulliez, Hilla Benzaken, Heather

Von Sacken, Dan Peyton, Erin Fessler, Aaron Arnoldy, Cassidy Rush, Tierra Kirby, Gaeten Moussa, Tess Bone, Kailynn Palaio, Sam Burke, Alison Tanker, James Frederick, Lusmai Diaz, Bo Peterson, Mike Belatti, Grace Galloway, Isabel Magnus, Elena Laswick, Ines Mazas, Kirby Landers, Terrill Kucera, Sarah Botton, Shanti Aguilar-Cardenas, Erin Fessler, Alexandra Lunt, Lindsay Horikoshi, Lara Pairceir and Florian Ostmann.

Definitely need to acknowledge the contributions of Jeff Hittner and Yulia Denisyuk. See anything familiar in this toolbox?

Thank you to the wonderful folks I had the opportunity to work with at Solutions Journalism Network (SJN). In addition to David (above), a huge thanks to Tina Rosenberg, Keith Hammonds, Sam, Taylor Nelson, Lita Tirak, Alec Saelens, Marie von Hafften, Samantha McCann, Katherine Noble, and Kerri Stokes. I hope that this is both reflective and supportive of your tremendous work.

Over the past few years, I've been afforded some wonderful opportunities to test new content and ideas with hundreds of students/professionals thanks to teaching/facilitation opportunities provided to me by Latika Kohli, Tim Levin, Kira Mendez, Fiona Wilson, Sara Boomsma, Kira Mendez, Michael Schaefer, Edward Jurkovic, Jane Thompson, Aaron Hubbard, Tara Czechowski, Don Kramer, Craig Vezina, Glenn Blumhorst, Dan Baker, and Bethany Leech. Thank you! Massive appreciation to Dr. Jack McGourty! Thank you Jack. (Sign up for his newsletter.)

Apart from Neil, there are so many folks who played a role in making our work and this toolkit possible from our Warby Parker collaboration. Thank you Dave Gilboa, Jesse Sneath, Hannah Kowalski, Kaki Read Mackey, and Paul Mackey.

Much appreciation to the folks at Deloitte who joined us and consulted for local organizations. I learned so much from you in the process. Thanks in particular to Tyler McKeeman and Rachel Ferber.

Ten years of collaborating with the Levi Strauss Foundation extended team taught me sooo much. Thank you Kim Almeida! Huge gratitude to Daniel Lee, Stan Wong, Fran Bitton, Tamar Benzaken Koosed, Carlued VE Leon, Eileen McNeely, Fatima Angeles, Jarek Borkowski, Bryn Philibert, Pankaj Kapoor, and Holdayara Hernandez. Thank you to all of the WWB Champions for sharing your insights and experiences. Thanks to Oscar Gonzalez and the whole AI team. Lots of photos of you in this book. And special thanks to my dear friend David Wofford. I so appreciate our conversations. Always a learning experience. And gratitude to Annie O'Connor, my amazing workshop design and facilitation partner

Over the past nearly 20 years I've had the opportunity to work with university leadership and faculty in more ways than I can think of. And I'm always learning something new. Thank you to Cynthia Franklin, Susan Dicklitch-Nelson, Abi Cavazos, David Kirsh, Yogesh Joshi, Christopher Stevens, Gabe Brodbar, Valerie Nightengale, Jacqueline Smith, Leanne Dunsmore, Eric Popkin, Patrick Eccles, Corey Anne Portel, Meghan Ann Ozaroski, Anke Wessels, Brian Hanson, Ivy Shultz, Rebecca Rodriguez, Alex Yepes, Heather Cohen, Caroline Payne, Dan Chong, Doug Woodward, Tricia Homer, Melissa Evens, Kristan Skendall, John Mayo, Eric Popkin, Makaela Kingsley, Jimena Holguin, Cheryl Kiser, Sara Minard, Todd Manwaring, Sarah Holloway, Patricia Culligan, Emily Pritchard, Rosann Spiro, Annie Kao, Inga Peterson, Thomas Phillips, Sarah Trent, Kavita Sharma, Gretchen Young, Rebecca Rodriguez, Lin Klein, Kent Trachte, Summer Spadera, Jennifer Krauser, Jay Smith, Sara Herald, Bruce Manciagli, Lisa Gavigan, Sandi Smoker, Chris Nayve, Stuart Napshin, Sheb True, Justin Cochran, Stacy Campbell, Drew Stelljes, Jill Kickul, Stacy Kosko, Matt Matsuda, Kerry O'Brien, Phoebe Punzalan, Michael Pirson, Debra Lynn Moesch, Lizzy Hazeltin, Monica Laidig, Karen Slaggert, Irina Adams, Martha Reeves, Lynne Goodstein, Elaine Mosakowsi, Lisa Wolfe, Francy Milner, Archana Shah, Michael Schaefer, Amanda McBride, Ted Fisher, Carolyn Jones, Michele Kahane, Yusi Terrell, Fabiola Berdiel, Cynthia Lawson, Manuel Montoya, Wynd Harris, Raluca Nohorniac, Rachel Tomas Morgan, Irina Adams, Elisabeth Frost Maring, Christine Garten, Abby Chroman, Melissa Carrier, Mark Hendersen, Monica Dean, Renee Heavlow, Cindy Cooper, Clay Cooper, Kathy Sikes, Nicole Patel, and Paul Arnston.

Matt Nash, you're an inspiration! A special shout out to Eric Mlyn and Ross Lewin. Your leadership helped make Social Entrepreneur Corps possible. And Jennifer Precht, what can I say?! Amazing.

Thank you to all of the wonderful folks who we've worked with through Miami University, my alma mater. Thanks to Mark Lacker, Clark Kelly, Diane Delisio, Brian Bergman, Heid Bortel, Martha Petrone, Anne Ferrell, Marek Dollar, Jim Friedman, Tim Holcomb, Katie Mulligan, Kim Taveres, and Brad Bundy.

I definitely have to acknowledge my Peace Corps and Nebaj people. Thanks for the friendship and support during those first few years in the field. Thank you Joe Damm, Sam Kazdal, Craig Badger, Chris Hansot, Sara DeRuyck, Nicole Manopol, Lisa Rudge, Alan Reade, Lynn Roberts, Will Pfaff, Kim Miller, Jules Wilkinson, and Leslie Burgess.

Thanks to my MIT DLab friends. I learned so much from you! Thank you Kofi Taha, Victor Grau Serrat, Sara Bird, and Jodie Wu.

We've had such generous support over the years from people I admire. Thank you Dave Peery, Jessamyn Lau, Andy Boszhardt, Frank Belatti, Dorothy Largay, Nancy Swanson-Roberts, John and Kelly Grier, Kelly Michel, the First Presbyterian Church of New Vernon, Ed Satell, Regina Black-Lennox, Mike and Margaret Kirby, Candace and Rich Weeks, and Susanna Place. You made this possible. Thank you Marjorie Raines! You're always there for me/ us.

Thank you Sean McCormick for the support, friendship, and ideation. Always great having a beer and running new ideas by you.

I've learned so much that contributed to this toolbox from my consulting work around the world. I'd like to acknowledge Brian Rudert, Dieter Fisher, Pia Reyes, Audra Renyi, Fares Zaki, Farid Azouri, Selcuk Tanatar, Chris Falco, Tatiana Dwyer, Teo Jakic, Vitali Vorona, Al Babbington, Raam Thakrar, Cesar Buenadicha and Aminta Perez-Gold.

Thanks to Philip Auerswald and Winthrop Carty for the MIT Innovation Journal article. You're master editors.

Appreciation and acknowledgment to my Ashoka and Ashoka adjacent community. Thanks to Bill Drayton, Diana Wells, Nadine Freeman, Amy Clark, Jack Edwards, Linda Peia, Beverly Schwartz, Tia Johnston Brown, Tim Scheu, Valentina Raman, Vipen Thekk, Mentor Dida, Angelika Roth, Armando Laborde, Fernande Raine, Henry De Sio, Lennon Flowers, Romina Laura Faub, Amy Satterthwaite, Mentor Dida, Paula Recart, Konstanze Frischen, Valeria Budinich, Itai Dinour, Aleta Margolis, Laura White, Dina Buchbinder Auron, Michael Zakaras, Luzette Jaimes, Cosmo Fujiyama Ghaznavi, David Castro, Gustavo Gennuso, Vera Cordeiro, Nancy Walsh, Brittany Koteles, Danielle Goldstone, Eric Dawson, Simon Stumpf, Reem Rahman, Maria Laura Acebal, Bill Carter, Barb Steele, Marie Ringler, Laura Hay Mack, Michael Vollman, Hanae Baruchel, Yuseul Kim, Autumn Breon, Dana Meckler, David Green, Ben Powell, Stephanie Schmidt, Marina Mansilla Herman, Douglas McMeekin, Jennifer Hoos Rothberg, George Khalaf, Megan Marcus, Sameh Seif, Natasha Walker, Oda Heister, Lucian Lucena de Lima, Katherine Lucy, Gonzalo Muñoz Abogabir, Abigail Sarmac, Andres Martinez, Sabine Baumeister, Carl Munana, Howard Weinstein, Tri Mumpuni, Sanjeev Arora, Bob Spoer, Lorena Garcia Duran, Ellen Moir, Jean Claude Rodriguez-Ferrera Massons, Felipe Vergara, Mathias Craig, Felix Oldenberg, Claire Fallender, Jack Sim, Salomon Raydan, and Meera Vijayaan.

AshokaU! Thank you! You catalyzed so much learning and so many opportunities. Marina Kim, Erin Boyd, Beeta Ansari, Ali Fraenkel, and Emily Lamb.

Thanks to the SVL team. I think we all learned a lot. We gave it a shot. Thanks to Marc Albanese, Kacci Li, Jesse Tang, Chika Ota, Steve Santiago, John Doskoczynski, Maya Major, Joel Wishkovsky, and Andre Cardadeiro. Thank you and I owe you, Christine Chmielewski. You are incredibly generous.

I learned so much from my structured finance colleagues. Thank you Chris Gould for giving me a chance. Thanks to Andrew Fishman. And gratitude to Mark Adiletta, Rakesh Kak, Maria Adams, Elaine Shore, Gail Hatch, Bunker Snyder, Angela Kalaygian, Vicky Hernandez, Stacy Lynch, Hidey Hiramatsu, John Faulkner, and Barry Boothe.

Thanks for the support, collaboration, and friendship Annie Richmond, Kate Otto Chebly, Rachel Botos, Audriana Stark, Tim Rann, Melissa Fisher, Rachel Hurley, Jenna Gebel Chaiken, Matthew Barr, Stewart Craine, Addie Thompson, Lara Galinsky, Susan Davis, Olivier Keyser, Namita Mody, Nadia Sandi, Julia Corvalan, Rachel Ferber, Beverly Tam, Stephanie Harrison, Kaveh Sadhegian, Roxanne Aragon, Leslie Joy, Shalena Broadnax, Ana Pau Cantu, Dave Dillman, Karen Davis, Erik Stangvik, Tod Gimbel, Armando Huerta, Diana Sierra, Allison Archambault, Ebaa Elkalamawi, and Dave Schwab.

So many wonderful friends I'd like to acknowledge for being there over the past few years in particular. Thank you Dave Hazelton, John and Kelly Grier, Chris and Kerry Watts, John Scuterud, Steven Nichols, Lee Whitaker, Mike Miller, Jon Otterberg, Mike Rucker, Chris Camp, Mike Gaby, Dave and Tiffany Grayson, Molly Balla, Liz Tahawi, Anne and Mike George, Gina and Kevin Watson, Hayley Marcous, Gary Kane, Stephanie Baker, Jay and Ali Zimner, Matthew and Sidaya Sherwood, Emily and George Haskell, Carol and Rafa, Maya and Carmi Margalit, Dave and Phebe Jacobsen, and Mark and Heather Tucci. John Fitch, I miss you!! Thanks for always being there my brother Matt Smith!

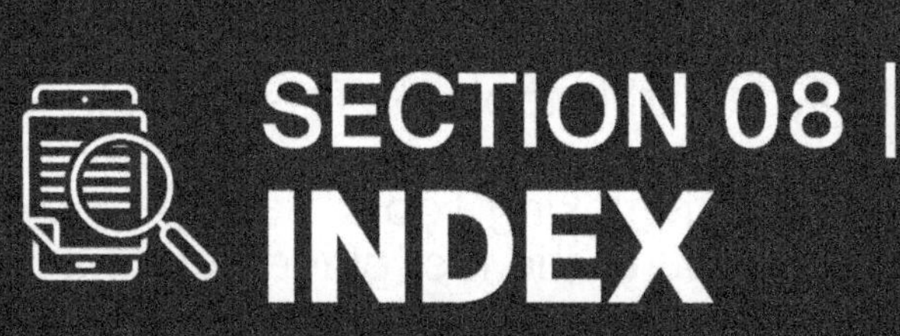

SECTION 08 | INDEX

Alyssa H. collaborating with communities in Nicaragua

Albina R. and Yoli G. collaborating in Antigua, Guatemala

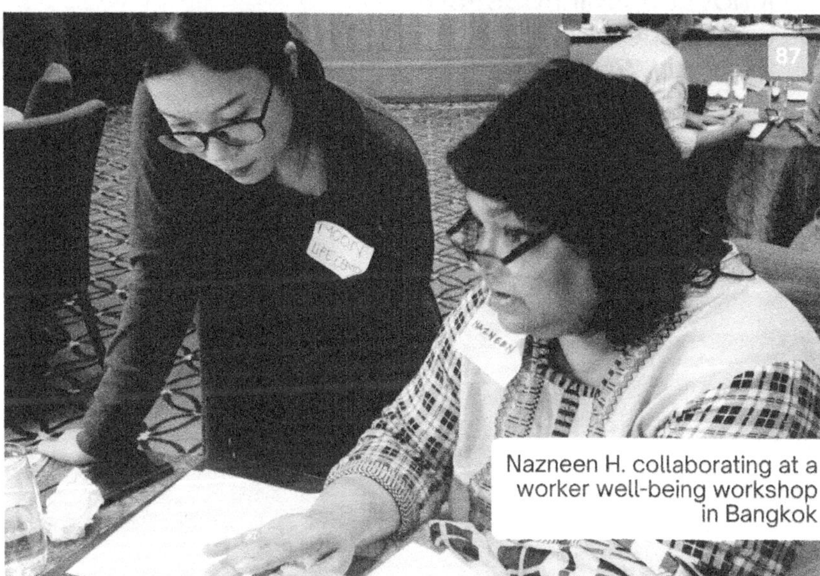

Nazneen H. collaborating at a worker well-being workshop in Bangkok

Holley G. collaborating with families in Guatemala

Jessica J. collaborating with entrepreneurs in Peru

Sarah W. collaborating with a community member in Ecuador

NOTES:

Following are a few things to keep in mind while using this INDEX:

- The priority goal is to help you navigate around this toolbox. This isn't all-inclusive. Forgive any omissions.
- I haven't included the terms used in the Changemaking Tools.
- For economy's sake, the INDEX often takes you to the first place where a term is used. You can follow the trail from there.
- Look to pages 345 - 356 as the priority indices for the Changemaking Innovation Mini-Cases.
- I didn't include all of the resources listed from pages 381 to 383 in RECOMMENDED RESOURCES FOR CHANGEMAKERS. Go to those pages to find the complete list.

NOTES:

NOTES:

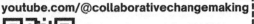

youtube.com/@collaborativechangemaking

Subscribe and find HOW-TO videos, additional Changemaking Innovation Mini-Cases, educational videos, and more.

ABOUT THE WRITER + DESIGNER

GREG VAN KIRK

Greg's worked in 25+ countries over the course of his career including the U.S., Canada, Mexico, Guatemala, El Salvador, Nicaragua, Colombia, Peru, Ecuador, Paraguay, Suriname, Brazil, Haiti, The Dominican Republic, The U.K., The Netherlands, France, Germany, Bosnia and Herzegovina, Saudi Arabia, Serbia, Egypt, Senegal, The Gambia, Guinea, South Africa, India, Thailand, and Japan.

He wears and has worn many hats during his changemaking journey. This toolbox is a product of his diverse experiences.

Greg is a partner to Ali, dad to EvaLuna and Hudson, and the feeder and walker of Lucy and Blu.

He was a Peace Corps Volunteer. He worked in micro-finance and helped start one of the first rural internet centers in the Western Highlands of Guatemala. During this time, he used his savings to start a restaurant, education center, cook stove business, and trekking business with local community members. He failed miserably trying to start a rabbit business with a community.

Greg is an award-winning social entrepreneur. Greg was the lead designer of the award-winning MicroConsignment Model featured on the NBC Nightly News, CNNMoney, and in The New York Times, amongst other media.

He's a World Economic Forum "Social Entrepreneur of the Year for 2012 (Latin America)," a two-time Ashoka Globalizer Fellow, and was awarded The Bishop Medal by the Miami University Alumni Assoc.

He co-founded and led Community Enterprise Solutions, which was awarded "Community Partner of the Year" by Levi Strauss & Co. and the "Irish Impact: Community Partner of Year" by the Mendoza College of Business at the University of Notre Dame. Greg co-founded and led Social Entrepreneur Corps, one of the first "Innovation Award" winners at AshokaU. He also co-founded Soluciones Comunitarias, winner of "Leveraging Business for Social Change" by Ashoka Changemakers.

He's been a "Social Entrepreneur-in-Residence" at Arizona State University, Marquette University, University of San Diego, and Indiana University, amongst others.

He's an expert in experiential/ service learning and study abroad. As president of Social Entrepreneur Corps, Greg led the start-up and overall operations in Guatemala, Ecuador, Nicaragua, South Africa, and the Dominican Republic. He created strategic partnerships with institutions including Columbia University, University of Connecticut, Cornell University, Deloitte, Duke University, Franklin & Marshall College, Kennesaw State University, University of Maryland, Miami University, University of New Mexico, University of Notre Dame, Northwestern University, NYU, Smith College, Stanford University, and Warby Parker amongst others. He led program and curriculum design.

He's an educator. Greg started his career teaching English in Japan. He's designed and taught entrepreneurship, social entrepreneurship, and social innovation courses/workshops at the professional, university, and high school levels. He's taught at Columbia University, Fordham University, Miami University, Lehigh University, University of Notre Dame, University of New Hampshire, University of Wisconsin, and The American School of Paris, amongst other institutions.

He works as a strategic consultant. Greg's led consulting engagements for organizations such as Levi Strauss Foundation, Visa Foundation, Bespoke Education, The Spaceship Academy, USAID, Chemonics, Inter American Development Bank, IFC, Solutions Journalism Network, VisionSpring, Soros Foundation, Church World Service, Water For People, World Wide Hearing, and Fundacion Paraguaya, amongst others. This work has included everything from co-leading the design of a global worker well-being strategy to designing an entrepreneurial ecosystem to inspire displaced populations to return to their communities, to supporting the design of a global vision program, to evaluating the impact of greenhouse projects, to designing a micro franchising strategy so that micro-entrepreneurs could access outboard boat engines.

He was a structured finance advisor. Before joining the Peace Corps, Greg worked for a boutique firm in San Francisco and for UBS in New York. He focused on aircraft, digital switching equipment, and power plants.